Hplc of small molecules

a practical approach

Edited by
C K Lim

Medical Research Council, Clinical Research Centre, Watford Road, Harrow, Middlesex HA1 3UJ, UK

IRL PRESS

Oxford · Washington DC

IRL Press Limited
P.O. Box 1,
Eynsham,
Oxford OX8 1JJ,
England

British Library Cataloguing in Publication Data

H.p.l.c. of small molecules: a practical approach.—(The Practical approach series)
1. Chemistry, Organic 2. Liquid chromatography
I. Lim,C.K. II. Series
574.19'24   QD272.C447

ISBN 0-947946-77-2 (softbound)
ISBN 0-947946-78-0 (hardbound)

Printed by Information Printing Ltd, Oxford, England.

Preface

High-performance liquid chromatography (h.p.l.c.) is one of the fastest developing analytical techniques which is rapidly becoming an integral part of many research and routine laboratories involving biomedical analysis. The aim of this book is to provide detailed practical h.p.l.c. procedures for the analysis of small molecules in life science. The topics covered include the introduction to h.p.l.c. of small molecules, amino acids and small peptides, biogenic amines, carbohydrates, lipids, bile acids, steroids, vitamins, nucleotides and nucleosides, porphyrins and bile pigments. The authors are all experts in their particular areas of analysis and have selected methods which, through their own experiences, are proven and reliable. These methods are expected to be widely applicable in biochemistry and cell biology, in the study of metabolic pathways, the biochemical diagnosis of diseases and in enzyme assays. Whenever possible, an introduction is given to each chapter for the benefit of workers contemplating entering the field. A few chapters have been extensively revised to conform with the theme of a practical approach. I thank the authors concerned for their understanding and cooperation.

C.K.Lim

Contributors

B.H.Billing
Medical Unit, The Royal Free Hospital, Pond Street, London NW3 2QG, UK

D.H.Curnow
Department of Clinical Biochemistry, Queen Elizabeth II Medical Centre, Nedlands, Western Australia 6009, Australia

J.W.Honour
Cobbold Laboratories, Middlesex Hospital Medical School, Mortimer Street, London W1N 8AA, UK

E.F.Hounsell
Applied Immunochemistry Research Group, Clinical Research Centre, Watford Road, Harrow, Middlesex HA1 3UJ, UK

M.H.Joseph
Department of Psychology, Institute of Psychiatry, De Crespigny Park, Denmark Hill, London SE5 8AF, UK

A.Karmen
Albert Einstein College of Medicine, Yeshiva University, 1300 Morris Park Avenue, Bronx, NY 10461, USA

S.Lam
Albert Einstein College of Medicine, Yeshiva University, 1300 Morris Park Avenue, Bronx, NY 10461, USA

C.K.Lim
Division of Clinical Cell Biology, Clinical Research Centre, Watford Road, Harrow, Middlesex HA1 3UJ, UK

C.A.Marsden
Department of Physiology and Pharmacology, Medical School, Queen's Medical Centre, Nottingham NG7 2UH, UK

S.McKavanagh
Medical Unit, The Royal Free Hospital, Pond Street, London NW3 2QG, UK

D.Perrett
Department of Medicine, St. Bartholomew's Hospital, London EC1A 7BE, UK

E.Rossi
Department of Clinical Biochemistry, Queen Elizabeth II Medical Centre, Nedlands, Western Australia 6009, Australia

M.J.Shearer
Clinical Science Laboratories, Guy's Tower (17th and 18th Floor), Guy's Hospital, London Bridge, London SE1 9RT, UK

B.Tracey
Section of Perinatalogy and Child Health, Clinical Research Centre, Watford Road, Harrow, Middlesex HA1 3UJ, UK

Contents

10. PORPHYRINS 261

E.Rossi and D.H.Curnow

Abbreviations

A	adrenaline
ACTH	adrenocorticotrophic hormone
ALA	δ-aminolaevulinic acid
APS	aminopropylsilane
AVP	arginine vasopressin
BMC	4-bromomethyl-7-methoxycoumarin
C11AA	11-amino undecanoic acid
CAH	congenital adrenal hyperplasia
CPB	competitive protein binding
DA	dopamine
DFQ	3-(1,2-dihydroxyethyl)furo[3,4-b]quinoxaline-1-one
DHBA	3,4-dihydroxybenzylamine
DHEA	dehydroepiandrosterone
DHEAS	dehydroepiandrosterone sulphate
DIPEA	diisopropylethylamine
DMSO	dimethyl sulphoxide
DOPA	3,4-dihydroxyphenylalanine
DOPAC	dihydroxyphenylacetic acid
EC	energy charge
ECD	electrochemical detection; electrochemical detector
EDTA	ethylenediaminetetraacetic acid
EGTA	ethyleneglycobis-(β-aminoethyl)ether tetraacetic acid
FAD	flavin−adenine dinucleotide
FAME	fatty acid methyl esters
FMN	flavin mononucleotide
5HIAA	5-hydroxyindoleacetic acid
3α-HSD	3α-hydroxysteroid dehydrogenase
5HT	5-hydroxytryptamine
5HTP	5-hydroxytryptophan
HVA	homovanillic acid
IP	ion-pair; ion pairing
$K_1(I-H_2)$	2,3-dihydrophylloquinone
LCEC	liquid chromatographic−electrochemical detection
MHPG	3-methoxy-4-hydroxyphenylglycol
MK-6	menaquinone-6
MO-TMS	methyloxime-trimethylsilyl ether
3MT	3-methoxytryptamine
N'-MN	N'-methylnicotinamide
NA	noradrenaline
NAD	nicotinamide adenine dinucleotide
NADP	nicotinamide adenine dinucleotide phosphate
NM	normetanephrine
NP	normal phase
NSB	non-specific binding
25-(OH)D	25-hydroxyvitamin D
1,25-$(OH)_2$D	1,25-dihydroxyvitamin D
24,25-$(OH)_2$D	24,25-dihydroxyvitamin D

ODS	octadecylsilyl
OPD	*o*-phenylenediamine
OPT-thiol	*o*-phthalaldehyde-thiol reagent
4-PA	4-pyridoxic acid
PBG	porphobilinogen
pBPB	*p*-bromophenacyl bromide
PBS	phosphate-buffered saline
PCA	perchloric acid
PL	pyridoxal
PLP	pyridoxal phosphate
PM	pyridoxamine
PMP	pyridoxamine phosphate
PN	pyridoxine
PNP	pyridoxine phosphate
2-Pyridone	N-methyl-2-pyridone-5-carboxylamide
RBC	red blood cell
RBP	retinol-binding protein
RI	refractive index
RIA	radioimmunoassay
RP	reversed-phase
SAX	strong anion exchange
SCX	strong cation exchange
SCID	severe combined immunodeficiency disease
SGOT	serum glutamic−oxalacetic transaminase
SGPT	serum glutamic−pyruvic transaminase
TBHS	tetrabutylammonium hydrogen sulphate
TCA	trichloroacetic acid
TEPA	tetraethylenepentamine
TMP	thiamin monophosphate
TPP	thiamin pyrophosphate
Tris	tris(hydroxymethyl)aminomethane
TTP	thiamin triphosphate
VFA	volatile fatty acids

CHAPTER 1

Introduction to h.p.l.c. of small molecules

C.K. LIM

1. INTRODUCTION

High-performance liquid chromatography (h.p.l.c.) is an ideal technique for the analysis of small molecules (mol. wt. <1000). The application of h.p.l.c. in virtually every facet of life science involving small molecules has been described. This chapter is primarily concerned with the practical aspects of the technique. It is essential, however, to be familiar with the fundamental h.p.l.c. equations so that the technique can be more fully understood and effectively applied.

2. FUNDAMENTAL H.P.L.C. EQUATIONS

The elution chromatogram (*Figure 1*) is used to calculate the following important h.p.l.c. parameters.

(i)   Capacity ratio or capacity factor (k')

$$k'_1 = \frac{t_1 - t_o}{t_o}$$

$$k'_2 = \frac{t_2 - t_o}{t_o}$$

where t_o is the retention time of an unretained compound, usually a solvent used to dissolve the solutes. It represents the column void volume and the peak is often referred to as the 'solvent front'; t_1 and t_2 are the retention times of compounds 1 and 2, respectively. k' is a measure of solute retention and should be quoted whenever possible.

(ii)   Selectivity (α)

$$\alpha = \frac{k'_2}{k'_1}$$

α measures the ability of a column to separate components 1 and 2 due to different affinity and therefore retention.

(ii)   Number of theoretical plates (N)

$$N = 16 \left(\frac{t_1}{w_1}\right)^2 = 5.54 \left(\frac{t_1}{w_{1/2}}\right)^2$$

where w_1 is the peak width of solute 1; $w_{1/2}$ is the peak width at half the peak height; 16 is a factor carry over from the distillation theory. N is a measure

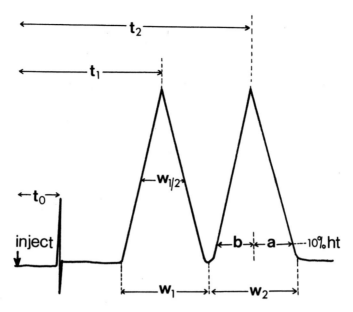

Figure. 1. Elution chromatogram for the calculation of h.p.l.c. parameters.

of zone or band spread of a peak throughout the chromatographic system. The smaller the band spread the larger the N and the more efficient the column.

(iv)   Height equivalent to a theoretical plate (H)

$$H = \frac{L}{N}$$

where L is the column length. H also measures column efficiency and is a more important parameter as it is independent of the column length. The smaller the H the better the column.

(v)   Reduced plate height (h)

$$h = \frac{H}{dp}$$

where dp is the mean particle diameter of the packing material. h is a measure of the degree of band dispersion produced by the packing considered in relation to the particle size. It is the best parameter for determining peak efficiency. It has no dimensions thus allowing different columns to be compared. A good column should have an h of between 2 and 3.5.

(vi)   Peak symmetry (A_{10})

The peak symmetry is calculated at 10% of peak height by the equation

$$A_{10} = \frac{a}{b}$$

where a is the distance to the training edge and b the distance to the front edge, respectively at 10% peak height. The ratio for a symmetrical peak is 1.0. Typical values for a good column are between 0.85 and 1.3.

(vii)   Resolution factor (R_s)

$$R_s = \frac{t_2 - t_1}{\frac{1}{2}(w_2 - w_1)}$$

R_s measures the resolution between two components and is dependent on k', α and N. The resolution equation is thus expressed as:

$$R_s = \frac{1}{4}\sqrt{N}\left(\frac{\alpha-1}{\alpha}\right)\left(\frac{k'}{k'+1}\right)$$

For more detailed theoretical descriptions and for the measurement of other h.p.l.c. parameters the publications of Knox are recommended (1,2).

3. H.P.L.C. MODES OF SEPARATION

These can be broadly classified as gel-permeation (g.p.c.), adsorption (normal phase or liquid—solid), partition (liquid—liquid), ion-exchange and reversed-phase (RP) chromatography.

3.1 Gel-permeation chromatography

G.p.c. is normally used for the separation of biological macromolecules and polymers. It separates compounds on the basis of size and solutes are eluted in the order of decreasing molecular size. The technique is less useful for small molecules.

3.2 Adsorption chromatography

Adsorption chromatography involves interaction between the adsorbent (usually silica) and the solute and solvent molecules in solution (3). The process can be considered as a competition between the solute and solvent molecules for adsorption sites on the solid surface. Since different molecules are absorbed and displaced differently, separation is effected. This simple model is probably true when non-polar organic solvents are used for elution. In the presence of polar liquids the solid surface may be coated with a layer of liquid and liquid—liquid partition may also effect the separation.

Adsorption chromatography is also referred to as normal phase (NP) or liquid—solid chromatography when relatively non-polar organic eluents (e.g. hexane, dichloromethane, ethyl acetate) are used with the polar adsorbent. Solutes are eluted in order of increasing polarity and retention decreases with increasing solvent polarity. The solvent strength parameter ($\epsilon°$) values (4) are useful for adjusting the mobile phase composition to obtain the right 'solvent strength' for a particular separation. The organic solvents used must be very dry. Water deactivates silica leading to variable retention. Organic solvents saturated with water may be used but the contents must be strictly controlled.

Adsorption chromatography is best for the separation of compounds which are highly soluble in organic solvents (e.g. fat-soluble vitamins, see Chapter 8) or have low stability or aggregation problems in aqueous mobile phases (e.g. phospholipid, see Chapter 5).

3

It has the unique ability to obtain class separation (e.g. porphyrin methyl esters, see Chapter 10), to separate isomers (e.g. biliverdin dimethyl ester isomers, see Chapter 11) and to separate highly hydrophilic species (e.g. carbohydrates, see Chapter 4) which are difficult to retain on RP columns.

The mainly organic mobile phase allows simpler, more efficient peak collection and concentration for off-line solute characterization or for on-line coupling to a mass spectrometer. The availability of a wide range of organic solvents may also be exploited to provide for special secondary or tertiary solvent effects which improve the separation (e.g. 24,25-dihydroxy vitamin D, see Chapter 8).

3.3 Partition chromatography

A partition packing may be in the form of a liquid phase coated on an inert solid such as silica or silica chemically bonded with various functional groups. Partition chromatography occurs when the separation is effected by the interaction of the solute between the mobile phase and the liquid stationary phase. Partition chromatography on liquid-coated silica is very seldom used because of instability due to 'bleeding' of the stationary liquid phase. The bonded phases are good substitutes but are not particularly widely used. The following chemically bonded polar phases are commercially available (5,6): amino, cyano, diol and nitro. They complement silica for NP chromatography.

An alternative to polar bonded phases is dynamic coating of silica *in situ*, e.g. a solution of tetraethylenepentamine in aqueous acetonitrile passed through a silica column will mimic an amino column for carbohydrate separation (see Chapter 4).

3.4 Ion-exchange chromatography

H.p.l.c. ion-exchangers are usually silica chemically bonded with anionic or cationic groups (7), commonly aminopropyl, tetraalkylammonium or sulphonic acid groups. Hydrophilic polymeric ion-exchange gels are also available but are mainly used for the separation of large molecules.

Ion-exchange chromatography separates molecules on the basis of their molecular charge. The separation proceeds because ions of opposite charge are retained to different extents. The resolution is influenced by the pH of the eluent which affects the selectivity and by the ionic strength of the buffer which mainly affects the retention.

Compounds capable of ionization, and particularly zwitterionic compounds which are always ionized, chromatograph well on ion-exchange columns. Rapid separation of nucleotides (see Chapter 9), for example, has been achieved on an aminopropyl-bonded (weak anion-exchange) column. Ionizable compounds, however, are now more often separated by RP chromatography with buffered eluents of controlled pH and molarity or in the presence of ion-pairing (IP) agents for RP-IP chromatography.

3.5 Reversed-phase chromatography

RP chromatography is so named because it behaves in the opposite way to NP chromatography. The stationary phase is silica chemically bonded with an alkylsilyl compound to give a non-polar, hydrophobic surface (6,8). Solute retention is mainly due to hydrophobic interactions between the solutes and the hydrocarbonaceous stationary phase surface. Polar mobile phases, usually water mixed with methanol, acetonitrile and/or other water-miscible organic solvents, are used for elution. Solutes are eluted in order of decreasing polarity (increasing hydrophobicity), and increasing the polar (aqueous) component of the mobile phase increases the retention of the solutes.

The most popular RP packing is the C_{18} type in which octadecylsilyl (ODS) groups are bonded to the silica surface. Silica with C_{22}, C_8, C_4, C_3, C_2 and C_1 groups attached are also available. Under identical h.p.l.c. conditions the retention of solutes usually increases proportionately with the carbon chain length of the bonded groups. In general, the more polar (less hydrophobic) compounds are best separated with mobile phases of low organic content and since shorter chain hydrocarbon phases interact best with mobile phase of lower organic content, they are more suited to the analysis of these compounds. The longer chain hydrocarbon phases interact best with mobile phases of higher organic content and are therefore best suited to non-polar, hydrophobic solutes.

RP columns are stable in the pH range $2-7$ and at elevated temperatures. The pH range can be exceeded for a short period of time, particularly with the longer carbon chain phases (C_{18}, C_{22}) which are more stable than the shorter C_1 or C_2 phases. At alkaline pH, however, silica begins to dissolve, although pre-saturating the mobile phase (using a pre-saturation column) with silicate may help to minimize the damage.

RP chromatography is the most versatile and most widely used h.p.l.c. mode. Apart from the usual methanol − water and acetonitrile − water solvent mixtures, additives can be used in conjunction with the mobile phase to give special selectivities. RP chromatography can therefore be further classified to include ion-suppression, ionization control, ion-pair (IP) and non-aqueous RP chromatography.

3.5.1 *Ion-suppression*

Weak acids and bases are often chromatographed with poor peak shapes at neutral pH due to partial ionization of the solutes. The simplest solution is to suppress the ionization (9) and separate the compounds in the unionized form which are usually chromatographed as sharp peaks. Phosphoric, sulphuric and perchloric acids are used to suppress the ionization of acids while dilute ammonia or ammonium carbonate are used for the bases.

3.5.2 *Ionization control with buffered mobile phase*

The ionization of a solute and therefore its hydrophobicity can be precisely adjusted by using a buffer of controlled pH and concentration (10). This powerful technique allows samples with a wide range of sizes and hydrophobicities (polarities) to be separated. The choice of a buffer is an important consideration when employing this technique because the nature of the buffer can significantly affect the selectivity, efficiency and resolving power of the column. An ideal buffer should have the following properties (11).

(i)   Chemically stable under h.p.l.c. conditions.
(ii) Uniform buffering capacity in the pH range $2-7$.
(iii) Optical transparency preferably down to 200 nm.
(iv) Highly soluble in the organic solvents used in RP chromatography, especially acetonitrile and methanol.
(vi) The facility to accelerate rates of proton equilibration. Rapid rates of proton trans-

fer are essential to reduce the kinetic contributions to band spreading of ionizable solutes.

(vii)   The potential of masking silanol groups of the stationary phase.

Residual silanol groups are related to the extent to which the silica surface is bonded or covered. The lower the coverage the higher the residual silanol content. As it is difficult to cover all the silanol groups with the relatively large hydrocarbon molecules due to steric hindrance, residual silanol groups are always present on RP packings. Residual silanol groups tend to cause a mixed retention mechanism, peak tailing (due to adsorption), reduced column efficiency and variable retention time. The mixed retention mechanism, however, may sometimes lead to better resolution but it is an unknown variable.

Residual silanol groups can be largely eliminated by 'end-capping', i.e. by further treating the bonded phase with a small silylating reagent such as trimethylchlorosilane. Alternatively, a buffer which can effectively mask and suppress the effects of residual silanol groups is used for elution. Such a buffer usually contains an amine or an ammonium component that interacts with silanol groups at the stationary phase surface. This leads to reduced peak tailing and improved resolution, particularly with positively charged compounds. Melander *et al.* (11) have shown that phosphates of vicinal diamines possess most of the desired chromatographic properties for RP chromatography. In the author's laboratory ammonium acetate buffer is preferred, and is used as a general purpose buffer (12) for RP chromatography. It has the added advantage of being highly soluble in acetonitrile and methanol. Very high molar concentration (1 M) can therefore be used to achieve separations otherwise difficult or impossible (e.g. porphyrin isomers, see Chapter 10). The main disadvantage of ammonium acetate is its relatively high u.v. cut-off (220 nm).

Ammonium acetate is also able to form IP with solutes, while the association of the NH_4^+ ions with the stationary phase may lead to ion-exchange properties. The retention of porphyrins, for example, decreases with increasing ammonium acetate concentration (Chapter 10 and ref. 13). This is typically an ion-exchange behaviour.

3.5.3 *Ion-pair chromatography*

IP chromatography (9) is based on the principle that ionic species can be extracted into organic solvents as neutral IP in the presence of a counter ion (species of opposite charge). In its simplest form a solute ion A^- is added to a mobile phase system containing a counter ion B^+. The partition equilibrium is represented by the equation

$$A^- \text{ (acid)} + B^+ \text{ (base)} \rightleftharpoons A^- B^+ \text{ (ion-pair)}$$

Formation of the neutral IP allows the compound to be chromatographed on RP columns. The roles of the anions and cations can obviously be reversed.

Compounds that are difficult to chromatograph by ion-suppression or ionization control, e.g. strong acids and bases or highly hydrophilic weak acids and bases, often require ion-exchange or IP chromatography for satisfactory separation. Alkyl sulphonates (e.g. heptanesulphonic acid) or sulphates (e.g. sodium laurylsulphate) are common IP agents for cations (bases) and tetraalkylammonium salts (e.g. tetrabutylammonium chloride, cetyltrimethylammonium bromide) are typical IP agents for anions (acids). Zwitterionic pairing agents (e.g. 11-aminoundecanoic acids, 12-aminododecanoic acid) have been used for the separation of nucleotides (Chapter 9 and ref. 14). RP-IP chromatography is especially valuable when the simultaneous separation of neutral, acidic and basic components is required. This can be achieved, for example, by using a mobile phase consisting of a methanol−buffer mixture at pH 2.5 and containing 1% of sodium lauryl-sulphate as the IP agent for elution. The neutral molecules are separated in the usual RP manner. The ionization of acids is suppressed at low pH and the bases are proton-ated and form IP with the IP agent. All three classes of compounds can thus be chromato-graphed with the same system.

IP agents with bulky hydrophobic groups such as sodium laurylsulphate and sodium dodecylsulphate may be strongly partitioned into the stationary phase and are difficult to remove by subsequent washing. It is recommended that a dedicated column is used for IP chromatography involving these detergents.

3.5.4 *Non-aqueous RP chromatography*

RP chromatography may be carried out with totally non-aqueous solvent as mobile phases. Lipophilic compounds which do not chromatograph well on silica or have in-sufficient solute solubility in the mobile phase for normal phase chromatography can sometimes be separated by non-aqueous RP chromatography. The following non-aqueous solvents are commonly employed: acetone, acetonitrile, dimethyl sulphoxide, dichloromethane, methanol and tetrahydrofuran. A single solvent (see Chapter 8, Sec-tion 2.5) or a binary (see Chapter 11, Section 3.3.1) or ternary solvent mixture (see Chapter 5, Section 4.4) may be used for elution. The main advantages of non-aqueous RP are increased solubility of solutes in the mobile phase, better column stability and efficiency.

4. CHIRAL SEPARATION

The resolution of racemate by h.p.l.c. can be achieved by one of the following methods.

(i)   Derivatization of the enantiomers and separation of the diastereomeric derivatives.
(ii)   Use of a chiral mobile phase for ligand-exchange chromatography.
(iii)   Formation of diastereomeric IP with a chiral counter-ion.
(iv)   Use of a chiral stationary phase.

4.1 **Optical resolution by chiral derivatization**

This method involves the derivatization of enantiomers with an optically pure reagent. The diastereoisomers formed are then separated by h.p.l.c. Enantiomeric alkanolamines, for example, have been resolved as the monoesters by reacting with optically pure and symmetrically O, O-disubstituted (R,R)- or (S,S)-tartaric acids (15). An ODS−Spheri-sorb column with methanol−2% acetic acid adjusted to pH 3.7 (1:1 v/v) as eluent was used for the separation.

The simultaneous analysis of common protein amino acid enantiomers has also been achieved by chiral derivatization. The amino acids were reacted with 2,3,4,6-tetra-O-acetyl-β-D-glucopyranosyl isothiocyanate to give diastereomeric thiourea derivatives which were effectively separated on an ODS column by gradient elution (16). The deriva-tives were detected by their absorbance at 254 nm.

4.2 **Optical resolution by using chiral mobile phase additives**

Optical isomers can be separated by adding a chiral metal chelate to the mobile phase for ligand-exchange chromatography. Lindner *et al.* (17) used L-2-isopropyl-4-octyl-diethylenetriamine-Zn(II) as the chiral additive and resolved most of the common amino acids into optical isomers as their dansyl derivatives. The column was 5 μm Hypersil bonded with n-octyl groups and the mobile phase was 0.8 mM metal chelate and 0.19 M ammonium acetate, pH 9, in acetonitrile−water [35:65 (v/v)]. By replacing the Zn(II) with Ni(II), D,L-dansyldipeptides can be similarly resolved.

Nimura *et al.* (16) employed the optically active binary Cu complex with N(*p*-toluene-sulphonyl)-D-phenylglycine as a chiral additive to the mobile phase and achieved resolution of underivatized D,L-amino acids. The amino acids were detected fluorometrically after reaction with O-phthalaldehyde.

4.3 **Optical resolution by ion-pair chromatography**

The separation is based on the formation of diastereomeric IP with a chiral counter-ion in the mobile phase. The diastereomeric IP are then separated by h.p.l.c.

Petterson and Schill (18) used (+)-10-camphosulphonic acid as a chiral IP agent for the direct resolution of some amino alcohols of the β-blocker series. The separation was performed on a LiChrosorb-Diol column with 1-pentanol-dichloromethane [1:199 (v/v)] containing 2.2×10^{-3} M of the IP agent as mobile phase.

Enantiomers of carboxylic and sulphonic acids have also been separated as diastereomeric IP on LiChrosorb-Diol with quinine as the counter-ion (19).

4.4 **Optical resolution by using a chiral stationary phase**

The recent works of Pirkle *et al.* (20) have led to the synthesis of a series of chiral stationary phases for optical resolution. The rational approach to the design of these highly effective phases allows a large number of enantiomers of amines, amino alcohols, amino acids, alcohols and diols to be resolved.

Chiral stationary phases for direct racemic separation are also commercially available, e.g. (R)-N-(3,5-dinitrobenzoyl) phenylglycine bonded to α-aminopropylsilanized silica (J.T.Baker, Regis Chem.), α-acid glycoprotein immobilized on silica (Enantio Pac, LKB), and bovine serum albumin covalently bonded to wide-pore silica (Resolvosil, Macherey-Nagel).

5. SAMPLE PREPARATION TECHNIQUES

The successful application of h.p.l.c. to biomedical analysis often depends on a good sample preparation procedure. In limited instances direct injection of biological fluids (bile, urine, serum) is possible. The great majority of analyses, however, require some form of sample preparation before chromatography to remove the large quantities of interfering materials and to prevent contamination of the analytical column. A good sample preparation technique also minimizes quantitative errors and places less demand on the chromatography leading to better separation and faster analysis.

The following sample preparation techniques are commonly adopted.

5.1 Solvent extraction

This method is useful for compounds which are soluble in organic solvents and can be selectively extracted. Soluble derivatives may also be prepared for compounds that are insoluble in organic solvents provided the reaction is quantitative and does not give multiple products. Ionizable compounds can often be extracted into organic solvents in the presence of a counter-ion as IP or at the isoelectric point by pH adjustment.

5.2 Ultrafiltration

Large molecules and particulate materials can be effectively removed by filtration under pressure using an ultrafiltration cell or by centrifugation in a membrane cone.

5.3 Precipitation

A suitable quantity of an organic solvent (e.g. acetone, acetonitrile, methanol, dimethyl sulphoxide) or a strong acid (e.g. perchloric acid, trichloroacetic acid) may be used to precipitate proteins or to homogenize solid materials like cells and tissues. The solids are removed by centrifugation. It is important to ensure that the extracted solutes are stable in the chosen precipitating agent and that co-precipitation of solutes and proteins is not a problem.

5.4 Solid phase extraction

Selective extraction of solutes onto a solid phase support allows sample concentration as well as effecting a partial sample clean-up. This can be carried out simply by using a small glass column (e.g. a pipette) filled with a suitable sorbent or with a disposable cartridge from Waters Associates (Sep-Pak) or Analytichem International (Bond-Elut). A wide variety of cartridges, packed with different sorbents to provide different selectivities, are available. These include silica and the bonded C_2, C_8, C_{18}, cyano, amino, diol, phenyl, cyclohexyl and ion-exchange phases. Examples of their applications can be found in nearly every chapter of this book. A typical extraction procedure, using a C_{18} cartridge, is as follows.

(i)   Wash the cartridge with methanol to solvate the sorbent.
(ii)   Condition the cartridge with water or a buffer solution with or without IP agent.
(iii) Load the sample solution either directly or after dilution with buffer, pH adjustment or IP formation.
(iv)   Wash the cartridge with a suitable solvent mixture to remove early eluting impurities.
(v)   Selectively elute the solutes with an appropriate eluent.
(vi)   Inject an aliquot directly or after evaporation and reconstitution.

Solid phase extraction has been extended and developed into an Advanced Automated Sample Processor (AASP) by Varian Associates for on-line injection of the total extract from the cartridge into the h.p.l.c.. A maximum of 10 cassettes (each comprising 10 cartridges) may be loaded into the AASP for automatic injection and elution. This technique greatly improved the precision, accuracy and sensitivity of analysis as well as sample through-put. Procedures developed for Sep-Pak or Bond-Elut extraction can often be transferred (with modifications) into an AASP system.

6. GUARD COLUMN

The main function of a guard column is to protect the analytical column from strongly adsorbed compounds, precipitated materials and fine particles. Guard columns are usually 2−5 cm long packed with pellicular materials, porous microparticles (5−10 μm) or large spherical porous particles (30−70 μm) identical or similar in nature to the h.p.l.c. packing. For example, use a silica guard column for NP and an ODS guard column for RP separation. Large spherical porous particles are preferred because they can be easily and conveniently dry packed and have a fair capacity.

A guard column may also act as a solvent pre-saturator when harsh eluents are used, e.g. basic solvents for silica or acid solvents below pH 2 for RP. The guard column will degrade before the analytical column.

7. COLUMN SWITCHING

In this technique (21,22) part of the solutes eluted from the first column are diverted by means of a switching valve into a second column for further separation (*Figure 2*). The second column may be of the same or of a different packing material (e.g. a more retentive phase) to the first column. Multi-column switching is also possible (23) by using more than one switching valve.

Column switching may be used as an alternative to gradient elution (24). Solutes which are not retained by the first column are diverted into a second column. The valve is then switched back to its original position for the separation of compounds retained on the first column. After this is completed the valve is again switched to divert the eluent through the second column for the separation of compounds temporarily held

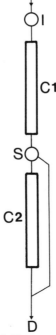

Figure 2. Schematic diagram of a column switching system. I=injector, S=column switching valve; C1= column 1, C2=column 2, D=detector.

on it. The same mobile phase is used throughout. By using columns of different selectivities, especially in multi-column switching operations, very high separation efficiency can be obtained.

Column switching is also a useful sample preparation technique (25,26) when a short pre-column is used as the first column. Only compounds of interest are allowed into the analytical column and unwanted substances are diverted to waste without entering the analytical column.

8. COLUMN TESTING

Columns may be bought pre-packed or packed in the laboratory. Slurry packing techniques are required for $3-10$ μm materials and various methods have been described (27,28). Column packing instruments, together with detailed operating instructions, are commercially available (Shandon Southern, Jones Chromatography).

Whether a column is bought or packed it is important that a standard column testing procedure is carried out to assess its kinetic performance. The test is not concerned with the thermodynamics of separation. A mixture of simple organic compounds showing ideal thermodynamic behaviour, i.e. giving sharp and symmetrical peaks, is therefore chosen as the test mixture.

A good test mixture should include an unretained peak for measuring t_0, a couple of minimally retained peaks to assess zone broadening due to extra column effects, a pair of moderately retained peaks and a well retained component to assess column efficiency and peak symmetry. The author uses a mixture (recommended by Shandon Southern) consisting of acetone, phenol, p-cresole, 3,5-xylenol, anisole and phenetole for testing RP columns packed in the laboratory.

The performance of the packed column is checked by calculating N, h and A_{10} from the chromatogram as described in Section 1. A good 10 cm $\times$ 5 mm column should have N $= 6000-8000$ (for the last peak), $h = 2.5-3.3$ and $A_{10} = 0.85-1.3$. A column of known efficiency should always be used to check instrument efficiency before testing the column. If peak tailing is observed, it is likely that a void space has developed at the top of the column due to settling of the packing materials and this can be solved by simply filling in the void with the packing material. Injecting too large a sample size will also cause peak tailing. If peak fronting is observed, this is most probably due to some of the sample travelling more rapidly down the wall region than the bulk of the sample which passes down the centre of the column. The column is badly packed and requires re-packing.

9. COLUMN MAINTENANCE

H.p.l.c. columns deteriorate gradually over long periods of use. A well maintained column, however, may still give a satisfactory performance after 1 or 2 years of continuous operation. The main causes of column deterioration and their possible remedies (29) are as follows.

(i)   Contamination of the column top by strongly retained and/or undissolved materials from the sample. This problem can be minimized by improving the sample preparation step or by using a guard column. Contaminated columns may be cleaned by washing with a strong solvent, for example removing lipids from RP columns by washing with a mixture of tetrahydrofuran in acetonitrile or methanol and removing proteins by gradient elution with a gradient mixture of acetonitrile, propanol and 0.1% trifluoroacetic acid. Some highly hydrophobic compounds may be removed by eluting the RP column with acetonitrile or methanol with the repeated injection of 100−200 μl of tetrahydrofuran. It is sometimes necessary to replace the top 1−2 mm of the column packing in order to restore a heavily contaminated column.

(ii)   The pH of the mobile phase is too low or too high for column stability. If it is necessary to use harsh solvents a pre-saturation column should be used to prevent the analytical column degrading too rapidly.

(iii)   Impurities in the mobile phase. These gradually collect on the column top and can be avoided by using h.p.l.c. grade solvents and filtration through a micropore filter.

(iv)   Incorrect column storage. Columns should never be stored in water or aqueous buffers as this will result in salt precipitation and microbial growth. RP columns should be flushed with water to remove all salts and then stored with methanol. Acetonitrile−water or methanol−water mixtures may be used for shorter term storage. Normal phase columns are usually stored with dry hexane. It is important to ensure that both ends of the column are tightly capped to prevent solvent evaporation and drying which may alter the column bed geometry.

10. REFERENCES

1. Knox,J.H. and Bristow,P.A. (1977) *Chromatographia*, **10**, 279.
2. Knox,J.H., ed. (1978) *High-Performance Liquid Chromatography*. Edinburgh University Press, Edinburgh, UK.
3. Snyder,L.R. (1974) *Anal. Chem.*, **46**, 1384.
4. Synder,L.R. (1968) *Principles of Adsorption Chromatography*. Marcel Dekker, New York.
5. Abbot,S.R. (1980) *J. Chromatogr. Sci.*, **18**, 540.
6. Major,R.E. (1980) *J. Chromatogr. Sci.*, **18**, 488.
7. Wood,R., Cummings,L. and Jupille,T. (1980) *J. Chromatogr. Sci.*, **18**, 559.
8. Cooke,N.H.C. and Olsen,K. (1980) *J. Chromatogr. Sci.*, **18**, 512.
9. Bidlingmeyer,B.A. (1980) *J. Chromatogr. Sci.*, **18**, 525.
10. Horváth,Cs., Melander,W.R. and Molnar,I. (1977) *Anal. Chem.*, **49**, 142.
11. Melander,W.R., Stoveken,J. and Horváth,Cs. (1979) *J. Chromatogr.*, **185**, 111.
12. Lim,C.K. and Peters,T.J. (1984) *J. Chromatogr.*, **316**, 397.
13. Lim,C.K., Rideout,J.M. and Peters,T.J. (1984) *J. Chromatogr.*, **317**, 333.
14. Knox,J.H. and Jurand,J. (1981) *J. Chromatogr.*, **218**, 341.
15. Lindner,W. and Leitner,Ch. (1984) *J. Chromatogr.*, **316**, 605.
16. Nimura,N., Toyama,A. and Kinoshita,T. (1984) *J. Chromatogr.*, **316**, 547.
17. Lindner,W., Le Page,T.N., Davies,G., Seitz,D.E. and Karger,B.L. (1979) *J. Chromatogr.*, **185**, 323.
18. Petterson,C. and Schill,G. (1981) *J. Chromatogr.*, **204**, 179.
19. Petterson,C. (1984) *J. Chromatogr.*, **316**, 553.
20. Pirkle,W.H., Hyun,M.H. and Bank,B. (1984) *J. Chromatogr.*, **316**, 585.
21. Huber,J.F.K., van der Linden,R., Ecker,E. and Oreans,M. (1973) *J. Chromatogr.*, **83**, 267.
22. Huber,J.F.K. and Vodenik,R. (1976) *J. Chromatogr.*, **122**, 265.
23. Alfredson,T.V. (1981) *J. Chromatogr.*, **218**, 715.
24. Huber,J.F.K. and Eisenbeiss,F. (1978) *J. Chromatogr.*, **149**, 127.
25. Erni,F., Keller,M.P., Morin,C. and Schmitt,M. (1981) *J. Chromatogr.*, **204**, 65.
26. Werkhoven-Goewie,C.E., De Ruiter,C., Brinkmann,U.A.Th., Frei,R.W., De Jong,G.J., Little,C.J. and Stahel,O. (1983) *J. Chromatogr.*, **255**, 79.
27. Bristow,P.A., Brittain,P.N., Riley,C.M. and Williamson,B.F. (1977) *J. Chromatogr.*, **131**, 57.
28. Martin,M. and Guichon,G. (1977) *Chromatographia*, **10**, 194.
29. Rabel,F.M. (1980) *J. Chromatogr. Sci.*, **18**, 394.

CHAPTER 2

Amino acids and small peptides

MICHAEL H.JOSEPH and CHARLES A.MARSDEN

1. INTRODUCTION

The first problem in amino acid analysis is one of resolution rather than sensitivity. Animal blood plasma and tissues contain relatively large pools of the principal protein amino acids in their free form. These fall into a number of groups based on classes of substituent (acid, basic, neutral, aromatic, etc), but within each group the structural differences are relatively subtle.

In the traditional ion-exchange procedure of Moore and Stein (1), free amino acids are separated on columns of sulphonated cation-exchange resins, and detection and quantification are achieved by a post-column reaction with ninhydrin and spectrophotometry in the visible range. The automated version of this system (2) has for several decades represented the commonest laboratory use of (moderately) h.p.l.c., pressures up to some hundreds of p.s.i. being used with relatively large columns. Automated apparatus of this type has reached a high level of sophistication and the technique has been refined in detailed studies by several groups (3−5).

The recent surge of interest in h.p.l.c. however is based on the development of columns packed with very uniform micro-particulate silica (3−10 μm) chemically modified to give a surface coating with different functional groups. This enables high resolution to be obtained with short columns (15−30 cm); high pressures (1000−3000 p.s.i.) then being required to obtain reasonable flow-rates. 'Reversed-phase' (RP) packings, in which silica particles are reacted with alkyl silylating reagents (covering the surface with hydrophobic hydrocarbon chains), and used with polar (principally aqueous) mobile phases have proved to be extremely versatile in the analysis of common components of physiological tissues and fluids and of drugs, many of which exhibit a mixed hydrophobic−hydrophilic character. It is estimated that 80% of current h.p.l.c. work is carried out on RP packings. This chapter is aimed therefore particularly at the investigator who possesses h.p.l.c. equipment and who wants to analyse amino acids and small peptides from time to time, but not at such intensity or frequency as to immediately justify the purchase of a dedicated automatic amino acid analyser. An h.p.l.c. amino acid system can be subsequently upgraded to a fully automatic system if this is required (6).

2. DERIVATIZATION

Few of the protein amino acids have side chains with physical characteristics which permit direct estimation in solution. The major group of those that do, phenylalanine, tyrosine and tryptophan, owe their u.v.-absorbing, fluorescent and electrochemical activities to their (substituted) aromatic nuclei, and these also confer reasonable retention on a RP column. Thus, as we shall see (Section 6.1), aromatic amino acids and their many biologically important metabolites can be determined in their free form by RP-h.p.l.c. For general determination of protein amino acids however, derivatization is universally used for detection and quantification. All derivatization reagents introduced to date interact with the amino group, although subsequent cyclization to the phenylthiohydantoin (PTH)-amino acid in the case of phenylisothiocyanate derivatives does also involve the carboxyl group. Thus the agents used will, in general, react with ammonia, with the N terminus of peptides and proteins, with other primary amines and diamines and, in appropriate cases, with other secondary amines. They will also derivatize non-α-amino acids; for example γ-aminobutyric acid (GABA) and taurine, two ω-amino acids which are particularly abundant in brain tissue. In general, with the exception of ammonia, this is not an analytical problem because of the relative abundance of amino acids, and indeed can be turned to advantage in the analysis of peptides (Section 5.3), amines (7) and diamines (Section 5.2).

The properties of a number of the principal derivatization reagents are compared in *Table 1*, and a fuller description of their development and properties can be found elsewhere (6,8,9). We wish to concentrate on *o*-phthalaldehyde-thiol reagent (OPT-thiol), because we believe this to be the most useful for the 'occasional' amino acid analyst. (OPT is more properly, but rarely called *o*-phthaldialdehyde.)

The reaction of OPT-thiol with an amino acid, or indeed any primary amine, is shown in *Figure 1*. It can be seen that a new heterocyclic species is generated, a substituted isoindole. This is the source of the fluorescence and the electrochemical activity of the OPT-amino acid derivatives and, as in the case of the aromatic amino acids, it also

Table 1. Comparison of some detection reagents for amino acids.

	Ninhydrin	*Dansylchloride (DNS-Cl)*	*Fluorescamine*	*o-Phthalaldehyde-thiol (OPT-thiol)*
Solvent	Aqueous	Anhydrous	Anhydrous	Aqueous
Incubation (typical)	20 min 100°C	30 min 37°C	Negligible (<1 sec) Room temperature	1–120 sec Room temperature
Detection	Absorbance 550, 470	Fluorescence 340/510	Fluorescence 390/475	Fluorescence 340/455
Sensitivity	Moderate to good (>100 pmol)	Good (10–50 pmol)	Good	Very good (<10 pmol)
Secondary amines	Yes[a]	Yes[a]	No	No
Pre-columm possible		Yes		Yes
Comments	Problems: NH$_3$, stability of reagent	Problems: fluorescence of DNS-OH[a] side reactions	Expensive	Derivatives Electrochemically active

[a]At different wavelengths

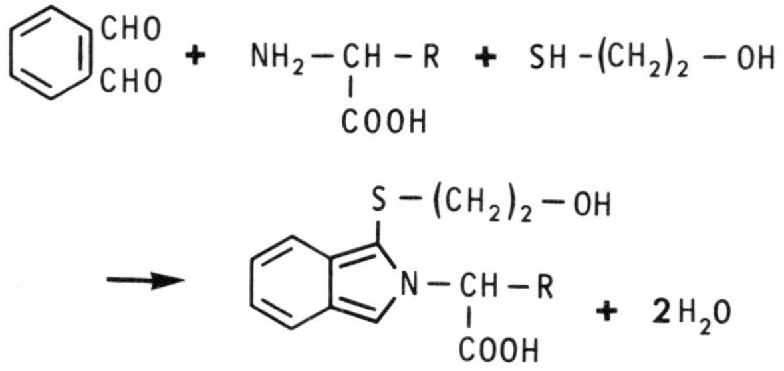

Figure 1. Reaction of OPT-thiol with amino acid.

results in a species which chromatographs well on RP packings. Thus pre-column derivatization can be used, which with multi-use h.p.l.c. equipment is preferable to the plumbing modification implicit in post-column derivatization. It is also more economical of reagents.

Other advantages are as follows.

(i)   The reagent does not react with water [contrast dansylchloride (DNS-Cl), fluorescamine] and can be made up as a stable solution in aqueous buffer.

(ii)   The reaction is fast $(1-2$ min) and carried out at room temperature (contrast ninhydrin, DNS-Cl), although not as fast as fluorescamine.

(iii)   Ammonia does not result in substantial interference.

(iv)   Single products in high yield are formed (contrast DNS-Cl).

(v)   The electrochemical activity of the OPT-amino acids means that dual series detection, with much improved specificity, is available.

(vi)   The reagent is cheap and freely available.

The drawbacks to the method include.

(i)   The OPT-amino acid derivatives are not stable indefinitely, and the stability varies between amino acids (but see Section 5.1).

(ii)   The OPT-thiol reagent will not react with secondary amines or amino acids unless they are first converted to primary amine derivatives (Section 5.4).

3. PRACTICAL H.P.L.C. SEPARATION OF OPT-AMINO ACIDS

Many descriptions have appeared of the application of conventional apparatus for RP-h.p.l.c. to the analysis of OPT derivatives of amino acids $(10-13)$. The high resolution of RP (typically C_{18}) columns means that it is unlikely to be possible to resolve the full range of protein amino acids under isocratic conditions. The solution is to use gradient elution, using either two pumps with high pressure mixing, or one pump with mixing on the inlet side using proportioning valves or a gradient former. Isocratic elution can be used for resolving the slow running group of large neutral amino acids which compete for the large neutral amino acid uptake system (13,14). If gradient equipment is not available, a cheap ($\sim$£200) alternative may be constructed from a pneumatic valve and cam timer, which permits switching between two eluting buffers and back again at pre-determined times (15,16). However, in what follows we will assume that some form of gradient h.p.l.c. apparatus is available.

We have used a 150 $\times$ 4.6 mm column of Hypersil ODS 5 μm or ultrasphere ODS with equal success. A short guard column containing the same packing or a 30 μm pellicular RP column is strongly advisable where physiological samples are to be handled. We have used phosphate buffers, with methanol as organic modifier. Acetonitrile may be useful as an additional/alternative modifier with columns with greater retaining power. For a detailed analysis of the influence of different buffer species on retention see (10). Either fluorescence or electrochemical detection (or preferably both in series) can be used. Normally a simple filter fluorimeter with low volume flow cell is used. Excitation and emission wavelengths are well separated at 360 and 455 nm, respectively [the suggestion that excitation at 230 nm gives higher sensitivity but with more risk of interference (17) may relate only to second order scatter from the excitation monochromator]. A suitable lamp and band pass filter will provide excitation at about 350 mm and a suitable cut off filter will restrict emission below 400 mm. For electrochemical detection (ECD), most commercially available models are suitable; these are provided with a glassy carbon or porous carbon working electrode whose potential can be set at least between 0.0 and 1.0 V.

3.1 H.p.l.c. conditions for separation of OPT-amino acids

Low (A) and high (B) strength methanol mobile phases are made up as folows.

(i)   Weigh out enough NaH_2PO_4 to make up one litre of 0.05 M phosphate buffer and dissolve in about 900 ml of water.

(ii)   Bring to the pH required (5.5) with 1 M NaOH with continual stirring; add water to 1 litre.

(iii)   Mix 800 ml with 200 ml of AnalaR methanol (buffer A) and 200 ml with 800 ml of methanol (buffer B).

(iv)   Thoroughly degas both solutions under reduced pressure (in an ultrasonic bath if necessary).

(v)   Prime the h.p.l.c. system with buffers A and B and equilibrate the column and detectors with buffer A.

We have used a gradient of $0-10\%$ in buffer B in 10 min, $10-85\%$ in 30 min, $85-0\%$ in 5 min and 10 min re-equilibration, but the slope and timing must be determined empirically for the column and system used.

3.2 Preparation of OPT-thiol reagent

The OPT-thiol reagent is made up at least 24 h before use (10,13), as follows.

(i)   Dissolve 27 mg of OPT in 500 μl of absolute alcohol, add 5 ml of a 0.1 M solution of sodium tetraborate dehydrate (borax).

(ii)   Mix.

(iii)   Add 50 μl of mercaptoethanol in a fume cupboard.

(iv)   Mix thoroughly, store in a tightly closed container in the dark.

This reagent can be kept for several weeks with periodic additions of 20 μl of mercaptoethanol to maintain the yield of OPT-amino acid. Ready to use OPT-thiol reagent solution is available from Sigma Chemical Co. Ltd.

3.3 **Preparation of OPT-amino acids**

To derivatize, mix thoroughly 200 μl of OPT reagent with 50 μl of amino acid solution (100 nmol/ml is convenient for standards), or distilled water for the blank, wait 2 min and inject 20 μl into the h.p.l.c. system, starting the gradient at the same time. Because of the limited stability of the OPT-amino acids, it is important that the time between mixing and injection into the h.p.l.c. is consistent. On the fluorescence detector a peak should be seen for each amino acid in the standard, with little or no unretained peak. Peaks on the electrochemical detector will depend on the potential set, but 0.6 V should give peaks for all the amino acids. In addition there is a marked unretained peak, the height of which will increase with working electrode potential. It will obviously be necessary to experiment with a variety of mixtures of a few amino acid standards to build up a picture of the separation achieved before going on to complete standard mixtures and physiological samples.

3.4 **Sample preparation**

Tissue or physiological fluids for amino acid analysis will need to be deproteinized. Homogenize the tissue in 4 volumes of methanol, let stand for 10 min at 4°C, centrifuge (5000−10 000 *g*; 10 min) to remove precipitated protein and treat the supernatant as the amino acid standard solution above. If acid is needed to efficiently disrupt the tissue

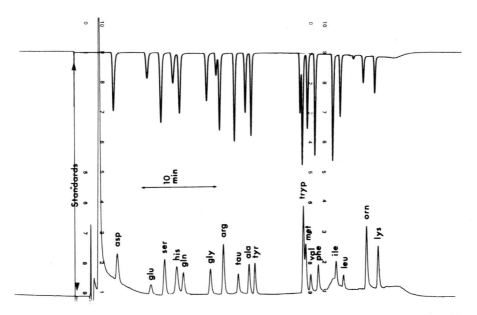

Figure 2. Gradient elution of OPT-amino acid standard mixture (400 pmol each) on 15 cm x 4 mm Hypersil ODS. Gradient mixture: **A**, 80% (v/v) 0.05 M sodium phosphate buffer, pH 5.5, in methanol; **B**, 20% of the same buffer in methanol. Elution 0−10% B in 10 min, 10−85% in 30 min, 85−0% in 5 min and 10 min re-equilibration. Lower, electrochemical trace at 0.5 V, f.s.d. 50 nA; upper, fluorimetric trace (Fluoromat 10 mV ×1 setting).

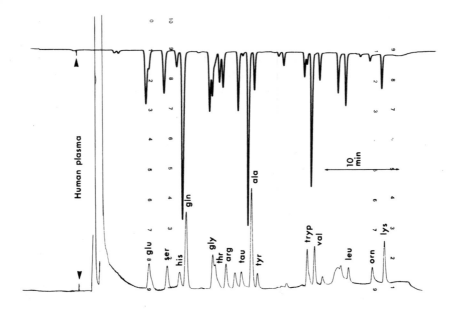

Figure 3. Separation of OPT-amino acids in human plasma. Conditions as in *Figure 2*.

and precipitate protein, then this will need to be neutralized since the OPT reaction is carried out at alkaline pH. Orthophosphoric acid is a useful possibility as this will not interfere with the chromatography after neturalization. Ammonia can interfere with the determination if present at very high concentrations, for example, some urine samples. It can be removed by precipitation with sodium tetraphenyl boron prior to derivatization (18).

3.5 Peak identification and quantification

The ratio of fluorescence to electrochemical peak height should be the same for each amino acid in the sample as for that amino acid in the standard. This provides a check on identity additional to that of retention time. Since the variation of peak height with electrochemical potential depends upon amino acid structure, even more positive identification can be obtained by varying the detector potential on successive runs (for details see ref. 13), or by using a multiple electrode detector (see ref. 19).

The concentration of each amino acid in the injected supernatants is then calculated using the response of either detector, provided that standards and samples have been run under the same conditions. The standard concentration is multipled by the ratio of the peak height of the sample to that of the standard for that amino acid to give the sample concentration. Since the total volume of supernatant is known, the total amount of amino acid in the tissue sample and thus its concentration per unit weight, can be calculated. For further details see (16). *Figures 2−8* show examples of amino acid determinations in standards and in various tissues and fluids.

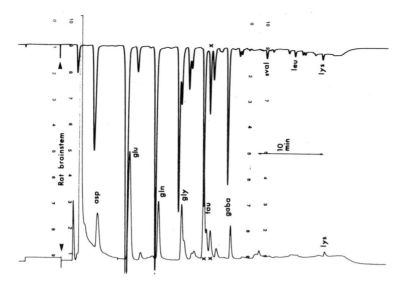

Figure 4. Separation of OPT-amino acids in rat brain stem. Conditions as in *Figure 2.*

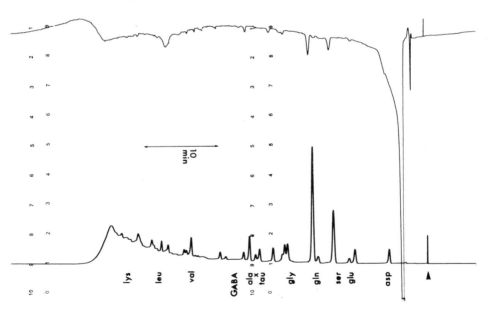

Figure 5. Separation of OPT-amino acids in push−pull perfusate of rat hippocampus. Upper, electrochemical trace at 0.5 V, f.s.d. 20 nA; lower, fluorimetric trace 10 mV × 0.2 setting. Other conditions as in *Figure 2.*

4. COMMON PROBLEMS ENCOUNTERED

4.1 Bubbles formed during the gradient

This is most likely to occur as the concentration of organic modifier (methanol) reaches a maximum and to affect the electrochemical detector more markedly ('spikes'). The

19

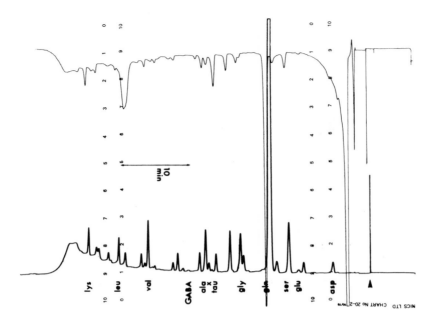

Figure 6. Separation of OPT-amino acids in human lumbar CSF. Conditions as in *Figure 5* except electrochemical trace at f.s.d. 50 nA.

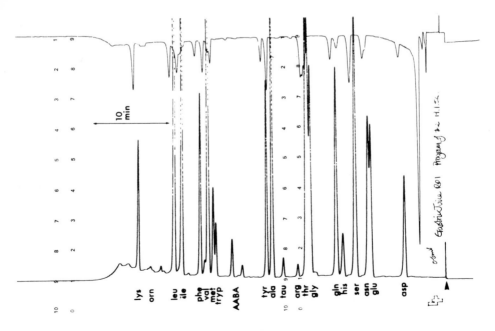

Figure 7. Separation of OPT-amino acids in human gastric juice. Conditons as in *Figure 6* except fluorimetric trace at 10 mV × 0.5 setting.

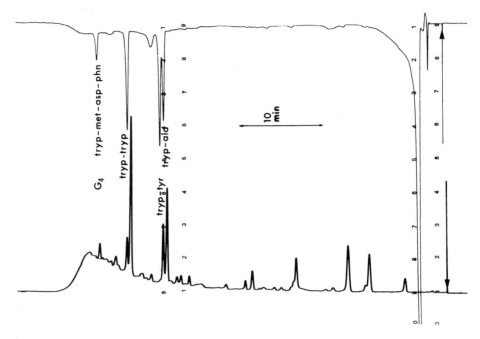

Figure 8. Separation of OPT-tryptophyl di- and tetra-peptide standards. Conditions as in *Figure 6* except fluorimetric trace at 10 mV × 0.1 setting.

problem is also liable to build up over time if the system is kept running overnight and the buffer reservoirs are not in a temperature-controlled environment. The best solution is to additionally degas the mobile phases with helium through a gas bubbler and, if possible, to sparge continually with a low flow-rate during operation of the h.p.l.c. system.

4.2 Rising electrochemical baseline during the gradient

That this is due to the operation of the gradient, rather than the high methanol buffer itself can be seen by holding the gradient at its highest point and observing the baseline. It appears to be due to a build up of metal ions in the slow flowing component of the buffer and can be markedly reduced by adding EDTA to both buffers (0.01% final concentration) and replacing the sintered metal submersible filters usually provided on h.p.l.c. pump inlet lines with sintered glass filters. Persistent problems may require passification of the pump and connecting tubing up to the junction point between buffers (but not the column ! − try a glass-lined one if this gives problems) with 3 M nitric acid.

4.3 Peaks present in the blank

This problem is variable from laboratory to laboratory and depends partly on batch to batch variation in reagents. When double detection is available it can often be seen that interfering peaks only show up on one detector and not the other, and can thus be distinguished from genuine amino acids showing up on both. Where very high sensitivities are being used, peaks in the blank may arise from amino acid contaminants in reagents, distilled water or on glassware, etc., reflecting the protean distribution of these compounds. Since the method has been used to determine amino acids in sea water (see 10), the basal level of environmental contamination is likely to underlie the realistic limit of detection.

4.4 Failure to adequately resolve certain amino acid pairs

We have problems with the pairs Gln and His, Gly and Thr and Met and Trp. When the amino acids differ in charge their relative retention is readily altered by changing the pH of the eluting buffer. This enables us to separate Gln and His. Gly and Thr is a common problem; the only published solution we have found is the inclusion of a small amount of tetrahydrofuran (ref. 11, concentration $1-2\%$) in buffer A (can be in buffer B also). Met and Trp are a continuing problem, although strangely not so with isocratic elution. If any readers have found a solution to the problem (other than running the electrochemical detector at a low voltage so that it sees Trp and not Met) the authors would be pleased to hear about it.

4.5 Increase in column back pressure over samples

Two laboratories have independently reported increases in back pressure when a series of brain perfusates or superfusates are successively chromatographed using the procedure described above for the analysis of amino acids. This appears to be due to high molecular weight material, since the problem can be solved by filtering the perfusate through a 10 000 molecular weight cut off filter using a centrifugal device (16) before derivatizing the free amino acids.

5. MODIFICATIONS AND EXTENSIONS TO THE OPT METHOD

5.1 Use of alternate thiols

As mentioned above, the stability of OPT-amino acid derivatives is limited and variable. This necessitates accurate timing of the procedure and makes automation of the procedure difficult unless the autoinjector can also do the mixing (Waters WISP or Anachem-Gilson). Ethane thiol in place of mercaptoethanol was reported to result in more stable derivatives of amines (20) but this has not been confirmed for amino acids (9,10,21). It appears that the limited stability is due to nucleophilic attack on the sulphur atom derived from the thiol (22) and that more sterically bulky amines produce more stable derivatives (23). This has led to the trial of more bulky thiols. Mercaptopropionic acid has been used with OPT as a post-column reagent (24) and in our hands does produce more stable derivatives, although the retention times of all the amino acids are altered somewhat, as might be expected. Recently t-butyl thiol has been introduced as a reagent which will sterically hinder attack on the S-atom (21,25). This results in very good stability, and electrochemical activity is little affected, although fluorescence is considerably reduced.

5.2 Extension to diamines

Biogenic diamines such as cadaverine and putrescine will also react with OPT and form stable derivatives which will chromatograph under the conditions for amino acids. If the gradient used is extended to 100% buffer B, then diamines can be eluted also. The stability of the spermine and spermidine derivatives is limited because of nucleophilic attack from the secondary amine groups in the chain (22). Again, steric hindrance could be exploited in the formation of more stable derivatives.

5.3 Extension to small peptides

As noted above (and ref. 13), OPT will react with the N-terminal amino acid of peptides. Fluorescence of the resulting derivatives rapidly falls off with increasing peptide chain length. However, the electrochemical activity is again considerably less affected. Thus, in principle, OPT derivatization can be used to determine a number of small peptides which are particularly abundant in, for example, brain tissue (carnosine, homocarnosine, CCK-4).

5.4 Extension to secondary amino acids and cysteine

Proline and hydroxyproline will not react with OPT-thiol as a primary amine group is required. Cysteine gives a poor fluorescence yield (although its electrochemical yield is less attenuated) presumably due to its dual amine and thiol functions. These amino acids can be determined separately using pre-column derivatization with NBD-Cl (26), or concurrently with the other protein amino acids using supplementary pre-column reactions prior to the OPT-thiol derivatization (27).

6. DIRECT H.P.L.C. OF AMINO ACIDS

6.1 Aromatic amino acids

As mentioned above the structures which confer u.v.-absorbing, fluorescence and EC activity on aromatic amino acids also allow them to be separated directly on RP columns without derivatization. *Table 2* gives relevant data on the aromatic amino acids found in proteins, and a number of related metabolites including the precursors of the biogenic amines. The capacity factors are given as an example for a 15 cm column of Hypersil ODS as described previously, but using a mobile phase of 0.1 M NaH_2PO_4:methanol (90:10). Fluorescence properties, and the approximate electrode potential needed for EC detection are indicated. Fuller details can be found in the references cited.

Table 2. LCEC properties of aromatic amino acids.

	FL	EC(V)	k'
Phe[a]	+	–	–
Tyr[b]	+	0.8	1.3
DOPA		0.4	Needs pairing agent, see Chapter 3
Trp[c]	+	0.9	5.4
5HTP[c]	+	0.5	2.85
Kyn[d]		1.1	2.7
3-HK[d]		0.4	1.75

[a]From ref. 28; [b]from ref. 14; [c]from ref. 16; [d]from ref. 29.
DOPA: dihydroxyphenylalanine; 5HTP; 5-hydroxytryptophan; Kyn: kynurenine; 3-HK; 3-hydroxykyn-urenine.

6.2 Cysteine and histidine

Cysteine is also electroactive and it, and other thiols, can be determined at a gold−mercury or gold electrode (8). Histidine and its metabolites are not electroactive, but can be determined using a specific reaction with fluorescamine (8).

7. LIQUID CHROMATOGRAPHIC−ELECTROCHEMICAL DETECTION (LCEC) OF SMALL PEPTIDES

Only two amino acids, tyrosine and tryptophan, are readily oxidized at a carbon-based electrode but at higher potentials (+0.9 V) than catechol and indoleamines (Chapter 3, Section 1.1). Many of the neuropeptides recently identified contain one or both of these amino acids and therefore are electroactive (*Table 3*, ref. 30). Radioimmunoassay (RIA) is the general method for measuring neuropeptides. There are, however, many examples of families of peptides whose sequence differs by only one amino acid which poses difficulties in producing absolutely specific antibodies. H.p.l.c. is increasingly used to separate closely related neuropeptides prior to RIA. An alternative approach is to combine h.p.l.c. with a sensitive on-line detection system. Neither u.v. nor fluorescence detection have adequate sensitivity to measure the low levels found in brain but LCEC has been shown to have the prerequisite sensitivity to measure certain neuropeptides in brain. These include cholecystokinin (31) and, from the studies of Johnson *et al.* (32), arginine vasopressin (AVP). This section will describe the LCEC detection of vasopressin using the Coulochem dual electrode detector (ESA) combined with a radial compression separation system (Waters).

Table 3. Peak oxidation potentials of tyrosine, tryptophan, cysteine and neuropeptides containing these amino acids at pH 4.6.

Substance	V
Tyrosine	0.84
Tryptophan	0.88
Cysteine	0.90−1.00
Neurotensin	0.78
Oxytocin	0.82
Vasopressin	0.82
Caerulein	0.83
Leu-enkephalin	0.84
Met-enkephalin	0.84
Somatostatin	0.86−0.90
Cholecystokinin (CCK-4)	0.88
Cholecystokinin (CCK-8)	0.88
LH-releasing hormone	0.83
β-MSH	0.80−0.86
ACTH1-24	0.80−0.88

The values (V) are the potential at which maximum current was generated.
Peptides containing neither tyrosine nor tryptophan are not electroactive (e.g. substance P, thyrotrophin-releasing hormone).
Amino acids (1 μm) and neuropeptides (0.1 μm) were dissolved in 5 ml of 0.15 M citrate/acetate pH 4.6 and electroactivity determined using differential pulse voltammetry. Data taken from ref. 30.

7.1 Method for arginine vasopressin (AVP) based on that described in references (32,33)

7.1.1 *H.p.l.c. technique*

RP isocratic h.p.l.c. separation of various neuropeptides can be performed using a Waters Z module radial compression separation system containing a radial-pak C_{18}, 10 μm cartridge. The mobile phase is 0.15 M NaH_2PO_4/methanol (60:40 v/v), pH 5.8, delivered at a constant flow-rate of 1.5 ml/min by a Waters 510 pump.

7.1.2 *Electrochemical detection*

The detector is an ESA Coulochem 5100A dual channel detector with two porous graphite in-line working electrodes (see Chapter 3). The current/voltage curve for AVP (20 pmol injected) shows that increasing the voltage at detector electrode 2 led to an increased peak height (nA) up to a plateau level of 800 nA between 0.80 V and 0.90 V. The optimum working potential (i.e. maximum response at lowest offset current) is 0.85 V at detector electrode 2 using electrode 1 at a screen potential of 0.40 V. Similar electrode conditions were found to be optimum for other peptides investigated. The system also incorporated a guard cell electrode prior to the injector and this was set at 0.90 V to act as a scrubber for the mobile phase.

7.2 Detection of neuropeptide standards

Using the above conditions the retention times (min) of the series of peptide standards (20 pmol injected) are as follows: AVP (5.0), Met-enkephalin (6.0), Leu-enkephalin (7.5), oxytocin (11.0), angiotensin II (12.5), neurotensin (15.5) and angiotensin III (17.5). Calibration curves for each of the above neuropeptides were constructed between 0.2 and 200 pmol injected by measuring the peak area. The limit of detection for each peptide at a signal-to-noise ratio of 3:1 is less than 200 fmol.

7.3 Measurement of AVP in tissues

Brain, pituitary or adrenal tissues are dissected out and homogenized by sonication (Ultrasonics Rapides Ltd, 100 W for 1 min) in 1 M acetic acid. The supernatant is separated by centrifugation (4000 *g* for 20 min), dried down in a vortex evaporator (Buchler) and stored at $-20°C$. The pellet is also kept at $-20°C$ so that the protein content can be determined. Samples are taken up in mobile phase prior to injection.

Tentative identification of peaks observed in brain tissue extracts can be made by comparing their h.p.l.c. retention times (R_T) with the R_T of pure synthetic standards and confirmed by adding similarly extracted standards to the tissue extract ('spiking') (see Chapter 3, Section 6.1). To test that each peak is made up of only one peptide and not a mixture of peptides with similar R_T, two oxidation peaks can be generated for each peptide using the dual electrodes (see Chapter 3, Section 5.2) and the ratio of the two peak heights measured. For example, AVP standards are injected onto the column with detector electrode 1 set at 0.60 V and detector 2 at 0.90 V. Some AVP is oxidized at detector 1 and the remainder at detector 2, the ratio of the two peak heights is recorded. This procedure is then repeated for AVP in extracts of neurointermediate lobe (NIL) and the two ratios compared. The peak height ratio for AVP standard under these conditions has been found to be 1.265 ± 0.005 ($n = 10$) and for AVP in the NIL extract 1.30 ± 0.02 ($n = 10$). There is no significant difference between these two values confirming that the AVP peak measured in the tissue extracts does not include other peptides with similar R_T. Similar procedures need to be repeated with other brain tissue extracts for other peptides before their identification can be accepted.

7.4 Advantages of the coulometric ESA detector combined with radial compression separation for peptide determination

We have found no particular advantage in using the ESA Coulochem detector for the assay of catechol and indoleamines (see Chapter 3) but for the assay of AVP its use has resulted in markedly improved signal-to-noise ratios compared with earlier studies using a Bioanalytical Systems (BAS) glassy carbon electrode system. The ESA detector enables operation in the 'screen mode' whereby the first detector can be set to oxidize substances at a lower potential (0.4 V) in order to remove background and unwanted peak currents at the second detector (set at 0.85 V). Thus peptide oxidations are monitored within the range $0.40-0.85$ V. This screening is possible since the large surface area graphite-porous detectors oxidize almost all of the eluate in contrast with more conventional amperometric detectors. Furthermore, a guard cell is present in the system prior to the injector set at a potential above the working range of detector 2, in order to oxidize and eliminate any contaminants in the mobile phase so allowing further improvement to the signal-to-noise ratio. The coulometric detector also offers improvements in sensitivity and reproducibility since much of the large electrode surface area of the detectors is not inactivated by neuropeptide adsorption to the electrode surface as occurs with small surface amperometric detectors.

The use of the Z module offers a number of advantages compared with the conventional column. Firstly, the uniformly compressed cartridge improves peak separation and reduces peak 'tailing' due to surface properties which are characteristic of column separation. Secondly, the reduced resistance to flow of the mobile phase through the cartridge compared with a column (with equivalent packing material) enables more rapid analysis at lower back pressures. Finally, the Z module cartridge contributed towards improvements in the signal-to-noise ratio and consequently in the overall improvement in sensitivity.

We (33) have compared ATP levels in the neurointermediate lobe using LCEC and RIA and the results have shown that the former method overcomes the problem of antibody specificity providing more accurate and specific measurement of tissue AVP.

8. CONCLUSIONS

Use of OPT derivatization provides a simple and robust way to determine free amino acids for the occasional user, and thus the metabolism of the transmitter amino acids, including taurine and γ-aminobutyric acid (GABA). The technique is also suitable for the determination of the primary amino acid composition of protein hydrolysates, although a preliminary reaction is required for secondary amino acids (26,27). H.p.l.c. separation of PTH-amino acids can also be used for protein sequencing. The OPT technique also shows promise for the determination of small peptides.

Direct detection following h.p.l.c. is also particularly useful in examining the metabolism of aromatic amino acids in relation to their role as precursors of physiologically important compounds. Direct detection following h.p.l.c. is also suitable for peptides containing aromatic amino acid residues.

9. ACKNOWLEDGEMENTS

We thank Philip Davies for technical assistance (M.H.J.) and the Wellcome Trust and the SERC for financial support (C.A.M.). The LCEC assay for AVP was developed by C.A.M. in collaboration with Dr G.Bennett and Janel Johnson. Figures $2-8$ are reproduced from ref. 13 by kind permission of the publisher, Elsevier, Amsterdam.

10. REFERENCES

1. Moore,S. and Stein,W.H. (1951) *J. Biol. Chem.*, **192**, 663.
2. Spackman,D.H., Stein,W.H. and Moore,S. (1958) *Anal. Chem.*, **30**, 1190.
3. Hamilton,P.B. (1960) *Anal. Chem.*, **32**, 1779,1782,
4. Perry,T.L. (1982) In *Handbook of Neurochemistry*, Vol. **I**, 2nd edition, Lajtha,A. (ed.), Plenum, New York, p. 151.
5. de Belleroche,J., Dykes,C.R. and Thomas,A.J. (1976) *Anal. Biochem.*, **71**, 193.
6. Chan,M.M.S. (1985) *Amino Acid Analysis by HPLC*, Bulletin GR 5925, Beckman Instruments, Fullerton, CA, USA.
7. Davis,T.P., Gehrke,C.W., Gehrke,C.W.,Jr., Cunningham,T.D., Kuo,K.C., Gerhardt,K.O., Johnson,H.D. and Williams,C.H. (1978) *Clin. Chem.*, **24**, 1317.
8. Perrett,D. (1984) In *The Chemistry and Biochemistry of the Amino Acids*, Barrett,G.C. (ed.), Chapman and Hall, London, p. 426.
9. Lee,K.S and Drescher,D.G. (1978) *Int. J. Biochem.*, **9**, 457.
10. Lindroth,P. and Mopper,K. (1979) *Anal. Chem.*, **51**, 1667.
11. Jones,B.N., Pääbo,S. and Stein,S. (1981) *J. Liquid Chromatogr.*, **4**, 565.
12. Turnell,D.C. and Cooper,J.D.H. (1982) *Clin. Chem.*, **28**, 527.
13. Joseph,M.H. and Davies,P. (1983) *J. Chromatogr.*, **277**, 125.
14. Joseph,M.H., Johnson,J.A. and Kennett,G.A. (1984) in *Progress in Tryptophan and Serotonin Research*, Schlossberger,H.G., Kochen,W., Linzen,B. and Steinhart,H. (eds), W.de Gruyter, Berlin, p. 387.
15. Joseph,M.H., Kadam,B.V. and Risby,D. (1981) *J. Chromatogr.*, **226**, 361.
16. Joseph,M.H. (1986) In *Working Methods in Neuropsychopharmacology*, Joseph,M.H. and Waddington,J.L. (eds), Manchester University Press, in press.
17. Hill,D.W., Walter,F.H., Wilson,T.D. and Stuart,V.D. (1979) *Anal. Chem.*, **51**, 1338.
18. Turnell,D.C. and Cooper,J.D.H. (1984) *Clin. Chem.*, **30**, 588.
19. Joseph,M.H. and Marsden,C.A. (1986) In *Monitoring Neurotransmitter Release During Behaviour*, Joseph,M.H., Fillenz,M., Macdonald,I.A. and Marsden,C.A. (eds), Ellis Horwood, Chichester, UK, p. 195.
20. Simons,S.S. and Johnson,D.F. (1977) *Anal. Biochem.*, **82**, 250.
21. Jacobs,W.A., Meyer,G.S., Hamilton,P.J., Leburg,M.L. and Shoup,R.E. (1986) In *Monitoring Neurotransmitter Release During Behaviour*, Joseph,M.H., Fillenz,M., Macdonald,I.A. and Marsden,C.A. (eds), Ellis Horwood, Chichester, p. 239.
22. Skaaden,T. and Greibrokk,T. (1982) *J. Chromatogr.*, **247**, 111.
23. Stobaugh,J.F., Repta,A.J., Sternson,L.A. and Garren,K.W. (1983) *Anal. Biochem.*, **135**, 495.
24. Kucera,P. and Umgat,H. (1983) *J. Chromatogr.*, **255**, 563.
25. Allison,L.A., Mayer,G.S. and Shoup,R.E. (1984) *Anal. Chem.*, **56**, 1089.
26. Umgat,H., Kucera,P. and Wen,L.F. (1982) *J. Chromatogr.*, **239**, 463.
27. Cooper,J.D.H., Lewis,M.T. and Turnell,D.C. (1984) *J. Chromatogr.*, **285**, 484.
28. Hyland,K., Smith,I. and Howell,D. (1985) In *Monitoring Neurotransmitter Release During Behaviour*, Joseph,M.H., Fillenz,M., Macdonald,I.A. and Marsden,C.A. (eds), Ellis Horwood, Chichester, p. 233.
29. Joseph,M.H. (1984) In *Progress in Tryptophan and Serotonin Research*, Schlossberger,H.C., Kochen,W., Lenzen,B. and Steinhart,H. (eds), W.de Gruyter, Berlin, p.55.
30. Bennett,G.W., Brazell,M.P. and Marsden,C.A. (1981) *Life Sci.*, **29**, 1001.

31. Sauter,A. and Frick,W. (1983) *Anal. Biochem.*, **133**, 307.
32. Johnson,J.V., Bennett,G.W., Marsden,C.A., Gardiner,S.M. and Bennett,T. (1984) *Clin. Exp. Theor. Practice*, **6A**, 1993.
33. Bennett,G.W., Johnson,J.V. and Marsden,C.A. (1986) In *Monitoring Neurotransmitter Release During Behaviour*, Joseph,M.H., Fillenz,M., Macdonald,I.A. and Marsden,C.A. (eds), Ellis Horwood, Chichester, UK, p. 244.

CHAPTER 3

Biogenic amines

CHARLES A.MARSDEN and MICHAEL H.JOSEPH

1. INTRODUCTION

The introduction of h.p.l.c. with electrochemical detection (LCEC) has provided the neurochemist with a major new tool to investigate the role of catechol and indoleamines in the peripheral and central nervous systems. These compounds, principally adrenaline (A), noradrenaline (NA), dopamine (DA), 5-hydroxytryptamine (5HT) and their metabolites can be detected by their oxidation at a carbon-based electrode following separation on an appropriate chromatographic column. This method provides a rapid, relatively cheap and very sensitive assay for the amines in small brain and plasma samples.

For successful LCEC there are three major stages that require detailed attention.

(i)   Pre-injection sample preparation.
(ii)   Consistent column chromatography with clear separation between compounds.
(iii)   Sensitive carbon-based detector electrodes. These are either made with carbon paste, glassy carbon or porous graphite.

This chapter describes briefly the electrochemical principles of electrochemical detection and its scope with reference to the amines and, in more detail, the requirements for successful use of LCEC for the measurement of amines in brain and plasma.

1.1 Electrochemical principles

In discussing the basic electrochemical concepts related to their use in neuropharmacology, it is important firstly to distinguish between electrochemical events in flowing solutions, i.e. those pertaining to the situation of an electrode placed at the end of the h.p.l.c. column, and those in a quiet or static solution which corresponds more closely to *in vivo* electrochemical electrodes implanted in the brain. The present discussion will be limited to the former.

Air oxidation of catecholamines is a well-known phenomenon and consequent problem for those working in the amine research field; in that reaction catecholamines are oxidized at the ring hydroxyl groups (*Figure 1*) to produce an orthoquinone derivative with the release of two electrons. The electrochemist has harnessed this oxidation by carrying it out at the surface of an electrode.

The oxidation is driven by applying a positive potential; electrons are transferred to the electrode, the resultant current being directly proportional to the number of molecules oxidized. Thus all the electrochemical techniques involve the application of a potential to an electrode (usually graphite paste, glassy carbon or carbon fibres),

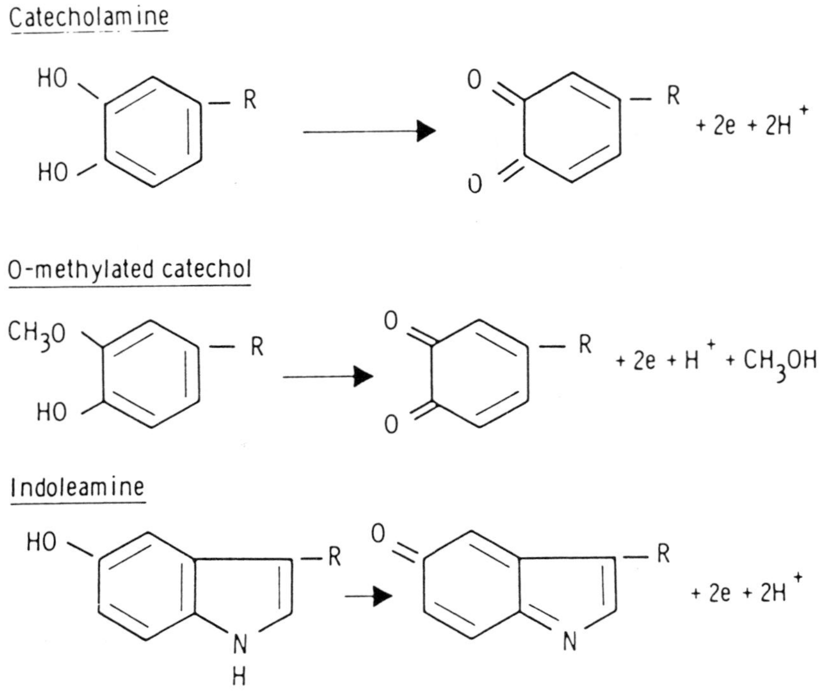

Catecholamine

O-methylated catechol

Indoleamine

Figure 1. Diagram showing the oxidation of catechol and indoleamines that occurs at the surface of the carbon electrode.

oxidation of the chemical being monitored near the surface of the electrode followed by amplification and measurement of the current produced.

When the solution containing the electroactive substances is flowing past the electrode (i.e. LCEC), an initial concentration gradient is set up due to the electrolysis of the substances near the electrode surface but this does not limit the oxidation as fresh unoxidized material is constantly being brought into contact with the electrode by the movement of the solvent. In the case of the quiet solution (i.e. *in vivo* electrodes in the brain) there is no forced convection to replenish the stock of electroactive substance at the electrode surface; consequently, the amount available for oxidation decreases with time. In this situation, therefore, experimental design is important so that such factors as electrode life and resolution of oxidation peaks can be optimized.

With LCEC it is usual to have a three-electrode system. The potential is applied to the working electrode and is maintained (via a reference electrode) by passing the required current through the working and auxiliary electrodes. A final important point is that in all the situations the electrochemical reaction *and* current measurement occur at the *working electrode*. The theoretical aspects of electrochemistry at solid electrodes has been given in more detail elsewhere (1).

The potential at which oxidation occurs depends on the ease with which the compound can be oxidized. Fortunately catechols and indoles oxidize relatively easily and therefore at relatively low potentials — mostly between 0.25 and 0.65 V using standard carbon paste or glassy carbon electrodes (*Table 1*). This makes LCEC of the amines

Table 1. Amines and related compounds showing electroactivity[a].

Catecholamines and precursors	Catecholamine metabolites	Indoleamines and precursors	Indoleamine metabolites	Amine-related compounds
1. Catechols	1. Catechols	1. 5-hydroxyindoles	1. 5-hydroxyindoles	α-methyl DOPA and metabolites
Dopamine (DA)	Dihydroxyphenylacetic acid (DOPAC)	5-hydroxytryptophan (5HTP)	5-hydroxyindole acetic acid (5HIAA)	Isoprenaline
Noradrenaline (NA)	Dihydroxyphenyl glycol (DHPG)	5-hydroxytryptamine (5HT)	5-hydroxytryptophol	Some:
Adrenaline (A)	2. Methoxyhydroxy	2. 5-methoxyindoles	2. 5-methoxyindoles	Neuroleptics
Dopa	Normetanephrine (NM)	Melatonin[b]	Bufotenin	MAO inhibitors
2. Phenols	Homovanillic acid (HVA)	3. Indoles	3. Indoles	β-blockers
Octopamine[b]	3-Methoxytyramine (3MT)	Tryptophan[b]	Indoleacetic acid[b]	Antidepressants
Tyramine[b]	Vanillylmandelic acid (VMA)	Tryptamine[b]		Ascorbic Acid
Tyrosine[b]	3-Methoxy-4-hydroxyphenylethyl alcohol (MOPET)	5-methyl-5HT (internal standard)		Uric Acid
	Metanephrine			
	3-Methoxy-4-hydroxyphenyl-glycol (MHPG)			
	3,4-Dihydroxybenzylamine (DHBA) (internal standard)			

[a]Precise potential at which oxidation occurs is dependent upon the type of electrode and pH (see ref. 1 for details). Within the first four columns, groups of compounds are arranged in order of increasing potentials required for oxidation (i.e. detection).
[b]Oxidized at +0.75 V or above, all the other compounds oxidized at potentials around +0.5 V.

a simpler matter than, say, LCEC of compounds with oxidation potentials of about +0.9 V, higher background oxidation currents due to the oxidation of components of the mobile phase being seen at higher potentials.

2. BASIC SET-UP FOR LCEC

2.1 **Minimal equipment necessary**

Essentially successful LCEC requires the equipment detailed below.

2.1.1 *A solvent delivery pump*

This should have as little pump 'noise' as possible, i.e. the pulsations in the mobile phase should be so low as to be undetectable by the electrochemical detection system. The pump should operate between 0.4 and 2.0 ml/min flow-rate or 0.2 ml/min or below if microbore LCEC is to be used (see Section 7).

2.1.2 *A sample injection system*

At present manual type filled loop valve injectors (e.g. Rheodyne) are used together with an appropriate syringe (Luer-Lok or Hamilton). Alternatively an automated injection system (e.g. Waters 'Wisp', Gilson, Varian) can be incorporated, though care in their use needs to be exercised particularly with regard to the stability of the indoleamines (see Section 3).

2.1.3 *Chromatographic column*

All the assays described in this chapter use either reversed-phase (RP) or reversed-phase ion pair (RP-IP) chromatography. In both cases 3 or 5 μm ODS columns of between 10 and 25 cm long are used (e.g. Biophase, Spherisorb, Ultrasphere, μ-Bondapak or 'Resolve'). When using 3 μm column materials with LCEC certain aspects require special attention. Low dead volumes are needed (i.e. 5 μl sample injected onto the column whereas with 5 μm material up to 100 μl samples can be injected). Furthermore the pumping system needs very effective mechanical damping and, in particular, a rapidly responding recorder with low electronic damping is required to prevent merging of peaks especially those that are eluted rapidly from the column. A pre-column can be placed before the main column to prevent contamination of the main column.

2.1.4 *Electrochemical detectors*

It is now possible to obtain amperometric or coulometric detectors with either single or dual electrode systems. There is an ever increasing range of commercial amperometric detectors using a variety of electrode materials. The original successful model was produced by Bioanalytical Systems (BAS) (*Figure 2*) who are still probably the market leaders. This company produces both single and dual electrode systems (LC4B) using glassy carbon or carbon paste electrodes (see Sections 5.1 and 5.2) (*Figure 2*). Other companies producing comparable models include Millipore Waters Chromatography Division (Waters 460 detector) and EDT Research (LCA 15). The major alternative is the dual electrode coulometric detector (ESA Inc. model 5100A) which has been used successfully both for the analysis of amines (2) and neuropeptides (3). The practical applications of the dual electrode systems will be discussed in Section 5.2.

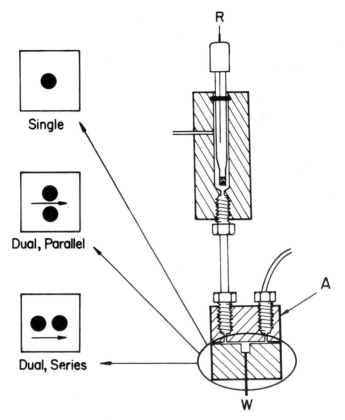

Figure 2. Diagram showing the arrangement of the Bioanalytical Systems Inc. (BAS) electrode system for use with their LCEC detector. Note the different electrode arrangements available — single, dual in parallel or series. A = auxiliary electrode, R = reference electrode and W = working electrode.

2.1.5 *Recording the output from the detector*

The simplest means is to use a single or dual channel pen recorder (depending on whether a single or dual electrode system is being used) of suitable quality (e.g. 'Omniscribe' Texas Instruments, Bryans, etc.). Alternatively the detector can be linked to a programmable h.p.l.c. integrator (e.g. Shimadzu, Spectra-Physics).

2.1.6 *Ancillary equipment*

The mobile phase should be prepared using double-distilled de-ionized water and must be filtered and degassed (e.g. 0.1 μm Millipore filter system) prior to use. All reagents used in the mobile phase should be h.p.l.c. grade. H.p.l.c. amine standards are prepared in 0.1 M perchloric acid (PCA) containing 0.4 mM sodium metabisulphite to prevent oxidation. Stock solutions (10^{-4} M) of the standards can be stored frozen at $-80°C$. It is best to make, say, a 50 ml stock solution and store this as individual $1-5$ ml samples. Fresh standards (10^{-7} M) can then be prepared daily by unfreezing one of the stock samples and diluting it with 0.1 M PCA/0.4 mM sodium metabisulphite or mobile phase. The diluted standard should be kept on ice during use.

3. PRE-INJECTION SAMPLE PREPARATION

3.1 **Brain samples**

These are dissected out over ice or on a commercial cool-tray, then frozen in dry ice or liquid nitrogen and stored in air-tight containers in the dark at $-80°$C until required for assay. Studies involving post-mortem human brain material should adopt the guidelines suggested by the MRC for the handling of such material. Mechanical slicing of human brain should be avoided as the heat produced appears to decrease amine levels.

The simplest and fastest pre-injection extraction method is to homogenize (Ultra Turrax) or to sonicate (Ultrasonics) at 4°C small (up to 100 mg wet weight) brain samples in $200-2000$ μl of 0.1 M PCA containing 0.4 mM sodium metabisulphite. The samples are then centrifuged (9000 g, 10 min), the supernatant retained and microfiltered (e.g. Acro aqueous filters) prior to injection onto the column. The indoleamines, in particular 5-hydroxyindoleacetic acid (5HIAA), are very sensitive to light and air, being rapidly oxidized, so it is sensible not to prepare more than 12 samples for injection at one time. Once ready for injection the samples should be kept on ice and ideally in the dark. An alternative approach is to sonicate or homogenize the tissue in the mobile phase being used for the chromatographic separation.

It is now known that several amines and their metabolites are present in brain both as free and sulphated conjugates $(4-7)$. The conjugated forms are not electroactive at accessible potentials so in order to be measured they need to be hydrolyzed either under controlled acid conditions (e.g. 8) or enzymatically. Both hydrolysis reactions result in interfering chromatographic peaks, particularly when dealing with 3-methoxy-4-hydroxyphenylglycol (MHPG). A suitable method for separating MHPG from other interfering substances following enzymatic hydrolysis and prior to injection onto an h.p.l.c. column using small silica columns (Sep Paks) has been described by Walter and Haynes (9).

Intracerebral dialysis involves the collection of amines and their metabolites into artificial cerebrospinal fluid perfused through a microdialysis loop or tube implanted into the brain (10,11). The perfusate is collected into a small 'Eppendorf' tube containing 1 μl of 0.1 M PCA with 0.4 mM sodium metabisulphite placed on the end of the outlet tube of the dialysis loop. The perfusate can then be directly injected onto the h.p.l.c. column.

3.2 **Whole blood samples**

Several studies have measured 5HT in whole blood, nearly all of which is found in the platelets. The main problem with measurement of 5HT in blood arises at the pre-injection extraction phase as many protein precipitants give poor 5HT recovery and 5HT is readily oxidized by oxyhaemoglobin. One approach is to separate platelets (12) though recovery may be incomplete. Alternatively the proteins may be precipitated with zinc hydroxide or perchloric acid with ascorbic acid or sodium metabisulphite added to prevent oxidation of 5HT. The blood should then be centrifuged and microfiltered prior to injection onto the column. There are, however, problems in using ascorbic acid as an anti-oxidant as it is readily oxidized at the potential used to oxidize and detect 5HT by LCEC, so markedly increasing the size of the solvent front. This can be overcome by using a dual electrode detector or fluorescence detector to avoid the ascorbate interference (see Section 5.2).

3.3 Plasma and urine samples

The early studies using LCEC to measure catecholamines in plasma commonly employed absorption onto alumina followed by elution of the amines from the alumina with per-chloric acid (13,14). This approach, however, is not specific for the catecholamines and while this non-specificity was not critical when strong cation ion-exchange chromatography (SCX) was used for the separation step, the advent of the more efficient RP-IP columns has necessitated an improved extraction to remove other compounds that interfere with the chromatography and extend the solvent front.

Macdonald and Lake (15) have described a two-stage extraction process, suitable for use with RP-IP chromatography. This firstly involves the extraction of the cations in the sample and then the separation of catecholamine cations from other cations. The cations are initially extracted using Sepralyte (Analytichem), a strong cation compound, and the catechols are then complexed with diphenylborate which is extracted into an organic phase by ion pairing with tetraoctylammonium bromide. The catechols are finally back-extracted into CH_3COOH prior to injection on the h.p.l.c. column. Prior to this extraction process blood should be collected into EDTA/lithium tubes containing 20 μl ml of EGTA/reduced glutathione mixture (4.75 g EGTA, 3 g glutathione in 50 ml double-distilled de-ionized water), the plasma separated within 1 h of collection and stored at $-80°C$.

Macdonald and Lake (15) have described the two-stage extraction in detail as well as the intra- and inter-assay variation observed in plasma A and NA levels measured following this extraction. Here we are only giving a short working guide to the extraction supplied by Dr I.A.Macdonald (Department of Physiology and Pharmacology, University of Nottingham Medical School).

(i)   Activate 50 mg of Sepralyte SCX (Analytichem International Inc.) with 1 ml of 0.2 M Na_2HPO_4 buffer (pH 7.5), by shaking for 1 min then centrifuging and discarding the buffer.

(ii)   Mix the plasma (0.5−2 ml) or urine (0.25−0.5 ml) sample with the internal standard (e.g. 10 pM of 3,4-dihydroxybenzylamine, see Section 6.2) and, if necessary, adjust the pH to 7.5−8.0 before the cations are extracted onto the SCX by mixing for 2 min. After centrifugation, discard the supernatant and wash the SCX twice with 1 ml of water, before eluting the cations into 1 ml of 1 M Na_2PO_4 buffer (pH 2.9) by mixing for 1.5 min.

(iii)   After centrifugation, transfer this eluate to a screw-topped glass tube, add sufficient NH_4OH (concentrated stock solution, ~8 M) to raise the pH to 8 (this usually requires 90−100 μl of NH_4OH) before adding 0.5 ml of 2 M $NH_4OH/$ NH_4Cl buffer (pH 8.5, containing 3.5 g of diphenylborate−ethanolamine complex and 5 g of EDTA per litre) to form a diphenylborate−catechol complex. Then add 2.5 ml of a mixture of heptane/octanol (1 vol octanol/99 vol heptane), containing 2.5 g tetraoctylammonium bromide per litre, put the Teflon-lined screw caps onto the tubes and shake for 2 min to extract the borate−catechol complex into the organic phase, forming an ion-pair with the tetraoctylammonium bromide.

(iv)   After centrifugation transfer 2 ml of the heptane/octanol supernatant to a glass centrifuge tube, add 1 ml of octanol and 0.2 ml of 0.08 M CH_3COOH and vortex mix the mixture for 1 min to back-extract the catecholamines into the CH_3COOH. After centrifugation, remove the CH_3COOH layer from below the organic supernatant, and store in Eppendorf tubes on ice prior to injection onto the chromatographic column.

This two-stage extraction excludes most, if not all, of the additional peaks seen on the chromatograms of plasma extracted onto alumina. This method can be used to measure basal levels of NA (2 nmol/l) and A (0.19 nmol/l) in 2 ml samples of human plasma with intra-assay coefficients of variation of 8% for both amines. The inter-assay variation is less than 10% for NA and less than 20% for A (15). This extraction method should markedly improve the inter-laboratory comparisons for RP-IP chromatography of plasma catecholamines which, in a recent inter-laboratory evaluation of available techniques, gave a rather poor performance (14).

4. HIGH-PERFORMANCE LIQUID CHROMATOGRAPHY

The first LCEC technique described used SCX columns to separate amines and strong anion exchange (SAX) for acid metabolites. These have now been superceded by RP and RP-IP column separation. This section will describe the basic mobile phases that can be used with these columns for the isocratic separation of amines and their metabolites together with notes on the general use and care of such columns with special reference to LCEC. It should, however, be remembered that no two columns are exactly alike and, while the mobile phases described may serve as guidelines, the exact nature of the mobile phase may be adjusted to suit the particular column and needs of the assay. More detailed theoretical information on the column materials is given elsewhere in this volume [see Chapter 1 and Adams and Marsden (1)].

4.1 Reversed-phase (RP) chromatography

Analytes are partitioned between a hydrophobic stationary phase and an aqueous mobile phase. Elution is in the order of increasing hydrophobicity. RP chromatography can be used to separate dihydroxyphenylacetic acid (DOPAC), 5HT, tryptophan, 5HIAA, homovanillic acid (HVA) with N-methyl-5HT as internal standard. The most commonly used mobile phase for this separation is given in *Table 2* (mobile phase A). Increasing the methanol concentration will shorten all the retention times (*Table 3*) by making the mobile phase less polar, i.e. allowing it to compete more effectively with the non-polar stationary phase. Decreasing pH, on the other hand, will selectively increase the retention of the acid metabolites by suppressing their ionization, increasing their hydrophobicity. RP chromatography is less suitable for the separation of catecholamines (A, NA, DA) as NA is eluted near the solvent front (i.e. it is too hydrophilic). This method does, however, provide a rapid and simple separation for indoleamines and most catecholamine metabolites (*Figure 3*). Thus it is useful for analysing amine metabolites in urine (16), cerebrospinal fluid (17) and brain (18).

Table 2. Summary of the conditions suitable for measuring amines and their metabolites by LCEC.

	Reversed-phase	Reversed-phase ion-pair
Column	3 or 5 μm ODS (C$_{18}$) (15–25 cm) e.g. Spherisorb, Ultrasphere, Biophase, μ-Bondapak	3 or 5 μm ODS 2 (C$_{18}$) (15–25 cm) Manufacturers as for reversed-phase
Mobile phase	Mobile phase A[a] 0.1 M Acetate/citrate buffer pH 4.6 with 10% (v/v) methanol Mobile phase E[e] 0.1 M Trichloroacetic acid Adjust to pH 3.0 with 1 M sodium acetate 0.1 M EDTA 20% Methanol	Mobile phase B[b,c] 0.1 M NaH$_2$PO$_4$ 0.1 mM EDTA 1.0 mM Sodium octylsulphate 9% Methanol. pH 3.6 Mobile phase C 0.15 M NaH$_2$PO$_4$ 0.1 mM EDTA 0.5 mM Sodium octanesulphonic acid 14% Methanol. pH 3.4 Mobile phase D[d] 0.1 M NaH$_2$PO$_4$ 1.0 mM EDTA 1.0 mM Sodium octanesulphonic acid Adjust to pH 4–4.4 with citric acid Mix with acetonitrile (see ref. 19 for details)
Electrode and potential	Below 15% methanol: Carbon paste or glassy carbon, pyrolytic and porous carbon. Above 15% methanol: Do not use carbon paste. Potential: 0.5–0.9 V. Most amines and their metabolites can be detected at potentials below 0.75 V. Amino acids (tryptophan, tyrosine) are only detected at potentials above 0.85 V.	
Amines detected	Mobile phase A[f] DOPAC, 5HT, tryptophan, 5HIAA, HVA, N-CH$_3$5HT Can include: DOPA, 5HTP Mobile phase E Developed specifically to measure 3-MT	Mobile phase B[g] MHPG, NA, A, DHBA, DOPAC, 5HIAA, DA Mobile phase C and D NA, A, DA, DOPAC, 5HT, 5HIAA, HVA[g]: (B, C and D can be adapted to include: DOMA, VMA, DOPA, DHPG, 5HTP, MHPG, NM, tryptophan, 3MT)
Flow-rate and run time	0.8–1.2 ml/min ~14 min (mobile phase A)	0.8–1.6 ml/min ~12–40 min
Internal standards	N-Methyl 5HT	3,4-Dihydroxybenzylamine (DHBA), N-methyl-5HT

[a]From ref. 31,32; [b]From ref. 28; [c]A modified form of mobile phase A has been used with the Coulochem detector (2.25); [d]From ref. 19; [e]From ref. 2; [f]5HT and 5HIAA are rapidly oxidized at room temperature in air — follow instructions in Section 3.1 to prevent loss; [g]See *Figure 4*.

Table 3. The effects of raising pH, methanol, ion-pair concentration or length on the separation of amines and their metabolites using RP or RP-IP columns[a].

	Range	Acid [VMA, DOPAC, 5HIAA, HVA]	Neutral [MHPG]	Amine [A, NA, DA, 5HT (3MT)]
pH	3→6	Faster	No change	No change
MeOH	0→20%	Faster	Faster	Faster
Ion pair concentration	50 μM ↓ 1 mM	No change	No change	Slower
Ion pair chain length	Pentyl ↓ Dodecyl	No change	No change	Slower
Temperature	20→35°C	Faster	Faster	Faster

[a]More detailed information is given in the following references: 1,19,21,22,24,33,34.

4.2 Reversed-phase ion-pair (RP-IP) chromatography

The catecholamines remain positively charged throughout the pH range (pH 2−8) compatible with RP columns. Thus it is not possible to overcome their hydrophilicity by increasing pH to suppress their ionization. The solution to this problem is the addition of ion pairing agents to the mobile phase (e.g. sodium octyl sulphate). The combination of a hydrophobic side chain and negatively charged group has the effect, once equilibrium has been reached with the stationary phase, of selectively retarding the elution of positively charged species, i.e. amines, in this pH range. The effect increases with concentration (up to a maximum) and with chain length (*Table 3*). However all amines, including 5HT, which is already sufficiently retarded, are slowed down. Thus, RP-IP is now the separation method of choice for the amines and their metabolites with the exception of 5HT. This has a long retention time using mobile phase B (*Table 2, Figure 4*) though, more recently, improved separation of 5HT has been achieved with mobile phase C and D [*Table 2, Figure 4*, (19)]. 3,4-Dihydroxybenzylamine (DHBA) or N-methyl-5HT can be used as internal standard. The compounds that can be separated include MHPG, NA, DOPA, DOPAC, normetanephrine (NM), DA, tryptophan, 5HIAA, 5-hydroxytryptophan (5HTP), HVA and 3-methoxytryptamine (3MT) (20). There are, however, problems with detecting and measuring 3MT in brain samples due to the very low levels present (0.79 nmol/g) but it has been successfully determined using LCEC and mobile phase E [*Table 2*, (21)].

It needs to be stressed again that no two columns behave in exactly the same way and small adjustments to the mobile phase are often needed to achieve the separation required. The main ways of altering the separation of amines on RP-IP columns by altering the composition of the mobile phase are given in *Table 3*.

A more complex situation arises when one wishes to alter the retention times of individual amines. Altering the ion pair reagent concentration while also changing the percentage methanol or acetonitrile may produce differential effects as demonstrated in *Figure 4* and *Table 3*. In this case, 5HT and DA have been eluted much faster using mobile phase C (*Table 2*) than with mobile phase B because the concentration of ion pair reagent has been reduced, while the acid metabolites are coming off the column more quickly due to the increased methanol level. An alternative approach to this problem

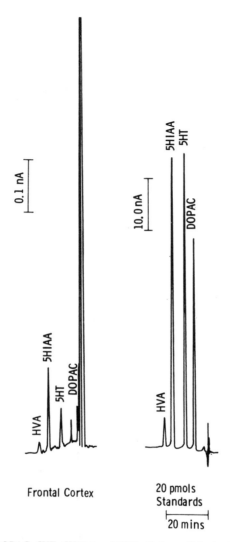

Figure 3. Separation of DOPAC, 5HT, 5HIAA and HVA. Column, Spherisorb 5 ODS 2 (25 cm); eluent, 0.1 M citrate−acetate buffer pH 4.0, (mobile phase A); flow-rate, 1 ml/min; electrode (BAS) potential, +0.65 V [this potential is not optimal for HVA oxidation (about +0.85 V)]. The figure shows a chromatogram obtained with injected standards (20 pmol) and an *in vivo* intracerebral dialysis sample obtained from the frontal cortex.

is to alter the nature of the pairing reagent. Joseph (22) has described the use of alkyl boronates to retard the catecholamines, by selectively pairing with them, while speeding up the elution of non-catechols including 5HT. Two mobile phases were tried. The first mobile phase contained 6 mM butane boronic acid in 0.05 M phosphate pH 7.5 with no methanol and separation was carried out under isocratic conditions. The second mobile phase contained 5 mM butane boronic acid in 0.1 M phosphate and separation was run in a gradient of 0−20% methanol. With both mobile phases it was possible to measure 5HT and NA in the same run. Further investigation into possible selective pairing reagents is needed.

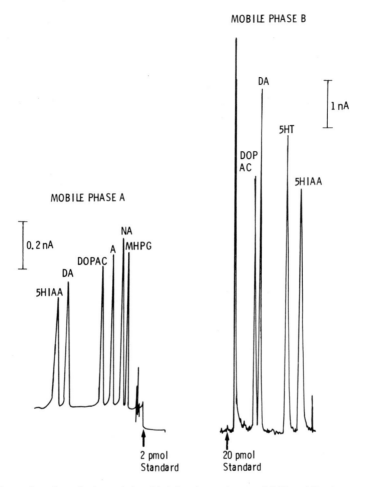

Figure 4. Separation of standard catechol and indoleamines using two RP-IP mobile phases. With mobile phase B (see *Table 2* for details) good separation of MHPG, NA, A, DOPAC, DA and 5HIAA is obtained but 5HT is retained on the column for over an hour. With mobile phase C (*Table 2*) the retention of 5HT is markedly shortened while MHPG, NA and A now come off in the solvent front. In both cases the potential of the electrode (BAS) was set at +0.65 V and the flow-rate of the mobile phase was 1 ml/min.

4.3 Care of columns

4.3.1 *Split peaks*

These are usually caused by settling of the packing material at the top of the column. If the settling has been uniform the easiest solution is to fill up the packed bed with more packing material or alternatively glass beads. It may also be possible to reverse the column so that the top becomes the bottom although extensive washing would be advisable (see Section 4.3.2).

4.3.2 *Poor resolution and broadening of the peaks*

This usually indicates that the column material requires washing. The simplest protocol to adopt is to wash the column with water (100 ml), methanol (100 ml), acetone (100 ml), methanol (100 ml), water (100 ml). The acetone removes the ion pair reagent from the column material.

4.3.3 *High offset current caused by impure water*

It is very important to make sure that only pure (double-distilled, de-ionized) water is used. Water with a high ion content will raise the offset current detected by the electrochemical system and can also disrupt separation. If impure water is used accidentally the entire h.p.l.c. system, including the column, will need to be washed as described in Section 4.3.2. In addition, if the Coulochem detector is being used the electrodes will need to be back-washed with nitric acid (see Section 5.1.2).

5. ELECTROCHEMICAL DETECTION

5.1 **Electrodes**

There are two basic types of electrodes used with amperometric detection — carbon paste and glassy carbon. The Coulochem coulometric detector uses a porous graphite electrode. The ideal working electrode material should be inert in the electrolytic mobile phase but able to oxidize the substances being analysed in a reproducible potential-dependent manner. In practice most carbon electrodes are almost inert to the mobile phases given in this chapter at potentials below +0.85 V (using the BAS electrode types). When potentials above +0.85 V are being used high offset currents are obtained but this can now be counteracted using a dual electrode system (see Section 5.2).

5.1.1 *Carbon paste and glassy carbon electrodes*

These, prepared and used under suitable conditions, provide the most sensitive electrodes with detection limits for the catecholamines as low as 0.1 pmol injected onto the column with a signal-to-noise ratio of 3:1, using oil-based carbon paste.

Oil-based carbon paste electrodes produce sharper voltammograms, and lower residual currents, compared with silicon- or wax-based carbon paste or glassy carbon. In practical terms the difference between carbon paste and glassy carbon is not very marked (*Table 4*), but it is possible to obtain the same amount of current from the oxidation of the catecholamines with the oil-based carbon paste electrode at a lower potential than with a wax-based carbon paste electrode (*Table 4*). When the electrode is first switched on, the current recorded rises very rapidly and then declines to an acceptable stable level. This decay time is often quite variable for different electrodes. Ideally

Table 4. Effect of electrode material on potential range required to oxidize NA (10^{-5} M) at pH 5.0[a].

Electrode	Potential range (V)
Carbon paste (oil-based)	+0.28 − +0.50
Carbon paste (wax-based)	+0.40 − +0.83
Glassy carbon	+0.29 − +0.55

[a]Oxidation measured by voltammetry in solutions of NA (10^{-5} M) prepared in acetate/citrate buffer (0.1 M), pH 5.0.

this residual (standing) current will show little or no drift with time during chromatographic operation. Large residual currents can often be decreased by using more purified buffer salts and in particular ensuring that very pure water is used in the mobile phase (see Section 4.3.3). Residual current also increases with larger applied potentials; therefore, it is always advisable to work at the lowest applied potential consistent with acceptable sensitivity. In this way one obtains the best signal-to-noise ratio. Superimposed on the residual current is noise which may be either spasmodic or regular in pattern. In the former case the source is often due to air bubbles passing over the electrode surface; these should be removed (see instruction manual) and the mobile phase degassed. Periodic noise may be related to pump pulsations affecting the flow of the mobile phase or to electrical noise. In general, the former is overcome by suitable pulse damping and the latter by comprehensive grounding of the system or checking the stability of the mains supply.

With time the surface of the carbon-based electrodes loses sensitivity due to passivation or becomes more noisy because the surface becomes uneven. Commercially available carbon paste electrodes and glassy carbon electrodes (e.g. BAS) are supplied with electrode resurfacing instructions, but some general points are worth making. With either electrode it is essential that not only the carbon electrode surface but also the surface of the Plexiglas (carbon paste) or Kel-F (glassy carbon) housing is smooth. The carbon paste electrode is resurfaced by gentle rubbing on a smooth surface (commonly a computer card). Metal polish is an excellent material for smoothing Plexiglas. Pits on the surface of the Plexiglas will affect the flow of the mobile phase over the electrode surface, leading to increased noise and a decreased signal-to-noise ratio. Other actions that influence the state of the surface of the carbon paste electrode are the flow-rate and pressure at which the mobile phase is pumped. Increased flow and pressure cause a decrease in the life of the electrode.

With paste electrodes it is also important that the pit into which the carbon paste is put does not have rounded edges. These make the flow of the mobile phase over the electrode surface uneven, so increasing background noise and residual current. The major limitation of carbon paste is that it cannot be used with a mobile phase containing more than $10-15\%$ methanol. Under such conditions it is essential to use glassy carbon electrodes.

Glassy carbon electrodes are excellent for routine assays not requiring maximum performance. The main problem with their use is the relatively high residual current observed and therefore poorer signal-to-noise ratio than with carbon paste. Particular attention has to be paid to the mobile phase; addition to it of EDTA sequesters any metals leaching out of the tubing and pumping system. Both carbon paste and glassy carbon electrodes benefit from continuous use and it is common practice not to switch off the pumps overnight, simply recycling the mobile phase. Glassy carbon electrodes supplied by BAS come with a cleaning kit (polishing pad and alumina) and full instructions. Anton (23) described a method for cleaning glassy carbon electrodes using a $CrO_3-H_2SO_4$ solution suggesting it improved sensitivity over alumina polishing but this needs confirming.

5.1.2 *Porous graphite electrode*

(Coulochem Detector ESA). These electrodes are sealed and so cannot be routinely resurfaced — we have found that the electrode units, under continuous use, last about 2 years. The electrodes can be cleaned by flushing sequentially with distilled de-ionized water, filtered 6 M nitric acid, water, filtered 4 M sodium hydroxide and finally water.

5.1.3 *Reference electrode*

This is normally an Ag/AgCl electrode with 3 M sodium chloride as the electrolyte and it functions to provide a stable potential with which the working electrode can be compared. If care is taken to avoid air bubbles around its surface or letting it dry out, there are few problems with the reference electrode. The stability of the reference electrode can be determined by comparing the potential difference between a new Ag/AgCl electrode and the suspect electrode with a voltmeter.

5.2 **Dual electrode systems**

Both amperometric and coulometric detectors are available as dual electrode systems. This section will briefly outline the possible uses of dual electrode systems though it should be stressed that plasma or brain amines and their metabolites can be successfully and reliably measured using a single electrode system.

The BAS dual electrode can either be used in a parallel configuration or in series (*Figure 2*).

(i) *Parallel.* In this situation the electrodes are placed side-by-side and each operated at different potentials. In this way simultaneous chromatograms (C) are produced and the ratios of the peaks (C_2/C_1) may be used to determine the purity of the peaks in samples compared with injected standards.

(ii) *Series.* In this case the eluate coming off the column is seen by one electrode before the other. With this arrangement it is possible to check the purity of the chromatographic peaks and improve the quality of the trace by oxidizing the amines at the first electrode and then reducing them at the downstream electrode. Only those showing a reversible oxidation (e.g. catechols) will be detected at the second electrode. Since ascorbic acid and uric acid are both present in relatively high concentration in brain, but are oxidized irreversibly, oxidation at one electrode followed by re-reduction at another can be especially useful in preventing interference with amine analysis. Ascorbate elutes with the solvent front, and is largely responsible for the unretained peak. An alternative approach with the coulometric detector is to use the first electrode at a lower positive potential to screen the eluate before detecting what one wishes to at the second electrode. This can be a particular advantage when one is detecting substances that oxidize at a high potential such as neuropeptides (3). In this way it is possible to (a) reduce the residual current and (b) oxidize all the compounds separated on the column that might interfere with the separation of the compounds of interest and so improve the resolution of those compounds. The full possibilities for using the electrode configuration of the Coulochem detector have been described elsewhere (2,24,25). The Coulochem detector has taken this process further by also introducing guard electrodes which can oxidize the mobile phase prior to entering the column to reduce the residual current.

5.3 **Trouble-shooting**

This section deals with a noisy baseline. Basically problems associated with noise come from two areas: (a) pump noise, (b) electrode noise. A third cause of noise can be the mobile phase and, as already mentioned, this can be overcome by using pure chemicals, pure de-ionized double-distilled water and by having a chelating agent (EDTA) in the mobile phase to remove any metals leached out of the pumping system and tubing.

Pump noise usually relates to:

(i)   insufficient damping on the pump — a factor that should be checked prior to purchase;

(ii)   faulty piston seals or check valves — it is worth maintaining a sufficient supply of spares;

(iii) more major faults with the pump.

All pump manuals provide a 'trouble-shooting' section that deals with the process of locating the source of pump noise and changes in the pressure generated by the flow of mobile phase.

Electrode noise usually relates to the state of the electrode surface. As already mentioned (Section 5.1.1) attention should be paid to both the surface of the electrode and electrode housing. Carbon paste electrodes should either be resurfaced or re-packed with new carbon paste and it should be remembered that carbon paste obtained from BAS does not have an indefinite shelf life once opened and there is variation in the quality of the paste between batches. Glassy carbon or porous graphite electrodes should be cleaned following the manufacturer's instructions.

6. PEAK IDENTIFICATION, SENSITIVITY AND CALIBRATION

6.1 Peak identification

The major approach to good peak identification is good chromatography — a factor already discussed (Section 4). The other essential steps are given below.

6.1.1 *Spiking*

Peaks in tissue samples should be identified by spiking with appropriate concentrations of standards added to the extract. The best way to do this is to split the extract, inject one half onto the column without added standards and the other half with added standard.

6.1.2 *Internal standards and recovery determinations*

Internal standards are regularly used with LCEC techniques. Any compound that is electroactive, not found in the sample, and elutes from the column closely but not identically with the substances being detected will serve this role. An internal standard serves two major functions.

(i)   It ensures that the injection onto the column has been made correctly. With the more sophisticated injection ports available today this is less of a problem than previously. Stainless steel fixed loop volume (1, 20, 50 or 100 μl) injection systems are recommended (e.g. Rheodyne) as these give reproducible injection volumes.

(ii)   It verifies the absolute recovery of the extraction method which precedes the column separation. The internal standard must behave during the extraction process in the same way as the substances being measured.

For catecholamine assays, dihydroxybenzylamine (DHBA) is commonly used as an internal standard since it elutes close to but separately from the catecholamines and behaves in a similar manner to catecholamines during the extraction process.

α-Methyldopamine can be used as internal standard, although it has a rather long retention time on the column and prolongs the assay time. Alternatively, N-methyl-dopamine can be used as internal standard for brain assays with RP separation where DHBA and A overlap (26). N-Methyl-5HT (27) and 3-methoxy-4-hydroxyphenylethyl alcohol (38) have proved to be successful internal standards for indoleamines with RP separation. The internal standard should be added at the *start* of the extraction process at an appropriate concentration to each sample, in which case the recovery can be stated in terms of *absolute recovery (%)*. When the internal standard is taken through the extraction process but not added to the tissue, it is referred to as *relative recovery (%)*. In both cases the current detected for the extracted internal standards is compared with that produced by its direct injection onto the column. Although it is desirable to obtain higher recoveries, it is more important that sample-to-sample recovery be consistent.

6.1.3 *Dual electrode systems*

This aspect is covered in Section 5.2.

6.2 **Sensitivity and calibration**

The limit of detection is usually considered as the lowest amount detected, preferably expressed as amount injected (moles) onto the column, when the signal-to-noise ratio is 3:1. For any practical assay or experiment involving biological material, the limit of detection should be determined in the light of existing conditions. It is important to state exactly what the limit of detection refers to, i.e. concentration in the original sample before extraction or amount injected onto the column. If the former is used, then this should be qualified by giving information about the recovery of the substance through the extraction method. Routinely, the limit of detection for catecholamines (NA, DA and A) injected onto the column is 0.1 − 1 pmol, through considerably lower limits can be achieved (0.02 − 0.1 pmol). The sensitivity for 5HT is similar to that for the catecholamines, while the catecholamine metabolites have a range of detection limits with MHPG, DOPAC and 5HIAA similar to the amines and HVA having a higher limit (5−10 pmol) at potentials optimal for the amines but this is improved (0.5 pmol) at the potential optimal for its own oxidation.

It is important to construct calibration curves by direct injection onto the column of standards of known concentrations (made with the same eluent as used for the tissue extracts) to determine the linearity range of the detector response. The results for such calibration curves should be expressed as detector current (nA) versus amount injected rather than peak height (cm). Similar calibration should be performed for any internal standard used.

7. FUTURE DEVELOPMENTS

It is now established that adoption of microbore h.p.l.c. can increase the sensitivity of LCEC by about 20-fold allowing detection limits for catechol and indoleamine in brain of 50−200 femtograms (29) and this approach has now been adapted for use with plasma samples (30). Microbore chromatography provides a marked fall in on-column sample dilution as the peak volume of the substances coming off the column is related to the volume of the column. Therefore decreasing the diameter and length of the column will decrease the peak volume increasing the concentration of the compounds in the eluent proportionately to the decrease in volume. Combined with the slower flow-rate this provides more compound at the surface of the working electrode for a longer time and therefore a greater coulometric yield. The net outcome is improved sensitivity with shorter chromatographic run times. There are, however, certain aspects that need to be considered to obtain the maximum effect with microbore LCEC.

(i)   The dead space should be minimal so the column should be directly connected to the microbore injector (Rheodyne) and the electrode holder and a small spacer (10 μm) should be used in the electrode block.

(ii)   The pumping system should be pulse free.

(iii)   The response time on the detector needs to be fast enough to separate the rapidly eluting peaks (0.5 sec).

In the next few years one can expect microbore LCEC to become a major method for the analysis of low amounts of amines in small sample volumes. At present however normal LCEC is the method of choice for measuring amines and their metabolites in many biological samples.

8. ACKNOWLEDGEMENTS

We should like to thank Drs Ian Macdonald and Keith Martin, Carol Routledge and Dennis Risby for their practical advice and constructive comments. The studies carried out in the authors' laboratories described in this chapter have been supported by the Wellcome Trust and the MRC.

9. REFERENCES

1. Adams,R.N. and Marsden,C.A. (1972) In *Handbook of Psychopharmacology,* Vol. **15**, Iversen,L.L., Iversen,S.D. and Snyder,S.H. (eds), Plenum Press, New York, p. 1.
2. Matson,W.R., Langlais,P., Volicer,L., Gamache,P.H., Bird,E. and Mark,K.A. (1984) *Clin. Chem.,* **30**, 1477.
3. Johnson,J.V., Bennett,G.W., Marsden,C.A., Gardiner,S.M. and Bennett,T. (1984) *Clin. Exp. Theor. Practice,* **A6**, 1993.
4. Buu,N.T., Duhaime,J., Savard,C., Truong,L. and Kuchel,O. (1981) *J. Neurochem.,* **36**, 769.
5. Dedek,J., Baumes,R., Tien-Duc,N., Gomeni,R. and Korf,J. (1979) *J. Neurochem.,* **33**, 687.
6. Karoum,F., Chuang,L.-W. and Wyatt,R.J. (1983) *J. Neurochem.,* **40**, 1735.
7. Rivett,A.J., Francis,A., Whittemore,R. and Roth,J.A. (1984) *J. Neurochem.,* **42**, 1444.
8. Hutson,P., Kantamaneni,B.D. and Curzon,G. (1984) *J. Neurochem.,* **43**, 151.
9. Walter,D.S. and Haynes,M.J. (1986) In *Monitoring Neurotransmitter Release During Behaviour,* Joseph, M.H., Macdonald,I.A., Fillenz,M. and Marsden,C.A. (eds), Ellis Horwood, Chichester, UK, 206.
10. Ungerstedt,U. (1984) In *Measurement of Neurotransmitter Release In Vivo,* Marsden,C.A. (ed.), J.Wiley, Chichester,UK, p. 81.
11. Zetterstrom,T., Sharp,T., Marsden,C.A. and Ungerstedt,U. (1983) *J. Neurochem.,* **41**, 1769.
12. Tagari,P.C., Boullin,D.J. and Davies,C.L. (1984) *Clin. Chem.,* **30**, 131.
13. Hallman,H., Farnebo,L.O., Hamberger,B. and Jonsson,G. (1978) *Life Sci.,* **23**, 1049.
14. Hjemdahl,P. (1984) *Acta Physiol. Scand. Suppl.,* **527**, 43.
15. Macdonald,I.A. and Lake,D.M. (1985) *J. Neurosci. Methods,* **13**, 239.
16. Joseph,M.H., Kadam,B.V. and Risby,I.D. (1981) *J.Chromatogr.,* **226**, 361.
17. Joseph,M.H., Baker,H.F. and Ridley,R.M. (1981) In *Central Neurotransmitter Turnover,* Pycock,C.J. and Taberner,P.V. (eds), Croom Helm, London, p. 162.

18. Cross,A.J. and Joseph,M.H. (1981) *Life Sci.*, **28**, 499.
19. Saller,C.F. and Salama,A.I. (1984) *J. Chromatogr.*, **309**, 287.
20. Wagner,J., Vitali,J., Palfreyman,M.G., Zraika,M. and Huot,S. (1982) *J. Neurochem.*, **38**, 1241.
21. Westerink,B.H.C. and Spaan,S.J. (1982) *J. Neurochem.*, **38**, 342.
22. Joseph,M.H. (1985) *J. Chromatogr.*, **342**, 370.
23. Anton,A.H. (1984) *Life Sci.*, **35**, 79.
24. Joseph,M.H. and Marsden,C.A. (1986) In *Monitoring Neurotransmitter Release During Behaviour,* Joseph,M.H., Macdonald,I.A., Fillenz,M. and Marsden,C.A. (eds), Ellis Horwood, Chichester, UK, 195.
25. Langlais,P.J., Bird,E.D. and Matson,R.W. (1984) *Clin. Chem.*, **30**, 1046.
26. Maruyarma,Y., Oshima,T. and Nakajima,E. (1980) *Life Sci.*, **26**, 1115.
27. Loullis,C.C., Felten,D.L. and Shea,P.A. (1979) *Pharmacol. Biochem. Behav.*, **11**, 89.
28. Mefford,I.N. (1981) *J. Neurosci. Methods*, **3**, 207.
29. Caligura,E.J. and Mefford,I.N. (1984) *Brain Res.*, **296**, 156.
30. Caligura,E.J., Capella,P., Bottari,L.G. and Mefford,I.N. (1986) In *Monitoring Neurotransmitter Release During Behaviour,* Joseph,M.H., Macdonald,I.A., Fillenz,M. and Marsden,C.A. (eds), Ellis Horwood, Chichester, UK, 216.
31. Mefford,I.N. and Barchas,J.D. (1980) *J. Chromatogr.*, **181**, 187.
32. Reinhard,J.F., Jr., Moskowitz,M.A., Sved,A.F. and Fernstrom,J.D. (1980) *Life Sci.*, **27**, 905.
33. Asmus,P.A. and Freed,C.R. (1979) *J. Chromatogr.*, **169**, 303.
34. Scratchley,G.A., Masoud,A.N., Stohs,S.J. and Wingard,D.W. (1979) *J. Chromatogr.*, **169**, 313.

CHAPTER 4

Carbohydrates

ELIZABETH F. HOUNSELL

1. INTRODUCTION

H.p.l.c. was introduced into the field of carbohydrates for the analysis of mono- to tetrasaccharides of neutral sugars found in natural products of interest to the food industries (1−7). More recent applications have included the analysis and purification of oligosaccharides containing neutral and acetamido sugars (8−16) and sialylated (8,17−20), sulphated (21−25) and phosphorylated (17) oligosaccharides. These oligosaccharides present their own specific problems for h.p.l.c. separation because of the differing chromatographic behaviour afforded by hydroxyl, acetamido and anionic groups and the diversity of structures that can be formed. Furthermore, because the constituent monosaccharides can be linked together at a variety of positions and with either α or β configuration, the need often arises for separation of oligosaccharide isomers with very similar chromatographic properties. These types of oligosaccharides are important components of body fluids, such as milk and urine, and of cell surface and secreted glycoconjugates (glycoproteins, glycolipids and glycosaminoglycans). Their purification is necessary for structural characterization and for assessing antigenicity and possible function. For example, it has been shown, by the use of purified and characterized oligosaccharides as inhibitors of monoclonal antibody binding to glycoproteins in radioimmunoassays, that several tumour-associated and differentiation antigens are specific, closely related oligosaccharide structures (26−28). Other workers have used h.p.l.c. to purify oligosaccharides synthesized by glycosyltransferases in order to establish the biosynthetic routes to the carbohydrate chains of glycoproteins (18).

Several different h.p.l.c. packing materials and solvent systems have been investigated for carbohydrate separation including native and derivatized oligosaccharides chromatographed on silica, silica chemicaly bonded with amino groups, silica modified with soluble amines *in situ*, reversed-phase (RP), anion- and cation-exchangers (with a variety of buffers and with aqueous−organic eluents) and size exclusion chromatography. In several instances a combination of different chromatographic modes was required for the complete separation of all of the isomers present in mixtures of oligosaccharides obtained from biological sources (16,29,30).

The present chapter describes the chromatographic behaviour of mono- and oligosaccharides using the different h.p.l.c. packings. This is followed by examples of specific applications reported in the literature for the analysis and preparative separation of mono- and oligosaccharides from which the conditions for further applications can be deduced.

2. DETECTION SYSTEMS FOR H.P.L.C. OF CARBOHYDRATES

2.1 **Refractive index**

Many of the early h.p.l.c. studies on carbohydrates used a differential refractive index detector because these studies were carried out on oligosaccharides containing neutral sugars only, which absorb weakly in the u.v. light range (1−7). The disadvantages of using a refractometer are that only isocratic elution is possible and the sensitivity is relatively low, 10−100 nmol being required for detection.

2.2 **U.v. absorbance**

Oligosaccharides containing acetamido groups or sialic acids can be detected by absorbance in the near-u.v. light range (180−220 nm) with a detection limit of approximately 1 nmol. Various u.v. absorbances have been used to achieve the best signal-to-noise ratio from 190 nm through 195, 200, 202, 206, 208 to 210 nm (e.g. references 15, 12, 20, 14, 9, 29 and 19, respectively).

For preparative separations, a higher wavelength can be used. An approximate 10 and 100 times decrease in sensitivity is achieved by increasing the wavelength of detection from 208 to 218 and 228 nm, respectively.

Oligosaccharides having unsaturated monosaccharides formed by enzymic digestion of sulphated glycosaminoglycans have u.v. absorption maxima at 232 nm. These can therefore be detected by u.v. in eluents which absorb at less than 230 nm, as in ion-pair chromatography (21−23). The sensitivity of detection of these oligosaccharides at 232 nm was less than 1 nmol (25).

The sensitivity can be further improved (down to 1 pmol) by introducing a strongly u.v. absorbing group such as the benzoyl (32) or phenylisocyanate (33) groups into the molecules.

2.3 **Post-column derivatization methods**

Early post-column derivatization methods for carbohydrate detection employed strong acids and thus required acid-resistant equipment. For example, the use of orcinol-concentrated sulphuric acid reagent required an elaborate carbohydrate analyser to be set up for direct post-column detection (34). Similar methods, such as the phenol/sulphuric acid assay, have proved useful for separate, off-column hexose determination, (e.g. see ref. 29 for its use to detect hexose in fractions obtained from Bio-Gel P4 chromatography). The sensitivity of detection for these methods is approximately 20 nmol hexose which is slightly less than by u.v. detection of native oligosaccharides containing hexose and hexosacetamido sugars, but represents a greatly improved sensitivity for detection of oligosaccharides containing neutral sugars alone.

More recent post-column derivatization methods have used non-corrosive reagents, particularly for detection of reducing sugars after borate-complex ion-exchange chromatography. The copper complex of 2,2'-bicinchoninate (35), ethanolamine−boric acid (36) and 2-cyanoacetamide (37), for example, were used to detect 1 nmol oligosaccharide. Detection of less than 1 nmol oligosaccharide has been reported (38) using tetrazolium blue reagent (3,3'-[3,3'-dimethoxy-1,1'-biphenyl-4,4'-diyl]bis [2,5-diphenyl-2H-tetrazolium] dichloride) which has the additional advantage of achieving this sensitivity in the absence of borate buffer and at a lower reaction temperature of 85°C. The method is suitable for both reduced and reducing mono- and oligosaccharides.

2.4 Detection of radioactively labelled carbohydrates

The sensitivity of carbohydrate detection can be greatly increased by introducing a radioactive label, either by reduction with sodium boro[³H]hydride or de-N-acetylation and re-N-acetylation with [¹⁴C]acetic anhydride. Oligosaccharides isolated from biological sources are often obtained in reduced and/or de-N-acetylated form. For example:

(i)   after mild alkali−borohydride degradation used to isolate oligosaccharides linked through the oxygen of serine or threonine amino acids of glycoproteins (O-glycosidically linked) where reduction stabilizes the released chain by preventing alkali-catalysed 'peeling' reactions (31), and,

(ii)   after hydrazinolysis to release oligosaccharides linked to protein through the nitrogen of asparagine (N-glycosidically linked) where there is concommitant release of N-acetyl groups, which can then be replaced using [¹⁴C]acetic anhydride (20), and production of a reducing end for labelling by reduction with sodium boro[³H]hydride (10,17).

Analysis of reduced oligosaccharides has an additional advantage in that reduction destroys the anomerization at the reducing end thus simplifying chromatography and subsequent structural analysis (29). Several h.p.l.c. systems gave separation of anomers when present. These included silica chemically bonded with primary amine groups using buffered eluents (2,8), RP (4,13,14) and ion-exchange (37) chromatography. The separation of anomers was also given by h.p.l.c. after pre-column derivatization of reducing oligosaccharides with acetyl (16), benzoyl (32) and phenylisocyanate (33) groups. Therefore, reduction is usually performed routinely as part of these derivatization procedures. The sensitivity of detection of the latter two derivatives by u.v. (which is comparable with the sensitivity of detection of radioactively labelled material using high specific activity sodium boro[³H]hydride) would usually obviate the need to introduce a radioactive label on reduction. However, analysis of reduced, radioactivity labelled and acetylated oligosaccharides has been employed (16).

An alternative method for introduction of a radioactive label, that of O-acetylation with [¹⁴C]acetic anhydride, has so far not been reported, probably due to the difficulties in handling small amounts of radiolabelled acetic anhydride (unpublished results).

Several on-line radioactive detection systems are available, for example, from Berthold, Beckman and Nuclear Enterprises. These are available with both solid scintillant cells and the possibility of addition of liquid scintillant (with or without stream splitting). For ³H-labelled oligosaccharides approximately 10^4 and 10^2 c.p.m. are required for detection by the two types of technique, respectively. The sensitivity of detection of ¹⁴C is of the order of 10^3 c.p.m.

2.5 Electrochemical detection of carbohydrates

Rocklin and Pohl (39) reported nanomolar detection of both reducing and reduced neutral mono- and oligosaccharides using pulsed amperometric detection employing a gold electrode. This method was stated to have advantages of increased response times and detector durability as compared with potentiometric and single potential (d.c.) detectors and detection of carbohydrates in the presence of a high concentration of potentially interfering salts. An increased sensitivity for detection of reducing sugars (down to 1 pmol) was reported by Watanabe and Inoue (40) using amperometric detection of carbohydrates chromatographed in sodium phosphate buffer after post-column reaction with copper bis(phenanthroline) in alkaline solution at 96°C. The advantages and disadvantages of these systems over the detection methods reported above await further investigations.

3. STATIONARY AND MOBILE PHASES FOR H.P.L.C. OF CARBOHYDRATES

3.1 **Silica chemically bonded with primary amine groups or modified with soluble amines**

3.1.1 *Normal phase silica adsorbents*

Aitzetmüller (4) showed that low percentages of water in organic eluents will rapidly elute monosaccharides from silica. Silica is thus not suitable for preparative separations due to inadequate aqueous content for solute solubilization. Some analytical applications are, however, possible. For example, separation of oligosaccharide isomers varying in their 1-4 or 1-3 linkage to N-acetylglucosamine using the acetylated, radioactively labelled alditols of chemically synthesized oligosaccharides has been reported (16) using a 25 cm × 5 mm Hypersil column (5 μm spherical silica) with 5% isopropanol in dichloromethane−hexane 70:30 (v/v) as eluent. The same column eluted with acetonitrile−water−heptane 84:14:2 (by vol) resolved similar oligosaccharides in non-acetylated form which were obtained from mucin glycoproteins and were not separated on Hypersil chemically bonded with aminopropyl groups (APS). Such analytical systems are of use in the estimation of purity of oligosaccharide preparations.

Addition of soluble amine to an acetonitrile−water eluent resulted in a dramatic increase in capacity factors (k') for neutral mono- to disaccharides chromatographed on silica (4). We have used tetraethylenepentamine (TEPA) as *in situ* modifier and shown that this gives similar chromatographic behaviour to APS with slightly increased resolution (16). Several workers have suggested that *in situ* modification of silica with amines has advantages over chemically bonded stationary phases in resolution, expense and column durability (5−7,11). The amine modifier 1,4-diaminobutane with silica and also with APS was shown to give better resolution than TEPA with silica (11) or APS without amine modifiers (20).

The chemically bonded phases are, however, increasingly popular as the presence of soluble amines in the mobile phase rules out the use of u.v. detection. Several commercial packings on the market are shown in *Table 1* with examples of their use in carbohydrate h.p.l.c. Silica eluted with solvents containing amines and silica chemically bonded with amino groups are not recommended for the preparative isolation of reducing mono- and oligosaccharides due to the potential of Schiff base formation. A significant increase in recovery is obtained by separation of the reduced derivatives where yields of 75−85% are usually obtained.

Table 1. Examples of the applications of h.p.l.c. using silica adsorbents having chemically bonded functional amine groups.

Adsorbent	Manufacturer	Examples of application[a]
μ-Bondapak carbohydrate	Waters	Monosaccharide analysis[b]
		Analysis of neutral and sialylated oligosaccharides and glycopeptides from urine, using either aqueous acetonitrile or acetonitrile − 1 M sodium acetate/acetic acid buffer 1, pH 5.6[c]
		Fractionation of high mannose-type oligosaccharides[d]
Partisil 10 PAC	Whatman	Separation of neutral oligosaccharides[e]
		Analysis of sulphated disaccharides using acetonitrile − methanol − 0.5 M ammoniom acetate, pH 6.5[f]
Lichrosorb-NH₂	Merck	Preparative separation of non-sialylated O-linked oligosaccharides[g]
		Separation of high mannose-type oligosaccharides[h]
		Analysis of sialylated O-linked oligosaccharides using acetonitrile − 15 mM potassium phosphate buffer, pH 5.2[i]
MicroPak NH₂	Varian	Preparative separation of high mannose oligosaccharides[j]
Amino AS 5A	Chromatem	Analysis of sialylated complex carbohydrate chains using acetonitrile − potassium phosphate − diaminobutane[k]
APS-Hypersil	Shandon	Analysis and preparative separation of oligosaccharide isomers containing neutral and acetamido sugars[l]
		Analysis of sulphated disaccharides using 0.1 M sodium sulphate containing 0.05 M sodium acetate, pH 5.0[m]

[a]Unless otherwise stated solvent systems are acetonitrile − water.
[b]From ref. 1; [c]From ref. 8; [d]From ref. 10; [e]From ref. 2; [f]From ref. 22, 25; [g]From ref. 9; [h]From ref. 11; [i]From ref. 18; [j]From ref. 15; [k]From ref. 20; [l]From ref. 16,29; [m]From ref. 24.

Table 2. The chromatographic behaviour of oligosaccharides containing neutral and acetamido sugars on h.p.l.c. using a column of silica chemically bonded with aminopropyl groups.

The retention times (min) are shown for oligosaccharides obtained from human meconium glycoproteins chromatographed on an APS-Hypersil column (0.46 × 25 cm) using gradient elution from 75:25 (v/v) acetonitrile/dilute HCl pH 3.0 to 65:35 (v/v) at 10 min and 35:65 (v/v) at 20 min. Preparative separation of some of the compounds was achieved by isocratic elution using 65:35 (v/v) acetonitrile: dilute HCl pH 3.0.

	Retention time (min)
GalNAc-ol	6.8
Galβ1-3GalNAc-ol	10.6
GalNAcα1-3GalNAc-ol	10.6
GlcNAcβ1-3GalNAc-ol	10.1
Galβ1-3GlcNAcβ1-3GalNAc-ol	12.9
Galβ1-4GlcNAcβ1-3GalNAc-ol	12.9
Galβ1-4GlcNAcβ1-6GalNAc-ol	13.8
GlcNAcβ1$\searrow$$^6_3$GalNacol Gal$\beta$1$\nearrow$	13.8
Galβ1-4GlcNAcβ1$\searrow$$^6_3$GalNAcol Gal$\beta$1$\nearrow$	16.0

3.1.2 *The retention behaviour of oligosaccharides on silica chemically bonded with primary amine groups*

In general, oligosaccharides containing hexosacetamido, deoxyhexose and/or hexose residues have been chromatographed with aqueous acetonitrile eluents and oligosaccharides containing anionic groups with buffer−acetonitrile. An acidic, rather than neutral eluent has usually been favoured (2,8,12,16−18,20,24) which in one report (2) was shown to give sharper peaks and shorter retention time.

The solubility of most oligosaccharides is poor below 35% water content in the mobile phase. This is recommended as the starting concentration for preparative separations (29). Increasing the water content of the eluent decreased the retention time and hydrophobic interaction with the stationary phase was reported to be negligible, indicating a normal phase chromatography (38). The total number of hydroxyl groups, their distribution on the molecule and the linkage positions are important factors for separation. For oligosaccharides isolated from human meconium (*Table 2*) solute elution was largely in the order of increasing molecular weight. However, retention was longer for oligosaccharides having a 1−6 linkage (*Table 2*) and, as reported previously (38), for compounds having residues with adjacent hydroxyl groups on the same plane of the molecule, e.g. galactose and N-acetylgalactosamine compared with N-acetylglucosamine. Similar findings have been reported for h.p.l.c. of oligosaccharides isolated from human bronchial mucins (9). An increased retention for oligosaccharides having a 1−6 linkage was also reported for oligosaccharides which form part of the complex chains linked via N-acetylglucosamine to protein, on normal phase h.p.l.c. using acetonitrile−potassium phosphate buffer pH 5.2 as eluent (12).

3.2 Reversed-phase and reversed-phase ion-pair h.p.l.c. of carbohydrates

3.2.1 *Reversed-phase packings and eluents*

The majority of studies on RP and ion-pair (IP) h.p.l.c. of carbohydrates have used an octadecylsilyl (ODS) column and the chromatographic behaviour of oligosaccharides on stationary phases having different alkyl chain length has not been studied in detail. In one report an octylsilyl column was shown to decrease resolution without significantly altering the retention of neutral oligosaccharides which was, however, influenced by pore size (7). It will be of interest to investigate the chromatographic behaviour of oligosaccharides containing neutral and acetamido groups on columns of different alkyl chain length and pore size particularly for reduced sugars, as reduced sugars having a small number of acetamido groups and/or one or more deoxyhexose (e.g. fucose) residues were not retained on commercial ODS packings using 100% water as eluent (16). Retention on ODS increased on addition of salt (0.5 – 1 M sodium chloride) and decreased when the pH, organic content and/or temperature of the eluent were increased (7,16).

Sulphated oligosaccharides have been separated by RP-IP h.p.l.c. with either tetra-butylammonium phosphate (21,22) or dodecyltributylammonium in sodium nitrate (23) as IP agents. The former pairing agent was used for separating oligosaccharides obtained from heparan sulphate (a sulphated polymer of N-acetylglucosamine, glucuronic acid and iduronic acid) and chondroitin sulphate (a sulphated polymer of N-acetylgalactosamine and glucuronic acid), and the latter for x-carrageenan (a sulphated polymer of galacturonic acid). Oligosaccharides differing in the number of sulphate constituents or the position of sulphate linkage were separated. RP chromatography has also been applied for the separation of derivatized mono- and oligosaccharides with either acetonitrile – water (32), acetonitrile – ammonium acetate pH 7.0 (16) or acetoni-trile – 0.01 M potassium phosphate pH 7.0 (32) as eluent for benzoyl, acetyl and phenylisocyanate derivatives, respectively.

3.2.2 *The retention behaviour of oligosaccharides on reversed-phase packings*

As shown in *Table 3*, for native oligosaccharides containing both neutral and acetamido sugars, separation on ODS was not based on size. Oligosaccharides with a higher acetamido/neutral sugar ratio were retained longer due to the relative hydrophobicity of acetamido compared with hydroxyl. Thus, a tetrasaccharide having two hexosacet-amido and two hexose residues co-migrated with a trisaccharide having two hexosacet-amido residues and two hexoses and both these oligosaccharides eluted before disaccharides having two hexosacetamido groups and no hexose. In contrast to the elution order on APS (Section 3.1.2), oligosaccharides having a 1 – 6 linkage had shorter retention times. Comparison of *Tables 2* and *3* illustrates how a combination of chromatographic techniques (normal and reversed-phase, respectively) can be used to separate a series of closely related oligosaccharides (29) as oligosaccharides with different composition and linkage may co-migrate in one system.

For a series of oligosaccharides isolated from human milk (13,14,16) it was shown that non-reduced oligosaccharides were retained longer than their reduced counterparts on RP chromatography as expected by the difference of two hydroxyl groups. The separation of the anomers of the reducing oligosaccharides was obtained and this was exploited to separate oligosaccharide isomers not resolved as their reduced derivatives (13,14,16). Decreasing the retention time by increasing the organic phase (7) or, in the case of IP h.p.l.c., by increasing the concentration of pairing ion (21) has been shown to result in co-migration of anomers in RP chromatography.

Table 3. The chromatographic behaviour of oligosaccharides containing neutral and acetamido sugards on h.p.l.c. using a column of silica chemically bonded with octadecyl silyl groups.

The retention times (min) are shown for oligosaccharides obtained from human meconium glycoproteins chromatographed on an ODS-Hypersil column (0.46 × 25 cm) using dilute HCl pH 3.0 as eluent. The two trisaccharide isomers having 1-3, 1-3 and 1-4, 1-3 linkages are not separated by this system or that using aqueous acetonitrile eluents.

	Retention time (min)
GalNAc-ol	3.8
Galβ1-3GalNAc-ol	3.6
GalNAcα1-3GalNAc-ol	4.4
GlcNAcβ1-3GalNAc-ol	4.9
Galβ1-3GlcNAcβ1-3GalNAc-ol	5.9
Galβ1-4GlcNAcβ1-3GalNAc-ol	5.9
Galβ1-4GlcNAcβ1-6GalNAc-ol	5.1
GlcNAcβ1$\diagdown$$^{6}_{3}$GalNacol Gal$\beta$1$\diagup$	4.0
Galβ1-4GlcNAcβ1$\diagdown$$^{6}_{3}$GalNAcol Gal$\beta$1$\diagup$	4.2

3.3 The retention behaviour of oligosaccharides on ion-exchange resins

Conventional ion-exchange chromatography of neutral mono- and oligosaccharides showed that, for cation-exchange resins eluted with water and anion-exchange resins eluted with water or borate buffers, the retention of oligosaccharides increased with decreasing number of hydroxyl groups (reviewed in ref. 30). Variation in the counter ion was shown to affect different separations by altering the efficiency of interaction of the counter ion with varying configurations of hydroxyl groups above or below the plane of the ring (30). The separation is thus achieved by size/ion exclusion. These ion-exchange systems offer an alternative to the classical size exclusion chromatography. However, resins with a relatively low percentage of cross-linking are required for resolution of oligosaccharides larger than disaccharide (39), for example the 4% cross-linked polystyrene from Durrum, DAX4 (9), and the 8% cross-linked polystyrene used in amino acid analysers (41). Such resins are at present not available for h.p.l.c. because of their high compressibility. Ion-exchange groups chemically bonded to silica are, however, available commercially and anion-exchange h.p.l.c. using sodium chloride or phosphate buffer gradients has been used to separate sialylated (17,19,20), sulphated (42) and phosphorylated (17) oligosaccharides. As expected, the retention increased with increasing number of anionic groups and the chromatography was relatively independent of other structural differences between the oligosaccharides studied.

Oligosaccharides which do not contain anionic groups have also been chromatographed on ion-exchange h.p.l.c. columns. An anion-exchange column (MicroPak AX-5; Varian) eluted with aqueous acetonitrile has been used to separate oligosaccharides containing neutral and acetamido sugars (10) and a cation-exchange resin of highly cross-linked sulphated styrene−divinyl benzene co-polymer (Shodex DC-613) has been used to separate monosaccharides with aqueous acetonitrile as eluent. The latter separation was reported to be little changed by alteration in counter ion, although h.p.l.c. in the [H^{+}] form was preferred as this did not lead to anomer separation (37). Ion-exchange resins eluted with aqueous ethanol or acetonitrile show a different type of separation to that obtained using buffers in the absence of organic solvents (30). The separation in the presence of organic solvents is based on the stronger interactions of oligosaccharides having a greater number of hydroxyl groups with the water-rich hydration sphere of the resin. Therefore, pentoses eluted before hexoses (37) and oligomers eluted in order of increasing molecular weight (10).

Following the studies of Mellis and Baenziger (10) we have used MicroPak AX-5 anion-exchange resin eluted with aqueous acetonitrile to separate oligosaccharide isomers containing neutral and acetamido sugars and particularly those varying in the presence of a 1-3 or 1-4 linkage to N-acetylglucosamine. Although changes in chromatographic behaviour afforded by different linkages has yet to be fully studied, this system appeared to offer an alternative to normal and RP chromatography for resolving isomers.

4. APPLICATION OF H.P.L.C. TO CARBOHYDRATE COMPOSITIONAL ANALYSIS

4.1 Stationary phases, mobile phases and detection methods

The modern ion-exchange packings now available are the method of choice for neutral and acetamido sugar analysis in addition to their applications to analytical and preparative separations of oligosaccharides. The use of the same column and/or apparatus for both oligosaccharide purification and determination of composition is attractive compared with the combined h.p.l.c. preparative separation of oligosaccharides and g.c. composition analysis technique of the constituent monosaccharides.

The early applications of h.p.l.c. to the field of carbohydrate analysis, using silica, silica chemically bonded with primary amine groups or silica modified with soluble amines, reported the separation of fructose and glucose, disaccharides such as sucrose, maltose and lactose and larger neutral oligosaccharide oligomers of glucose and galactose (1−7). Resolution of other monosaccharides commonly found in the oligosaccharides of body fluids such as milk and urine and in the carbohydrate chains of glycoproteins and glycolipids were not reported. These include the epimers glucose, galactose and mannose, and related monosaccharides rhamnose, fucose, xylose and arabinose. Separation of all the monosaccharides, together with ribose and fructose, has been reported in one run using ion-exchangers, such as DAX4 anion-exchange resin (Durrum) with borate buffer as eluent (34,35) and a cation-exchange resin (Shodex DC-613) in the hydrogen form with aqueous acetonitrile as eluent (37). Detection in these ion-exchange systems was by post-column derivatization which gave an increased sensitivity over the refractive index monitoring used in the earlier applications. Other examples of the h.p.l.c. analysis of monosaccharides are given in a recent review by Honda (43).

Ion-exchange adsorbents have also been reported for the separation of acetamido sugars, for example that of N-acetylglucosamine and N-acetylgalactosamine, found as common constituents of glycoproteins and glycolipids, and N-acetyl- and N-glycolyl-mannosamines, formed from the sialic acids, N-acetyl- and N-glycolyl-neuraminic acid, by the action of N-acetylneuraminate pyruvate lyase (37). Glucosamine and galactosamine (in their non-N-acetylated form) and their reduced derivatives have been routinely analysed in many laboratories using commercial amino acid analysers with

Table 4. Methods for carbohydrate analysis.

Hydrolysis

The sample is hydrolysed using one of the following conditions

0.5 N Sulphuric acid in 90% acetic acid	80°C	4 − 16 h
1 − 2 N Hydrochloric acid	100°C	6 h
0.2 − 1 N Sulphuric acid	100°C	8 − 16 h
2 N Trifluoroacetic acid	120°C	1.5 h
0.01 N Hydrochloric acid containing Dowex 50X2 resin in the [H$^+$] form	95°C	48 h

Re-N-acetylation

The sample is neutralized after hydrolysis and re-N-acetylated by addition of acetic anhydride (5 × 10 μl aliquots at 10 min intervals) to a solution (0.5 ml) in saturated sodium bicarbonate at ambient temperature.

O- and N-acetylation

The sample can be O- and N-acetylated by the addition of acetic anhydride to the dry material or in solution in dry pyridine, and heating at 100°C for 1 h.

De-O-acetylation

The sample is dissolved in dry methanol and is stood for 3 h at ambient temperature with a catalytic quantity of barium or sodium methoxide or KOH pellets dissolved in 3:1 methanol/toluene (v/v) to a final concentration of 0.1 M.

Deamination of de-N-acetylated monosaccharides

Solid sodium nitrite is added to the acidic conditions of hydrolysis to give a final concentration of 20 mg/ml.

Methanolysis

The sample is dissolved in dry methanol containing 1 M HCl and heated at 80°C for 16 h followed by neutralization with solid silver carbonate or pyridine and re-N-acetylation by the addition of acetic anhydride to a final concentration of 10% acetic anhydride.

detection by ninhydrin (41). We have recently used a Micropak AX-5 h.p.l.c. anion-exchange column (Varian) with aqueous acetonitrile as eluent and u.v. detection at 208 nm for the separation of N-acetylglucosaminitol and N-acetylgalactosaminitol. This separation was previously achieved by paper chromatography or t.l.c. of radioactively labelled monosaccharides in microscale studies to identify these monosaccharides at the reduced end of oligosaccharides released from N- and O-glycosidically linked chains, respectively. Anion-exchange h.p.l.c. therefore offers an alternative method for this anlaysis.

4.2 **Hydrolysis and derivatization techniques for carbohydrate compositional analysis**

Except for isolated cases where mono- and disaccharides are present in food preparations (1 − 7), and body fluids (33), carbohydrate analysis usually requires a hydrolysis step to generate monosaccharides from oligosaccharides and the carbohydrate chains of glycoproteins and glycolipids. Hydrolysis results in de-N-acetylation of acetamido groups. A re-N-acetylation step is generally included in the derivatization procedure although the resulting monosaccharides can be analysed as their non-N-acetylated amines (41) and after deamination of de-N-acetylated glucosamine and galactosamine to yield 2,5-anhydromannose and 2,5-anhydrotalose, respectively (*Table 4*). The hydrolysis conditions shown in *Table 4* have the disadvantage that the resulting reducing monosaccharides are unstable in the acidic conditions and, as monosaccharide stability and the rates of interglycosidic bond cleavage vary depending on monosaccharide type, neutral, deoxyhexose and acetamido sugars and the uronic and sialic acids cannot be analysed quantitatively using one hydrolysis condition. On the other hand, during methanolysis the methyl glycosides formed from neutral and acetamido sugars and the methyl ester, methyl glycosides formed from the uronic and sialic acids are relatively stable in the methanolic acid conditions used. Thus, quantitative recovery of all different types of monosaccharide can be achieved in one analysis by this method. However, the one to four possible methyl glycosides (α and β pyranose, α and β furanose) for each monosaccharide produced by this technique may be difficult to separate by h.p.l.c. Their detection by g.c. in reproducible ratios has proved to be very useful for unambiguous identification of sugars in biological samples. The alternative, popular method for g.c. analysis using alditol acetates which give only a single peak for each monosaccharide can be inaccurate due to completely overlapping non-sugar contaminants (unpublished observations). Presumably, derivatization reagents more specific for monosaccharides could be used for h.p.l.c. detection as has been proposed for the post-column reaction with 2-cyanoacetamide (37). Other derivatization methods for sensitive detection of carbohydrates by h.p.l.c. analysis include post- (34−39) and pre-column (32,33) methods.

One additional method for analysis of carbohydrates, using hydrolysis of permethylated oligosaccharides followed by reduction and acetylation to yield partially methylated alditol acetate derivatives, has the same problems in the production of reducing sugars and thus in the choice and control of hydrolysis conditions for reproducible production of both neutral and acetamido sugars. However, this method has the advantage of providing compositional and linkage data in one analysis. The several possible derivatives given for each monosaccharide in the chain which vary depending on the original position of linkage of the monosaccharide in the oligosaccharide are separated and identified by capillary g.c. with combined mass spectrometry. This analysis is routinely performed on $10-20$ μg of material purified after methylation with Sep-Pak or Bond-Elut C_{18} cartridges (obtained from Waters Associates and Analytichem International, respectively). Other methods of identifying these derivatives include t.l.c. with calorimetric detection or the detection of a radioactive label introduced by reduction with sodium boro[^{3}H]hydride. H.p.l.c. may therefore have a role to play in analysing these derivatives using sensitive radioactive detection. There are reports of h.p.l.c. separation of several partially methylated alditol acetates using RP and anion-exchange chromatography (43).

5. ANALYTICAL AND PREPARATIVE SEPARATIONS OF OLIGOSAC-CHARIDES CONTAINING NEUTRAL AND ACETAMIDO SUGARS

5.1 Oligosaccharides obtained by chemical or enzymic synthesis

Characterization of the specificity of carbohydrate-binding proteins such as lectins, anti-carbohydrate antibodies, glycosidases and glycosyltransferases requires highly purified oligosaccharides for use in binding/inhibition studies and as acceptor substrates. Oligo-saccharides produced by chemical and enzymic synthesis have been invaluable in many studies several of which required h.p.l.c. analysis as a criterion of purity and for iden-

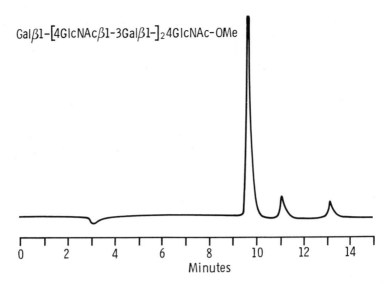

Figure 1. H.p.l.c. of a chemically synthesized preparation of the oligosaccharide methyl glycoside Galβ1-4GlcNAcβ1-3Galβ1-4GlcNAcβ1-3Galβ1-4GlcNAc-OMe. Column, ODS-Hypersil; gradient elution, from 100% acetonitrile to acetonitrile − water 85:15 (v/v) in 15 min. The minor components are isomers of the oligosaccharide.

tification of biosynthetic products.

For example, oligosaccharides related to poly-N-acetyllactosamine obtained from natural sources (human milk) and by chemical synthesis have been used in studies on the characterization of the fine specificities of anti-i and anti-I antibodies (27). The largest oligosaccharide of linear poly-N-acetyllactosamine sequence that has been synthesized so far (A.Veyrìeres, C.Augé and S.David, Universite d'Orlay France) is the hexasaccharide Galβ1-4GlcNAcβ1-3Galβ1-4GlcNAcβ1-3Galβ1-4GlcNAcβ1-OMe. H.p.l.c. of the synthetic preparation of this oligosaccharide on ODS showed the presence of three component methyl glycosides which were particularly well separated by RP chromatography (*Figure 1*). Their preparative separation could be readily achieved by h.p.l.c. and analysis by n.m.r. showed them to be isomers which could have arisen by branching. Although the minor components were obtained in too small an amount for complete structural determination, their removal from the main product was important for interpreting the results of antibody inhibition studies and of endo-β-galactosidase digestion (27).

A series of oligosaccharides (di- to heptasaccharide) containing galactose, N-acetylglucosamine and mannose, related to the backbone structures of complex carbohydrate chains N-glycosidically linked to protein, have been chemically synthesized and analysed by h.p.l.c. prior to use in studies to characterize the specificities of glycosyltransferases (12). H.p.l.c. using Lichrosorb-NH$_2$ eluted with acetonitrile − 15 mM potassium phosphate gave a separation mainly by size with the larger oligosaccharides having a longer retention time. However, as discussed in Section 3.1.2, the replacement of a galactose by an N-acetylglucosamine residue caused an elution-accelerating effect and the presence of a 1-6 linkage (either at a branch point or in straight chain) a retardation. This study therefore emphasized the importance of characterizing h.p.l.c. systems before their application to identify products of enzyme synthesis, as oligosaccharides with both different composition and different linkages may co-migrate. In addition, h.p.l.c. systems exhibiting different chromatographic properties can be used for analysis (Section 3).

As discussed in Section 3.3, ion-exchange h.p.l.c. offers an alternative method for the separation of oligosaccharides not resolved by normal and RP chromatography although few studies have been carried out on commercially available h.p.l.c. ion-exchangers. As an example of the types of separation that may be achieved, the following oligosaccharides, prepared from the oligosaccharides of milk (Section 5.2) by partial acid hydrolysis and enzymic synthesis, were completely separated as their de-N-acetylated and reduced derivatives (41) using the column of an amino acid analyser (40 × 1 cm of Locarte No 12 resin, an X8 cross-linked sulphonated polystyrene) eluted at 50°C with sodium citrate/borate buffer, flow-rate 45 ml/h:

$$GlcNAc\beta1-3Gal-ol$$
$$GlcNAc\beta1-6Gal-ol$$
$$GalNAc\alpha1-3Gal-ol$$
$$Gal\beta1-3GlcNAc-ol$$
$$Gal\beta1-4GlcNAc-ol$$
$$GalNAc\alpha1-3Gal\beta1-3GlcNAc-ol$$
$$GalNAc\alpha1-3Gal\beta1-4GlcNAc-ol$$

One additional method which achieved the separation of isomers produced by chemical synthesis was their reduction, acetylation and h.p.l.c. on silica with organic eluents (16). Such methods should be considered when h.p.l.c. is being used as a criterion of purity of oligosaccharides.

5.2 The oligosaccharides of human milk, urine and faeces having lactose at their reducing end

Human milk, urine and faeces are a rich source of oligosaccharides for studies of the antigenicities, biosynthesis and biodegradation of carbohydrates. They have been particularly useful in studying the structure and biosynthesis of the blood group and related antigens. The non-sialylated oligosaccharides so far identified from human milk are shown in *Table 5* together with the designations of their antigenicities (26,28). The oligosaccharides having fucosylated galactose residues are substrates for the glycosyltransferases coded for by the blood group A and B genes which catalyse the transfer of an N-acetylgalactosamine and a galactose residue, respectively, in $\alpha1-3$ linkage to the galactose residue already having fucose in $\alpha1-2$ linkage. For example, oligosaccharides with the blood group A (GalNAcα1-3[Fucα1-2]Galβ1-) and ALe[b] (GalNAcα1-3[Fucα1-2]Galβ1-3[Fucα1-4]GlcNAcβ1-) structures were isolated by classical chromatographic techniques using paper and celite column chromatography from the faeces of infants breast-fed by blood group A mothers and also from human urine (gifts of H.Sabharwal, A.Lundblad and G.Strecker) and used in studies to show that several antibodies raised against the cell surface receptor for epidermal growth were recognizing these structures on this glycoprotein (44). The blood group and related antigens found on secreted and cell surface glycoproteins are usually present in amounts too small for direct structural analysis of individual sugar components. The use of anti-

Table 5. The neutral oligosaccharides of human milk.

Antigenicity	Structure	Name
	Galβ1-4Glc	Lactose
	Galβ1-4Glc 2 | Fucα1	2'Fucosyllactose
	Galβ1-4Glc 3 | Fucα1	3'Fucosyllactose
	Galβ1-4Glc 2 3 | | Fucα1 Fucα1	Lacto-difucotetraose
FC10.2	Galβ1-3GlcNAcβ1-3Galβ1-4Glc	Lacto-N-tetraose (LNT)
	Galβ1-4GlcNAcβ1-3Galβ1-4Glc	Lacto-N-neotetraose (LNNT)
H	Galβ1-3GlcNAcβ1-3Galβ1-4Glc 2 | Fucα1	Lacto-N-fucopentaose I (LNFI)
Lewis[a]	Galβ1-3GlcNAcβ1-3Galβ1-4Glc 4 | Fucα1	Lacto-N-fucopentaose II (LNFII)
SSEA-1,Y Le[x]	Galβ1-4GlcNAcβ1-3Galβ1-4Glc 3 | Fucα1	Lacto-N-fucopentaose III (LNFIII)
Lewis[b]	Galβ1-3GlcNAcβ1-3Galβ1-4Glc 2 4 | | Fucα1 Fucα1	Lacto-N-difucohexaose I
Lewis[a]/ SSEA-1,Le[x]	Galβ1-3GlcNAcβ1-3Galβ1-4Glc 4 3 | | Fucα1 Fucα1	Lacto-N-difucohexaose II
SSEA-1,Le[x]	Galβ1-4GlcNAcβ1-3Galβ1-4Glc 3 3 | | Fucα1 Fucα1	Lacto-N-difucohexaose III

carbohydrate antibodies, the antigenic determinants of which have been established by studies involving purified and characterized oligosaccharides from large-scale natural sources such as milk, has therefore made possible the identification and tissue localization of these antigens.

As the interest in carbohydrate structures as antigens and as components of receptors increases, h.p.l.c. will have an increasing role to play in their purification. Of the studies reported so far, partial purification of the oligosaccharides LNT, LNNT, LNFI, LNFII and LNFIII (*Table 5*) by h.p.l.c. separation of their α and β anomers has been achieved using water as eluent on RP columns (13,14). Their reduced derivatives were not retained sufficiently on ODS-Hypersil for separation (16) and the alditol isomers were not separated by h.p.l.c. on APS-Hypersil using water—acetonitrile eluents or on silica with TEPA—water—acetonitrile (16,30). The separation of LNT from LNNT and LNFII from LNFIII has also not been achieved using their acetylated derivatives chromatographed on a silica adsorbent with organic solvents (16) or anion-exchange h.p.l.c. using water—acetonitrile eluents. The fucosylated and non-fucosylated oligosaccharides are well separated in these systems and on the APS-Hypersil column, for example with isocratic elution in 65:35 (v/v) acetonitrile—water (30). T.l.c. of the resulting isomeric mixtures after reduction and acetylation was then used to separate LNT-ol from LNNT-ol and LNFII-ol from LNFIII-ol (30). An h.p.l.c. separation of the latter isomers has been achieved (16) using the acetylated derivatives on an ODS column eluted with a linear gradient of 30—60% (over 20 min) acetonitrile in 0.5 M ammonium acetate followed by isocratic elution at 60:40 (v/v) acetonitrile—0.5 M ammonium acetate (for 10 min). The purified oligosaccharides after deacetylation have been used in studies to characterize several monoclonal antibodies raised against tumour-associated and differentiation antigens (28) which could thus be shown to recognize the 3-fucosyl-N-acetyllactosamine structure termed SSEA-1 (Galβ1-4[Fucα1-3]GlcNAcβ1-).

5.3 Oligosaccharides having the complex and high mannose structures of N-glycosidically linked chains of glycoproteins

The carbohydrate chains of glycoproteins linked via the nitrogen of asparagine residues (N-glycosidically linked) are of three main types, high mannose, hybrid and complex, as shown in *Table 6*. High mannose-type chains can be released from protein by the endo-β-glucosaminidase enzymes H and D yielding oligosaccharides having a reducing end -Manβ1-4GlcNAc sequence (10). The urine of patients with lysosomal storage diseases is a rich source of oligosaccharides terminating at the reducing end with this sequence (8,15,32). The deficiency of carbohydrate chain degrading enzymes in these disorders produces oligosaccharides of various sizes. The urine of mannosidosis patients for example was shown by h.p.l.c. to contain partially mannosylated tri- to decasaccharides of the high mannose chains (32). Oligosaccharides having a -4GlcNAcβ1-4GlcNAc reducing end sequence are released: (i) from protein by hydrazinolysis (10,31) and by peptide-N-glycosidase and (ii) from lipid of biosynthetic intermediates by mild acid hydrolysis (11).

H.p.l.c. of non-anionic oligosaccharides obtained from these sources has been carried out in silica chemically bonded with primary amine groups and/or eluted in the presence of amine modifiers (*Table 1*). Where the presence of amino acids (glycopeptides) was suspected, elution has been carried out in acetonitrile buffer, e.g. 0.1 M sodium acetate—acetic acid buffer pH 5.6 (8) and 0.05 mM phosphate buffer (31). Otherwise elution was with acetonitrile—water. Other examples of the h.p.l.c. of N-glycosidically linked oligosaccharides and glycopeptides are given in ref. 43.

Table 6. The N-glycosidically linked chains of glycoproteins.

The tri- to decasaccharides identified in the urine of patients with mannosidosis have one GlcNAc residue (that linked at C4 by Manβ) and the combinations of mannose residues within the high mannose structure shown below. The urine from patients with other lysosomal storage diseases contain fragments of the complex chains, the majority of which terminate at the reducing end with Manβ1-4GlcNAc. Several complex-type chains have been identified on different glycoproteins, for example, the tetraantennary structure shown below is present in orosomucoid, whereas the triantennary structure (lacking the Galβ1-4GlcNAcβ1-6 branch) is present in fetuin and ceruloplasmin. Fucose residues, Galβ1-3GlcNAc linkges and longer Gal-GlcNAc sequences may also be present in some complex chains and sialic acid residues are often found linked at the non-reducing termini.

Oligosaccharide chain

High mannose

```
Manα1-2Manα1 ──────┐
                    ⁶₃Manα1 ─────┐
Manα1-2Manα1 ──────┘             ⁶₃Manβ1-4GlcNAcβ1-4GlcNAc
Manα1-2Manα1-2Manα1 ─────────────┘
```

Hybrid

```
      Manα1 ──────┐
                   ⁶₃Manα1 ─────┐
      Manα1 ──────┘             ⁶₃Manβ1-4GlcNAcβ1-4GlcNAc
Galβ1-4GlcNAcβ1-2Manα1 ─────────┘
```

Complex

```
Galβ1-4GlcNAcβ1 ──────┐
                       ⁶₂Manα1 ─────┐
Galβ1-4GlcNAcβ1 ──────┘             ⁶₃Manβ1-4GlcNAcβ1-4GlcNAc
Galβ1-4GlcNAcβ1 ──────┐             │
                       ⁴₂Manα1 ─────┘
Galβ1-4GlcNAcβ1 ──────┘
```

5.4 Oligosaccharides released from glycoproteins by mild alkali/borohydride degradation: O-glycosidically linked carbohydrate chains

Although a proportion of N-glycosidically linked chains may be released from glycoproteins by mild alkali−borohydride degradation typically, this reaction, with 0.05−0.1 M sodium hydroxide in 1−2 M sodium borohydride for 16 h at 56°C or 48 h at 37°C (31), is used to release chains linked to protein through the hydroxyl groups of serine and threonine (O-glycosidically linked). The released chains characteristically have N-acetylgalactosaminitol at the reduced end although other mild alkali-susceptible linkages such as Xyl-Ser are also found in glycoproteins.

Mucin glycoproteins are a major source of oligosaccharides having GalNAc-Ser/Thr linkages which have been termed mucin-type chains. Many such chains are present in mucins which are large molecular weight glycoproteins having, on average, one carbohydrate chain for each four amino acids. The released chains are heterogeneous ranging in size from GalNAc-ol to oligosaccharides having 20 or more monosaccharides with many different possible types of sequence and linkage. Although the number of possible structures is great, oligosaccharides are in general built up via core regions having Galβ1-3, GlcNAcβ1-3 and GlcNAcβ1-6 linked to GalNAc-ol with backbones of Galβ1-4GlcNAcβ1-3 or Galβ1-3GlcNAcβ1-3 sequences in straight chain and with Galβ1-4GlcNAcβ1-6 sequences forming branch points. Peripheral, chain terminating sugars characteristically have an α anomeric configuration (e.g. Fucα, Galα, GalNAcα, GlcNAcα, sialic acid α).

The large number of possible oligosaccharides that can be formed in this way, and released from mucins by mild alkali/borohydride degradation, poses a difficult task for separation techniques. So far only a relatively small number of these oligosaccharides has been studied by h.p.l.c. The h.p.l.c. separation of the oligosaccharides representing the majority of the possible core region structures has been described using ODS- and APS-Hypersil (*Tables 2* and *3*) and also using Lichrosorb-NH$_2$ and μ-Bondapak Carbohydrate (9). The different amine-bonded silicas have shown similar retention of oligosaccharides, however they can vary in separation of particular isomers. For larger oligosaccharides where the number of possible structures increases rapidly with increasing molecular weight, ODS and ion-exchange stationary phases may be required for additional separation. The increased retention of the larger oligosaccharides in this series allows for a greater flexibility in choice of solvents, for example, gradient elution in RP systems and the introduction of additional organic solvents besides acetonitrile to normal phase systems to give increased resolution (e.g. the use of heptane in Section 3.1.1).

In summary, the h.p.l.c. of non-ionic di- to tetrasaccharides can be achieved by normal phase chromatography on silica chemically bonded with primary amine groups or eluted with soluble amine modifiers, the starting eluent being 65:35 (v/v) acetonitrile−water (representing the least amount of water for adequate solubility in preparative separations) and by RP chromatography using water as eluent. For larger oligosaccharides increasing concentrations of water are used in the normal phase system and, as the number of residues having acetamido groups increases, eluents having increasing concentrations of acetonitrile can be used in the RP system. H.p.l.c. using anion-exchange resins (e.g. MicroPak AX-5) with acetonitrile−water eluents can be used as an additional separation technique (10,30).

6. H.P.L.C. FOR THE ANALYTICAL AND PREPARATIVE SEPARATION OF ANIONIC OLIGOSACCHARIDES

6.1 Sialylated oligosaccharides

The sialic acids are common chain-terminating groups of the oligosaccharides of milk and the N- and O-glycosidically linked carbohydrate chains of glycoproteins. Within the general term, sialic acids, there are a number of neuraminic acids which vary in their acyl substituents on the C5 nitrogen and the oxygens at C4, 6, 7, 8 and 9. The reported h.p.l.c. of sialylated oligosaccharides are largely for those containing N-acetyl-neuraminic acid residues and in many studies the methods used for isolation of oligosaccharides would release the O-acyl substituents which are labile to mild base (e.g. 10 mM NaOH 50°C; 50 mM NaOH 4°C) and to mild acid (e.g. 0.01 M HCl 70°C). The N-glycolyl (-NH-CO-CH$_2$OH) substituent affects normal phase h.p.l.c. separations by increasing the retention relative to molecules having the N-acetyl group (-NH-CO-CH$_3$). Oligosaccharides isolated from bovine submaxillary mucins containing N-glycolyl-neuraminic acid residues were studied by Tsuji *et al.* (19) using an Hitachi custom anion-exchange resin (No. 2630) eluted with various gradients containing different concentrations of sodium chloride, but their chromatographic behaviour was not directly compared with those having N-acetylated neuraminic acids. This study of the application of anion-exchange h.p.l.c. to the purification of sialylated oligosaccharides showed separation of isomers and other oligosaccharides having the same number of sialic acid residues, whereas h.p.l.c. on another anion-exchange system using MicroPak AX-10 (Varian) and potassium phosphate as eluent (17) showed a separation by number of sialic acids only. Separation of three monosialylated oligosaccharides reported in the first study was also achieved using APS-Hypersil with acetonitrile−0.15 M potassium phosphate buffer, pH 5.2 (65:35 v/v) as eluent. The overall elution time was much shorter (15 min rather than 53 min reported for the study of Tsuji *et al.*) and decreased in the order:

APS-Hypersil

NeuAcα2-6Galβ1-4Glc > NeuAcα2-6Galβ1-4GlcNAc > NeuAcα2-3Galβ1-4Glc;

Hitachi No. 2630

NeuAcα2-3Galβ1-4Glc > NeuAcα2-6Galβ1-4Glc > NeuAcα2-6Galβ1-4GlcNAc.

These results reflect the chromatographic behaviour of oligosaccharides reported in Section 3.1.1, in that in normal phase the presence of a 1-6 linkage has a retardation effect and replacing galactose or glucose with an N-acetylglucosamine (an exchange which reduces the number of hydroxyl groups in one plane of the molecule) has an elution accelerating effect. The separation of several other monosialylated oligosaccharides by h.p.l.c. using primary amine-bonded silica has also been reported using aqueous buffer−organic solvents (8,18). At present the primary amine-bonded silica offers a faster and less expensive alternative to anion-exchange separation of isomers and oligosaccharides varying in the number of sialic acid groups. However the use of anion-exchange resins with aqueous buffer−organic solvent systems should be investigated for the separation of anionic isomers, independent of the number of anionic groups.

6.2 Sulphated and phosphorylated oligosaccharides

It is becoming increasingly apparent that the N- and O-glycosidically linked carbohydrate chains of secreted and cell surface glycoproteins discussed in Sections 5.3 and 5.4 contain anionic groups different to the sialic acids. For example, a phosphate group is now known to be an integral part of the N-linked carbohydrate chains of lysosomal hydrolases and involved in their recognition by cell membrane receptors. A phosphorylated oligosaccharide released from human β-glucuronidase by endoglycosidase H digestion has been analysed by h.p.l.c. using gradient elution of 25−500 mM phosphate buffer (17). Similar sulphated sequences have yet to be analysed by h.p.l.c. In contrast, several h.p.l.c. systems have been investigated for the separation of the polysulphated oligosaccharides obtained by heparinase, chondroitinase and endo-β-galactosidase treatment of the glycosaminoglycans, heparin and heparan sulphate (22), chondroitin and dermatan sulphate (21,24,25) and keratan sulphate (42), respectively (*Table 1* and Sections 3.2.1 and 3.3).

The separation of larger polysaccharides has been achieved by size exclusion h.p.l.c. The separation of heparan sulphate fractions using a Fractogel (Toyopearl) TSK HW.45 (45) is an example. Although these columns have not yet gained widespread use in carbohydrate separation, their potential for replacing classical gel filtration column materials such as Bio-Gel should be explored. At present a size exclusion chromatography step using this latter material is often used prior to further purification of both anionic oligosaccharides (using buffers such as ammonium acetate or ammonium bicarbonate) and non-anionic oligosaccharides (29,42). However the high compressibility of Bio-Gel dictates that relaively long elution times are used. Our rapidly increasing knowledge of the chromatographic behaviour of oligosaccharides in normal and RP h.p.l.c. and the rapidly increasing number of column packings on the market including ion-exchange and size exclusion columns, should in future obviate recourse to any chromatographic system besides h.p.l.c. for oligosaccharide separations.

7. ACKNOWLEDGEMENTS

The author is grateful to Mrs Teresa Barrett for typing this manuscript.

8. REFERENCES

1. Linden,J.C. and Lawhead,C.L. (1975) *J. Chromatogr.*, **105**, 125.
2. Rabel,F.M., Caputo,A.G. and Butts,E.T. (1976) *J. Chromatogr.*, **126**, 731.
3. Jones,A.D., Burns,I.W., Sellings,S.G. and Cox,J.A. (1977) *J. Chromatogr.*, **144**, 169.
4. Aitzetmüller,K. (1978) *J. Chromatogr.*, **156**, 354.
5. Shaw,P.E. and Wilson,C.W.,III. (1982) *J. Chromatogr. Sci.*, **20**, 209.
6. Wade,N.L. and Morris,S.C. (1982) *J. Chromatogr.*, **240**, 257.
7. Verhaar,L.A.T., Kuster,B.F.M. and Claessens,H.A. (1984) *J. Chromatogr.*, **284**, 1.
8. Ng Ying Kin,N.M.K. and Wolfe,L.S. (1980) *Anal. Biochem.*, **102**, 213.
9. Lamblin,G., Boersma,A., Lhermitte,M., Roussel,P., Van Halbeek,H., Mutsaers,J.H.G.M. and Vliegenthart,J.F.G. (1983) in *Proceedings of the 7th International Symposium on Glycoconjugates*, Chester,M.A., Heinegård,D., Lundblad,A. and Svensson,S. (eds.), Rahms, Lund, p. 565.
10. Mellis,S.J. and Baenziger,J.U. (1981) *Anal. Biochem.*, **114**, 276.
11. Turco,S.J. (1981) *Anal. Biochem.*, **118**, 278.
12. Bergh,M.L.E., Koppen,P., Van den Eijnden,D.H., Arnarp,J. and Lönngren,J. (1983) *Carbohydr. Res.*, **117**, 275.
13. Cheetham,N.W.H. and Dube,V.E. (1983) *J. Chromatogr.*, **262**, 426.
14. Dua,V.K. and Bush,C.A. (1983) *Anal. Biochem.*, **133**, 1.
15. Warren,C.D., Schmit,A.S. and Jeanloz,R.W. (1983) *Carbohydr. Res.*, **116**, 171.
16. Hounsell,E.F., Rideout,J.M., Pickering,N.J. and Lim,C.K. (1984) *J. Liquid Chromatogr.*, **7**, 661.
17. Baenziger,J.U. and Natowicz,M. (1981) *Anal. Biochem.*, **112**, 357.
18. Bergh,M.L.E., Koppen,P. and Van den Eijnden,D.H. (1981) *Carbohydr. Res.*, **94**, 225.
19. Tsuji,T., Yamamoto,K., Konami,Y., Irimura,T. and Osawa,T. (1982) *Carbohydr. Res.*, **109**, 259.
20. Parente,J.P., Leroy,Y., Montreuil,J. and Fournet,B. (1984) *J. Chromatogr.*, **288**, 147.
21. Ototani,N., Sato,N. and Yosizawa,Z. (1979) *J. Biochem.*, **85**, 1383.
22. Lee,G.J. and Tieckelmann,H. (1980) *J. Chromatogr.*, **195**, 402.
23. Heyraud,A. and Rochas,C. (1982) *J. Liquid Chromatogr.*, **5**, 403.
24. Hjerpe,A., Antonopoulos,C.A., Engfeldt,B. and Nurminen,M. (1982) *J. Chromatogr.*, **242**, 193.
25. Seldin,D.C., Seno,N., Austen,K.F. and Stevens,R.L. (1984) *Anal. Biochem.*, **141**, 291.
26. Gooi,H.C., Williams,L.K., Uemura,K., Hounsell,E.F., McIlhinney,R.A.J. and Feizi,T. (1983) *Mol. Immunol.*, **20**, 607.
27. Gooi,H.C., Veyrières,A., Alais,J., Scudder,P., Hounsell,E.F. and Feizi,T. (1984) *Mol. Immunol.*, **21**, 1099.
28. Gooi,H.C., Hounsell,E.F., Edwards,A., Majdic,O., Knapp,W. and Feizi,T. (1985) *Clin. Exp. Immunol.*, **60**, 151.
29. Hounsell,E.F., Lawson,A.M., Feeney,J., Gooi,H.C., Pickering,N.J., Stoll,M.S., Lui,S.C. and Feizi,T. (1985) *Eur. J. Biochem.*, **148**, 367.
30. Hounsell,E.F., Jones,N.J. and Stoll,M.S. (1985) *Biochem. Soc. Trans.*, **13**, 1061.
31. Hounsell,E.F., Pickering,N.J., Stoll,M.S., Lawson,A.M. and Feizi,T. (1984) *Biochem. Soc. Trans.*, **12**, 607.
32. Daniel,P.F., DeFeudis,D.F., Lott,I.T. and McCluer,R.H. (1981) *Carbohydr. Res.*, **97**, 161.
33. Dethy,J.-M., Callaert-Deveen,B., Janssens,M. and Lenaers,A. (1984) *Anal. Biochem.*, **143**, 119.
34. Voelter,W. and Bauer,H. (1975) *Clin. Chem.*, **21**, 1882.
35. Sinner,M. and Puls,J. (1978) *J. Chromatogr.*, **156**, 197.

36. Kato,T. and Kinoshita,T. (1980) *Anal. Biochem.*, **106**, 238.
37. Honda,S. and Suzuki,S. (1984) in *Proceedings of the XIIth International Carbohydrate Symposium*, Vliegenthart,J.F.G., Kamerling,J.P. and Veldink,G.A. (eds.), Vonk Publishes, Zeist, The Netherlands, p. 501.
38. D'Amboise,M., Noël,D. and Hanai,T. (1980) *Carbohydr. Res.*, **79**, 1.
39. Rocklin,R.D. and Pohl,C.A. (1983) *J. Liquid Chromatogr.*, **6**, 1577.
40. Watanabe,N. and Inoue,M. (1983) *Anal Chem.*, **55**, 1016.
41. Donald,A.S.R. (1977) *J. Chromatogr.*, **134**, 199.
42. Scudder,P., Tang,P.W., Hounsell,E.F., Lawson,A.M., Mehmet,H. and Feizi,T. (1986) *Eur. J. Biochem.*, in press.
43. Honda,S. (1984) *Anal. Biochem.*, **140**, 1.
44. Gooi,H.C., Hounsell,E.F., Lax,I., Kris,R.M., Liberman,T.A., Schlessinger,J., Sato,J.D., Kawamoto,T., Mendelsohn,J. and Feizi,T. (1985) *Biosci. Rep.*, **5**, 83.
45. Irimura,T., Nakajima,M., Di Ferrante,N. and Nicolson,G.L. (1983) *Anal. Biochem.*, **130**, 461.

CHAPTER 5

Lipids

BERYL TRACEY

1. INTRODUCTION

Lipids are a large group of naturally-occurring compounds characterized by their hydrophobic properties. These compounds are found in all biological systems, in great variety and with enormous diversity of incidence and function. Before the advent of modern h.p.l.c., thin-layer chromatography (t.l.c.) was used to separate involatile or thermolabile lipids and gas chromatography (g.c.) was used extensively for quantitative separation and identification of volatile lipids or volatile lipid derivatives.

H.p.l.c. is now used increasingly for the analysis of all classes of lipids. Good resolution of complex and thermolabile compounds can be obtained and also easy recovery of intact material for further analysis.

Lipids comprise a heterogeneous group of compounds. They have been divided on the basis of susceptibility to hydrolysis into two main groups, simple lipids such as fatty acids, prostaglandins, steroids and terpenes which contain no hydrolysable bonds, and complex lipids which usually contain fatty acids esterified to polyfunctional alcohols such as glycerol (triglycerides), glycerol-3-phosphate (phospholipids) and sphingosine (sphingolipids).

The latter two groups are further esterified to highly polar groups which confer surface activity on the molecule. The diversity of structure and function of lipids demands different analytical procedures to suit the chemical properties of each group and the environment in which it occurs, but h.p.l.c. on a reversed-phase (RP) column using either a variable wavelength u.v. detector or a refractive index (RI) detector will yield useful results in most instances, although other detectors such as the infra-red detector have been used, and liquid chromatography−mass spectrometry (l.c.−m.s.) can be used to identify complex lipids in a single analysis where several steps were required before.

Lipids usually require several sample preparation steps before h.p.l.c. analysis and although crude solvent extracts of lipids can be separated on h.p.l.c., indeed h.p.l.c. can be used to separate lipid classes (1), it is better to pre-fractionate the sample into lipid classes before analysis. This is done, classically, by t.l.c. but can now be done rapidly using disposable bonded silica columns in a vacuum elution system.

2. H.P.L.C. OF FATTY ACIDS

2.1 Introduction

Fatty acids are a major component of cells and tissues as building blocks in the complex lipids. The proportion which is found unesterified is usually small. Structurally fatty acids contain a single carboxyl group at one end of a long generally unbranched hydrocarbon chain. There may be one or more double bonds, usually *cis*, in the chain. The most naturally abundant fatty acids have even-numbered chain lengths between C_{14} and C_{22}. Unsaturated fatty acids predominate over saturated ones. Fatty acids are insoluble in water except for C_6 chain length and below, these are all liquids with an appreciable volatility at working temperatures and are referred to as volatile fatty acids.

As part of the strategy for identification of species of phospholipids, triacylglycerols and other complex lipids it is usually necessary either to hydrolyse or transesterify the component fatty acids and chromatograph them for quantitation and identification. An intermediate clean-up step to separate the fatty acids from the hydrolysate can be done using t.l.c. or column chromatography before derivatization or analysis.

The standard method used for the analysis of fatty acids is usually g.c. of their methyl esters (FAME). Recently this has been improved by the introduction of narrow-bore capillary columns with very much greater resolving capacity, and capillary g.c. of methyl esters is the most powerful technique for resolving the many isomeric unsaturated and saturated fatty acids found in biological materials. H.p.l.c. of fatty acids, however, has not been neglected and several methods are used.

Reversed-phase h.p.l.c. (RP-h.p.l.c.) on C_8 or C_{18} hydrocarbon-bonded microparticulate ($3-10$ μm) silica columns will separate *cis*$-$*trans* isomers and saturated from unsaturated fatty acids. Elution is in order of increasing chain length with unsaturated acids eluting before saturated ones of the same chain length. As in g.c., special fatty acid analysis columns are available tailored to produce the desired separations. The use of low-wavelength u.v. detectors enables the detection of free fatty acids and FAME at $202-215$ nm or a RI detector can be used. A similar order of sensitivity is obtained using these methods of detection. For the greatest sensitivity and accurate quantitation it is better to chromatograph the fatty acids as strongly u.v. absorbing phenacyl esters or as 4-bromomethyl-7-methoxycoumarin (BMC) esters for fluorescence detection.

For analysis of underivatized short-chain fatty acids, anion exchange or 'ion' chromatography is suitable or RP-h.p.l.c. of u.v.-absorbing phenacyl esters.

2.2 Methods of extraction of free fatty acids from tissues

The classical method of obtaining a relatively pure free fatty acids fraction from total lipids isolated by solvent extraction using chloroform:methanol (2:1) is separation by preparative t.l.c. or silicic acid chromatography. The methodology for this is available in several textbooks on lipid analysis (2,3).

More recently, methods have been published using manufactured bonded-phase extraction columns such as Bond-Elut (Analytichem) (4) (see Section 5.3).

These methods can also be used to separate fatty acids obtained from hydrolysis of complex lipids.

2.3 Preparation of methyl esters of fatty acids

Several methods are available for preparing fatty acid methyl esters. The methods vary in the cost and ease of preparation of reagents and derivatives. For esterification of free fatty acids the most common methods are reaction with diazomethane in ethereal solution at room temperature, or esterification in excess anhydrous methanol catalysed by boron trifluoride (BF_3) or boron trichloride or anhydrous HCl. Diazomethane must be prepared with care because the precursors used are toxic and diazomethane can be explosive. The cheapest reagent is prepared by bubbling dry HCl gas into anhydrous methanol. Ready-prepared mixtures of BF_3 in methanol (14% w/v) can be purchased for rapid sample preparation but the methyl esters must be extracted from the reaction mixture into hexane or salted out of solution before chromatography to avoid contaminating the column with boron.

(i)   To 100 mg of fatty acid in a 5 ml Reacti-vial add 3 ml of BF_3 − methanol (14% w/v).

(ii)   Heat to 60°C for 5 − 10 min.

(iii)   Cool and transfer to a separating funnel with 30 ml of hexane.

(iv)   Wash (×2) with an equal volume of saturated NaCl solution and discard the aqueous layers.

(v)   Dry the hexane extract over Na_2SO_4 and evaporate the solvent under nitrogen.

(vi)   Re-dissolve the methyl esters in an appropriate solvent (acetone or acetonitrile) for RP-h.p.l.c..

Another rapidly reacting reagent is DMF − dimethylacetal. This reacts rapidly at room temperature with fatty acids, although heating to ensure solution of the acids may be necessary. This reagent can be used dissolved in a variety of solvents or purchased as a ready-prepared solution in pyridine (Pierce). Once reaction has been completed no further work-up is required before injection.

2.4 Preparation of fatty acid methyl esters by transesterification of lipids

Methanolic HCl (5% w/v), BF_3 − methanol and sodium or potassium methoxide have all been used successfully as reagents for transesterification of fatty acids in glycerolipids and phospholipids. The reaction time is usually short but heating to moderate temperatures (60 − 80°C) may be necessary to ensure solution of the lipid. Reaction with sodium methoxide can be carried out in different dry solvents enabling a choice of solvent compatible with the material being subject to methanolysis and the h.p.l.c. system. A method of methanolysis suitable for glycerolipids, phospholipids and cholesteryl esters is set out below (5).

(i)   Dissolve 1 − 10 mg of glycerolipid (or other complex lipid) in 1 ml of sodium-dried ether.

(ii)   Add 20 μl of dry methyl acetate.
        N.B. This is added to prevent hydrolysis and must be added before the sodium methoxide.

(iii)   Add 20 μl of 1 M sodium methoxide in dry methanol and mix. The solution will become cloudy as sodium glycerol derivatives are precipitated.

(iv)   Stop the reaction after 5 min at room temperature by adding 30 μl of saturated oxalic acid in ether. Mix.

(v)   Centrifuge the mixture at 1500 g for 2 min to precipitate sodium oxalate.

(vi)   Remove the ether with a stream of dry nitrogen taking care not to disturb the precipitate.

(vii)   Add 1 ml of fresh ether or hexane and aliquot directly for analysis.

For amounts less than 1 mg reduce the reagents proportionately. A longer reaction time

Table 1. Absorption characteristics of phenacyl groups.

Chromophore reagent	Molar extinction coefficient ϵ	Wavelength of detection/λ_{max} nm
α-bromo-2'-acetonaphthone	37 000	254
α,p-dibromoacetophenone	28 000	260
α-bromoacetophenone	35 000	243
α-bromo-p-nitroacetophenone	14 590	263
	20 000	266

(1 h) is required at room temperature for cholesteryl esters. If shorter chain esters are present (C_{12} and below) the solvent evaporation step can be omitted but there may be interference in the chromatography (g.c.) with methanol-soluble side products and reagents.

There is a modification available to this method which increases the compatibility with RP-h.p.l.c. systems (6).

(i)   Dissolve glycerolipids in 1 ml of acetonitrile with slight warming.

(ii)   Add 25 μl of methyl acetate.

(iii)   Add 50 μl of 1 M potassium methoxide in methanol.

(iv)   Stop the reaction after 5 min by addition of 6 μl of acetic acid.

(v)   Clean up samples by centrifugation (2 min at 1500 g) through a column of neutral alumina (1 cm) in a disposable Pasteur pipette.

(vi)   The solution can be chromatographed directly.

2.5 Derivatization of fatty acids to enhance detection

Esters of u.v.-absorbing alkyl groups are prepared to facilitate detection and quantitation of fatty acids. A number of different chromophores have been used for this purpose, the estimated molar extinction coefficients ϵ at λ_{max} or the wavelength of detection are given in *Table 1*.

The choice of phenacyl ester may depend on the solubility, chromatographic properties and sensitivity of detection. The limit of detection is in the nanogram range, 10^3 times better than free fatty acids.

Quantitative measurements of sample components are simply related to integrated peak area on a molar basis. Esterification with fluorescent alkyl groups can also be employed.

Techniques for microscale derivatization of fatty acids to form esters with u.v. chromophores or fluorophores are all base-catalysed or crown ether-catalysed alkylating reactions in an aprotic solvent.

A typical reaction is the one which has been developed to prepare p-bromophenacyl derivatives (7). If p-bromophenacyl derivatives are unsuitable the same basic method can be used to prepare phenacyl, naphthacyl or p-nitrophenacyl esters instead.

(i)   For 0.001 −0.5 mM total fatty acids, prepare the potassium salts by dissolving the fatty acids in methanol or water and titrating to phenolphthalein end-point using methanolic KOH solution (10%). The solvent can be removed either by a rotary evaporator or lyophilization or blowing down with nitrogen.

(ii)   Transfer the potassium salts to a 3 ml Reacti-vial (Pierce) fitted with a stirring bar.

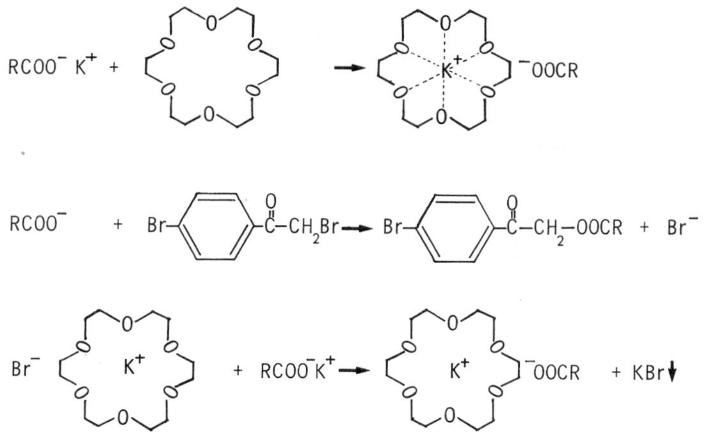

Figure 1. Phase transfer catalysis reaction for preparation of *p*-bromophenacyl esters of fatty acids.

(iii)   Add a 3- to 10-fold molar excess of alkylating reagent containing *p*-dibromoaceto-phenone:18-crown-6 (10:1) in acetonitrile to the fatty acid potassium salts. Add sufficient acetonitrile to bring the volume to 0.5−1.0 ml.

(iv)   Stir the mixture continuously in the sealed Reacti-vial at 80°C for 15 min. Cool the solution and chromatograph directly using a u.v. detector at 260 nm.

If it is undesirable to prepare potassium salts step (i) can be eliminated. Instead the fatty acids are dissolved in an appropriate excess of alkylating reagent in the Reacti-vial and solid potassium carbonate in 3−5 molar excess is added. The heating time should be extended to 30 min.

The reaction is a phase transfer catalysis reaction. The crown ether solvates the potassium ion enabling solution of the carboxylate anion in the aprotic solvent (*Figure 1*). Under these conditions the anion is very reactive and displaces the α-bromine in α,p-dibromoacetophenone by a nucleophilic displacement reaction.

2.5 **Method for preparation of 4-methyl-7-methoxycoumarin esters** (8)

Fluorescent derivatives can be prepared using a similar type of phase-transfer catalysed reaction in which the reagent is BMC. 4-Methyl-7-methoxycoumarin fatty acid esters are formed which have an excitation maximum at 362 nm and an emission λ_{max} at 415 nm in the solvents used for RP-h.p.l.c. of fatty acid esters. The greatest intensity occurs in 20% water in methanol.

(i)   Prepare stock solutions of 18-crown-6 (70 mg in 100 ml) in acetonitrile and BMC (110 mg in 100 ml) in acetone. Protect the BMC in acetone solution from light by wrapping the bottle in aluminium foil.

(ii)   For 2−4 mg of fatty acid neutralize to phenolphthalein end-point in methanolic solution with 10% KOH in methanol in a 50 ml flask. Remove the solvent from precipitated K^+ salts.

(iii)   To the potassium salts add 1 ml of crown ether solution and 5 ml of BMC solution (corresponding to $10-20\%$ molar excess) and reflux for 15 min. The molar ratio of BMC to 18-crown-6 is 8:1.

(iv) The product solution can be injected directly into the h.p.l.c. or purified by filtration through a short column of silica gel prepared in a disposable Pasteur pipette.

This reaction can be scaled down and carried out in a Reacti-vial fitted with a stirrer bar, heated at 80°C in a heating block. The reaction can be modified by the use of solid potassium carbonate catalyst instead of neutralization with KOH in which case the heating time should be increased to 25 min.

2.6 Methods of h.p.l.c. analysis of fatty acids

Fatty acids can be separated on RP columns either as free acids (*Table 2*) or derivatized as esters (*Tables 3* and *4*).

Table 2. Conditions for separation of free fatty acids.

1.	*Column*	25 cm × 4.6 mm i.d. octyl-silica (C8) 5 μm.
	Solvent	acetonitrile:tetrahydrofuran:10% phosphoric acid (pH 2) (50.4:21.6:28). Temperature 36°C; flow-rate 1.6 ml/min.
	Detector	U.v. 190−215 nm or RI.
	Sample	10 μl (1 μg/μl) in mobile phase.
2.	*Column*	30 cm × 3.9 mm i.d. Waters 'Fatty Acid' column 10 μm.
	Solvent	acetonitrile:tetrahydrofuran:water (45:20:35); flow-rate 1−2 ml/min.
	Detector	RI or u.v. 190−215 nm.

[a]Detection is possible between 190 and 215 nm using a u.v. detector but the response of each acid will depend on the degree of unsaturation in the chain. Acids with two or more double bonds give a greater response at 192 nm but saturated acids give a better response at 205 nm. Limits of detection are $2-10$ μg.
[b]Gradient elution is not possible using either method of detection because both are sensitive to solvent changes.
[c]The peak area is linearly related to sample concentration in the range $10-400$ μg injected using a refractometer.
[d]The need to use low solvent pH to improve peak shape will depend on the residual activity of the column.
[e]Elution is in order of carbon number with unsaturated acids eluting before saturated ones in order of degree of unsaturation.

Table 3. Conditions for separation of fatty acid methyl esters (FAME).

1.	*Column*	25 cm × 5 mm i.d. + 5 cm × 5 mm i.d. (guard column) ODS-silica 10 μm.
	Solvent	acetonitrile:water (95:5); flow-rate 1 ml/min.
	Detector	RI or u.v. 190−215 nm.
	Sample	1 mg in acetonitrile.
2.	*Column*	(3×) 25 cm × 4.6 mm i.d. ODS-silica 5 μm.
	Solvent	acetone:acetonitrile:tetrahydrofuran (50:42.4:7.6); flow-rate 1 ml/min.
	Detector	RI.
	Sample	10 μg/ml (total) in mobile phase.

[a]Sensitivity of detection is the same as for free fatty acids.
[b]FAME are less polar than free fatty acids and less soluble in aqueous eluants thus only a small percentage of water can be used in the solvent.
[c]If a totally non-aqueous solvent is used the retention on the column is less and long columns are required to obtain good resolution.

Table 4. Conditions for analysis of fatty acid phenacyl esters and BMC esters.

Column	25 cm × 4 mm i.d. ODS-silica 5 μm.
Solvent	acetonitrile (or methanol):water gradient from 70−80% to 95−98% acetonitrile; flow-rate 1−2 ml/min.
Detector	phenacyl esters u.v. 254 or 260 nm; BMC esters fluorimetric λ_{ex} = 360 nm, λ_{em} = 400 nm.
Sample	10 ng−10 μg in acetonitrile.

[a]Limits of detection 10−100 pmol.
[b]*Cis/trans* isomers can be separated using these conditions as well as saturated and unsaturated acids. The order of elution is similar to that for free acids and methyl esters, *cis* isomers elute before *trans* isomers. Certain 'critical pairs', e.g. C20:4 and C16:1 cannot be separated using a single organic modifier, but methanol/acetonitrile or tetrahydrofuran/acetonitrile mixtures can be used to obtain resolution (9).
[c]Two or more 25 cm columns can be connected together to obtain resolution using acetonitrile and water only.

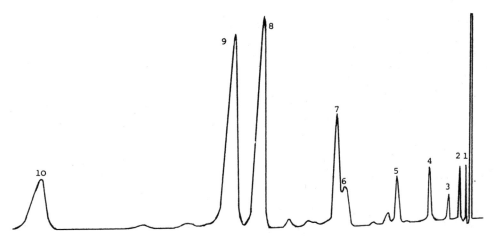

Figure 2. RP-h.p.l.c. of FAME prepared by transesterification of milk fat. Column, 250 × 5 mm i.d. (Lichrosorb 10-RP18) + 50 × 5 mm i.d. guard column; isocratic elution with acetonitrile−water (95:5) at 1 ml/min; differential RI detection. Sample equivalent to 1 mg milk fat in 50 μl acetonitrile. Fatty acid identification **1** = 4:0; **2** = 6:0; **3** = 8:0; **4** = 10:0; **5** = 12:0; **6** = 16:1; **7** = 14:0; **8** = 18:1; **9** = 16:0; **10** = 18:0. (Reproduced from ref. 6 with permission.)

An example of analysis using the conditions in *Table 3*, condition 1, is shown for milk fat derivatives (*Figure 2*) prepared by transesterification (see Section 2.4).

The degree of resolution which can be obtained is shown in *Figure 3* from work by Borch (10). A 90 cm × 0.64 mm i.d. μ-Bondapak-C$_{18}$ (10 μm) (Waters) column was eluted using a gradient of 67−97% acetonitrile in water at a flow-rate of 2 ml/min. The use of this long column required a running time of 250 min for a sample containing C12:0−C24:0 fatty acid phenacyl esters.

2.7 Analysis of volatile fatty acids (VFA)

Short-chain VFA can be chromatographed using all the preceding techniques for free acids, methyl esters and phenacyl or BMC esters. Generally less organic modifier and more aqueous solvent will be needed to separate VFA and VFA esters on ODS- or octyl-bonded silica columns.

Alternatively, free VFA can be separated using 'ion partition' techniques on the Ami-

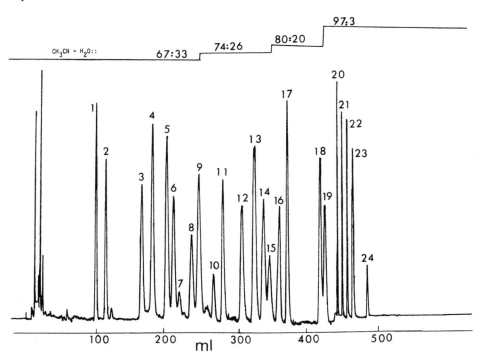

Figure 3. RP-h.p.l.c. of fatty acid phenacyl esters. Column, 90 cm × 0.64 mm i.d. μ-Bondapak C_{18}; eluent, 67–97% acetonitrile in water at 2 ml/min; detection, u.v. at 254 nm. **Peak 1** = 12:0; **2** = 14:1; **3** = 18:3; (α- and γ-linolenic); **4** = 14:0; **5** = 16:1; **6** = 20:4; **7** = *trans* 16:1; **8** = 18:2; **9** = 15:0; **10** = *trans* 18:2; **11** = 20:3; **12** = 16:0; **13** = 18:1; (Δ^9 and Δ^{11}); **14** = 18:1 (Δ^6); **15** = *trans* 18:1; **16** = 20:2 ($\Delta^{11,14}$); **17** = 17:0; **18** = 18:0; **19** = 20:1 (Δ^{11}); **20** = 19:0; **21** = 20:0 and 22:1; **22** = 21:0; **23** = 22:0 and 24:1; **24** = 24:0. (Reproduced from ref. 10 with permission.)

nex HPX-87H (Bio-Rad) cation-exchange column for organic acids. This column contains a strong cation-exchange resin from which organic acids are eluted using dilute sulphuric acid (typically 0.005 M H_2SO_4) in order of increasing pKa. Up to 40% acetonitrile can be used to reduce the retention time of strongly bound organic acids. The column cannot be used with a solvent gradient. Detection of the underivatized acids is with a variable wavelength u.v. detector at 210 nm. Resolution of particular component pairs can be altered by variation of temperature, pH and concentration of acetonitrile. No other organic modifier can be used.

2.7.1 *Extraction of VFA*

Solvent extraction with ether from biological fluids which have been previously acidified to pH 1 and saturated with salt is the simplest method of isolation of VFA (11)

(i)   Acidify 1 ml of sample to pH 1 using 9 M H_2SO_4 in a stoppered tube.

(ii)   Add solid NaCl until no more will dissolve.

(iii)   Add 5 ml of ether + 25 μl of acetonitrile and vortex for 1 min to mix.

(iv)   Centrifuge at 1000 *g* for 1 min to break any emulsion.

(v)   Transfer the ether layer to another container with a Pasteur pipette taking care not to transfer any aqueous layer.

(vi)   Add 200 μl of 0.1 M NaOH to ethereal solution of VFA and vortex for 1 min. Test the pH of the NaOH layer and add 1 M NaOH dropwise to pH 9 or greater if necessary.

(vii)   Centrifuge to separate the layers and discard the ether layer.

(viii) The basic aqueous solution of Na salts can be chromatographed directly on the Aminex HPX-87H column after addition of 25 μl of acetonitrile. It should be acidified to pH 2 with phosphoric or another non-interfering acid just before analysis for chromatography on octyl- or ODS-bonded silica columns.

Quantitative extraction of free VFA is extremely difficult. Many different methods have been used such as steam distillation, vacuum distillation, liquid–liquid 'ion pair' extraction as well as simple ether extraction and none is entirely satisfactory. If derivatives are to be prepared, the VFA must be dissolved in a solvent suitable for the derivatization procedure.

2.7.2 *Derivatization of VFA*

In order to prepare methyl esters, the following steps should be carried out.

(i)   Take the alkaline solution of VFA from step (vii) Section 2.7.1 and neutralize to pH less than 2 with 6 M HCl in a screwcap vial (5 ml).

(ii)   Add an equal volume of methanol to the solution and 1 ml of BCl_3–methanol reagent, mix and heat for 5 min at 85°C.

(iii)   Cool to room temperature and extract with 1 ml of hexane/diethyl ether (50:50) by mixing gently in the same tube.

(iv)   Discard the aqueous phase (lower) and wash the organic layer with 3 ml of 0.3 M NaOH by mixing gently. If an emulsion forms centrifuge at 1000 g for 1 min.

(v)   Transfer the organic layer to a clean sample vial and cap to prevent any loss of sample.

(vi)   Methyl esters can be chromatographed in the same way as long-chain FAME.

The *p*-bromophenacyl esters of VFA can be prepared according to the method given in ref. 12.

(i)   Take the alkaline solution of VFA from step (vii) of the ether extraction (Section 2.7.1) and adjust to phenolphthalein end-point using 1 M methanolic HCl in a stoppered tube. Add three extra drops of 1 M HCl.

(ii)   Add a 2–3 molar excess of a solution of *p*-bromophenacyl bromide in methanol.

(iii)   Heat at 80–85°C for 10 min.

(iv)   Cool and extract with ethyl acetate. Add ice-cold water to the mixture until the ethyl acetate layer separates clearly.

(v)   Take off the ethyl acetate layer with a Pasteur pipette into a clean container. Chromatograph in the same way as long-chain fatty acid *p*-bromophenacyl esters.

2.7.3 *Method of h.p.l.c. analysis of VFA*

Table 5 shows the h.p.l.c. conditions for the analysis of VFA on Aminex resin and an example of the use of this type of analysis is the work of Guerrant *et al.* (11) who analysed bacterial culture medium short-chain acids after a simple ether extraction pro-

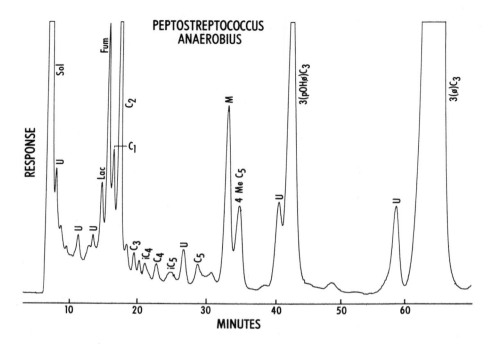

Figure 4. H.p.l.c. of free acids of *Peptostreptococcus anaerobius*. Column, Aminex HPX-87H cation-exchange (30 cm × 7.8 mm i.d.) plus Micro-guard column (Bio-Rad); eluent, 0.007 M $H_2SO_4 - 10.8\%$ acetonitrile; detection, u.v. at 210 nm. Peak identification Sol = solvent front; U = unknown; Lac = lactic acid; Fum = fumaric acid; C_1 = formic acid; C_2 = acetic acid; C_3 = propionic acid; iC_4 = isobutyric acid; C_4 = butyric acid; iC_5 = isovaleric acid; C_5 = valeric acid; M = PYG medium component; 4 Me C_5 = 4-methyl-valeric acid; $3(pOH\phi)C_3$ = 3(p-hydroxyphenyl)propionic acid; $3(\phi)C_3$ = 3-phenylpropionic acid. (Reproduced from ref. 11 with permission.)

Table 5. Conditions for analysis of VFA on Aminex resin.

Column	30 cm × 7.8 mm i.d. Aminex HPX-87H, cation-exchange resin (Bio-Rad).
Solvent	10.8% acetonitrile in 0.0035 M H_2SO_4 (0.19 ml H_2SO_4/litre); flow-rate 0.5 ml/min.
Detector	u.v. 210 nm.
Sample	VFA in alkaline solution.

[a]The flow-rate must not be increased above 0.5 ml/min, otherwise column blockage will result due to very high back pressure.
[b]Analysis time can be reduced by operating at higher temperatures or increasing the % acetonitrile up to 40%.
[c]n-Valeric acid elutes in 30 min, n-heptanoic acid in 60 min under these conditions. Branched-chain acids elute before n-acids.

Table 6. Conditions for analysis of VFA *p*-bromophenacyl esters.

Column	25 cm × 4.6 mm i.d. octadecyl silica 5 μm.
Solvent	methanol/water gradient 55% methanol to 95% methanol; flow-rate 1 ml/min.
Detector	u.v. 254 or 260 nm.

[a]Separation of branched-chain from n-acyl esters requires longer running times.
[b]Acetonitrile can be used instead of methanol, gradient 45−85% acetonitrile.

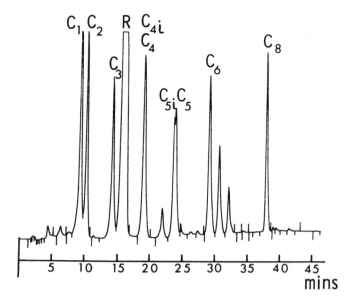

Figure 5. H.p.l.c. of volatile fatty acid *p*-bromophenacyl esters. Column, 25 cm × 4.6 mm i.d. 5 μm Hypersil ODS; gradient elution 45% acetonitrile, 55% water to 65% acetonitrile, 35% water in 25 min, then to 85% acetonitrile, 15% water by 35 min and hold to 47 min; detection, u.v. 260 nm. Sample 2 μl (VFA concentration 1 μg/μl). Peaks C_1 = formic acid; C_2 = acetic acid; C_3 = propionic acid; R = *p*-bromophenacyl Br; C_{4_i} = isobutyric acid; C_4 = n-butyric acid; C_{5_i} = isovaleric acid; C_5 = n-valeric acid; C_6 = hexanoic acid; C_8 = octanoic acid.

cedure, as a means of identifying the bacterial species present (*Figure 4*). *Table 6* shows the conditions for the separation of VFA *p*-bromophenacyl esters by RP-h.p.l.c.. A typical chromatogram is shown in *Figure 5*.

3. H.P.L.C. OF PROSTAGLANDINS

3.1 **Introduction**

Prostaglandins belong to a group of biologically active substances, referred to as the eicosanoids, which are found naturally occurring in most tissues. Arachidonic acid (5,8,12,14-*cis*-eicosatetraenoic acid) is the precursor for the synthesis of prostaglandins and other eicosanoids such as leukotrienes, thromboxanes and prostacyclins. Synthetic analogues of the naturally-occurring substances with pharmacological activity are used in medicine.

Many of the naturally-occurring and synthetic eicosanoids are geometric or stereo isomers containing several substituted hydroxy and keto groups, some of these are labile and subject to loss when undergoing analytical procedures. The use of h.p.l.c. allows for the separation of prostaglandins and related substances under mild conditions. Prostaglandins can be separated from thromboxanes, leukotrienes and hydroxyeicosatetraenoic acids using RP systems and gradient elution. Isomeric prostaglandins can be successfully separated using either long silica columns or argentation chromatography.

Detection and quantitation of prostaglandins by h.p.l.c. presents some problems. Naturally-occurring levels of prostaglandins are so low that they cannot be detected without either radiolabelling, a technique suitable for '*in vitro*' enzyme studies, or derivatization to introduce a chromophore which will enhance the u.v. absorption or fluorescence of the compound. Detection of large amounts of material (micrograms) by u.v. absorption at 192 nm (or 280 nm for leukotrienes) is possible without derivatization in suitable solvent systems.

3.2 Extraction of eicosanoids from tissues

Eicosanoids are usually found only in the tissue in which they are produced and active. They are produced in very small amounts and some intermediates have very short lives. The levels in blood and urine are negligible and seminal fluid is the only biological fluid containing amounts detectable by the usual techniques of extraction and chromatography, with or without derivatization.

Most work on the detection and identification of prostaglandins and related eicosanoids is done using '*in vitro*' stimulation of tissue preparations in suitable buffered media. Similarly the search for pharmacologically active inhibitors of prostaglandin, prostacyclin or leukotriene synthesis, is conducted by measuring the radioactively labelled products of '*in vitro*' enzyme preparations using either ^{3}H- or ^{14}C-labelled arachidonic acid as a substrate. Eicosanoids are soluble in polar solvents such as methanol which can be used for extraction.

(i)   Add methanol or ethanol to the prostaglandin-containing material to 80% (v/v) and mix well.

(ii)   Centrifuge at 2000 g for 5 min to pellet the precipitated protein.

(iii)   Remove the supernatant and evaporate to dryness either by a rotary evaporator (heat to $30-35°C$) or under a nitrogen stream.

(iv)   Reconstitute the sample in 100% methanol or 30% methanol in water. (The latter solvent gives better recovery but also dissolves any salts which are present. If detection is principally of radiolabelled compounds these will be undetectable and do not interfere with the chromatography.)

(v)   Centrifuge the sample at 2000 g for $1-2$ min to separate any undissolved material. Directly inject the supernatant onto the h.p.l.c.

Less polar solvents such as chloroform:methanol (1:1) which do not dissolve interfering salts can also be used. Extraction with chloroform:methanol will give a purer fraction which is more suitable for derivatization reactions.

(i)   Add methanol or ethanol to 50% of the sample volume. Vortex.

(ii)   Centrifuge the sample at 2000 g for 5 min to pellet the precipitated protein.

(iii)   Remove the supernatant and acidify to pH 3 using a weak acid such as citric or formic acid.

(iv)   Saturate with sodium sulphate.

(v)   Extract with an equal volume of chloroform three times. This can be done on a small scale using glass-stoppered centrifuge tubes which can be centrifuged, if it is necessary to break an emulsion.

(vi)   Pool the chloroform extracts and blow to dryness with a gentle nitrogen stream.

(vii) Use the dry extract for one of the derivatization procedures or dissolve in methanol/water (30/70) or other suitable h.p.l.c. solvent for direct injection onto the h.p.l.c. column. If necessary filter the sample before injection using a 0.5 μm filter.

Some workers have used extraction on silica gel columns (13) or XAD-7 resin (14) but in most circumstances this is not essential in order to obtain greater than 90% recovery of eicosanoids as shown by studies with radiolabelled material (15).

3.3 Derivatization for detection by u.v. and fluorescence detectors

3.3.1 *U.v. detection of underivatized eicosanoids*

A few eicosanoids have u.v.-absorbing chromophores with large ϵ values, these include the leukotrienes and related hydroxyeicosatetraenoic acids (λ_{max} = 280 nm), prostaglandin A_2 (λ_{max} = 217 nm), prostaglandin B_2 (λ_{max} = 280 nm) and 15-keto-PGE_2 (λ_{max} = 228 nm). However, the majority have no useful absorption band suitable for detection above 200 nm although it has been found (16) that for a number of prostaglandins at λ_{max} = 192.5 nm the value for ϵ is in the region of 14 000 – 18 000 (see *Table 7*) and this wavelength can be used for detection if solvent systems transparent below 200 nm are used. For RP-h.p.l.c. acetonitrile and water with a non-u.v.-absorbing buffer such as phosphate can be used, and for normal phase h.p.l.c. mixtures of hexane and acetonitrile acidified with a non-u.v.-absorbing acid. The detection limit using absorbance at 192.5 nm is about 30 ng.

3.3.2 *Derivatization of eicosanoids*

In circumstances when detection at low u.v. wavelengths is not possible, an alternative is to use a higher wavelength and prepare derivatives which have a high ϵ at the selected wavelength. In order to detect eicosanoids at higher wavelengths the 1-carboxyl group is esterified with an aryl group possessing the necessary chromophore. Several reagents have been used for this purpose (see Section 2.5).

Of the derivatization methods which have been developed for these reagents the one which is satisfactory for eicosanoids uses diisopropylethylamine as a basic catalyst and is carried out at 25 – 45 °C using a 3- to 10-fold molar excess of reagent in acetonitrile.

Table 7. Molar extinction coefficients of prostaglandins at 192.5 and 217 nm[a].

Compound	*Molar extinction coefficient (ϵ)*	
	λ = 192.5 nm	λ = 217 nm
6-keto $PGF_{1\alpha}$	14 300	1730
6-keto PGE_1	14 200	1950
TXB_2	15 400	1590
PGE_2	16 500	2230
PGE_1	15 800	2480
PGD_2	17 100	2800
15-keto PGE_2	13 800	10 060
PGA_2	18 500	10 830
PGB_2	15 600	3460
$PGF_{2\alpha}$	17 100	1770
$PGF_{1\alpha}$	16 400	1540

[a]From ref. 16.

The use of high temperatures and alkali metal salts must be avoided to prevent dehydration or isomerization of eicosanoids.

The reagents used are: *p*-bromophenacyl bromide (pBPB) (5 μM/ml) in acetonitrile, diisopropylethylamine (DIPEA) (5 mg/ml) in acetonitrile.

(i)   For samples containing $0.5-1.5$ μM prostaglandin use 1 ml of pBPB reagent plus 100 μl of DIPEA reagent. Dissolve the prostaglandins in the reagent solution and leave at room temperature for 30 min. $2-10$ μl aliquots of the sample may be chromatographed directly.

(ii)   For samples containing $1-300$ nM use $100-200$ μl of pBPB reagent and 10 μl of DIPEA reagent. Ensure that the molar excess of pBPB is at least 3-fold. Leave at room temperature for $2-3$ h to complete the reaction. The reaction time may be reduced by warming at 45°C or increasing the molar excess of the reagent.

Reagents should be stored in dark, moisture- and oxygen-free conditions, e.g. in a sealed septum-vial at 4°C, otherwise prepare fresh daily. Use dry acetonitrile. Raising the temperature of the reaction increases the likelihood of dehydration. Increasing the molar excess of pBPB reagent may give rise to chromatographic problems from the large reagent peak.

Derivatives for fluorescence detection can be prepared in the same way substituting 4-bromomethyl-7-methoxycoumarin in acetonitrile for pBPB. This reagent must be protected from light during storage.

3.4 **H.p.l.c. of eicosanoids**

3.4.1 *H.p.l.c. of underivatized eicosanoids*

Elucidation of the pathways of arachidonate metabolism in different tissues has been made possible by the technique of separation and detection of the metabolites of arachidonic acid labelled with either ^{14}C or [3]H. H.p.l.c. using a single 25 cm $\times$ 4.6 mn i.d. column packed with 5 μm ODS-silica and a methanol/water or acetonitrile/water solvent system (*Table 8*) is used to separate the major metabolites of both the cyclo-oxygenase and lipoxygenase pathways. Detection is usually carried out by monitoring the eluate in the u.v. at 192.5 nm and collecting 1 ml fractions for measurement of radioactivity in a scintillation counter.

On some columns improved peak shape may be obtained by lowering the pH of the eluent to 2 or 3. The elution order does not appear to be pH dependent except for the conjugated leukotrienes (LTC$_4$, LTD$_4$, LTE$_4$) which have shorter retention times at higher pH.

Table 8. Conditions for analysis of underivatized eicosanoids.

Column		25 cm $\times$ 0.46 mm i.d. 5 μm ODS-silica.
Solvent	(i)	Methanol (acetonitrile)/water (buffer with phosphate or ammonium acetate pH ~7). Gradient from 50 to 100% methanol (acetonitrile).
	(ii)	Methanol (acetonitrile)/water (acidified pH $2-3$ with acetic or phosphoric acid) Gradient as above.
Detection	(i)	U.v. 192.5 nm (acetonitrile/phosphate).
	(ii)	Fractions collected for liquid scintillation counting.
	(iii)	Radioactivity monitor.

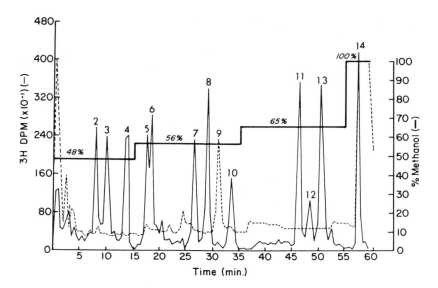

Figure 6. RP-h.p.l.c. of tritiated eicosanoids standards (—) and unlabelled LTE$_4$ (- - -). Column, Radial-Pak C$_{18}$ 5 μm (10 cm × 8 mm i.d.); column conditions were 48% methanol for 15 min, 56% methanol for 20 min, 65% methanol for 20 min and 100% methanol for 5 min. The remainder of the solvent is buffered water:ammonium acetate 0.017 M (pH 5.8). Flow-rate 3 ml/min; detection, u.v. at 280 nm; fractions were collected every 30 sec for radioactivity measurements. **Peaks 1** = 6-keto-=PGF$_{1\alpha}$; **2** = TXB$_2$; **3** = PGE$_2$; **4** = PGF$_{2\alpha}$; **5** = LTC$_4$; **6** = PGA$_2$; **7** = LTD$_4$; **8** = LTB$_4$; **9** = LTE$_4$; **10** = HHT; **11** = 15-HETE; **12** = 12-HETE; **13** = 5-HETE; **14** = arachidonic acid. (Reproduced from ref. 15 with permission.)

The use of methanol instead of acetonitrile raises the u.v. cut off of the solvent to approximately 205 nm. It also reverses the elution order of prostaglandins F$_{2\alpha}$ and E$_2$ and PGE$_2$ and PGD$_2$ are not resolved.

In general the retention time increases with the number of double bonds and hydroxy groups. Some *cis/trans* and diastereoisomers cannot be separated unless a longer column is used, and may require alternative chromatographic techniques.

An example of this method is the separation by Henke, Kouzan and Eling (15) of prostaglandins and leukotrienes using tritiated eicosanoid standards. The column was a Radial-Pak C$_{18}$ 5 μm 100 × 8 mm i.d. column (Waters). The solvent system was methanol and ammonium acetate 0.017 M (pH 5.8). A series of step changes in solvent composition were made from 48 to 100% methanol. The final elution time was 60 min.

Figure 6 is a chromatogram constructed from the counts in each fraction collected with the absorbance at 280 nm superimposed. The authors compared this method with the use of an Altex C$_{18}$ 250 mm × 4.6 mm i.d. column (Beckman) (*Table 9*). They achieved a similar separation using stepwise solvent changes from 55 to 100% methanol in 100 min with a solvent flow-rate of 1 ml/min.

The authors then used this system to study the arachidonate metabolites in guinea pig lung microsomes and rat alveolar macrophages. A modification required by these workers was the washing of their columns with 0.5% EDTA in methanol/water 10:90 prior to analysis to prevent decomposition of conjugated leukotrienes.

Table 9. Comparison of retention times of eicosanoids[a] on Waters Radial-Pak C_{18} 5 μm 10 cm $\times$ 8 mm i.d. and Altex C_{18} 5 μm 25 cm $\times$ 4.6 mm i.d.

Metabolites	*Retention time (min)*	
	Waters Radial-Pak C_{18}	*Altex C_{18}*
6-Ketoprostaglandin $F_{1\alpha}$	3.5	10
Thromboxane B_2	8.5	20
Prostaglandin E_2	10.5	24
Prostaglandin D_2	11.0	25
Prostaglandin $F_{2\alpha}$	15	29
Leukotriene C_4	18	39
Prostaglandin A_2	19	39
11-*trans*-leukotriene C_4	19.5	41
Leukotriene D_4	27	50
Leukotriene B_4	29.5	53
5S,12S-dihydroxyeicosatetraeneoate	29.5	53
Leukotriene E_4	32	54
12-hydroxyheptadecatrienoate	43	62
15-hydroxyeicosatetraenoate	47	73
12-hydroxyeicosatetraenoate	49	75
5-hydroxyeicosatetraenoate	51	78
Arachidonic acid	58	87

[a]From ref. 15.

(i) *Analysis of leukotrienes.* The conjugated triple bond in leukotrienes and other arachidonate metabolites from the lipoxygenase pathway makes them detectable at the nanogram level using u.v. absorption at 280 nm. A specific assay for leukotrienes can be devised by detection at this wavelength. Quantitative determinations can be made by using as the internal standard prostaglandin B_2 which also absorbs at 280 nm, but is not produced by the lipoxygenase pathway of arachidonate metabolism. LTB_4, LTC_4 and LTD_4 can be separated in 32 min on a 25 cm $\times$ 0.46 cm i.d. column packed with 5 μm Nucleosil C_{18} (Alltech) using a solvent system containing 65% methanol 35% water buffered to pH 5.7 by 3 $\times$ 10^4 M acetic acid adjusted to pH 5.7 with 10% NH_4OH. Under these conditions the isomer of LTB_4, 5(S), 12(S) dihydroxyeicosatetraenoic acid co-elutes with LTD_4. Reducing the solvent pH to 4 considerably extends the retention times of LTC_4 and LTD_4 and allows separation of LTD_4 and 5,12-diHETE isomers when this is needed (14).

Large volumes of extracts from tissue studies can be injected without loss of resolution, using this solvent system, if the samples are prepared in 30% methanol in water. Detection down to 2 ng per peak can be obtained. This is as sensitive as the currently used guinea pig ileum bioassay.

(ii) *Analysis of prostaglandins.* Although the majority of prostaglandins have no u.v. absorption bands above 200 nm, they do have an absorption band with a λ_{max} = 192.5 nm with a molar extinction coefficient ϵ of 14 000 − 18 000. Using a variable wavelength u.v. detector which will detect down to 190 nm, and a solvent system which does not absorb in that region, prostaglandins can be detected with sample peaks in the nanogram range. For example, Terragno *et al.* (16) separated nine prostaglandins in 20 min using a single 25 cm $\times$ 0.46 cm i.d. Ultrasphere C_{18} column (Beckman)

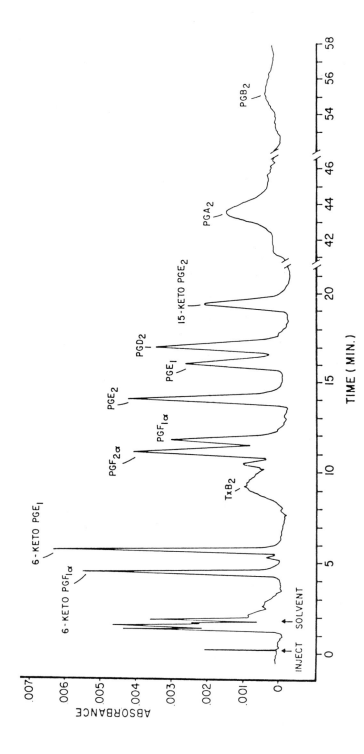

Figure 7. RP-h.p.l.c. of underivatized prostaglandins. Column, 25 cm × 4.6 mm i.d. Ultrasphere C_{18}; isocratic elution with $CH_3CN:0.017$ M H_3PO_4 (32.8:67.2 v/v); detection, u.v. at 192.5 nm, 0.008 AUFS. Sample = 100 ng each component. (Reproduced from ref. 16 with permission.)

with an ODS pre-column. These workers used pre-mixed solvents and isocratic elution in order to reduce perturbations of the detection baseline. Because it was not possible to use gradient elution or flow programming without causing baseline drift, it took 60 min to elute all of the prostaglandins when PGA_2 and PGB_2 were included. After investigation of several pH modifiers and proportions of acetonitrile and water, they established that 32.8% acetonitrile and 67.2% water buffered to pH 3.5 with 0.017 M orthophosphoric acid at a flow-rate of 1.7 ml/min separated prostaglandins in the following elution order: 6-ketoPGF$_{1\alpha}$, 6-ketoPGE$_1$, TXB$_2$, PGF$_{2\alpha}$, PGF$_{1\alpha}$, PGE$_2$, PGD$_2$, 15-ketoPGE$_2$, PGA$_2$, PGB$_2$ (*Figure 7*).

Quantitative determinations can be made using a calibration curve of peak area versus weight of sample injected for each prostaglandin. This is necessary because the ϵ value can be different for each one. The limit of detection using this system is 30 ng.

3.4.2 *H.p.l.c. of prostaglandins as u.v.-absorbing derivatives*

Most of the derivatizing agents used to enhance detection of prostaglandins result in the formation of aryl esters of the 1-carboxyl group. This reduces the polarity of the eicosanoids but does not prevent the use of RP chromatography to achieve separation.

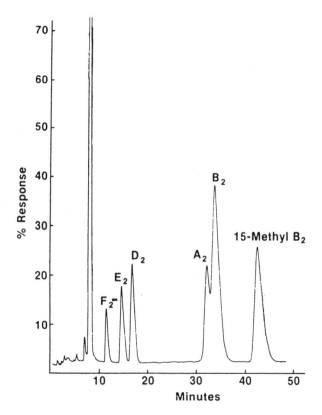

Figure 8. RP-h.p.l.c. of *p*-bromophenacyl esters of prostaglandins. Column, 25 cm × 4 mm i.d. *μ*-Bondapak C$_{18}$; eluent, acetonitrile/water (50:50) at 1.2 ml/min; detection, u.v. at 254 nm 0.32 AUFS. Sample 5 – 10 *μ*g each component. (Reproduced from ref. 17 with permission.)

Table 10. Conditions for reversed-phase chromatography of *p*-bromophenacyl esters of prostaglandins.

Column	25 cm × 0.46 mm i.d. 5 μm ODS-silica.
Solvent	Acetonitrile/water (methanol/water); flow-rate 1−2 ml/min. 50% acetonitrile in water[a] isocratically or gradient elution (50−100% acetonitrile).
Detection	U.v. 254 nm or 260 nm[b].

[a]Using acetonitrile as organic modifier the elution order is $PGF_{2\alpha}$, PGE_2, PGD_2, PGA_2, PGB_2.
[b]The peak area is linearly related to the molar concentration for all the sample components. A synthetic analogue of PGB_2, 15-methyl PGB_2 is suitable for use as an internal standard.

Table 11. Conditions for normal-phase chromatography of *p*-bromophenacyl esters of prostaglandin isomers.

Column		50 cm × 4.6 mm i.d. (2 × 25 cm coupled) 5 μm silica.
Solvent[a]	(i)	Hexane:methylene chloride[b]:methanol (45:55:5); flow-rate 0.8−1 ml/min.
	(ii)	Methylene chloride/acetonitrile:dimethylformamide (160:40:1); flow-rate 0.8−1 ml/min.
Detection		U.v. 260−280 nm

[a]Using solvent system (i) analogues with one double bond elute before those with two double bonds, *cis* before *trans* and keto groups before hydroxy groups. The elution order changes with the use of different solvent systems. Solvent system (i) is suitable for F-series prostaglandins, (ii) for E-series prostaglandins. The use of acetonitrile instead of methanol changes the order of elution of the 5 *cis/trans* pair and PGE_1 elutes after PGE_2.
[b]Methylene chloride has a u.v. cut-off of 235 nm.

Care must be taken to avoid interference in the chromatography from peaks due to reagents and the products of side reactions.

Fitzpatrick (17) separated *p*-bromophenacyl esters of prostaglandins in 50 min using 50% acetonitrile in water at a flow-rate of 1.2 ml/min (*Figure 8*). He used this method for determining the effect of indomethacin on prostaglandin synthesis by sheep seminal vesicle synthetase.

Normal-phase chromatography of prostaglandins is used to separate epimers and analogues of naturally-occurring prostaglandins.

Morozowitch and Douglas (18) separated 10 F-series isomers and eight E-series isomers on two coupled 25 cm × 2.1 mm i.d. Zorbax-sil columns. They used solvent (i) in *Table 11* for the F series at a flow-rate of 0.3 ml/min and eluted all 10 isomers with baseline resolution in some and partial resolution in all cases (*Figure 9*).

4. H.P.L.C. OF TRIGLYCERIDES

4.1 Introduction

Triacylglycerols (triglycerides) are naturally-occurring esters of fatty acids and glycerol. Fatty acids are a fuel source for energy metabolism in living tissues and triacylglycerols are the main storage and transport form of fatty acids, although small amounts of mono- and diacylglycerols can be found. Over 100 different naturally-occurring fatty acids have been identified, hence the potential combinations in triacylglycerols are very great. However, relatively few combinations are commonly found in most tissues. Generally triacylglycerols contain 70% unsaturated and 30% saturated fatty acids. About 60% of triacylglycerols contain the same fatty acid esterified to all three hydroxyl groups of glycerol. The remainder contain a mixture of fatty acids. Glycerol is not an asym-

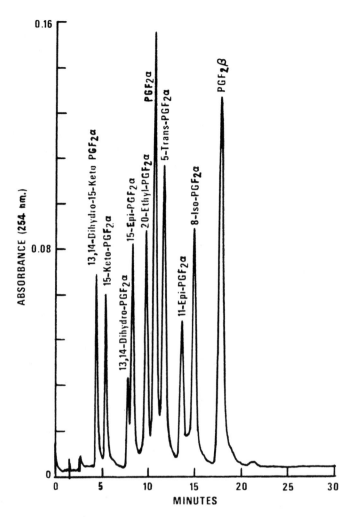

Figure 9. H.p.l.c. of *p*-nitrophenacyl esters of F-series prostaglandins. Column, two series coupled 2.1 mm i.d. × 25 cm Zorbax-sil; eluent, methanol (55:45:5) 0.3 ml/min; detection, u.v. at 254 nm. (Reproduced from ref. 18 with permission.)

metric molecule but triacylglycerols which have different acids on the 1 and 3 carbons of glycerol become optically active at the 2 carbon and stereo isomers are then possible.

It is not possible to determine the positional and fatty acid composition of a triglyceride, nor the triglyceride composition of a tissue lipid, using any single chromatographic technique and even quite complex strategies still fail to yield all the complex positional and compositional information about individual triglycerides.

The classical methods of separating and identifying triglycerides have been t.l.c. to separate the individual triglycerides, using argentation − t.l.c. to separate them in order of degree of unsaturation if required, followed by methanolysis of the recovered t.l.c. fractions to give FAME. These are separated, quantitated and identified by g.c.

Recently h.p.l.c., particularly on RP columns (19) has provided better resolution of triglycerides than t.l.c. and the peak fractions can readily be collected for further analysis to identify the fatty acid composition. Recent advances in l.c.−m.s. interfaces have now enabled direct identification of triglycerides from their mass spectra after separation by h.p.l.c. (20).

4.2 **Extraction of triglycerides from tissue**

A simple mixture of chloroform:methanol 2:1 will extract all neutral lipids from tissues or biological fluid but some free fatty acids and phospholipids will also be extracted. It is usually necessary to purify the triglyceride fraction before further analysis either by t.l.c. on silica gel or using the more recently introduced sample preparation columns containing bonded silica adsorbent.

(i)　Homogenize the tissue (20 ml/g) with chloroform:methanol (2:1) in a suitably sized homogenizer.

(ii)　If the sample is a liquid, vortex mix thoroughly in a suitable stoppered tube with a similar proportion of $CHCl_3 - MeOH$.

(iii)　Centrifuge briefly at 1000 g for 1−2 min to separate the layers.

(iv)　Remove the chloroform layer to a clean, dry container and blow to dryness with a stream of nitrogen.

(v)　If the sample is to be stored it should be kept frozen in a sealed container away from light to prevent oxidation.

4.3 **Purification of triglycerides for h.p.l.c.**

4.3.1 *T.l.c.*

Standard size 20 × 20 cm plates coated with 0.25 mm silica gel G are used with a solvent mixture of heptane:isopropyl ether:acetic acid (50:40:4). The triglyceride bands can be detected with 2,7-dichlorofluorescein and recovered by extraction from the silica gel with chloroform:methanol (2:1). The fluorescein can be removed by washing with dilute ammonia (21).

4.3.2 *Bonded-silica sample preparation column*

The method used for purification of triglycerides can also be used for phospholipids (Section 5.3). 4 ml of chloroform:isopropanol (2:1) will elute neutral lipids only from an aminopropylsilica Bond-Elut column (*Table 12*). This fraction contains cholesteryl esters, mono-, di- and triglycerides. The elution scheme is shown diagrammatically in *Figure 10*.

Table 12. Solvents used in Bond-Elut purification of neutral lipids.

Solvent	*Elution volume ml*	*Lipid fraction*
1. Chloroform:isopropanol (2:1)	4	All neutral lipids
2. Hexane	4	Cholesteryl esters
3. Hexane:dichloromethane:ether (89:10:1)	8	Triglycerides
4. Hexane:ethyl acetate (95:5)	16 (col 2) + 4 (col 3)	Cholesterol
5. Hexane:ethyl acetate (85:15)	8	Diglycerides
6. Chloroform:methanol (2:1)	4	Monoglycerides

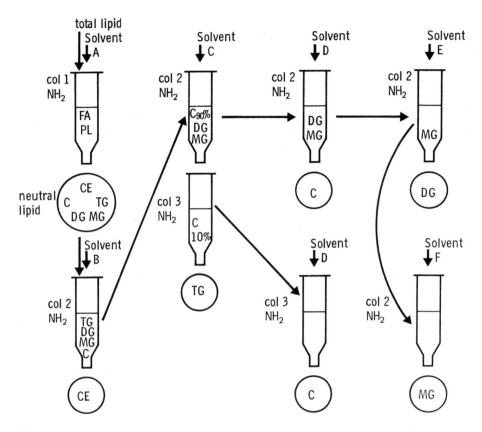

Figure 10. Elution scheme for separation and isolation of neutral lipid classes from total lipid extracts on Bond-Elut aminopropyl columns ($-NH_2$). Solvents are tabulated in *Table 12*. *Key*: FA = fatty acids; PL = phospholipids; C = cholesterol; CE = cholesteryl esters; TG = triglycerides; DG = diglycerides; MG = monoglycerides. (Redrawn from ref. 14 with permission.)

It is important to maintain solvent proportions and volumes as stated. All the columns should be prepared beforehand by washing twice with 2 ml of hexane. The sample is applied to the first column dissolved in the minimum of chloroform. The neutral lipid fraction from the first aminopropyl column should be dried down under nitrogen and dissolved in 200 μl of hexane. This fraction is then processed using a new column to separate triglycerides from cholesteryl esters, cholesterol and mono- and diglycerides. If only triglycerides are required the elution series can be stopped after elution with hexane:dichloromethane:ether (89:10:1). The triglyceride fraction should be dried down under nitrogen and dissolved in acetone or tetrahydrofuran for h.p.l.c.. All the other neutral lipids can be saved if desired and analysed using the same h.p.l.c. conditions as for triglycerides. The load limit for a 500 mg aminopropyl column is 10 mg total lipid (4).

4.4 **H.p.l.c. of triglycerides**

H.p.l.c. of triacylglycerols on RP octadecyl-bonded silica columns of standard dimensions 25 or 30 cm × 4 mm i.d. will resolve most species including some 'critical pairs'

Table 13. Conditions for RP-h.p.l.c. of triglycerides[a].

1.	*Column*	25 cm × 4.6 mm i.d. 5 μm C_{18}-silica (e.g. Supercosil-LC18).
		For better separations couple two 25 cm columns together.
	Solvent	*Isocractic*, acetone/acetonitrile (63.6:36.4); flow-rate 1−2 ml/min.
	Detector	RI or mass spectrometer.
2.	*Column*	As above.
	Solvent	*Gradient*, 30−90% propionitrile in acetonitrile in 60 min; flow-rate 1.5 ml/min.
	Detector	Mass spectrometer or u.v. at 205 nm.
3.	*Column*	Waters 'Triglyceride Analysis' column 30 cm × 7.8 mm i.d. ('semi-prep') 10 μm C_{18}-silica.
	Solvent	*Isocratic*, acetonitrile/tetrahydrofuran (50:50); flow-rate 2 ml/min.
	Detector	RI.
4.	*Column*	25 cm × 4.6 mm i.d. 5 μm C_{18}-silica, e.g. Zorbax-ODS.
	Solvent	*Isocratic*, acetonitrile/dichloromethane/tetrahydrofuran (60:20:20); flow-rate 1−2 ml/min.
		Gradients are possible.
	Detector	Infra-red at 5.75 μm.

[a]From refs. 19−23.

which were unresolved by previous methods such as t.l.c. or g.c. RP- h.p.l.c. will give better resolution than $AgNO_3$−t.l.c. Triglycerides are eluted in order of carbon number and degree of unsaturation on C_{18}-silica columns. Several different non-aqueous solvent systems (19−23) have been used depending on which method of detection is used (*Table 13*).

4.4.1 *Detectors for h.p.l.c. of triglycerides*

(i) *U.v. detectors*. These are not very suitable for h.p.l.c. of triglycerides. There is an absorption band due to the ester carbonyls and also to double bonds in the carbon chain, between 190 and 215 nm but in order to utilize this, solvents transparent in this region must be used. Of the solvents commonly used for elution of triglycerides, aceto-nitrile, acetone, tetrahydrofuran, hexane and dichloromethane, only acetonitrile is trans-parent below 200 nm. Solvent systems containing acetonitrile and propionitrile have been used (20), which are transparent and give excellent separations but propionitrile is toxic and must be handled with care.

(ii) *Refractive index detectors*. These are most commonly used to detect triglycerides. The sensitivity is in the range of 50 μg − 100 mg/sample. Solvents with high refractive indices lower the sensitivity so chloroform, hexane and dichloromethane are usually avoided. Acetonitrile with acetone or tetrahydrofuran as the less polar modifier are used. It is not possible to perform gradient elution.

(iii) *Infra-red detectors*. These have the advantage of allowing gradient elution, although some baseline drifting can be seen at the wavelength used for detection (5.75 μm car-bonyl absorbance) with either dichloromethane or tetrahydrofuran as modifier. A balanc-ed mixture of both can be used in an increasing gradient with acetonitrile to avoid baseline drift. Either sodium chloride or calcium fluoride cells can be used, but the solvents must be strictly anhydrous to prevent damage to the flow cell (19). The sensitivity is about the same as that of the RI detector.

(iv) *A mass spectrometer*. When directly connected to h.p.l.c. this is now proving to be an excellent, if expensive, detector for triglycerides. The column eluent can be intro-

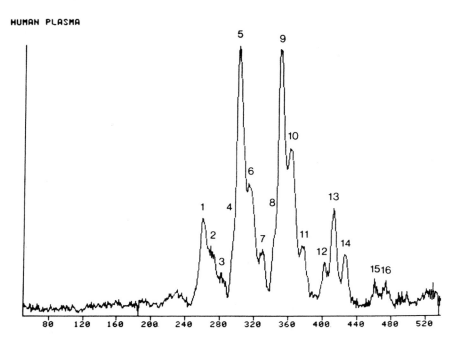

Figure 11. L.c. −m.s. of human plasma triacylglycerols separated on 25 cm × 4.6 mm i.d. Supelcosil C_{18} 5 μm using 30−90% propionitrile in acetonitrile gradient in 60 min at a flow-rate of 1.5 ml/min. L.c. −m.s. condition as in text. The major peaks are **(1)** 16:0 18:2 18:2 **(5)** 16:0 18:1 18:2 **(6)** 16:0 16:0 18:2 **(9)** 16:0 18:1 18:1 **(10)** 16:0 16:0 18:1. (Reproduced from ref. 20 with permission.)

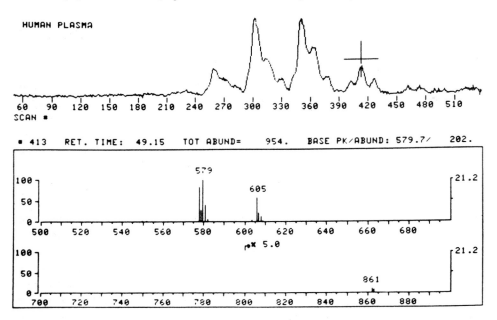

Figure 12. Chemical ionization spectrum of peak (13) in *Figure 11*. Upper panel, total ion current profile; lower panel, mass spectrum of palmitoyloleoylstearoylglycerol (16:0 18:1 18:0). Conditions as in *Figure 11*. (Reproduced from ref. 20 with permission.)

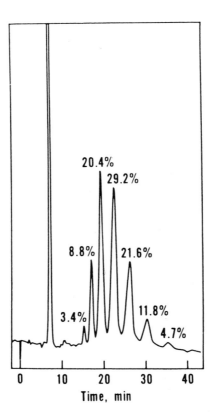

Figure 13. H.p.l.c. of soybean oil. Column, 60 cm × 3.8 mm μ-Bondapak C_{18}; eluent, acetonitrile–acetone (2:1); detection, RI. Sample 2 mg. The percentage of the total weight represented by each peak calculated from quantitative g.c. of the peak fractions is given. (Reproduced from ref. 19 with permission.)

duced into the mass spectrometer either directly (20,21) (usually with 100/1 split) or with a moving belt interface. If acetonitrile is used as solvent it can act as reagent gas in the chemical ionization mode. Spectra obtained give a detectable protonated molecular ion and also mass ions corresponding to all the component diacylglycerols in roughly the correct proportions. If direct introduction is used there is a problem of sensitivity because of the solvent splitting before introduction into the mass spectrometer.

An example of the power of using l.c.–m.s. for resolution and identification of triglycerides is the work of Kuksis *et al.* (20,21) who used an l.c.–m.s. interface based on Baldwin–McLafferty direct liquid introduction (100/1 split of eluent at a flow-rate of 1.5 ml/min) chemical ionization using the h.p.l.c. solvent (acetonitrile/propionitrile) as reagent gas on a Hewlett Packard 1084B LC and 5985B quadrupole m.s. These workers separated most of the critical pairs of triglycerides using 30–90% propionitrile in acetonitrile gradients on a 25 cm × 4.6 mm i.d. column packed with 5 μm Supelcosil C_{18} (Supelco) in samples of peanut oil, stripped lard, bovine milk fat, human plasma (*Figure 11*) and rat liver triglycerides and were able to identify the peaks directly using the characteristic mass spectra (*Figure 12*).

Plattner *et al.* (19) used RP-h.p.l.c. on 60 cm × 3.8 mm i.d. μ-Bondapak C_{18} with acetonitrile:acetone (2:1) as the eluting solvent and a RI detector to separate 2 mg of soybean oil into six fractions (*Figure 13*) which were collected and analysed further by g.c. of the intact triglycerides in each fraction and g.c. of the FAME after transesterification. These workers calculated the percentage of triglycerides in each fraction by adding an internal standard (tripentaelecoin) to each before g.c. triglyceride analysis. The fractions contained more than one species of triglyceride and, even after the constituent fatty acids were identified and quantified, it was not possible to calculate the composition of the different triglyceride species.

4.4.2 *Quantitation*

Unless pure standards of the correct composition are available for calibration it is not possible to determine individual triacylglycerols quantitatively using any of the available h.p.l.c. detectors. The best way to get quantitative results is to collect the individual peak fractions from h.p.l.c. analysis, prepare the FAME of the component fatty acids in the presence of an added internal standard and analyse them using quantitative capillary g.c. From this the proportions and identity of the component fatty acids can be obtained and the amount of triglyceride can be estimated.

5. H.P.L.C. OF PHOSPHOLIPIDS

5.1 **Introduction**

Phospholipids are a group of complex lipids which are an essential component of cell membranes. The structure consists of a polar head carrying one or more ionizable groups and a non-polar tail consisting of two hydrocarbon groups of C_{16} or more. This structure endows the molecule with surface-active properties. The phospholipids (phosphodiacylglycerides) are of the general formula shown in *Figure 14*.

Two of the hydroxyl groups of glycerol are esterified to long-chain fatty acids and the third to phosphate. The phosphate is further esterified to an alcohol which may contain other charged groups. The phosphoglycerides are classified on the basis of the head group esterified to phosphate (*Table 14*). Within each class are many 'species' containing different combinations of fatty acids.

There are two other phospholipids which are not phosphoglycerides but which behave in the same way. Sphingomyelin is a sphingolipid in which sphingosine (2-amino-1,3-

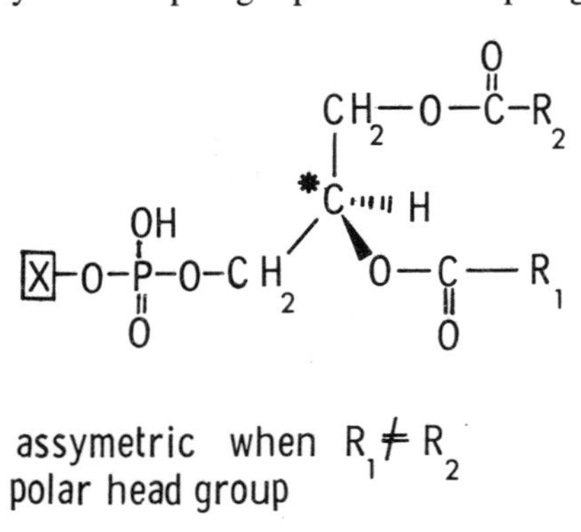

* C is assymetric when $R_1 \neq R_2$
X is polar head group

Figure 14. General formula for phosphodiacylglyerides.

Table 14. Classes of phosphoglycerides.

Phosphoglyceride	Head group (X)		Net charge at pH=7
Cephalin	Ethanolamine	$-O-CH_2-CH_2-\overset{+}{N}H_3$	0
Lecithin	Choline	$-O-CH_2-CH_2-\overset{+}{N}(CH_3)_3$	0
Phosphatidylserine	Serine	$-O-CH_2-CH\overset{\overset{+}{N}H_3}{\underset{COO^-}{}}$	−
Phosphatidylinositol	Inositol		−
Phosphatidylglycerol	Glycerol	$-O-CH_2-CHOH-CH_2OH$	−
Phosphatidyllysylglycerol	3'-O-lysylglycerol	$-O-CH_2-CHOH-CH_2$ O $^+NH_3CH_2-(CH_2)-CH-C=O$ $\underset{\overset{+}{N}H_3}{\mid}$	−
Cardiolipin	Glycerol bridge of two phosphatides	$-O-CH_2-CHOH-CH_2-O-$	2−

diol-transoctadec-4-ene) is esterified to choline phosphate at the 1 position and forms an amide bond at 2 with a mono-unsaturated fatty acid. Sphingomyelin has no net charge at pH 7.

Plasmalogen is similar in structure to cephalin with the difference that the hydrocarbon group attached to the first carbon of glycerol is an α-β unsaturated alcohol and the linkage formed is an α-β unsaturated ether. This bond is acid labile and under the analytical conditions used for the separation of phospholipid classes, it is hydrolysed and the compound chromatographed is 1-lysophosphatidylethanolamine.

The phospholipid composition of whole tissues, membrane fractions and biological fluids has been studied for many years using solvent extraction, silica column chromatography and t.l.c., with the use of g.c. −m.s. and infra-red spectrometry to identify the structure of isolated phospholipid classes. Now h.p.l.c. is used more since the introduction of low-wavelength u.v. detectors has overcome the problem of the detection of phospholipids, the only useful absorption band of which is below 210 nm. Derivatization has been used to a limited extent to aid detection of these compounds. Phospholipids are extracted from tissues by solvent extraction using the Folch system, followed by a t.l.c. or column separation step to separate neutral and phospholipids. Separation of phospholipid classes by h.p.l.c. is carried out on 5 μm silica columns. Fractions from h.p.l.c. separation of phospholipids on silica can be collected and further analysed to identify the species of each phospholipid class. RP-h.p.l.c. on octadecyl-bonded silica separates species containing different fatty acids. These can be identified if the peak fractions are collected, the fatty acid ester bonds hydrolysed and the fatty acids further analysed by h.p.l.c. or capillary g.c.

5.2 Tissue extraction

The most commonly used methods are based on the system devised by Folch *et al.* (24). Solvent extraction is with chloroform:methanol (2:1, v/v) as detailed below.

(i)   Homogenize the tissue with chloroform:methanol (2:1) (20 ml/g of tissue) in a suitably sized homogenizer.

(ii)   Separate the solvent from the homogenized tissue using either filtration with fat-free filter paper or centrifugation. If centrifugation is used it may be necessary to lower the specific gravity of the homogenate by adding extra methanol (0.2 vol is sufficient).

(iii) Retain the filtrate and restore the solvent proportions to $CHCl_3$:MeOH (2:1) if necessary. Wash the filtrate with 0.2 vol solution of the chloride of one of the following cations: Ca^{2+}, Mg^{2+} (0.0015 M), Na^+, K^+ (0.05 M). The ratio of $CHCl_3$:MeOH:aqueous solution should be kept at 8:4:3.

(iv)   Separate the mixture into aqueous and organic layers by centrifugation at 2000 *g* for $1-2$ min.

(v)   Separate the upper (aqueous) and lower (chloroform) layers. To aid separation of the phases without contamination or loss of the lower phase, after removing the majority of the upper phase, wash the interface with 1.5 ml of $CHCl_3$:MeOH: H_2O (3:48:47) — theoretical upper phase × 3 *without mixing*, then add methanol until the interface becomes miscible.

(vi)   Evaporate the chloroform:methanol extract to dryness under nitrogen and re-constitute in the desired solvent for further analysis.

The salt solution prevents back-extraction of phospholipids into the aqueous solution in which some have considerable solubility. $CaCl_2$ is the most effective salt for this purpose but it may be necessary to use an alternative if it causes precipitation of insoluble Ca^{2+} salts.

The yield is greater than 90% total lipids using this method. This extract has been used for h.p.l.c. of phospholipids without further purification (25).

5.3 Purification of phospholipid extract

5.3.1 Fractionation of total lipid extract using bonded silica columns

Recently Kaluzny (4) has used Bond-Elut aminopropylsilica disposable columns to fractionate total lipid extracts obtained by the Folch method. Separate fractions containing neutral lipids, fatty acids and phospholipids can be eluted in serial fashion from the column. The neutral lipids can be further fractionated if required.

(i)   Prepare 500 mg of Bond-Elut aminopropylsilica columns (with SS frits) by washing twice with 2 ml of hexane. Do not allow the columns to dry out completely after the second wash.

(ii)   Apply the lipid extract reconstituted in 0.5 ml of chloroform, under vacuum.

(iii) Elute the column in series with the following solvents. Put a fresh collection tube into the apparatus before each change of solvent.

      (a) chloroform:2-propanol (2:1)   4 ml — neutral lipids

      (b) 2% acetic acid in diethyl ether   4 ml — fatty acids

      (c) methanol   4 ml — phospholipids

(iv)   Use the fractions for further analysis or blow down to dryness under nitrogen for reconstitution in another solvent.

Using the Vac-Elut apparatus, 10 lipid fractions can be processed at once in 15 – 20 min. The columns can be regenerated by washing in the reverse elution order.

5.3.2 *Acetone precipitation*

A simple method for separating 'surface active' phospholipids from a total lipid extract is precipitation from ice-cold acetone (26).

(i)   Dissolve the dry residue from a Folch extraction in the minimum of chloroform 2.5 – 5 μl/mg and cool in a deep freeze for 10 min.
(ii)   Add excess ice-cold acetone until no more milky precipitate is formed. Vortex mix.
(iii) Centrifuge the mixture at 2000 g for 10 min at 0.4°C to pellet the precipitate and transfer the supernatant to another stoppered tube.
(iv)   Wash the precipitate with a further 1 ml/mg of ice-cold acetone.
(v)   Allow both tubes to stand in a freezer overnight and collect the precipitates the following day. Dry thoroughly.

5.4 **H.p.l.c. of phospholipid classes**

Separation of phospholipids on the basis of the polar head group esterified to phosphate is best carried out on a silica or a bonded polar column such as the DIOL or CN column (*Table 15*). A solvent system containing a small percentage of water with (25,28) or without (26,27) a pH modifier will separate most of the phospholipid classes. Most of the methods developed for the analysis of phospholipids have used variable wavelength u.v. detectors for detection at 203 – 205 nm. In order to achieve sensitivity of detection at this wavelength only a limited number of solvents are suitable. There are two frequently used solvent systems, either acetonitrile and water or hexane, isopropanol and water.

Some phospholipids can have broad tailing peaks and others are separated or partially separated into two or three peaks containing species of different fatty acid composition. The use of a small percentage of concentrated acid greatly improves the peak shape. Either phosphoric (25) or sulphuric acid (28) can be used. If quantitation of the phosphate content of collected fractions is intended the latter must be used. A 3 – 4 cm × 4 mm i.d. guard column packed with 5 – 40 μm silica is used to protect the analytical columns.

5.4.1 *Gradient elution*

Gradient elution can be used to reduce analysis time and improve peak shape. The percentage of water in the solvent is increased from about 2 to 15% when acetonitrile is the organic solvent. A lower percentage is used with a hexane, isopropanol and water system. Here the isopropanol content and water content must both be increased during gradient elution, isopropanol from about 4 to 24% and water from 0 or 0.4% to about 1%. If an acidic modifier is used, the concentration of this must also be increased as the water content is increased.

In order to achieve complete solubility of the water and acid in the hexane/isopro-

Table 15. Conditions for separation of phospholipid classes[a].

Column	Solvent system	Elution order[b]
Silica (10 μm; 25 cm $\times$ 4 mm i.d.)	*Isocratic* acetonitrile/methanol/ 85% phosphoric acid (130:5:1.5)	PI,PS,PE,PC,LysoPC,S (CL in solvent front PA and PG co-elute with PC)
	Solvent A: acetonitrile	CL,PI,PS,PE,LysoPE,PC
	Solvent B: acetonitrile/water (80:20)	(two peaks)
	Gradient 12.5%B to 75%B (3−15 min)	S (two peaks), LysoPC (three peaks)
Silica (10 μm; 30 cm $\times$ 4 mm i.d.)	*Isocratic* hexane/isopropanol/ water (6:8:1.15)	PE,PG,PI,PS,PC,S_1,S_2
Silica (5 μm; 30 cm $\times$ 4 mm i.d.)	*Solvent A:* hexane/isopropanol/ water/H_2SO_4 (97:3:0:0.02%)	PA,CL,PG,PS,PI,Cer,PE (two peaks)
	Solvent B: hexane/isopropanol/ water/H_2SO_4 (75:24:0.09:0.1%)	LysoPE (three peaks)
	Gradient 4%B to 100%B (2−50 min)	PC_1,PC_2 + S (two peaks)
DIOL (5 μm; 25 cm $\times$ 4.6 mm i.d.)	*Solvent A:* acetonitrile *Solvent B:* acetonitrile/water (3.5:1) *Gradient* 12%B to 75%B (4−12 min), temp. 38°C	PG,PI,PS,PE,PC,S
CN (5 μm; 25 cm $\times$ 4.6 mm i.d.)	*Solvent A:* acetonitrile *Solvent B:* acetonitrile/water (5:1) *Gradient* 10%B to 75%B (4−12 min), temp. 38°C	PG,PI,PS,PE,PC,S

[a]From refs. 25−28.
[b]*Key*: PA = phosphatidic acid, CL = cardiolipin, PG = phosphatidylglycerol, PE = phosphatidylethanol-amine, PS = phosphatidylserine, PC = phosphatidylcholine, PI = phosphatidylinositol, LysoPE = 1-lyso-phosphatidylethanolamine, S = sphingomyelin, LysoPC = 1-lysophosphatidylcholine, Cer = ceramides.

panol mixture during gradient elution with this system, it is best to use two pre-mixed solvent mixtures containing all the components. A linear gradient increasing the percent-age of the mixture high in water is then performed. This is more complicated to set up than the simpler acetonitrile/water system but gives good resolution of phospholipid classes and partial resolution of the classes into component species.

5.4.2 *Column conditioning*

Silica columns are usually stored in hexane when not in use. It is necessary to establish a routine conditioning procedure when changing from hexane to the solvent system used for separating phospholipid classes if reproducible results are to be obtained. The column conditioning procedures are shown in *Table 16.* DIOL and CN columns do not require such long periods of conditioning but should be well equilibrated with the starting solvent before each analysis. It is advisable to use a guard column to keep the column in good condition.

Table 16. Silica column conditioning procedures.

	Conditioning solvent
After use of acetonitrile/water system	Pass 30 ml of methanol/water 1/1, 30 ml of methanol, 30 ml of dichloromethane, store in n-hexane overnight.
Before use of acetonitrile/water system	Equilibrate with starting solvent for $1-5$ h.
After use of hexane/isopropanol/water gradient system	Pass 100 ml of isopropanol, 100 ml of n-hexane, store in n-hexane overnight.
Before use of hexane/isopropanol/water gradient system	Equilibrate with hexane/isopropanol/water/ (H_2SO_4) 75/24/0.9 (0.1) Solvent B 20 column volumes.
Between gradient runs	(1) 20 column volumes 50% isopropanol, 50% starting solvent. (2) Gradient over 20 column volumes to starting solvent. (3) 20 column volumes starting solvent (30 min total).

5.4.3 *Quantitation*

It has been generally accepted that absorption at 205 nm by phospholipids depends upon their content of unsaturated C-C bonds which will vary with the proportion of different fatty acids contained. As this changes with the species and tissue from which the phospholipids are obtained it is difficult to perform absolute quantitation on the basis of the peak areas in a chromatogram. There is a dissenting view (27) which is supported by experimental work showing that phosphatidylethanolamines of different double bond content gave nearly identical u.v. absorbances when they were analysed at the same concentration. This would indicate that the absorbance was also due to functional groups present in equal amounts in both samples such as carboxyl, phosphate and amino groups. In this case calibration curves can be prepared from commercially available phospholipid standards. The limits of sensitivity are found to vary for the different phospholipid classes, phosphatidylserine being particularly difficult to quantitate.

Quantitative determination of surface-active phospholipids has been used clinically to determine foetal lung maturity in premature births (*Figure 15*). The phospholipid composition in the amniotic fluid has been shown to be related to the incidence of respiratory distress syndrome (RDS) in premature infants and its determination can predict the necessity for therapeutic measures. Andrews (26) used h.p.l.c. on a 5 μm DIOL or CN column to separate and quantitate, using an internal standard, the surface-active phospholipids phosphatidylcholine (PC), sphingomyelin (S), phosphatidylglycerol (PG), phosphatidylinositol (PI), phosphatidylethanolamine (PE) and phosphatidylserine (PS).

5.5 **RP-h.p.l.c. separation of phospholipid species**

Under some analytical conditions separation of phospholipid classes on silica will give multiple peaks with varying degrees of resolution. Nissen and Kreysel (27) found that sphingomyelin gave two peaks which proved to contain species with different fatty acid

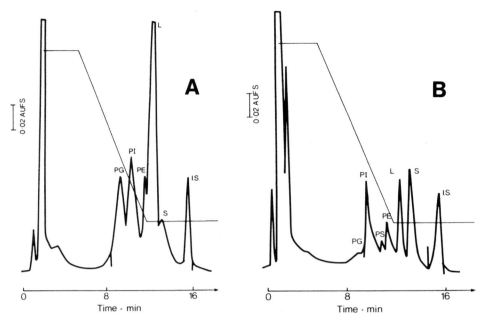

Figure 15. H.p.l.c. of phospholipids in amniotic fluid. Column, 12.5 cm × 4.6 mm i.d. 5 μm DIOL fitted with 30 cm × 14.6 mm i.d. guard column packed with 5 μm silica Si60; gradient elution with 88% solvent A (acetonitrile) and 12% solvent B (acetonitrile/water 3.5:1) to 25% A and 75% B, flow-rate 2 ml/min; temperature, 38°C; detector, u.v. 203 nm. **(A)** Mature amniotic fluid (gestation 37 weeks) phospholipid concentration as % of total phospholipids:lecithin (L) 48.82%; sphingomyelin (S) 12.48%; phosphatidyl-glycerol (PG) 7.11%; phosphatidylinositol (PI) 16.26%; phosphatidylethanolamine (PE) 15.31%; phospha-tidylserine (PS) <0.01%. (L/S ratio = 3.9:1.) **(B)** Immature amniotic fluid (L/S ratio = 1.2:1), phosphatidylglycerol (PG) is not present. Internal standard (IS) γ-caproyllysolecithin. (Reproduced from ref. 27 with permission.)

Table 17. Conditions for RP-h.p.l.c. of phospholipid species.

Column	(i) 30 cm × 4 mm 5 μm ODS-silica <u>or</u>
	(ii) 10 cm × 4.6 mm 3 μm ODS-silica.
Solvent system	90−98% methanol or acetonitrile/methanol (70:30−60:40)
	10−2% potassium phosphate buffer pH 7.4 1−10 mM either isocractic elution or methanol gradient from 90−98%.
Flow-rate	1−2 ml/min. Separation time 60−90 min.
Detection	U.v. absorption 203−208 nm.
Sample size	0.1−2 mg in 10−100 μl CHCl$_3$ or CHCl$_3$:MeOH.

Elution is in order of increasing fatty acid carbon number. The presence of unsaturated bonds in a fatty acid reduces the retention time of a species relative to those containing fewer or no unsaturated C-C bonds. Retention time and resolution is dependent on the buffer concentration and pH. Retention time increases with increasing concentration and pH. Poor resolution is obtained below pH 6.5 indicating that ionization of the phosphate group is necessary for the best separation of phospholipid species.

composition while phosphatidylcholine gave two peaks which appeared to contain the same fatty acids.

The properties of biological membranes containing phospholipids may be dependent on the fatty acid content of those phospholipids as well as on the nature of the polar

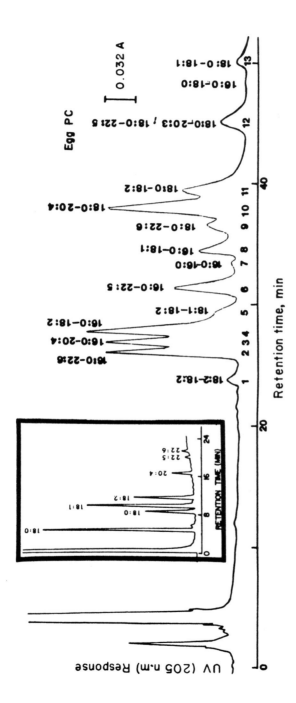

Figure 16. RP-h.p.l.c. of egg phosphatidylcholine. Column, 30 cm × 4 mm i.d. Nucleosil-5-C₁₈; eluent, methanol – 1 mM phosphate buffer pH 7.4 (9.5:0.5 v/v); flow-rate 1 ml/min. Sample injected 500 μg PC in 10 μl dichloromethane:methanol (1:1). The major fatty acid composition of the PC in an individual peak is given near the peak. **Inset:** g.c. analysis of fatty acid methyl esters of egg total PC on SP2340 column. (Reproduced from ref. 29 with permission.)

head group.

To obtain information about the proportions and identities of the fatty acids in phospholipids, the latter must be hydrolysed to give the free fatty acids which can be further characterized by h.p.l.c. analysis, or the phospholipids can be transesterified to form the methyl esters of the constituent fatty acids for analysis by capillary g.c. (see Section 2.4). RP-h.p.l.c. on ODS-bonded silica columns is used to fractionate a phospholipid into its component species. The same transesterification procedure can be used on the collected fractions to determine the exact fatty acid composition of each species. This can provide information about the identity and abundance of particular species in different tissues or subcellular fractions (29–31).

The conditions for RP-h.p.l.c. of phospholipid species are shown in *Table 17* .

Figure 16 is an example of RP-h.p.l.c. analysis of egg phosphatidylcholine (29). The conditions used are described in the figure. The composition of each peak was determined by analysing the collected peak fractions. Quantitation and identification of the fatty acids found in each peak fraction was done by g.c. and g.c. –m.s. of the fatty acid methyl esters formed from methanolysis of the phospholipids.

6. REFERENCES

1. Payne-Wahl,K., Spencer,G.F., Plattner,R.D. and Butterfield,R.O. (1981) *J. Chromatogr.*, **209**, 61.
2. Christie,W.W., ed. (1982) *Lipid Analysis*, 2nd Edn., Pergamon Press, New York, p. 96.
3. Marinetti,G., ed. (1982) *Lipid Chromatographic Analysis*, Vol. 1, Marcel Dekker Inc., New York.
4. Kaluzny,M.A., Duncan,L.A., Merritt,M.V. and Epps,D.E. (1985) *J. Lipid Res.*, **26**, 135.
5. Christie,W.W. (1982) *J. Lipid Res.*, **23**, 1072.
6. Christie,W.W., Connor,K. and Noble,R.C. (1984) *J. Chromatogr.*, **298**, 513.
7. Durst,H.D., Milano,M., Kikta,E.J., Connelly,S.A. and Grushka,E. (1975) *Anal. Chem.*, **47**, 1797.
8. Lam,S. and Grushka,E. (1978) *J. Chromatogr.*, **158**, 207.
9. Ryan,P.J. and Honeyman,T.W. (1984) *J. Chromatogr.*, **312**, 461.
10. Borch,R.F. (1975) *Anal. Chem.*, **47**, 2437.
11. Guerrant,G.O., Lambert,M.A. and Moss,C.W. (1982) *J. Clin. Microbiol.*, **16**, 355.
12. Umeh,E.O. (1971) *J. Chromatogr.*, **56**, 29.
13. Kissinger,L.D. and Robins,R.H. (1985) *J. Chromatogr.*, **321**, 353.
14. Mathews,W.R., Rokach,J. and Murphy,R.C. (1981) *Anal. Biochem.*, **118**, 96.
15. Henke,D.C., Kouzan,S. and Eling,T.E. (1984) *Anal. Biochem.*, **140**, 87.
16. Terragno,A., Rydzik,R. and Terragno,N.A. (1981) *Prostaglandins*, **21**, 101.
17. Fitzpatrick,F.A. (1976) *Anal. Chem.*, **48**, 499.
18. Morozowich,W. and Douglas,S.L. (1975) *Prostaglandins*, **10**, 19.
19. Plattner,R.D. (1981) in *Methods in Enzymology*, Volume **72**, Lowenstein,J.M. (eds.), Academic Pres, New York, p. 21.
20. Kuksis,A., Marai,L. and Myher,J.J. (1983) *J. Chromatogr.*, **273**, 43.
21. Marai,L., Myher,J.J. and Kuksis,A. (1983) *Can. J. Biochem. Cell Biol.*, **61**, 840.
22. Herslof,B.G. and Pelura,T.J. (1982) *J. Am. Oil Chem. Soc.*, **59**, 308A Abstr. No. 295.
23. El Hamdy,A.H. and Perkins,E.G. (1981) *J. Am. Oil Chem. Soc.*, **58**, 867.
24. Folch,J., Lees,M. and Sloane Stanley,G.H. (1957) *J. Biol. Chem.*, **226**, 497.
25. Shi-Hua Chen,S. and Kou,A.Y. (1982) *J. Chromatogr.*, **227**, 25.
26. Andrews,A.G. (1984) *J. Chromatogr.*, **336**, 139.
27. Nissen,H.P. and Kreysel,H.W. (1983) *J. Chromatogr.*, **276**, 29.
28. Yandrasitz,J.R., Berry,G. and Segal,S. (1981) *J. Chromatogr.*, **225**, 319.
29. Smith,M. and Jungalwala,F.B. (1981) *J. Lipid Res.*, **22**, 697.
30. Jungalwala,F.B., Hayssen,V., Pasquini,J.M. and McCluer,R.H. (1979) *J. Lipid Res.*, **20**, 579.
31. Teng,J.I. and Smith,L.L. (1985) *J. Chromatogr.*, **339**, 35.

CHAPTER 6

Bile acids

STANLEY LAM and ARTHUR KARMEN

1. INTRODUCTION

Bile acids are synthesized from cholesterol involving a series of enzymic reactions in the mitochondria and microsomes of the hepatocytes. Cholic acid and chenodeoxycholic acid are the major bile acids synthesized in the human liver and are referred to as the primary bile acids (*Figure 1*). The bile acids are excreted in the bile after conjugation with amino acids (mainly glycine and taurine) at the carboxyl group or with sulphuric or glucuronic acid at the hydroxyl groups. Bile acids are actively and passively (non-ionic diffusion) re-absorbed at the terminal ileum and the jejunum, respectively, during passage down the small intestine. All re-absorbed bile acids return to the liver via the portal blood system for re-hydroxylation and conjugation. Those which escape re-absorption are extensively metabolized by bacteria (e.g. deconjugation, 7α-dehydroxylation) on reaching the colon and give rise to a complex mixture of secondary bile acids (*Figure 1*) which are excreted in the faeces. The most commonly found

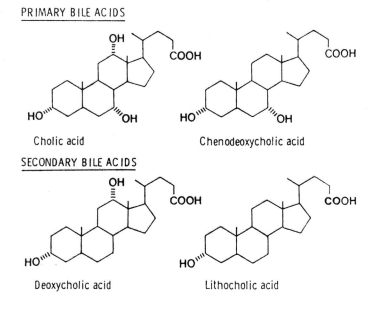

Figure 1. Structures of bile acids.

Table 1. H.p.l.c. systems for the separation of conjugated bile acids in bile.

Column	Mobile phase	Detector
1. 'Fatty acid analysis'	2-propanol:8.8 mM potassium phosphate buffer, pH 2.5 (32:68 v/v)	RI
2. μ-Bondapak C_{18}	methanol:water:acetic acid/NaOH, pH 4.7 (65:35:3.27 by vol.)	RI
3. μ-Bondapak C_{18}	acetonitrile:methanol:0.03 M potassium phosphate buffer, pH 3.4 (10:60:30 by vol.)	u.v. 200 nm
4. MicroPak SP-C_{18}-IP-4	0.5 mol/l tetrabutylammonium phoaphate in acetonitrile: water (54:46 v/v)	u.v. 210 nm

secondary bile acids in man are deoxycholic acid and lithocholic acid (*Figure 1*). Bile acids are amphiphilic and act as natural detergents. Their major role is to aid the absorption of fats and fat-soluble vitamins. The emphasis of this chapter is on the methods for the analysis of serum bile acids although procedures for analysis of bile acids in bile will also be discussed. The h.p.l.c. behaviour of bile acids and their conjugates, particularly on reversed-phase (RP) columns, have been studied (1−3).

2. H.P.L.C. OF BILE ACIDS IN BILE

The glycine and taurine conjugates of bile acids in bile are present in sufficiently high concentrations for detection with a refractive index (RI) or an u.v. detector set in the range 195−214 nm. Bile samples may be processed for h.p.l.c. as follows.

(i)   Add 2 ml of methanol to 1 ml of bile and vortex-mix.

(ii)   Centrifuge at 2000 *g* for 5 min.

(iii)   Filter the supernatant through a 0.22 μm Millex filter (Millipore).

(iv)   Inject 10−100 μl.

The conjugated bile acids can be separated by using a 'Fatty acid analysis' column from Waters Associates (4), by RP (5,6) or RP-IP chromatography (7,8). The h.p.l.c. systems are summarized in *Table 1*. The RP-IP technique has been shown to be more suited for the routine analysis of bile acids in bile (7).

Like the fatty acids (Chapter 5) the sensitivity of detection can be improved by preparing the u.v.-absorbing esters with reagents such as *p*-bromophenacyl bromide (9), *p*-nitrobenzoyl chloride (10) and 1-naphthyldiazomethane (11). The derivatization procedures are generally similar to those described for fatty acids (Chapter 5). The esters chromatograph well on RP columns. They are useful for the analysis of bile acids in bile and in faeces but are still inadequate for the determination of low concentrations of bile acids in serum.

3. H.P.L.C. OF BILE ACIDS IN SERUM

3.1 Introduction

One of the more clinically promising parameters of liver function and clinical status to be measured in recent years has been the serum bile acid concentration. It proved to be a sensitive indicator of liver dysfunction in a variety of diseases. Three general approaches have been used to make the measurement. The first is based on the specificity of the bacterial enzyme, 3α-hydroxysteroid dehydrogenase. When a serum preparation is reacted with NAD^+ in the presence of the enzyme, the NADH formed is a measure of the total bile acids. The NADH is measured either by absorbance at 340 nm, its fluorescence or by coupling to the dye, resazurine, which, in the presence of the enzyme diaphorase, is converted into the highly fluorescent resorufine. The second approach involves immunoassay with one of several antibodies with different specificities toward the different steroid portions of the bile acid molecules. The third is quantitative chromatography, particularly g.l.c., sometimes in conjunction with detection by mass spectrometry (12). Because of the low volatility of the bile acids and the small concentrations present, g.l.c. requires that the samples be cleaned up carefully, the conjugated bile acids hydrolysed and volatile derivatives such as methyl esters and acyl or trimethylsilyl derivatives synthesized prior to analysis. The complexity of sample preparation made g.l.c. unattractive as a routine method. H.p.l.c. was similarly difficult to apply because the variety of similar compounds in serum interfered with detection by the usual, non-specific u.v. absorbance detector which is relatively insensitive to bile acids. To overcome these problems highly sensitive methods based on either pre-column derivatization or post-column enzyme reaction followed by fluorescence detection have been developed. Pre-column labelling of bile acids with 4-bromomethyl-7-methoxy-coumarin (13), 1-bromoacetylpyrene (14) and 1-anthroyl nitrile (15) have been reported for the sensitive determination of serum bile acids. These methods, however, require extensive sample clean-up on a Sep-Pak C_{18} cartridge followed by group separation on a PHP-Sephadex LH-20 column before derivatization. They are therefore, like the g.l.c. procedure, unattractive as routine methods.

The introduction, by Baba *et al.* (16), of a semi-specific and highly sensitive h.p.l.c. system based on the use of a post-column enzyme reactor followed by a fluorometer, promised an improvement. Various modifications of the method have been described (17,18). Our experience with this approach, using the system offered commercially by JASCO, is described in detail in the following sections. We have used it to study the serum bile acid profiles of more than 200 patients with a variety of liver diseases.

3.2 Analysis of serum bile acids by h.p.l.c. coupled to post-column enzyme reaction and fluorescence detection

3.2.1 *Sample preparation*

Preparation of serum samples for h.p.l.c., usually a very tedious procedure, is simplified by use of the micro-protein precipitation procedure developed in our laboratory for assaying therapeutic drugs.

(i)   Pipette 100 μl of serum into a test tube.
(ii)   Sequentially add 10 μl of 10% $ZnSO_4$ and 100 μl of methanol.
(iii)   Vortex-mix and centrifuge for 1 min at 2000 *g*.
(iv)   Remove the supernatant into a clean test tube.
(v)   Wash the precipitate twice with 100 μl of methanol. Centrifuge and recover the supernatant after each washing.
(vi)   Combine the supernatants and inject 150 μl.

This procedure gives good recovery of bile acids and reproducible results (*Tables 2 and 3*). An alternative method (19) is to add 2.5 ml of ethanol to 0.5 ml of serum

Table 2. The recovery of bile acids from pooled serum ($n=5$).

	(%, mean ± S.D.)
UDC	96.5 ± 2.4
C	90.0 ± 2.2
GUDC	88.0 ± 2.8
GC	91.8 ± 3.0
TUDC	84.1 ± 3.0
TC	101.1 ± 4.1
CDC	91.9 ± 2.1
DC	90.1 ± 2.5
GCDC	108.0 ± 3.4
GDC	90.5 ± 1.6
TCDC	89.7 ± 1.4
TDC	90.3 ± 0.8
LC	85.3 ± 8.3
GLC	95.0 ± 11.2
TLC	103.0 ± 18.6

For abbreviations see *Figure 4*.

Table 3. The reproducibility of bile acid measurements by h.p.l.c. after protein precipition ($n=5$).

	(μM, mean ± S.D.)	C.V. (%)
UDC	4.77 ± 0.15	3.1
C	5.15 ± 0.25	4.8
GUDC	5.24 ± 0.28	5.4
GC	5.32 ± 0.28	5.3
TUDC	5.57 ± 0.30	5.5
TC	5.02 ± 0.54	5.3
CDC	4.85 ± 0.20	4.2
DC	4.86 ± 0.20	4.1
GCDC	4.91 ± 0.21	4.5
GDC	4.93 ± 0.21	4.3
TCDC	5.06 ± 0.21	4.2
TDC	5.10 ± 0.18	3.5
LC	5.05 ± 0.30	5.9
GLC	4.98 ± 0.34	6.5
TLC	4.92 ± 0.89	9.1

For abbreviations see *Figure 4*.

and to stir the mixture for 1 min in a water bath at 85°C, followed by centrifugation at 3500 *g* for 5 min. The procedure is repeated three times, and the combined supernatants are evaporated to dryness under reduced pressure. The residue is re-dissolved in 100 μl of methanol and 10 μl of the solution is injected.

3.2.2 *H.p.l.c. and post-column enzyme reaction conditions*

The bile acids are most conveniently separated on RP columns by gradient elution. To effect the gradient, the JASCO h.p.l.c. bile acid analyser system uses a GP-A40 gradient programmer and a TRI ROTAR-V pump (*Figure 2*). The sample is introduced

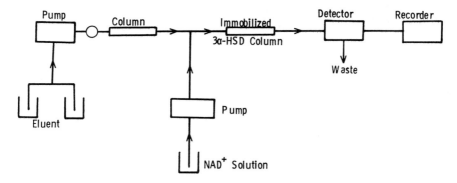

Figure 2. Schematic diagram of the bile acid analyser.

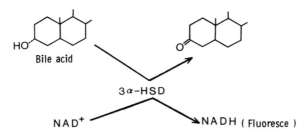

Figure 3. In the presence of 3α-hydroxysteroid dehydrogenase, NAD$^+$ oxidizes bile acids and the fluorescence of the NADH produced is proportional to the concentration of bile acid.

via the injector into the analytical column (25 cm × 4.6 mm) packed with a proprietary packing material (BilePak). Eluent A consists of 69% phosphate buffer (0.02 M KH$_2$PO$_4$, pH 7.80) and 31% acetonitrile, and eluent B 82% phosphate buffer (0.03 M KH$_2$PO$_4$, pH 7.80) and 18% acetonitrile. Elution starts with 100% eluent B (0% A) and continues with constantly increasing concentrations of eluent A, from 0% to 25% at 25 min, 65% at 50 min and 100% at 65 min. The flow-rate is 1 ml/min.

A post-column reactor is used to detect the bile acids in the column effluent (*Figure 2*). The post-column reagent consists of 1.0 mM EDTA, 0.3 mM NAD$^+$ and 0.5 ml of 2-mercaptoethanol in 0.01 M phosphate buffer, pH 7.0. The mixture is added to the column effluent at 0.5 ml/min. The combined stream is then passed into the post-column reactor, which consists of a chromatographic column containing covalently bound 3α-hydroxysteroid dehydrogenase (3α-HSD), supplied by JASCO as EnzymePak-HSD. The fluorescence of the NADH produced by the reaction of NAD$^+$ and bile acids (*Figure 3*) in the presence of the enzyme is monitored in the FP-115 fluorometric detector with excitation at 365 nm and emission at 470 nm.

3.2.3 *H.p.l.c. and post-column enzyme reaction behaviour of bile acids*

With the specified linear gradient elution protocol, the complete spectrum of bile acids elutes in slightly over 1 h. The bile acids emerge from the column in three groups (*Figure 4*). In the first are ursodeoxycholic and cholic acids, each followed shortly thereafter by their glycine and then their taurine conjugates. The second group contains chenodeoxycholic and deoxycholic acids, each followed by their conjugates, and the third

107

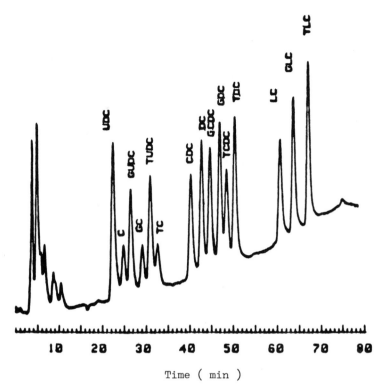

Figure 4. A chromatogram of bile acid standards. H.p.l.c. conditions are as described in Section 3.2.2. C, cholic acid; CDC, chenodeoxycholic acid; DC, deoxycholic acid; GC, glycocholic acid; GCDC, glyco-chenodeoxycholic acid; GDC, glycodeoxycholic acid; GLC, glycolithocholic acid; GUDC, glycoursodeoxy-cholic acid; LC, lithocholic acid; TC, taurocholic acid; TCDC, taurochenodeoxycholic acid; TDC, taurodeoxycholic acid; TLC, taurolithocholic acid; TUDC, tauroursodeoxycholic acid; UDC, ursodeoxycholic acid.

group, lithocholic acid and its conjugates. Detection of the different compounds after the post-column reaction is not uniform: the primary bile acids yield somewhat smaller quantities of NADH than the secondary bile acids indicating that the reaction with the bound enzyme is incomplete in the time which the primary acids remain in the reactor and that the affinity of the enzyme for different bile acid derivatives varies. Quantification therefore requires careful reproduction of the time which the derivatives spend in the reactor, through control of the flow-rate and through use of a calibration curve to compensate for the differences in response. The post-column reactor also changes with time. We found the response to be constant for about 200 injections, after which the fluorescence yield gradually decreased, requiring even more frequent calibration.

Over a considerable period early in our studies, the baseline was observed to drift during the course of each analysis. This drift is apparent on several of the figures shown here. The repetition of similar drift patterns with each analysis, even when samples that did not contain bile acids were assayed, suggested the eluting solvent as the cause. We found that the drift could be eliminated by preparing fresh mobile phase daily. We postulated that it was caused by accumulation of fluorescent metabolites of bacteria growing in the mobile phase.

4. CLINICAL STUDIES

We have used the above procedure (Section 3) to study the changes in serum bile acid profiles in more than 200 patients with different diseases of the liver, selected on the basis of abnormalities in serum liver function tests. These are described in the following sections.

4.1 **Cirrhosis**

Eight patients with far advanced Laennaec's cirrhosis had similar patterns of serum bile acid profiles. These patterns persisted throughout the period of the patients' hospi-

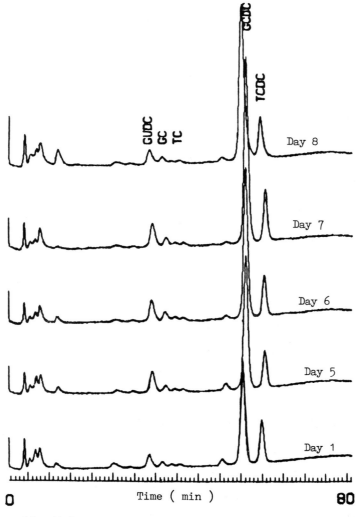

Figure 5. Serum bile acid chromatograms of serial samples from a patient with Laennaec's cirrhosis. The individual records are labelled with the patient's day of hospitalization. The patterns remained constant despite increases in the total bile acid concentration from 100 to 180 μM. For abbreviations see *Figure 4*.

talization through rises and falls in the total bile acid concentrations. The total bile acid concentrations ranged up to 150 μM. The chenodeoxycholic acid derivatives were found in much higher concentrations than those of cholic acid (*Figure 5*), exceeding 80% of the total. Twice as much of these acids was conjugated with glycine as with taurine. In one patient, a man who died in hepatic failure, the specimens taken just before death showed the appearance of unconjugated bile acids and the secondary bile acid, lithocholic acid. In all these patients the serum bilirubin was markedly elevated and the serum enzymes only moderately elevated in the patterns characteristic of cirrhosis; serum glutamic−oxalacetic transaminase (SGOT) more than serum glutamic−pyruvic transaminase (SGPT) and alkaline phosphatase 2−4 times more than the normal upper limit. The changes in bile acid concentrations did not parallel the changes in serum enzyme or bilirubin concentrations.

There were similar patterns in three of four patients thought clinically to have less advanced cirrhosis associated with alcoholism. One of the four had appreciably more

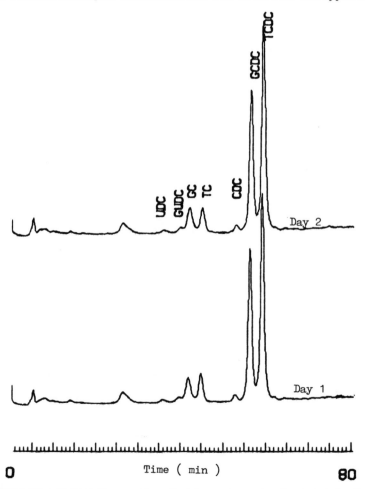

Figure 6. Serum bile acid chromatograms of samples taken on two consecutive days during the hospitalization of a patient thought to have acute alcoholic hepatitis as well as gallstones. For abbreviations see *Figure 4*.

of the cholic acid derivatives, up to 35% of the total, despite an appreciably elevated total bile acid concentration of 150 μM and similar pattern of serum enzyme elevations and jaundice.

One patient with alcoholic hepatitis and gallstones also had very high levels of chenodeoxycholic acid but a glycine to taurine ratio of less than 1, showing that the taurine, thought to be the preferred substrate for the conjugating system, was conserved (*Figure 6*). This patient was not jaundiced but had similar enzyme elevations and elevations of the total bile acids to a concentration of 100 μM. In this group the serum alkaline phosphatase and lactate dehydrogenase activities were only slightly elevated and the bilirubin ranged only up to 4 mg/100 ml. The transaminases were both elevated 3−6 times over the normal upper limit, with SGOT values approximately twice those of SGPT.

4.2 Hepatitis

In one patient with viral hepatitis, who had characteristic elevations of transaminases up to more than 50 times normal, with SGPT greater than SGOT, and jaundice, the total bile acid concentration was 216 μM in the first sample collected, in which the SGPT was 7074 i.u./l. The total bile acids fell gradually to a concentration of 145 μM during the next week, in parallel with the fall in SGPT to 1600 i.u./l. Over the same period the bilirubin rose gradually from 5.6 to 12 mg/100 ml. The bile acid patterns showed approximately equal concentrations of glycocholic and glycochenodeoxycholic acids. Taurocholic and taurochenodeoxycholic acids were both found at appreciably lower concentrations (*Figure 7*). There were no unconjugated or secondary bile acids present.

Three other patients thought also to have viral hepatitis, but who had histories of drug abuse as well, had more modest elevations of SGOT, that were greater than those of SGPT, and only slight hyperbilirubinaemia. All had approximately equal elevations of cholic and chenodeoxycholic acids, again conjugated mostly with glycine rather than taurine. The patterns were similar in these three patients during their hospitalization, despite marked drops, or, in one instance, rises, in the total concentration. In one patient with chronic hepatitis whose total bile acid increased from 28 μM to 68 μM the predominant metabolite was glycocholic acid.

4.3 Cholecystitis

In five patients with cholecystitis with jaundice, elevations of serum transaminase to 300 i.u./l, and total bile acids prior to surgical treatment up to 300 μM, cholic acid was the predominant bile acid showing more conjugation to glycine than taurine. There were easily detectable quantities of glyco- and taurodeoxycholic acids. Following surgery, the total bile acid fell more rapidly than the bilirubin or the serum enzymes (*Figure 8*).

4.4 Obstructive jaundice

One patient with obstructive jaundice, with characteristically marked elevations of serum alkaline phosphatase to 14 times normal, bilirubin to 21 times normal, and the relatively smaller elevations of SGOT and SGPT (with SGPT greater) had bile acid con-

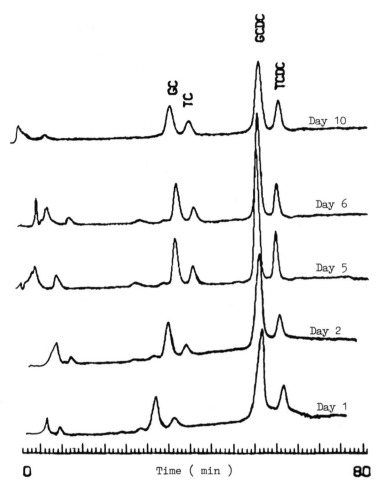

Figure 7. Serum bile acid chromatograms of samples from a patient with acute viral hepatitis taken over a 10-day period in the mid-course of the illness when the serum enzymes were decreasing and the bilirubin still rising. For abbreviations see *Figure 4*.

centrations up to 132 μM (*Figure 9*). Unlike the samples from the patients with the diagnoses described above, these had high concentrations of bile acids conjugated with taurine as well as glycine.

4.5 Cholangitis

One patient with cholangitis had serum bilirubin that increased from 0.9 mg/100 ml on admission to a high of 6 mg/100 ml on the third day of hospitalization followed by a return to 2 mg/100 ml, 3 days later. The alkaline phosphatase rose from 300 to 370 i.u./l during the same period with parallel, approximately equal, increases in both transaminases from 47 to 120 i.u./l. During the same period the total bile acid rose from 2 μM to 133 μM in 2 days, followed by a similarly rapid fall to 8 μM, 4 days later (*Figure 10*). As in the case of the patient with obstructive jaundice, conjugation

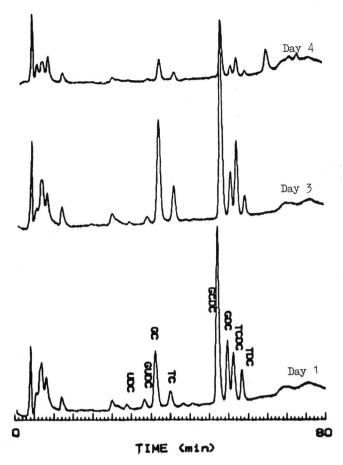

Figure 8. Serum bile acid chromatograms of samples from a patient with acute cholecystitis. A cholecystectomy was performed shortly after the sample was taken on day 3 of the patient's hospitalization. Deoxycholic acid conjugates appeared during the acute phase of the disease. For abbreviations see *Figure 4*.

of the bile acids to taurine was approximately equal to that to glycine. At the high point the concentrations of cholic and chenodeoxycholic acids were approximately equal. As the concentrations fell, the elevations of chenodeoxycholic conjugates predominated.

4.6 General discussion on h.p.l.c. serum bile acid profiles and liver diseases

The patient samples described above were selected because of marked elevations in the more usual serum liver indicators, such as bilirubin, alkaline phosphatase and the transaminases. Serial samples from each patient were assayed. In analysing the data, we considered the results in groups according to the primary presumptive diagnosis, rather than the most apparent pathologic mechanism. It soon became apparent that the total bile acids were elevated to approximately the same extent during the course of most of the diseases studied, indicating that elevation of total bile acid could not be specific for any individual liver disease. To derive further information about the mech-

113

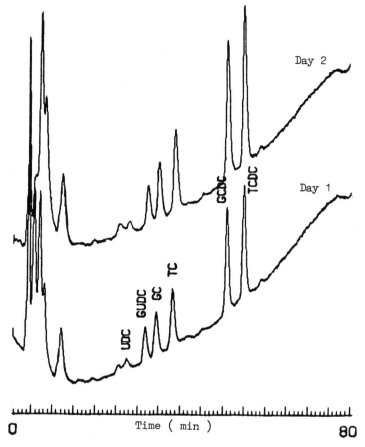

Figure 9. Serum bile acid chromatograms of samples taken on two consecutive days during the hospitalization of a patient with obstructive jaundice. The total bile acid concentrations were 90 μM on the first day,
132 μM on the second. After surgical relief of the obstruction on the second day the total concentration fell
to 46 μM on the third day and to 4 μM on the seventh day. For abbreviations see *Figure 4*.

anism of the observed changes, we studied the changes in bile acid quantity and composition during the course of each patient's disease and attempted to determine the
parallelism, if any, between changes in bile acids and those in the other liver function
tests.

Several consistent patterns of abnormality became apparent. As has been observed
previously, serum bile acids circulate as conjugates with glycine or taurine, except in
patients with severe liver failure in whose sera unconjugated as well as secondary bile
acids become detectable (20).

The high levels of bile acids observed in patients in the terminal stage of cirrhosis
suggest that the ability to synthesize bile acids is largely preserved. The preponderance
of chenodeoxycholic conjugates in these patients is consistent with the idea that the
ability of the liver to synthesize cholic acid may be compromised more than the ability
to synthesize chenodeoxycholic acid (21). We hypothesize that the predominance of
chenodeoxycholic acids indicates loss of much of the liver function.

Bile acids are conjugated to both glycine and taurine. In almost all patients with

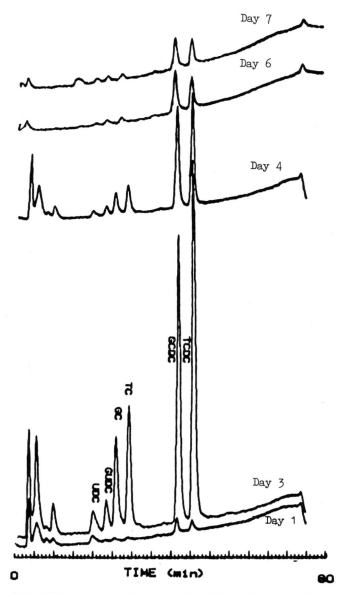

Figure 10. Serum bile acid chromatograms of samples taken during the first week of hospitalization of a patient with acute cholangitis. The total bile acid concentration rose from 3 μM on the first day to 132 μM on the third day and then fell back towards normal on succeeding days. Note the similarity of the patterns when the total concentrations were high to those in *Figure 9* from the patient with obstructive jaundice. For abbreviations see *Figure 4*.

markedly high levels of bile acids there was more conjugation to glycine than to taurine. The exceptions were those patients with acute cholecystitis in whom the bile acids fell rapidly with treatment and in whom, we hypothesize, liver architecture and function was otherwise intact. It has been reported that conjugation to taurine, which is ordinarily present at a lower concentration than glycine, is favoured. Since acute obstruction of

115

the bile duct results in diminution of the enterohepatic re-circulation of the bile acids, taurine is conserved and the taurine conjugates are observed in higher concentration than in other diseases. Conversely, the presence of substantial concentrations of taurine conjugates could be taken as an indicator of diminished enterohepatic circulation and, therefore, biliary obstruction.

The observation of taurine conjugates at a comparatively high concentration in one patient with acute hepatitis, who simultaneously had a markedly elevated serum bilirubin but a relatively normal alkaline phosphatase, may be consistent with this patient being in what is termed the 'obstructive phase' of his disease.

The total bile acid concentration changed more rapidly than any of the other liver indicators during acute diseases, suggesting that it may be a more sensitive indicator of change in liver status or, conversely, of the stability or chronicity of the disease. The total bile acid concentration and the patterns were not consistently related to each other. During the course of acute diseases, with relatively rapid increases or decreases in the total concentration, there was a marked consistency of the pattern, suggesting that the relative concentrations may indicate the nature of the abnormal mechanism, while the total concentration indicates its severity. Because of the inevitable uncertainty associated with the clinical data, samples from more patients must be analysed to substantiate the hypotheses presented here concerning relationships and associations between bile acid profiles and pathophysiology or clinical diagnoses. From the analyses of patient samples described here, neither the total nor the patterns could be predicted from the other indicators of liver disease, either individually or all together. This suggests that the bile acid patterns can provide diagnostic and prognostic information in addition to that provided by the more currently used serum indicators of liver disease.

5. REFERENCES

1. Goto,J., Kato,H., Saruta,Y. and Nambara,T. (1980) *J. Liquid Chromatogr.*, **3**, 991.
2. Shaw,R., Rivetna,M. and Elliott,W.H. (1980) *J. Chromatogr.*, **202**, 347.
3. Elliott,W.H. and Shaw,R. (1985) In *Methods in Enzymology.* Law,J.H. and Rilling,H.C. (eds), Academic Press, NY, Vol. **111**, p. 51.
4. Shaw,R., Smith,J.A. and Elliott,W.H. (1978) *Anal. Biochem.*, **86**, 450.
5. Block,C. and Watkins,J.B. (1978) *J. Lipid Res.*, **19**, 510.
6. Nakayama,F. and Nakagaki,M. (1980) *J. Chromatogr.*, **183**, 287.
7. Wildgrude,H.J., Füssel,U., Lauer,H. and Stockhausen,H. (1983) *J. Chromatogr.*, **282**, 603.
8. Wildgrude,H.J., Stockhausen,H., Petri,J., Füssel,U. and Lauer,H. (1986) *J. Chromatogr.*, **353**, 207.
9. Mingrone,G., Greco,A.V. and Passi,S. (1980) *J. Chromatogr.*, **183**, 277.
10. Shaikh,B., Pontzer,N.J., Molina,J.E. and Kelsey,M.I. (1978) *Anal. Biochem.*, **85**, 47.
11. Matter,D.P. and Purdy,W.C. (1979) *Anal. Chim. Acta*, **109**, 61.
12. Street,J.M. (1983) In *Proceedings of the First International Symposium on Bile Acids in Hepatobiliary and Gastrointestinal Diseases.* IRL Press, Oxford and Washington, D.C., p. 9.
13. Okuyama,S., Uemura,D. and Hirata,Y. (1979) *Chem. Lett.*, 461.
14. Kamada,S., Maeda,M. and Tsuji,A. (1983) *J. Chromatogr.*, **272**, 29.
15. Goto,J., Saito,M., Chika,T., Goto,N. and Nambara,T. (1983) *J. Chromatogr.*, **276**, 289.
16. Baba,S., Uenoyama,R., Suminor,K., Takeda,F., Hasegawa,S. and Kameno,Y. (1980) *Kobe J. Med. Sci.*, **26**, 89.
17. Ohnishi,S., Itoh,S. and Ishida,Y. (1982) *Biochem. J.*, **204**, 135.
18. Hasegawa,S., Uenoyama,R., Takeda,F., Chuma,J. and Baba,S. (1983) *J. Chromatogr.*, **278**, 25.
19. Niijima,S.-I. (1985) *Paediatr. Res.*, **19**, 302.
20. Javitt,N.B. (1982) In *Diseases of the Liver.* 5th edition, Schiff,L. and Schiff,E.R. (eds), J.B.Lippincolt Co., Philadelphia, PA, p. 119.
21. Goldman,M., Reno Vlahcevic,Z., Schwartz,C.C., Gustafsson,J. and Sewell,L. (1982) *Hepatology*, **2**, 59.

CHAPTER 7

Steroids

J.W.HONOUR

1. INTRODUCTION

The practical aspects of this chapter are directed to the extraction, separation and analysis of steroids in whole blood, plasma, urine or tissues for diagnostic and clinical research purposes. The selected applications thus extend from the measurement of a single steroid, for example cortisol in plasma, to a more general need to examine tissue extracts and biological fluids for a range of steroid products in order to acquire detailed information on the physiology or pathophysiology of steroid secretion. Publications on the h.p.l.c. separation of steroids abound. Usually a chromatogram illustrates the separation of reference steroids but few papers offer a copy of the data from a clinical specimen. In this respect the quality of each method needs careful scrutiny before application to clinical problems.

The principles of the methods described later in detail are applicable to the h.p.l.c. analysis of the range of naturally-occurring steroids. Where possible, methods have been selected which incorporate recent developments in solid state extraction of steroids from the biological matrix. Although not extensively covered in the present chapter, h.p.l.c. is also valuable for studying the pharmacology of the many steroid-based drugs used in medicine today. In some cases it is necessary to complement h.p.l.c. analysis with other analytical techniques.

2. BIOCHEMISTRY OF STEROIDS

Steroid hormones are elaborated in man by the adrenals, gonads and placenta largely from esters of cholesterol. *De novo* synthesis of cholesterol provides variable though generally small amounts of substrate for steroidogenesis. Cholesterol (C_{27}) (*Figure 1*) is reduced in carbon number to C_{21} (pregnane), C_{19} (androstane) and C_{18} (oestrane). Representative hormones of these steroid classes are shown in *Figure 1*, all are based on the cyclopentanoperhydrophenanthrene nucleus. Naturally-occurring hormones have from two up to occasionally six oxygen functions substituted most commonly at C-3, 6, 11, 16, 17, 20 and 21. All steroids have an oxygen function at C-3 and, in the case of androgens and oestrogens, oxygen at C-17, for example testosterone and oestradiol (see *Figure 2*). In general active hormones have a 3-keto-4-ene configuration.

The biosynthetic pathways for steroid hormones are summarized in *Figure 2*. Androgens and oestrogens are important secretory products of the gonads but are also synthesized by the adrenals. Adrenocorticosteroids are derived in the adrenal cortex. They influence carbohydrate, protein, fat and purine metabolism, electrolyte and water balance, cardiovascular and renal function, skeletal muscles and the nervous system. The

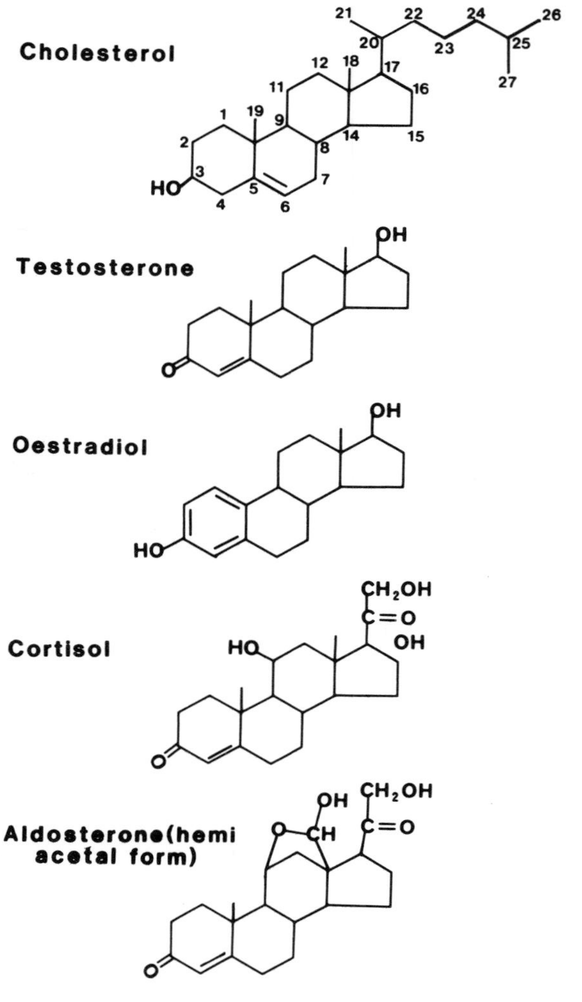

Figure 1. Steroid structures.

mineralocorticoid steroids, for example aldosterone, are generally C_{21},17- deoxy steroids with marked effects on sodium retention in the body. Glucocorticoids, for example cortisol in man and corticosterone in many animal species, have profound effects on glucose metabolism. The biological properties of natural and synthetic corticosteroids vary within a spectrum of each of the above activities.

The secretory activity of the adrenal cortex is regulated by pituitary adrenocortico-trophic hormone (ACTH) particularly with regard to the production of cortisol and cor-ticosterone. However secretion of aldosterone by the adrenal cortex although influenced by ACTH is significantly less dependent on the pituitary and is markedly affected by other factors of which the release of renin from the kidney in response to low sodium is the most important mechanism. Renin is an enzyme which influences the production of angiotensin which in turn stimulates the adrenal synthesis of aldosterone. The pro-duction of androgens and oestrogens by the gonads is also regulated by the pituitary.

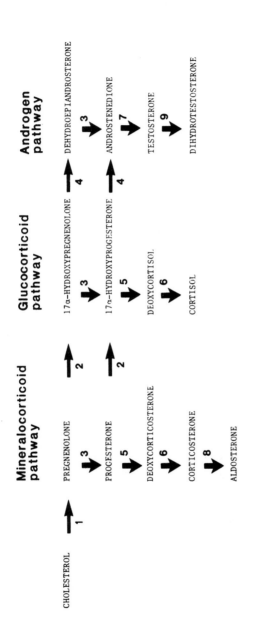

Figure 2. Biosynthesis of steroids.

Table 1. Typical plasma concentrations of steroid hormones in adult humans.

	nmol/l	ng/ml
Cortisol	100 – 700	120
Corticosterone	5 – 30	6
11-Deoxycorticosterone	0.2 – 1.2	0.24
11-Deoxycortisol	4 – 40	7
Progesterone	<2	0.14 males and follicular phase
	>20	
		1.0 (luteal phase)
Testosterone	10 – 30	7
Dehydroepiandrosterone (DHEA)	7 – 30	5
DHEA-sulphate	1000 – 6000	1430
Oestradiol	0.07	0.02
Androstenedione	1 – 3	0.8
11β-Hydroxyandrostenedione	3 – 8	2

Steroid hormones circulate in plasma partly bound to specific (e.g. sex hormone-binding globulin) and non-specific binding (e.g. albumin) proteins. Typical concentrations of total steroids in plasma are summarized in *Table 1*. The general concept of steroid hormone action involves specific binding of the hormone to cytoplasmic receptors, activation and translocation of the steroid – receptor complex to the nucleus, DNA-dependent RNA synthesis and induced protein synthesis which then evoke the appropriate physiological response. Not all steroids conform to this model. Steroids may be metabolized at target tissues and in peripheral tissues. Hence 5α- reduction of androgens is an important step in the action of androgens (and possibly other steroids). In fat tissues androgens may be aromatized to oestrogens. This is possibly the major site of oestrogen production in post-menopausal women. Aldosterone too is rapidly metabolized, principally by the liver but also in the kidney, into a variety of metabolites and conjugates (1) which may be biologically active.

The major metabolic pathways for inactivation of steroids involve reduction of steroid hormones notably by hepatic reduction of the A-ring giving tetrahydro derivatives and by reduction of the C-17 and C-20 carbonyl groups. Most of these reductions give rise to epimeric products although 3α,5β and 20α reductions predominate. In the newborn infant and in adults during drug treatment (e.g. barbiturates, diphenylhydantoin) further hydroxylations of the steroid nucleus at C-1, 6, 16 and 15 are not uncommon and indeed the enzymes may be induced by the drugs. Cortoic acids are a group of cortisol metabolites in which the C-21 hydroxyl group has been oxidized to carboxylic acids recently recognized which represents about 6% of the urinary excretion of the hormone (2).

Following the metabolic reduction of steroid hormones in the liver, conjugates are formed which are regarded as important to aid renal excretion. Typically glucuronides and sulphates are formed by transfer of the acidic groups. Some steroids prefer to be excreted in bile. During passage through the gut these latter steroids may be hydrolysed and acted upon by bacteria in the intestine (3). Some of their products may be re-absorbed, the remainder are excreted in faeces.

Prior to the introduction of radioimmunoassay (RIA) as a technique for measuring steroid hormone concentrations in biological fluids much useful information was gained from the chemical analysis of steroids in urine. The steroid content of a 24 h urine

Table 2. Genetic disorders of steroid biosynthesis in which measurement of precursor concentration in plasma is possible by using h.p.l.c. with current detectors.

	Clinical manifestations	Steroid markers	Typical plasma concentrations (nmol/l)
3β-Hydroxysteroid dehydrogenase/ 5-4 isomerase	Ambiguous genitalia, salt loss	DHEA	50−500
17α-Hydroxylase	Phenotypic female, amenorrhoea, hypertension	Corticosterone	300−2000
21-Hydroxylase	Virilization	17α-hydroxyprogesterone	30−600
11β-Hydroxylase	Virilization, hypertension	11-Deoxycortisol	100−2000
5α-Reductase	Phenotypic female, some masculinization at puberty	5α-Dihydro-testosterone	5−15

collection is an integer of the daily production. When steroids are measured in plasma by RIA very small aliquots can be used (e.g. 50 μl) for the assay. It has been possible to demonstrate not only diurnal variations in steroid concentrations but also pulsatile secretory patterns. Measurement of a steroid concentration in plasma provides insight into the tissue exposure of the hormone so that plasma is a more popular medium for analysis than urine although the latter still provides an important source of information.

The synthesis of steroid hormones from cholesterol involves a number of enzymes. Genetically based disorders of certain of the enzymes have been described and *Table 2* lists their effects on steroid production and metabolism and the extent to which normal corticosteroid levels are perturbed. Most of these conditions are treatable with replacement therapy.

The commercial synthesis of steroids was originally intended to provide hormones for the treatment of adrenal failure. Research into the endocrine physiology of pregnancy and the observation that rheumatoid arthritis improves during pregnancy led to a trial of hydrocortisone in patients with crippling rheumatic diseases. The prompt and striking clinical improvement signalled a new era in modern medicine. On account of their ability to suppress inflammatory and immunological reactions, glucocorticoids are now used in the treatment of a host of diseases. *Figures 3* and *4* include a number of steroidal and non-steroidal drugs which mimic the enzyme deficiencies (Trilostane, aminoglutethimide, metyrapone), which act to inhibit the secretion of trophic peptide hormones, or which inhibit the interaction of steroids with specific target receptors. The contraceptive steroids currently employed were directly derived from basic clinical studies of the endocrinology of the female reproductive system.

3. ROLE OF H.P.L.C. IN STEROID ANALYSIS

Chromatographic techniques have played an important part in the analysis of steroids from a variety of biological fluids (4), tissues as well as in pharmaceutical preparations and food. Final identification of steroids has been based on classical chemical techniques and on physicochemical properties, for example i.r., n.m.r., m.s.

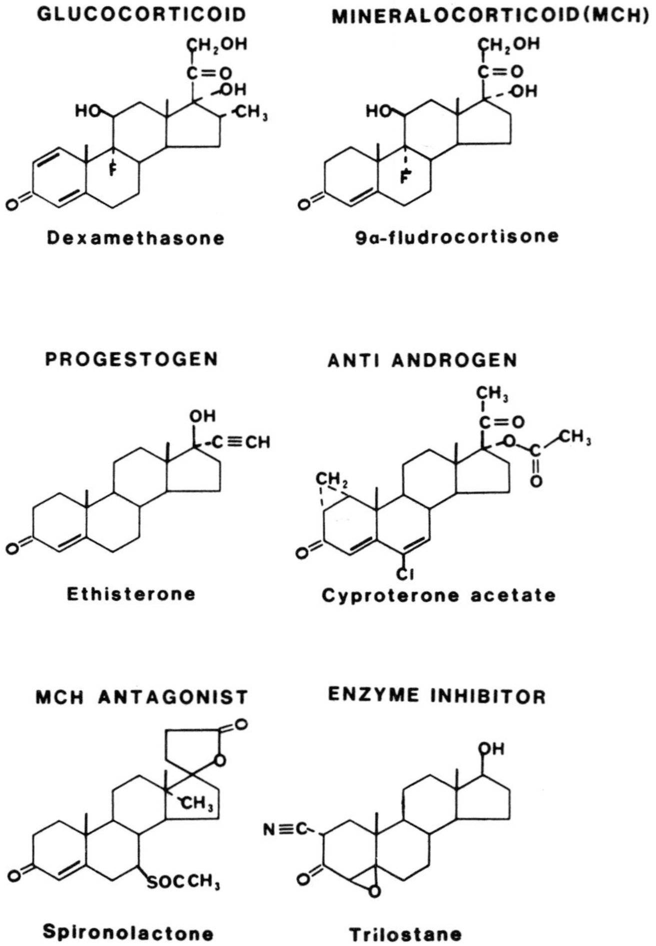

Figure 3. Steroid-based pharmaceuticals in common use. Trilostane is claimed to be an inhibitor of 3β-hydroxy-steroid dehydrogenase.

H.p.l.c. has become an important technique for steroid analysis because:

(i)   it does not require high temperatures;
(ii)   material can be recovered from the column eluate for further analytical procedures;
(iii) it has superior resolution to t.l.c. and paper chromatography;
(iv)   it offers the potential and versatility for separation of intact conjugates.

4. ANALYSIS OF STEROIDS USING H.P.L.C.

4.1 Columns

The separation of steroids with h.p.l.c. is largely directed by the choice of the support. Absorption, partition, ion-exchange, reversed-phase (RP) and reversed-phase ion-pair (RP-IP) chromatography can all effect separation. High-performance silica and alumina

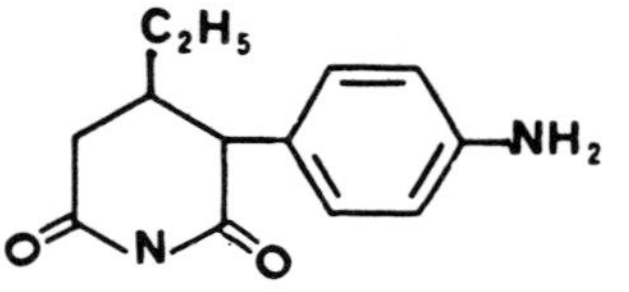

Aminoglutethimide

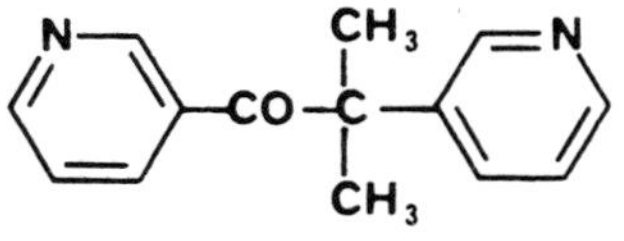

Metyrapone

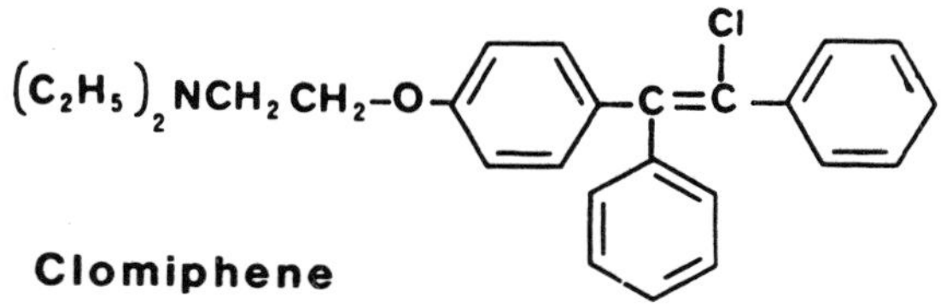

Clomiphene

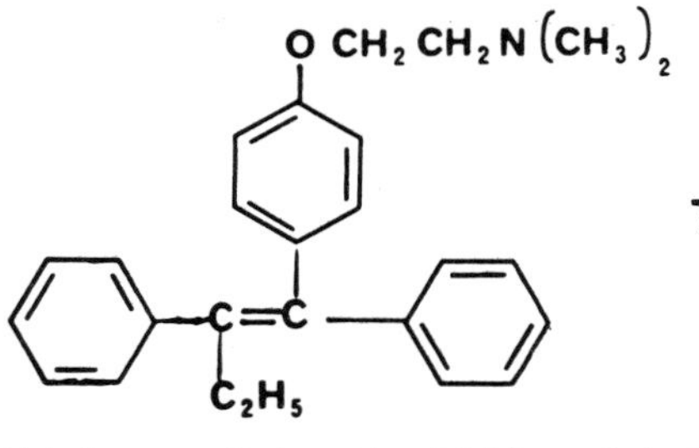

Tamoxifen

Figure 4. Non-steroidal pharmaceuticals used as inhibitors of steroidogenesis or of steroid action.

columns give excellent separation of steroids. RP columns eluted with polar solvent mixtures, usually methanol or acetonitrile with water, are now widely used. Columns with 60 000 − 80 000 theoretical plates per metre are common. These offer excellent resolution and sharp peaks to permit detection to around 1 ng of steroid. Typically columns are 250 − 300 mm in length and around 5 mm internal diameter. Narrow bore columns (1 − 2 mm) may permit increased sensitivity but depending on the volume of sample and the total mass of material in the extract there may be a loss of peak shape and resolution. The risk with RP packings is that very non-polar material will accumulate on the column and reduce selectivity of separation. This can be reduced by the use of a guard column (30 − 70 mm in length) containing the pellicular equivalent of the analytical column. These guard columns are cheap and can be dry-packed. It can also be useful to replace at intervals the first few millimeters of packing from the analytical column.

The complete separation of naturally-occurring mixtures of steroid hormones poses problems due to the wide range of polarities and the tendency for steroids of similar polarity derived from different metabolic pathways to elute in clusters. Careful selection of the stationary phase from the range of commercially available products can enable a system to be devised with high selectivity (5,6). Silica bonded with octadecylsilyl (ODS) or diol groups are most favoured for general use. Packings differ in particle size, porosity and levels of residual accessible silanol groups. O'Hare and Nice have compared the physical characteristics of many packings and established, for various solvent gradients, the resolution and elution order of up to 43 steroids (7). There seems to be no easy means to identify the most suitable packing for a particular separation. Selective properties cannot be firmly attributed to alkyl chain length or to shape of the packing. Certain supports have incomplete coverage of residual silanol groups which affects separation, peak shape and recovery. In some packings about 5% of uncapped silanol groups are particularly reactive due to intramolecular hydrogen bonding. This leaves the phase acidic and may explain the instability of certain steroids. Such supports are not recommended for certain steroids, for example 18-hydroxycorticosterone (8). The extent to which a packing is not covered can be determined by a methyl red absorption test (7).

4.2 Mobile phase

Chromatographic systems suitable for h.p.l.c. of steroids are based upon or can be tested with t.l.c. for the analysis of a single steroid. Useful separations of steroids can be achieved using isocratic chromatography on silica gel with binary solvents. The separation of a range of steroids is best achieved with gradient elution. Retention times are reproducible between runs provided that the column is equilibrated to the starting solvent mixture. Methanol:water gradients effect the separation of the major adrenal steroids. Dioxane is a better choice for the separation of polar adrenal steroids and acetonitrile is preferred for resolving testicular steroids (5). Peak shape and resolution can be improved by maintaining the column at a fixed temperature above ambient, for example $45-60°C$. At these temperatures the eluent viscosity is reduced. If working at ambient temperature, it is advisable to have a room with well controlled temperature to achieve reproducible retention times.

The difficulties in choosing the appropriate column packing for a particular separation have been eased to some extent by using three and four solvents in a mobile phase system. Systematic, statistical procedures for solvent optimization have been developed (9,10). Derks and Drayer (11) reported the separation of very polar 6α and 6β hydroxylated metabolites of cortisol by isocratic elution from a silica column with water:chloroform:methanol. The continued efforts of O'Hare *et al.* (10) to optimize separation of steroids isolated from human tissues have concentrated on the manipulation of mobile phases for selectivity and separation. In order to achieve separation of aldosterone and 18-hydroxycorticosterone in the presence of a large excess of cortisol they used an ODS Hypersil column held at 45°C and a mobile phase of methanol: tetrahydrofuran:water in the ratio 22:4.3:73.3 at 1 ml/min.

When salts are used in the eluting solvent (see Section 6.3.4 on analysis of oestrogen conjugates) these may in the long-term corrode the steel of the columns and tubing.

Oestrogens can be effectively separated when silver nitrate is included in the mobile phase to give 2 g of silver nitrate with 60 ml of methanol, 40 ml water at 0.55 ml/min (12). To prevent metallic silver building up, a water:methanol (50:50 v/v) mobile phase is used each evening to flush excess silver nitrate from the system. Even so a small build-up can occur which requires a rinse with dilute nitric acid or replacement of the tubing when back-pressure rises.

4.3 **Detection**

The α, β unsaturated ketone in the A-ring of naturally-occurring steroid hormones absorbs u.v. light with a maximum around 240 nm and extinction coefficients of 12 000 − 20 000. Isolated carbonyl groups absorb with a maximum at 280 (275 − 285) nm and extinction coefficients 17 − 155. The natural oestrogens have a peak absorption at 280 nm due to the aromatic A-ring. Underivatized phenolic steroids can be detected with sensitivity limits of 100 − 10 pg/ml. Although steroids can absorb u.v. below 200 nm, in practice it is difficult to attain a clear signal from noise without a reduction in sensitivity particularly when solvent gradients are used to elute the steroids. With some gradient elution systems it is necessary to correct for baseline variation by comparison of the response of the eluate from the analytical column with the flow of solvent alone through a reference cell.

The detection and quantitative determination of nanogram quantities of steroids has also been realized by the use of fluorescence (13), refractive index (14) and electrochemical detectors (15). In some cases it has been necessary to react the steroids in the eluate from the column with reagents to form u.v.-absorbing derivatives. Post-column derivatization methods are however restricted to very fast reactions limiting the scope of application (13).

By reference to *Tables 1* and *2*, one can see the limited potential for achieving measurement of steroids in small volumes of plasma or urine, both in normal and pathological situations, by using h.p.l.c. with u.v. absorption with detection limits of nanogram amounts of steroid. The selected applications of this technique (see Section 6) offer useful information.

Flow-through radioactivity detectors are potentially useful for examining the reactions with labelled substrates (16). The short resolution time of the compound in the counting chamber limits sensitivity. Several laboratories have demonstrated the variety and complexity of intermediates and products formed when radioactive steroids are incubated with steroid-metabolizing tissues. Current detection limits for tritium are 10 000 d.p.m. with flow cells incorporating scintillant (∼ 1 % efficiency) to 1000 d.p.m. (50 % efficiency) when the column effluent is mixed with liquid scintillant before passing through a flow cell.

Moving wire flame ionization detection has poor sensitivity (1 μg/ml) and is unsuited to gradient elution systems. Recent reports on coupling h.p.l.c. with mass spectrometry (m.s.) have been reviewed (17) and this method is becoming more widely available.

4.4 **Identification**

The identification of material in chromatograms is usually assumed from a homogeneous peak with an elution time which coincides with that of the reference compound under identical conditions. Since the detectors currently in use are not selective for distinct classes of substances, some further demonstration of specificity is required. 3-Keto-4-ene steroids can be distinguished from other possible compounds eluted from the column by monitoring the u.v. absorption at further wavelengths using a photodiode array detector (18). The sample can also be analysed separately with a different column (preferably of opposite polarity) or a different gradient elution system. Should the identification in each system coincide with the same standards it is highly probable that each chromatogram reflects the same steroid content. These criteria have not been rigidly applied in the published work relating to steroid hormones.

The ultimate system for identification will be h.p.l.c. − m.s. One disadvantage of the use of m.s. with underivatized steroids is the absence of significant molecular ions and the ease with which steroids dehydrate at high temperatures. Transfer of the sample onto a moving belt by a spray depositor/heated nebulizer should prove a reliable l.c. − m.s. interface. Soft ionization techniques may reveal more information than that gained from the fragmentation pattern derived by electron impact m.s. (19) and should be particularly beneficial in the case of steroid conjugates. The potential of h.p.l.c. − m.s. has been recognized for some time but has yet to be realized. The combination of microbore column h.p.l.c. with thermospray m.s. seems to be a most promising system.

4.5 Quantitative method

The height or area of the chromatographic peak is measured manually or with the aid of an integrator and ideally the response of the analyte is compared with the response of an appropriate internal standard. The ratios for standards are plotted for the concentration range of interest. The concentration of an unknown amount of steroid in the sample is determined from the calibration curve. There are a vast number of synthetic steroids available which can be used as internal standards. Typical examples are included in the applications of h.p.l.c. described later in this chapter. Since a number of steroid-based drugs are widely used in hospital patients the use of two very different internal standards, for example 19-nortestosterone and 6α-methyl prednisolone, prevents erroneous results in the case of medication by either one of the steroids selected as internal standard provided that they behave in a similar way to the analyte during the analytical procedure. When internal standards are not used the extraction and injection must be carefully controlled before peak response can be reliably derived from a calibration curve on injected standards. A deferred standard technique can be adopted in which a known amount of the analyte is injected in pure form some time after, but during the chromatographic run of, the unknown sample.

One major drawback to h.p.l.c. lies with the inadequacy of u.v. detectors to provide suitable sensitivity and selectivity for analysis of steroid hormones in plasma or tissue extracts. Coupling with RIA provides the most viable approach (see Sections 6.1.1, 6.1.4 and 6.2.4).

5. PREPARATION OF SAMPLES

5.1 Extraction

5.1.1 *Biological fluids*

Internal standards of tritium-labelled steroids can be added to a sample or extract in

order to check recovery. The sample should be left for some time, for example overnight at 4°C, in order to attain equilibrium of labelled with endogenous hormone.
Steroids have been traditionally extracted from aqueous solutions and tissues by use
of organic solvents, e.g. dichloromethane, ethyl acetate. A high ratio of solvent to
aqueous phase is required to avoid emulsions. Serum is usually mixed for several minutes
by vortexing or rotation. The layers are separated by centrifugation and the aqueous
layer is usually removed by suction. Freezing the aqueous phase (in a bath of dry ice
and methanol) provides a useful method of retaining water in the tube while decanting
an organic layer. To avoid large 'solvent front' effects in the chromatogram the extracts
are washed with 0.1 M base or with hexane to remove saponifiable lipids or non-polar
materials. The organic phase is partly dried by addition of anhydrous sodium sulphate.
A completely dry extract is produced by evaporation under nitrogen or by rotary evaporation under vacuum.

Bradlow first described the use of Amberlite XAD-2 for the extraction of steroids
from an aqueous phase. This resin is a polymer of divinylbenzene as beads which are
packed in a column or used in a tube as a batch extraction procedure. The aqueous
solution of steroids is passed through the column or the resin is mixed continuously
with the solution in a tube before pouring off the supernatant. The XAD-2 is washed
with water and steroids are eluted with an organic solvent, e.g. ethanol. The quality
of Amberlite XAD-2 has not be sustained (20) and some changes in recovery of steroids
have been reported. Also, selective absorption of polar metabolites has been recognized
when monitoring the recovery of radioactivity from kidney extracts after incubation
with radioactive aldosterone (1).

Recently small cartridges containing silica modified by covalently bonding a functional group to the surface, e.g. ODS groups (Sep-Pak C_{18} of Waters Associates, Bond-
Elut C_{18} of Analytichem) have been shown to be ideal for extraction and recovery of
steroids including metabolites and conjugates which are very water soluble (21,22).
Some metabolites of cortisol (notably 1β and 6α hydroxylated metabolites of cortisol
which are important excretory products of the hormone in urine of newborn infants)
(23) and aldosterone (found particularly in renal tissue) are highly polar and are poorly
recovered from water with organic solvents. The particle size and character of the solvent requires that the sample be forced through or sucked through the columns. The
following basic steps are utilized:

(i)   column preparation;
(ii)   sample application and clean-up;
(iii) analyte elution.

Methanol is passed through the column to wet the surface of the packing material. A
flush of water or buffer is then used to displace the methanol. The volumes of washes
used in these steps are not critical — typically being 2 − 5 ml. The sample is then passed
through the column and the compound(s) of interest are retained. One or more washes
with water or solvents can be used to selectively remove salts and other undesirable
compounds. The compound(s) of interest are then eluted with a relatively small amount
of solvent (such as methanol, acetone or ethyl acetate).

Sep-Pak cartridges fit the luer fittings of glass syringes. Practical aspects of the use
of other solid extraction methods are summarized in *Figure 5*. Typically samples can

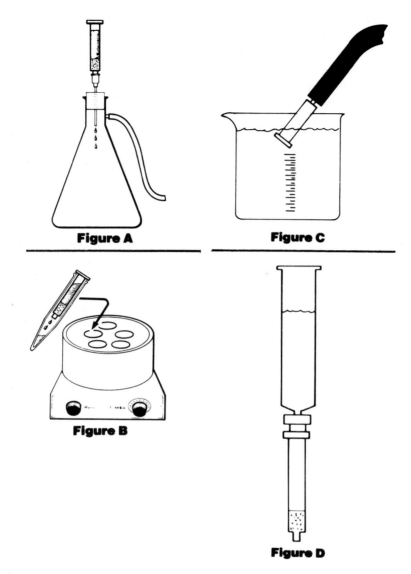

Figure A

Figure C

Figure B

Figure D

Figure 5. Solid-state extraction procedures. For small volume sample equip a sidearm flask with a vacuum source on the sidearm and a rubber stopper in the opening. Push a hypodermic luerhub needle (16 gauge) through the rubber stopper (**A**). Attach a Bond-Elut column to the needle hub. Place sample liquid in column and apply vacuum to draw sample through the column sorbent. Place rinse solutions in column to be drawn through sorbent bed by the vacuum. The column is then detached from the vacuum and suspended in an appropriate test tube. The test tube containing the column is placed in a centrifuge (**B**). Elution solvent is added to the column which is forced through the sorbent and collected in the test tube by centrifugation. For large volume samples attach a vacuum line directly to the column luer tip, immerse the open end of the column in a sample liquid and draw the sample through the column sorbent with vacuum (**C**). Rinses may be drawn by vacuum through the column sorbent to effect removal of residual sample liquid and further purification. Detach Bond-Elut column and proceed with sample elution by centrifugation as previously discussed. For sample volumes larger than the capacity of the Bond-Elut columns, reservoirs and adaptors to attach these reservoirs to Bond-Elut columns are available from Analytichem to accommodate a variety of sample volumes. All adaptors accept any of the reservoirs (**D**). Figure courtesy of Analytichem International.

be processed in a few minutes. The volume of solvent to elute material from the column is usually low (2 – 5 ml) so that solvent can be subsequently evaporated rapidly to leave a dry extract. Certain undesirable compounds which are absorbed on the column may be selectively removed by washing with a specific solvent or buffer prior to final elution. Compounds of interest can be eluted with a solvent selected on the basis of polarity and/or acidity. These columns have also improved markedly the purity of mixtures injected onto h.p.l.c. columns, essentially acting as pre-columns.

Disposable extraction cartridges for liquid – liquid extraction (Clin-Elut, Analytichem) are also available which contain an inert matrix of large surface area. Steroids from an aqueous solution absorb into the matrix, whilst the liquid is allowed to pass through the cartridge. An organic solvent when added interfaces with the sample and passes through the cartridge with dissolved steroids ready for analysis (24). With these cartridges pigments and polar compounds are retained in the cartridge leaving clean extracts for direct h.p.l.c. analysis.

The techniques based on extraction of solutes with solid matrix cartridges are at the point of further refinement to offer the potential for automated analysis. With the commercial systems available at the present time the initial extraction is still a manual or semi-automated process. However, Schoneshofer (25) has reported an automated sample pre-treatment procedure and illustrated the value of the system in the analysis of Triamcinolone in urine. The steroid is extracted from the urine on a pre-column containing PRP-1 (20 – 30 μm). This column is washed with a basic then an acidic solvent and an enriched extract transferred to a second pre-column containing ODS-silica. From this column the purified extract is 'back-flushed' onto the analytical column. Triamcinolone is quantified without an internal standard on the basis of the response of a u.v. absorption detector. This method permits Triamcinolone assays in 48 samples during 1 day. Compared with classical techniques the advantages are:

(i)   unattended analysis;
(ii)   extraction of large volumes of body fluids without contaminating the analytical column;
(iii)   the pre-columns are re-usable.

5.1.2 *Extraction of steroids from tissues*

The analysis of steroids in tissues usually involves lengthy extraction and purification procedures. Chloroform:methanol and acetone:ethanol have been extensively used for extraction of lipids from homogenates of tissues. A cleaner extract is obtained when lipids are extracted with hexane:isopropyl alcohol (26). A method for the combined extraction and purification of steroids from testicular tissue is as follows.

(i)   Cut 1 g of rat testes into pieces.
(ii)   Homogenize with 20 ml of n-hexane/isopropyl alcohol (3:2 v/v).
(iii)   Transfer the homogenate to a flask in an ultrasonic bath for 5 min.
(iv)   Filter into a 100 ml round-bottom flask.
(v)   Wash the homogenate residue with 3 ml of the above solvent and transfer to a round-bottom flask. Repeat twice more.
(vi)   Add 4 ml of Lipidex 1000 previously equilibrated overnight in the above solvent.
(vii)   Evaporate the solvents under vacuum at 25°C in a rotary evaporator.

(viii) Transfer the dry gel to a column (10 mm × 30 cm) with sintered glass at the base and the tip tapered to accept a Sep-Pak cartridge. Wash out the flask with 3 ml of water (repeat three times) in order to transfer all of the gel.

(ix) Suck water through the gel at 0.5 ml/min followed by 20 ml of water.

(x) Elute the steroids with 15 ml of methanol:water (85/15 v/v) at 0.5 ml/min. Collect the eluate.

(xi) Prepare the column (80 × 0.4 cm) of Lipidex 5000 in methanol:water:acetic acid (70:30:0.05 by vol).

(xii) Dilute the steroid eluate with 1 ml of 0.01 M aqueous acetic acid. Pass through the Lipidex column followed by 15 ml of solvent.

(xiii) Collect the eluate and dry.

Lipidex 1000 is inert with low polarity and with the absence of irreversible absorption. The gel acts as a solvent with high capacity for lipids. Inorganic and polar organic materials are readily removed with water. This extraction procedure is superior to the use of silica which binds steroids strongly and causes decomposition of some steroids.

5.2 Pre-column derivatization

Steroid hydrazones formed by reaction of ketosteroids with 2,4-dinitrophenylhydrazine have strong u.v. absorption (maximum 260 nm and extinction around 10 000) as well as visible absorbance (maximum 350 nm, extinction 10 000) giving detection limits for dehydroepiandrosterone sulphate (DHEAS) of 80 ng/ml (27). Kawasaki *et al.* (28) have recently described the measurement of 17-oxosteroid conjugates in urine and serum by h.p.l.c. of dansyl hydrazine derivatives coupled with a fluorescence detector.

5.3 Injection of sample

Extracts are usually dissolved in the mobile phase. The addition of a suitable macro-molecular matrix, e.g. polyethylene glycol to the extracting solvent prior to evaporation improves the recovery of steroids (29) suggesting that the steroids dissolve poorly in the mobile phase alone. Injectors which encompass rubber septa should be avoided. At the high instrument sensitivities often used for the analysis of steroid hormones spurious and irreproducible peaks may occur in the chromatogram. These may reflect the action of injected solvents on the septum. Injection valves are, therefore, preferred.

6. APPLICATIONS

A number of clinical applications have been selected from the literature and from experiments in this laboratory. These include:

(i) methods for direct measurement or purification of a limited number of steroid hormones in biological fluids for diagnostic purposes or for studies of drug kinetics and metabolism;

(ii) separation of a large number of steroid hormones or metabolites after extraction from fluids or tissues.

These studies have enabled:

(i) separation of steroid conjugates;

(ii) metabolic studies of the fate of radioactive steroids and drugs;

(iii)   quantitative determination of several steroids by RIA after separation for purification and for economy of sample size.

6.1 Measurement of selected hormones by h.p.l.c.

The quantitative analysis of cortisol and other endogenous hormones is important in assessing adrenal function. The low physiological concentrations of most steroids have necessitated the use of sensitive assays of which RIA is the most widely used. This latter technique is ideally suited to the measurement of one hormone concentration in a large number of samples and has revolutionized endocrinology. The specificity of each determination is not assured particularly when the current practice of direct estimation is adopted. Methods which incorporate extraction and chromatography are much more reliable. In some cases steroid concentrations have been obtained directly after h.p.l.c. separation with u.v. detection.

6.1.1 *Cortisol*

Solid-state extraction offers significant advantages over liquid—liquid extraction procedures with good recovery and reduction of contamination by the sample extract. Plasma cortisol can be measured (30) as follows.

(i)   Condition a C_{18} extraction column (Baker, Phillipsburg, NJ) with 2×1 ml of methanol followed by 2×1 ml of water under suction.
(ii)   Add corticosterone (as internal standard at 328 ng in 350 μl of methanol) to the serum. Mix and centrifuge for 5 min at 700 *g*.
(iii)   Add serum plus internal standard to the conditioned extraction column. Adjust the negative pressure to a flow of 1 ml in 30 sec.
(iv)   Wash the column with 1 ml of acetone:water (20:80 v/v). Repeat.
(v)   Wash the column with 1 ml of water. Repeat.
(vi)   Elute the cartridge with 200 μl then 100 μl of methanol. Collect the two eluates of methanol. Dry. Dissolve in solvent for h.p.l.c.

The concentration of cortisol is determined from the u.v. response (at 240 nm) of the analyte with reference to added corticosterone as internal standard. The addition of methanol to the sample (as solvent for the corticosterone) seems to improve the recovery of cortisol. An isocratic h.p.l.c. system is adequate for this type of analysis. A μ-Bondapak C_{18} column (300×4.6 mm) is eluted with methanol:water (60:40) at 1 ml/min.

6.1.2 *Corticosterone*

In rats and mice corticosterone is the principal steroid secreted by the adrenals. This hormone has been measured in plasma of both species although 200 μl of plasma is required for the analysis (31) limiting the number of samples of blood which can be taken from small animals.

6.1.3 *Aldosterone*

Aldosterone in solution is generally considered to exist as an equilibrium of the 11,18-hemiacetal form and the free C-18 aldehyde form. A third form has a hemiketal bridge between C-11 and C-18 and C-18, C-20. There is i.r. and n.m.r. evidence for all three species which can be separated by h.p.l.c. using a Si-10 column (Chrompak) with a mobile phase of chloroform:iso-octane:methanol:water (71:25:3.75:0.25 by vol) at a flow-rate of 80 ml/h (32). The conversion between forms does not take place in acidified water or acidified methanol but is rapid (100 min) in 0.067 M NaOH in 85% methanol and slow when in contact with the support phase of the h.p.l.c. column suspended in ethanol.

6.1.4 *18-Hydroxycorticosterone*

Marked elevation of 18-hydroxycorticosterone, a major by-product of adrenal aldosterone biosynthesis, is found in primary aldosteronism due to adrenal adenoma and with 17α-hydroxylase deficiency syndrome but not in idiopathic aldosteronism due to adrenal hyperplasia and with normal and low renin essential hypertension. Measurement of plasma 18-hydroxycorticosterone, together with aldosterone, is very useful in the differential diagnosis of certain hypertensive disorders.

H.p.l.c. has been applied to the separation and measurement of 18-hydroxycorticosterone in serum and adrenal tissue extracts (33).

(i)　　To 0.5 ml of plasma add 1 ml of 1 M NaOH and 20 ml of dichloromethane. Shake. Remove the aqueous layer.

(ii)　　Wash the dichloromethane extract with water before drying under nitrogen.

(iii)　　Dissolve the extract in methanol:water (2:1 v/v).

The conditions for h.p.l.c. are:

Pre-column:　　　　　　Finepak SIL C_{18} (10 μm)
Analytical column:　　　Finepak SIL C_{18} (5 μm)
Column temperature:　　37°C
Eluent:　　　　　　　　0.005 M aqueous HCl:methanol (35:65 v/v) at 1 ml/min
Detector:　　　　　　　245 nm.

An RP-h.p.l.c. system is used so as to elute 18-hydroxycorticosterone with an isocratic solvent system at a relatively early retention time. The mean recovery of 18-hydroxycorticosterone is 70%. 18-Hydroxycorticosterone is measured by RIA (34).

6.1.5 *Oestriol*

Oestrogens are measured when evaluating the integrity of the foeto-placental unit during the third trimester of pregnancy. In pregnancies complicated by toxaemia, hypertension and diabetes mellitus where the foetus may be distressed, oestriol production is lowered and this determination is used in association with the measurement of human placental lactogen and of foetal monitoring with ultrasound scanning to define foetal distress. Problems with collection of accurate 24 h urines have prompted the development of oestriol assays for serum.

(i)　　Pipette 1 ml of serum onto a dry Clin-Elut cartridge (Analytichem). Wait 3 min for the serum to absorb into the column.

(ii)　　Place an acid-washed 12 ml glass centrifuge tube under the column.

(iii)　　Elute the column with 5 ml of extraction solvent (dichloromethane:propan-2-ol 95:5 v/v).

(iv)   Wait 5 min.
(v)   Add 4 ml of extraction solvent.
(vi)   Combine the extracts.
(vii)   Discard the column.
(viii)   Evaporate the solvent to dryness.
(ix)   Reconstitute the extract in 50 μl of h.p.l.c. mobile phase.

H.p.l.c. conditions are:

Column:	250 × 4.6 mm Ultrasphere octyl (Beckman)
Mobile phase:	acetonitrile:phosphate buffer 23:77 (v/v)
Flow:	3 ml/min
Column temperature:	50°C
Detector:	fluorescence — 280 nm excitation (308 nm emission).

Using fluorimetric detection, oestriol sensitivity to 500 ng/l is adequate for quantification of the hormone in 1 ml of serum (28). Oestriol is eluted rapidly from the column so that 10 serum samples can be processed in 1.5 h.

6.1.6 *Testosterone*

Testosterone is the major androgen synthesized by the mammalian testis. The concentration of the hormone in spermatic venous effluent (1 ml) of rabbit testis can be determined using RP-h.p.l.c. with a flow-through spectrophotometer (35). 11β-hydroxy-4-androstene-3,17-dione is a sensible choice of internal standard, with similar behaviour to the analyte in the procedure whilst being an androgen derived only by the adrenal gland. Such an assay would not be sufficiently specific for measurement of peripheral concentrations of testosterone.

6.1.7 *Dehydroepiandrosterone sulphate*

The quantitative determination of DHEAS, one of the principle adrenal secretory products in man, is valuable for assessing certain adreno-cortical disorders (36).

(i)   To 0.1 ml of human serum in a centrifuge tube add 2 ml of acetonitrile.
(ii)   After extraction separate the layers by centrifugation.
(iii)   Add 2-hydroxyoestrone-3-methyl ether as an internal standard (100 ng) to the organic phase and dry the solvent at 40°C under nitrogen.
(iv)   To the residue, add 10 μl of p-nitrophenylhydrazine, 100 μl of trichloroacetic acid (TCA)−benzene (30 mg/10 ml) and heat the mixture at 60°C for 20 min.
(v)   Evaporate the reagents and re-dissolve the residue in 200 μl of methanol.

A μ-Bondapak C_{18} column is most suitable for separation of conjugated steroids using methanol:0.5% ammonium dihydrogen phosphate (8:3 v/v) as mobile phase. Using an electrochemical detector, DHEAS is detected at 360 pg. Interference from unused reagents and endogenous polar substances due to saturation of the output of the detector is a problem that may be overcome by removing the connection to the detector for about 5 min after injection. For the purpose of assessing the reliability of the method, DHEAS determined by h.p.l.c. in 14 normal male volunteers aged 24−38 years agrees with results from direct RIA without hydrolysis (Y = 0.98X + 0.011).

6.1.8 *Re-purification of partly degraded radiolabelled steroids*

Radiolabelled steroids are widely used these days as analytical reagents in competitive protein binding assays. In these assays degradation of radiolabelled steroids stored in phosphate-buffered saline (PBS) is detected by an increase in the non-specific binding (NSB). When the NSB relative to total counts exceeds 5% the label can be purified by differential partitioning of intact and degraded molecules between the aqueous phase and anhydrous diethyl ether as follows.

(i)   Transfer the stock solution of [^{3}H]progesterone (of $\sim$ 150 000 c.p.m./100 μl) in 1.0 M PBS containing gelatin (0.1%).

(ii)   Add 5 volumes of anhydrous diethyl ether.

(iii)   Vortex mix for 2 min.

(iv)   Leave to stand for 5 min.

(v)   Freeze the aqueous phase at $-40°$C.

(vi)   Decant the organic phase.

(vii)   Evaporate the ether under a nitrogen stream at 50°C.

(viii) Re-dissolve the label in buffer.

(ix)   Measure the radioactivity and NSB relative to total counts.

(x)   Adjust the counts to 10 000 c.p.m. per 100 μl.

(xi)   Take 600 μl of diluted label, add 400 μl of distilled water containing 1 μg of radio-inert steroid.

(xii)   Mix. Inject 100 μl onto a h.p.l.c. column (μ-Bondapak) equilibrated and eluted with methanol:water (3:2 v/v) at 1.0 ml/min.

(xiii) Collect 1 ml aliquots of the eluates.

(xiv)   Transfer the fraction to a liquid scintillation vial containing 10 ml of scintillant cocktail.

(xv)   Count the radioactivity.

The degree of purification can be checked by collecting fractions from an h.p.l.c. column (C_{18} μ-Bondapak) (37) eluted with a mobile phase of methanol:water (3:2 v/v) at 1 ml/min. Partly degraded material elutes as polar material ($\sim$ 5 min) relative to the native labelled progesterone (retention time 37 min). The purified progesterone gives lower NSB (1%) when re-tested in the assay. Chromatographic conditions have also been reported for the purification of oestradiol labelled with [^{125}I]iodine (38).

6.1.9 *Preparative purification of synthetic steroids*

In order to develop methods for measuring the concentration of steroids in plasma it may be necessary to synthesize the required compounds. Semi-preparative h.p.l.c. (for $1-10$ mg of steroid) can be used to purify the material using a wide bore column ($2-3$ cm). Some applications of this technology follow.

Excessive production or administration of certain adrenal steroids is known to produce hypertension in clinical and experimental situations. ACTH will stimulate adrenal steroid synthesis and cause an increase in blood pressure. In sheep this is associated with highly significant increases in the blood levels of cortisol, 11-deoxycortisol, corticosterone and deoxycorticosterone. Infusion of these steroid hormones (at rates appropriate to give blood concentrations similar to conditions of ACTH stimulation) do not reproduce the blood pressure effects of ACTH. Additional steroid hormones are postulated for the rise in blood pressure. 20α-Dihydroprogesterone and 20α-dihydro,17α-hydroxyprogesterone have been identified in sheep adrenal venous blood. Their concentration increases on ACTH stimulation of the adrenal. With the addition of these steroids to the above-mentioned steroid infusion it is possible to reproduce the blood effects of ACTH (39).

In order to synthesize these C-20-reduced steroids, progesterone and 17α-hydroxy-progesterone are reacted with lithium aluminium hydride before oxidation of the oxygen at C-3 with manganese dioxide. The total products are probably best identified by g.c. and g.c. −m.s. analysis.

The extract, after reduction and re-oxidation of progesterone, is converted to a methyloxime-trimethylsilyl ether form (MO-TMS) which is analysed on g.c. and g.c. −m.s. The g.c. chromatogram shows a number of peaks, two of which have the same retention times as reference 20β- and 20α-dihydroprogesterone. These represent about 68% and 12% of the total steroid. The g.c. −m.s. analysis of the crude extract of C-20-reduced progesterone indicates the presence of isomers of pregn-4-ene-3,20-diol. The four isomers of pregnene-3,20-diol can be identified by their g.c. retention times and comprise the following proportions of the crude extract:

Pregn-4-ene-3α,20β-diol	(5.1%)
Pregn-4-ene-3α,20α-diol	(0.7%)
Pregn-4-ene-3β,20β-diol	(10.1%)
Pregn-4-ene-3β,20α-diol	(1.3%)

A g.c. profile of the MO-TMS derivatives of 17α-hydroxyprogesterone reduced in the above manner also indicates several products of the reaction. G.c. −m.s. analysis confirms the presence of four isomers of pregnene-triol, presumably with the same configuration for the C-3 and C-20 hydroxyl groups as in the above pregnenediols and with the C-17α-hydroxyl retaining its configuration. With this extract, the pregnene-triols and the unreacted 17α-hydroxyprogesterone represent 28% of the total steroid impurity in the extract, with 25% of 20α-reduced 17α-dihydroxyprogesterone and 46% of 20β-reduced isomer. In contrast to the number of peaks detected in the g.c. analysis, the h.p.l.c. separation (gradient elution) of the above extracts shows few u.v.-absorbing peaks. The steroids can be eluted from an ODS-Hypersil column (0.5 × 28 cm) with a solvent gradient from 10 to 90% acetonitrile in water over 20 min at 1 ml/min. The steroids of interest have the following retention times:

17α,20α-dihydroxyprogesterone	10.7 min
17α,20β-dihydroxyprogesterone	11.4 min
20α-dihydroprogesterone	13.8 min
20β-dihydroprogesterone	15.6 min

The required products can be purified from the extracts by using semi-preparative h.p.l.c. coupled with a u.v. detector set at 254 nm. For the separation of free steroids a RP column (2.0 cm i.d. × 25 cm) with ODS-Hypersil packing is eluted isocratically for reduced 17α-hydroxyprogesterone using 50% acetonitrile in water and for reduced progesterone 60% acetonitrile in water. The required steroids in the extract are identified by comparison of their retention times with those of reference steroids. The peaks

Table 3. Applications of semi-preparative h.p.l.c. in purification of synthetic steroids.

2-Hydroxyoestrone-3-methyl ether
4-Hydroxyoestrone-3-methyl ether
16,18-Dihydroxy DHEA
18-Hydroxycorticosterone
11-hydrogen succinate and 11-glucuronic acid of oestriol
[26,27-^{2}H$_6$] and ^{2}H-labelled 24,25-dihydroxycholesterols

---

Taken from references 40,41.

corresponding to the compounds of interest are collected. A portion of the purified extract is again derivatized as MO-TMS and analysed by g.c. The g.c. profiles of the purified extracts confirmed the purity of 20α-dihydroprogesterone at 95% and about 82% for the 20α,17α-dihydroprogesterone after one purification step. Greater purification is possible by re-cycling of the fractions.

Further examples of the use of semi-preparative h.p.l.c. can be found in publications of Professor D.N.Kirk of the MRC Steroid Reference Collection (40,41). Some recent examples are summarized in *Table 3*. Ethyl acetate:hexane and ethyl acetate:light petroleum (b.p. 60−80°C) are favoured for these separations with a silica column of 2−3 cm × 25 cm.

6.2 Diagnostic profiles

6.2.1 *Congenital adrenal hyperplasia*

In normal and certain pathological situations concentrations of a limited number of steroid hormones are within the range of detection with current h.p.l.c. techniques. Hence, in congenital adrenal hyperplasia (CAH), due to deficiencies of the 21-hydroxylase or 11β-hydroxylase, high circulating levels of cortisol precursors are found in plasma. 17α-Hydroxyprogesterone and 11-deoxycortisol respectively are markers for these disorders (see *Table 2*). In 21-hydroxylase deficiency 17α-hydroxyprogesterone has been determined in plasma both by h.p.l.c. and by RIA (42).

(i)   Pipette 1 ml of serum into an extraction tube.
(ii)   Add [^{3}H]17α-hydroxyprogesterone and [^{3}H]11-deoxycortisol.
(iii)   Vortex for 2 min.
(iv)   Centrifuge for 10 min at 3000 *g*.
(v)   Remove the aqueous layer.
(vi)   Wash the organic layer with 1 ml of 0.1 M NaOH.
(vii)   Wash the organic layer with 1 ml of water.
(viii) Repeat the water wash.
(ix)   Dry the organic layer under nitrogen.
(x)   Dissolve the extract in 0.5 ml of mobile phase.
(xi)   Inject an aliquot of extract onto a C$_{18}$-μ-Bondapak column.
(xii)   Elute the column with acetonitrile:water (43:57 v/v) for 17α-hydroxyprogesterone; methanol:water (60:90 v/v) for 11-deoxycortisol and cortisol at 1 ml/min.
(xiii) Collect the eluates as peaks of 17α-hydroxyprogesterone and 11-deoxycortisol are eluted (previously determined by injection of standards and detected by their u.v. absorbance).

(xiv) Count the radioactivity for calculation of recovery.
(xv)   Measure the peak heights.
(xvi) Compare the result with a standard curve covering the range $5-6$ ng of steroids.
(xvii) Correct the results for method losses.

The results by the two methods over the range $9-56$ ng/ml are in good agreement. 11-Deoxycortisol is present at $36-80$ ng/ml in subjects with CAH due to 11β-hydroxylase deficiency.

6.2.2 *Metyrapone test*

The administration of metyrapone (11β-hydroxylase inhibitor, see *Figure 4*) results in elevated 11-deoxycortisol concentrations in plasma. The concomitant analysis of cortisol (43) provides a measure of adrenal inhibition. In most RIA methods the elevated 11-deoxycortisol concentrations may cause falsely elevated cortisol values because of cross-reaction with the antibodies. One further problem is that even in the single dose version of the metyrapone test the drug is present in plasma in μg/ml quantities.

(i)   Pipette 1 ml of plasma into an acid-washed glass extraction tube with PTFE-lined screwcap.
(ii)   Add dexamethasone (300 μl of 5 μg/ml in acetonitrile:methanol 1:1 v/v).
(iii)   Add 0.3 ml of 1 M HCl and 15 ml of dichloromethane.
(iv)   Cap the tube. Shake for 15 min.
(v)   Centrifuge at 2000 *g* for 10 min.
(vi)   Aspirate the aqueous layer and creamy interface.
(vii)   Wash the organic phase with 1 ml of 0.1 M NaOH.
(viii) Wash the organic phase with 1 ml of water.
(ix)   Add 1 g of anhydrous sodium sulphate.
(x)   Dry the organic phase under nitrogen.
(xi)   Reconstitute the residue in 250 μl of mobile phase.
(xii)   Couple the pre-column (HC-Peltosil 70 $\times$ 6 mm) to the analytical column (Zorbax-SIL 250 $\times$ 6 mm).
(xiii) Equilibrate the column with hexane:dichloromethane:ethanol:acetic acid (26:69:3.4:1 by vol). Elute the column at 2 ml/min.
(xiv)   Detector — u.v. absorption 254 nm.

This method has achieved simultaneous measurement of cortisol and 11-deoxycortisol and the selective extraction of steroids without metyrapone.

Retention times of steroids (natural and synthetic) are found in *Table 4*. This method is also applicable to the diagnosis of CAH due to a defect of the 11β-hydroxylase.

6.2.3 *Metabolism and pharmacokinetics of steroid-based drugs*

The capability of h.p.l.c. for the analysis of pharmaceuticals and for pharmacokinetic studies has been reviewed by Smith (44). The following examples illustrate the value of other techniques in complementing h.p.l.c. data.

Cyproterone acetate and its metabolites can be identified in urine by capillary column

Table 4. Relative chromatographic retention times of steroids (cortisol = 10 min) for h.p.l.c. separation (Zorbax-SIL) using hexane:dichloromethane:ethanol:acetic acid (26:69:3.4:1 by vol).

Deoxycorticosterone	0.31
11-Deoxycortisol	0.45
Fluocinolide	0.51
Cortisone	0.56
Corticosterone	0.57
Methyl prednisone	0.58
Prednisone	0.66
Beclomethasone	0.73
Aldosterone	0.84
Betamethasone	0.86
Dexamethasone	0.93
Cortisol	1.00
Methylprednisolone	1.2
Prednisolone	1.3

g.c. of steroids isolated from the urine of a patient receiving this drug (*Figure 6*) (4). A Sep-Pak extract of urine can be separated on a C_{18} h.p.l.c. column with a u.v. spectrometer set at 286 nm. *Figure 7* shows the h.p.l.c. response of the extract. The peak corresponding to cyproterone acetate (20.5 min) and its metabolite (16.8 min) can be collected for further characterization by m.s. Methyloxime trimethylsilyl ether derivatives can be prepared and analysed on g.c. and g.c.−m.s. The mass spectrum of the metabolite (mol. wt 562) indicates monohydroxylation of cyproterone acetate and the hydroxyl group is assumed to be at C-15 (45). This metabolite is thought to be more active than the native drug (46).

The metabolism of trilostane has also been studied by using h.p.l.c. analysis of the drug in plasma.

(i)   Add 1 ml of sodium acetate buffer (0.05 M, pH 5.0) to 2.0 ml of plasma in a stoppered tube. Mix.

(ii)   Add 10 ml of chloroform. Mix for 5 min on a rotating mixer.

(iii)   Centrifuge the tubes at 2000 *g* for 5 min.

(iv)   Remove the upper aqueous layer.

(v)   Dry the chloroform by addition of 1 g of anhydrous sodium sulphate.

(vi)   Transfer 5 ml of the chloroform extract to a clean glass vial. Dry in a vacuum at 45°C.

(vii)   Dissolve the extract in the mobile phase (methanol:0.1 M aqueous formic acid 1:1 v/v).

(viii) H.p.l.c. column: 5 μm ODS Hypersil (150 × 4.6 mm) at 30°C.

(ix)   Eluent flow: 2 ml/min.

(x)   U.v. detector: 254 nm.

(xi)   Trilostane: 6 min; 17-ketotrilostane: 7 min; ethisterone (internal standard): 12 min.

In plasma taken at intervals over 8 h after a 120 mg dose of trilostane the native drug and a metabolite (17-ketotrilostane) can be detected by their u.v. absorption. Concentrations greater than 200 pM in the ratio of 1 to 3 are found within 1 h of taking the drug (47). Both compounds are cleared from the blood in 6−8 h although the time

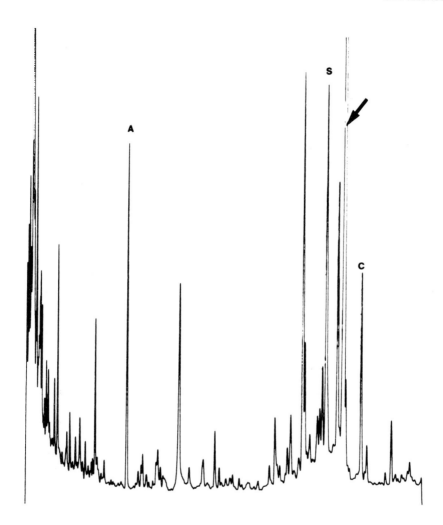

Figure 6. G.c. profile of steroids in urine of a child treated wtih cyproterone acetate. Conjugated steroids were hydrolysed enzymatically and all native steroids were analysed as MO-TMS (persilyl) derivatives. The arrow indicates the peak due to an important metabolite of cyproterone acetate.

of peak level varies considerably between individuals. The h.p.l.c. separation with u.v. detection revealed only limited information on the drug metabolism because other metabolites have been reduced in the A-ring and have minimal u.v. absorption. H.p.l.c. may be useful for separation and isolation of the metabolites which can be best characterized, when purified, by their properties in i.r. and n.m.r. spectroscopy. It is necessary to use g.c. as a non-specific detection system for purified materials. In the analysis for metabolites of trilostane in urine by using capillary column g.c. separation of an MO-TMS derivative of the urine extract, at least eight metabolites can be detected by their response in a flame ionization detector. This profile does not display the diagnostic features of a profile of steroids from urine of a child with a deficiency of 3β-hydroxy-steroid dehydrogenase and the data for the trilostane-treated subjects do not support

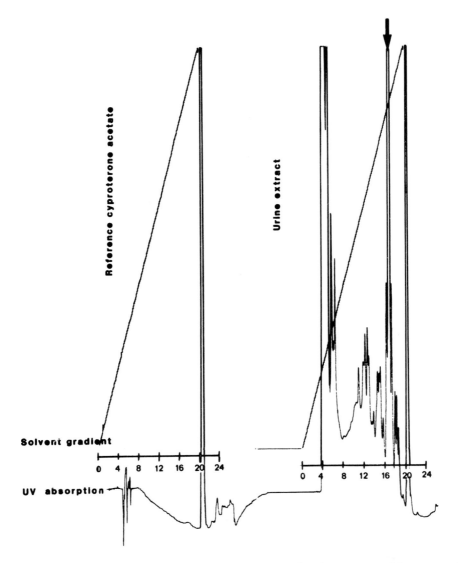

Figure 7. RP-h.p.l.c. separation of reference cyproterone acetate and a urine extract containing a more polar metabolite (arrowed) using gradient elution of acetonitrile:water and u.v. detection (286 nm).

inhibition of the adrenal enzyme. In a separate g.c. − m.s. analysis mass spectra can be obtained of each metabolite but, in common with electron impact m.s. of drugs, structural information is lacking in the fragmentation pattern of these compounds. Hence, h.p.l.c. and g.c. can be complementary although l.c. − m.s. will prove valuable in such investigations.

6.2.4 *Multiple measurements of steroid hormones by combination of automated h.p.l.c. and RIA*

If several steroids have to be determined simultaneously in one sample a separation

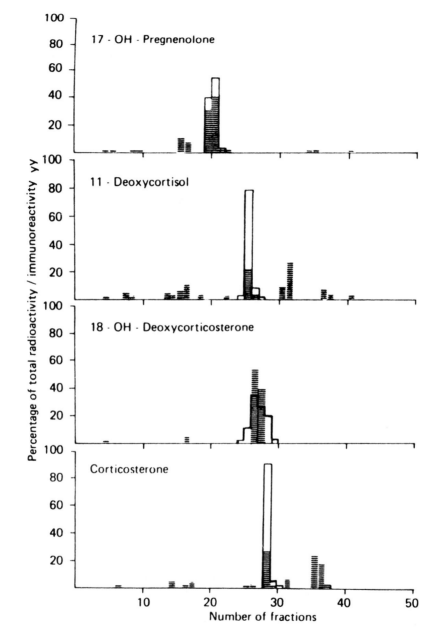

Figure 8. Profiles of immunoreactivity (hatched area) and [³H]steroid radioactivity (open area) arising in the h.p.l.c. fractions of the ether extracts of normal serum samples. Values are plotted as percentage of total immunoreactivity and radioactivity, respectively. Volume of each fraction is 1.3 ml. ³H-Radioactivity added to the serum sample was 4×10^3 d.p.m.

of steroids is obligatory. This is particularly true of a requirement in paediatric endocrinology to economize on sample size. Separation of steroids by h.p.l.c. with gradient elution not only permits the analysis of several hormones in the same extract but also

Table 5. Recovery of [^{3}H]steroids during the h.p.l.c. assay procedure preceding RIA.

Steroid	Overall recovery mean ± S.D. (%)
Progesterone	59.5 ± 7.5
Pregnenolone	62.1 ± 7.8
Deoxycorticosterone (DOC)	62.4 ± 4.9
17α-Hydroxyprogesterone	63.6 ± 8.0
17α-Hydroxypregnenolone	63.3 ± 17.6
11-Deoxycortisol	69.4 ± 15.1
18-Hydroxy-DOC	43.5 ± 15.0
Corticosterone	60.2 ± 15.8
Aldosterone	56.7 ± 13.6
Cortisol	66.0 ± 8.4
18-Hydroxycorticosterone	55.3 ± 4.4

increases the specificity of the RIA determination by removing steroids which are known (or not known) to react with the antibodies. Schoneshofer *et al.* (48) illustrate this point by collecting fractions from an h.p.l.c. separation of plasma steroids and for each antibody looking for immunoreactivity in all fractions of the column eluates. Considerable immunoreaction can be detected in some fractions (see *Figure 8*) remote from the elution position of the required analyte. This would be accounted for in a direct RIA analysis for the steroid without a chromatographic separation.

A method for simultaneous measurement of steroids in plasma can follow the approach given below.

(i)   *Extraction.*

(a)   To 1 ml of serum add ^{3}H -labelled steroids (about 5000 d.p.m. of each dissolved in 100 μl of water) (see *Table 5*).

(b)   Transfer to an 'Extrelut' column.

(c)   Elute with 20 ml of ether.

(d)   Evaporate.

(e)   Re-dissolve in 150 μl of n-hexane:iso-propanol (95:5, v/v).

High-performance liquid chromatography.

(a)   Transfer to an autosampler.

(b)   Automatic injection and chromatography.

(c)   Automatic collection of individual steroid fractions.

(d)   Evaporate the individual fractions.

(e)   Re-dissolve in appropriate amounts of water.

(f)   Count for ^{3}H-radioactivity in the appropriate aliquots for recovery of each steroid.

(iii)   *Radioimmunoassay.*

(a)   100 μl of sample (duplicate) or standard (1600−6.26 pg) in triplicates + 800 μl of γ-globulin buffer containing [^{3}H]steroid (RIA radioactivity) and steroid antiserum.

(b)   Incubate for at least 2 h at 4°C.

(c)   Add 100 μl of charcoal suspension.

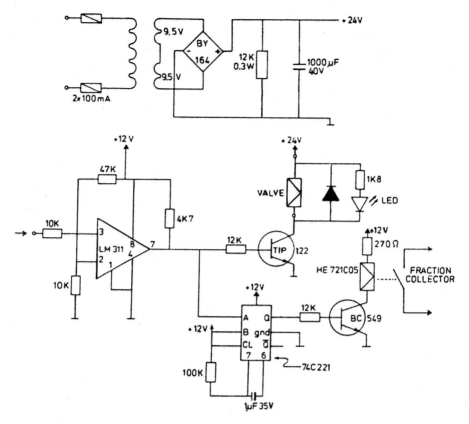

Figure 9. Circuit diagram of interface and connections between data module, fraction collector and steroid valve. The 12 V d.c. output on the data module is used to feed the interface. The timed event output (normally + 5 V d.c.) drops to ground potential upon activation, thus triggering the voltage comparator LM 331 which in turn triggers transistor TIP 122 and the valve is actuated. When the timed event output reverts to + 5 V d.c. the valve returns to its normal position, diverting the eluate from the l.c. column to a waste container. Through IC SN74C221 triggering transistor BC 549 the voltage comparator activates the Reed relay which causes the fraction collector to step. A light-emitting diode is connected in parallel to the valve's coil and provides visual inspection of the switching of the valve.

(d)   Shake and centrifuge (10 min at 4°C, 3300 *g*).

(e)   Decant.

(f)   Count for ^{3}H-radioactivity of the bound fraction.

(g)   Calculate the results.

The following seem to be crucial to the success of the h.p.l.c. manipulation before the RIA of the steroids:

(i)   establishing reproducible conditions (see Section 4.2);

(ii)   collection of fractions of the column eluate;

(iii)   establishing recovery of the steroids throughout the procedure.

Recoveries of steroids throughout such a procedure are high (*Table 5*). A practical solution to the issue of fraction collection is considered in a paper by Stoks and Benraad (*Figure 9*). These workers selected h.p.l.c. conditions to concentrate the elution of compound from the column to within 1 ml and achieved total separation of steroids in 15 ml. A data module (Waters Associates model 730) is coupled to an interface which activates a 3-port solenoid switching valve to allow collection of appropriate timed fractions in a fraction collector or to direct the eluate to waste (49).

In paper chromatography it has been common practice to include certain coloured dyes in the separation and to relate the retention of the steroids to the dyes. This may be a worthwhile approach when identifying the relative location of tubes filled with h.p.l.c. eluates.

6.3 H.p.l.c. analysis of steroids in urine

Steroid concentrations in blood can exhibit episodic variation and diurnal periodicity. Also the circulating concentration of total hormone does not always correlate with the bioactivity because the levels of binding protein vary. For these reasons, and others, steroids in a 24 h urine are measured as an integer of daily production. Also the excretion in urine of free steroid hormones is a useful index of circulating free hormone and correlates with the bioactivity of the available hormone.

6.3.1 *Cortisol in urine*

Urinary free cortisol is generally accepted to give a reliable index of plasma free cortisol in the diagnosis of glucocorticoid excess. When free cortisol in urine is analysed by h.p.l.c. after pre-treatment by the usual organic extraction, interfering substances having chromatographic behaviour similar to cortisol and the internal standard preclude accurate measurement. To remove these substances (50) the organic extract can be cleaned up by normal phase h.p.l.c. (Zorbax-SIL, 150 × 4.6 mm) prior to the analytical RP separation (Zorbax-CN, 250 × 4.6 mm). The mobile phase for the first column is the organic layer of a mixture of 20 ml of water, 40 ml of ethanol and 960 ml of dichloromethane. For the RP column, methanol:water (40:60) enables separation in 30 min.

A ternary system of tetrahydrofuran:methanol:water (24.5:2.5:73 by vol) containing ammonium acetate (0.05% w/v) has potential for the analysis of cortisol in urine with isocratic solvent elution. In this system retention times are:

Prednisone:	15.5 min.
Cortisone:	17.7 min.
Prednisolone:	20.8 min.
Cortisol:	22.3 min.
Fludrocortisone:	27.1 min.
11-Deoxycortisol:	32.8 min.

This separation affords discrimination of an abnormal cortisol production (*Figure 10*) and 9α-fludrocortisone could be incorporated as an internal standard (Bartlett and Wright, personal communication).

6.3.2 *Analysis of steroid carboxylic acids by h.p.l.c.*

Cortoic acids are devoid of chromophores which absorb in the near u.v. In order to measure these steroids in the urine it is necessary to convert them to derivatives. *p*-Bromophenacyl esters can be formed quantitatively and reproducibly, absorb in the

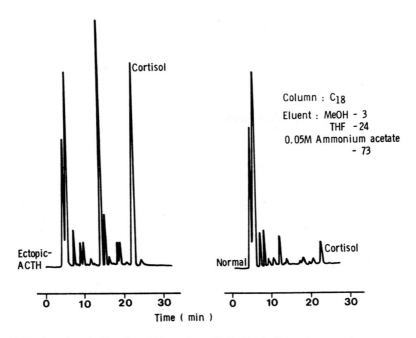

Figure 10. H.p.l.c. of cortisol in urine of **(a)** a patient with Cushing's disease due to cortisol excess provoked by an ectopic ACTH-secreting tumour and **(b)** a normal subject.

Table 6. Retention times of steroid acids as *p*-bromophenacyl esters separated on Zorbax ODS with methanol: water mobile phase.

	min
20α-Cortisoloic acid	18.1
20β-Cortisoloic acid	28.6
20α-Cortisonic acid	20.7
20β-Cortisonic acid	38.7
20α-Cortolic acid	24.0
20β-Cortolic acid	48.0
20α-Cortolonic acid	30.9
20β-Cortolonic acid	51.6
Dibromoacetophenone	7.1

u.v. with maximum at 254 nm and are separated on Zorbax ODS columns (250 by 5 mm) with methanol:water mixtures (2.2 ml/min) as mobile phase (51). The column is maintained at 40°C. Acids can be derivatized by reaction with alkyl bromides under basic conditions with 18-crown-6-ether as catalyst. Derivatives are prepared in screw-cap vials with Teflon-covered rubber septa (supplied by Pierce Chemical Company). Reagents are mixed using Teflon-covered magnets. Steroid acids epimeric at C-20 are well separated (*Table 6*). Improved resolution of 11-oxo and 11-hydroxy equivalents requires a second column to be coupled in series. This raises back pressure from 3000 to 4000 p.s.i. and flow-rate is reduced to 1.5 ml/min. The lower limit of detection with an 8 mm flow cell is 0.5 nM which is adequate for the estimation of steroid acids in human urine. Further improvements in sensitivity are likely with fluorescent chromophores.

6.3.3 *Assay of aldosterone in urine*

Aldosterone-18-glucuronide is an important urinary metabolite of aldosterone. This conjugate is uniquely hydrolysed at pH 1 at room temperature for 24 h. Hence, urine can be extracted with an organic solvent, e.g. dichloromethane to remove free steroids and, after hydrolysis of the aldosterone-18-glucuronide, free aldosterone is extracted with dichloromethane. The liberated aldosterone has been quantified by using RIA, by g.c. of the γ-lactone (periodate oxidation product) and by g.c. −m.s. De Vries *et al.* (52) have described an h.p.l.c. analysis of a urine extract. Aldosterone is quantified against prednisolone as an internal standard. The assay is said to be more precise and more sensitive than the g.c. assay with which it is compared, although the method is extremely tedious, relying upon three separations including t.l.c. prior to the h.p.l.c. separation.

6.3.4 *Analysis of oestrogen conjugates by using h.p.l.c.*

Several methods have been published for separation of oestrogen conjugates but few have achieved meaningful results from clinical samples, partly due to a shortage of synthetic reference materials. It is worth mentioning at this point that an electrochemical detector is not suitable for conjugates of oestrogens at the C-3 position.

Oestrogen conjugates may be separated by using h.p.l.c. columns operated in ion-pair mode, e.g. ODS and cetyltrimethylammonium bromide (CTMaBr) (53). The result of a separation of oestrogen conjugates in an XAD-2 extract of pregnancy urine indicates resolution of oestriol-3-glucuronide (E_3-3-G) from oestriol-16-glucuronide (E_3-16-G) which are the two major conjugates of oestriol in urine. Five other peaks have not been identified. The oestrogen conjugates are detected by their u.v. absorption at 220 nm. Since detergents are difficult to remove from the column this would need to be a dedicated system.

Oestrogen conjugates are isolated from urine then separated by using h.p.l.c. with a strong anion-exchange column (micro-Partisil-SAX) (54).

(i)   Pack the column (2×30 cm) with Amberlite XAD-2 in water.
(ii)   Wash with acetone.
(iii)   Wash with water.
(iv)   Run 50 ml of urine into the column.
(v)   Wash the column with water (50 ml).
(vi)   Elute the steroids with ethanol (100 ml).
(vii) Evaporate the ethanol to dryness. Dissolve in 2 ml of 20% aqueous methanol.

Oestrogen conjugates are eluted within 15 min by potassium dihydrogen phosphate (0.02 M). Even at 0.008 M the conjugates elute too fast to permit resolution of all eight conjugates in the mixture. Sodium chloride (0.1 M) without pH adjustment affords maximum resolution of the conjugates at a flow-rate of 0.4 ml/min and low pressure (500 p.s.i.). The oestrogen conjugates in this system elute in reverse order of their polarity. Resolution can be improved by coupling two columns in series (back pressure 1200 p.s.i.) with sodium chloride solution at a flow-rate of 0.8 ml/min. The steroid conju-

Table 7. Retention times of oestrogen conjugates eluted from a strong anion-exchange column (μ-Partisil 10 SAX, 25 cm × 4.6 mm) with 0.01 M sodium chloride pH 4.8 at 0.8 ml/min.

Oestriol-16-glucuronide	9.0
Oestriol-17-glucuronide	9.0
Oestriol-3-glucuronide	10.5
Oestradiol-17-glucuronide	14.5
Oestradiol-3-glucuronide	15.1
Oestrone-3-glucuronide	18.0
Oestradiol-3-sulphate	20.7
Oestrone-3-sulphate	23.3

gates are detected by their u.v. absorption at 254 nm. The analysis can be completed in 30 min. Previous l.c. systems for separation of oestrogen conjugates (ion-exchange, Sephadex) took 15 h or longer. E_3-16-G is not resolved from oestriol-17-glucuronide (E_3-17-G). The latter is not an important excretory conjugate in urine. Neither does this system permit the separation of mixed conjugates of oestrogens — but this is not achieved either by other l.c. systems. The system achieves stable retention times of conjugates added to extracts of urine (*Table 7*). Elution volumes increase with continued injection of urine extracts over several months. This effect can be reduced by protecting the analytical column with a guard column. The method has been applied to the analysis of metabolites of oestrone in plasma following intravenous injection of tritium-labelled oestrone. The eluates (0.6 ml/min) are collected in fractions at 20 sec intervals for counting of radioactivity. The pattern of elution of radioactivity resembled that of standards. The major metabolites identified are oestradiol-17-glucuronide (E_2-17-G), oestrone glucuronide (E_1-G) and oestrone sulphate (E_1-S).

6.3.5 Tetrahydrosteroid metabolites in urine

Detection of steroids after h.p.l.c. has usually been performed by u.v. absorption at 240 nm of the 3-keto-4-ene groups or by derivatization with fluorescent compounds. These methods cannot be applied to the analysis of urine in which most corticosteroids are present in tetrahydro form. Furthermore most urinary steroids are excreted as conjugates and in most methods for measuring these steroids it is first necessary to release the free steroid by using enzyme hydrolysis.

Kawasaki *et al.* (28) have described a fluorescence method for the direct determination of conjugated 17-oxosteroids in urine. Steroid conjugates are extracted from urine using a Sep-Pak C_{18} cartridge. Derivatives are prepared prior to h.p.l.c. separation using a μ-Bondapak C_{18} column and 0.01 M sodium acetate:methanol:acetic acid (65: 35:1 by vol) as the eluent. The eluate is monitored at 365 nm from 520 nm (excitation). Linearity of peak height response is obtained between 10 and 100 pM. Representative chromatograms display plausible results for a normal adult, a female with an ovarian tumour and a female with thyroiditis.

A fluorimetric method for 17-hydroxycorticosteroids has been described (13) using post-column derivatization with benzamidine.

(i)   Pipette 2 ml of urine into a 10 ml glass-stoppered test tube. Adjust to pH 6.5.

(ii) Add 0.1 ml of β-glucuronidase (500 Fishman units/ml from *Escherichia coli*), 0.2 ml of phosphate buffer pH 6.5 and one drop of chloroform. Mix.

(iii) Incubate the mixture for 24 h at 37°C.

(iv) Add 2 μg of betamethasone (20 μl of 100 μg/ml in methanol).

(v) Shake the solution with 4 ml of methylene chloride for 3 min.

(vi) Discard the urine layer.

(vii) Wash the organic layer with 0.5 ml of 0.1 M NaOH and 0.5 ml of water successively.

(viii) Transfer 2 ml of organic layer to another tube and dry.

(ix) Add 100 μl of mobile phase (50% aqueous methanol).

(x) Inject 30 μl onto a h.p.l.c. column (Finepak C_{18}, 10 μM, 4.6 mm × 25 cm).

The effluent from the column is mixed with sodium hydroxide (0.4 M) and a solution of benzamidine hydrochloride (0.5% w/v in a mixture of 2-propanol:water 1:1 v/v). A reciprocal pump equipped with two pump heads delivers the latter solutions alternately at 0.5 ml/min. The solutions are mixed in a T-shaped connector. The mixed reagents are added to the effluent from the column via a further T-shaped connection and passed through a PTFE tube (0.5 mm × 30 cm) immersed in a water bath, then cooled to room temperature before measuring fluorescence at 480 nm with excitation at 370 nm. The method is based on reaction with the dihydroxyacetone side chain of steroids, i.e. cortisol metabolites. A previous publication (55) used a reaction with glycinamide which also reacts with the glycol side chain of corticosterone metabolites.

During the third trimester of human pregnancy the concentrations of deoxycorticosterone in maternal plasma are 4−50 times those in non-pregnant women due to 21-hydroxylation of progesterone (56). This conversion can be proven by demonstrating *in vivo* the formation of [^{3}H]deoxycorticostersone from injected [^{3}H]progesterone. In order to quantify such conversion it is necessary to achieve a high degree of purification of the product or its metabolite. In the past, low resolution separation techniques have been used in conjunction with repeated crystallization of the product until constant specific activity was achieved. Purification of tetrahydrodeoxycorticosterone (THDOC) can incorporate h.p.l.c. separation.

(i) Adjust urine to pH 5.

(ii) Add 250 000 U/l of β-glucuronidase. Incubate for 3 days at room temperature.

(iii) Extract free steroids with ethyl acetate and dry by evaporation.

(iv) Separate free steroids from the residue by gradient elution chromatography on ethylene glyco-celite.

(v) Purify the THDOC fraction by t.l.c. — silica gel G with methylene chloride:diethyl ether (7:3 v/v).

(vi) Purify the THDOC fraction by h.p.l.c. (see *Table 8*).

(vii) React the THDOC fraction with pyridine and acetic anhydrade.

(viii) Purify the THDOC diacetate by t.l.c. using iso-octane:ethyl acetate (1:1 v/v).

(ix) Elute the THDOC diacetate, mix with authentic non-radioactive THDOC diacetate.

(x) Crystallize the THDOC diacetate from diethyl ether:petroleum ether (20−40°C).

Table 8. Retention times of C_{21} steroids on h.p.l.c. μ-Bondapak C_{18} (Waters) 30 cm $\times$ 4 mm eluted with MeOH/H_2O (7:3 v/v) at 2 ml/min.

Steroid	Retention time (min)
3α,21-Dihydroxy-5β-pregnan-20-one	5.04
5β-Pregnane-3,20-dione	7.64
5β-Pregnane-3α,20α-diol	9.84
5β-Pregnane-3β,20α-diol	7.60
3β-Hydroxy-5β-pregnan-20-one	8.40
3α-Hydroxy-5β-pregnan-20-one	9.08
20α-Hydroxy-5β-pregnan-3-one	8.48
3α,11β,21-Trihydroxy-5β-pregnan-20-one	2.80
5β-Pregnane-3α,17,20α-triol	7.56
3β,17-Dihydroxy-5β-pregnan-20-one	4.24
11β,17,21-Trihydroxy-5β-pregnane-3,20-dione	2.36
3α,11β,17,21-Tetrahydroxy-5β-pregnan-20-one	2.40
3α,17,21-Trihydroxy-5β-pregnane-11,20-dione	2.48
5α-Pregnane-3,20-dione	8.04
5α-Pregnane-3β,20α-diol	7.72
5α-Pregnane-3α,20α-diol	11.70
20α-Hydroxy-5α-pregnan-3-one	7.88
20β-Hydroxy-5α-pregnan-3-one	10.00
3β-Hydroxy-5α-pregnan-20-one	9.00
3α-Hydroxy-5α-pregnan-20-one	9.80
3β,17-Dihydroxy-5α-pregnan-20-one	3.88
3α,11β,17,21-Tetrahydroxy-5α-pregnan-20-one	2.40
4-Pregnene-3,20-dione	4.96
21-Hydroxy-4-pregnene-3,20-dione	3.12
20α-Hydroxy-4-pregnen-3-one	6.60
20β-Hydroxy-4-pregnen-3-one	9.28
17,20α-Dihydroxy-4-pregnen-3-one	3.40
17,20β-Dihydroxy-4-pregnen-3-one	3.64
17,21-Dihydroxy-4-pregnen-3,20-dione	2.44

The retention times of C_{21} steroids on the chosen h.p.l.c. system are summarized in *Table 8*. A-ring saturated metabolites were detected by using a refractive index detector.

6.3.6 *Multiple steroid measurements of free hormones in urine*

Using a protocol similar to that of the multiple steroid assay in serum (57) it is possible to split an extract of urine and with two h.p.l.c. systems to measure androstenedione, dihydrotestosterone, testosterone, 17α-hydroxyprogesterone, 11-deoxycortisol, corticosterone, aldosterone, cortisol and 18-hydroxycorticosterone then in the second run progesterone, pregnenolone, dehydroepiandrosterone, deoxycorticosterone and 18-hydroxydeoxycorticosterone.

(i)   *Extraction*

(a)   2 ml of urine plus [^{3}H]steroid (each dissolved in 100 μl of water).

Table 9. Excretion rates of urinary free steroids from normal males.

Steroid	Lower and upper limit (nmol/24 h)
Progesterone	0.23 − 0.56
Androstenedione	4.55 − 20.90
Pregnenolone	0.42 − 1.93
Dihydrotestosterone	0.27 − 1.37
Dehydroepiandrosterone	2.69 − 16.97
Testosterone	0.65 − 3.16
11-Deoxycorticosterone (DOC)	0.21 − 0.59
17α-Hydroxyprogesterone	0.59 − 1.80
17α-Hydroxypregnenolone	0.10 − 0.42
11-Deoxycortisol	0.15 − 0.39
18-Hydroxy-DOC	1.10 − 4.03
Corticosterone	0.85 − 2.62
Aldosterone	0.29 − 0.74
Cortisol	35.01 − 133.0
18-Hydroxycorticosterone	3.62 − 8.10

(b)   Transfer to an 'Extrelut' column.

(c)   Elute with 20 ml of ether.

(d)   Evaporate.

(e)   Re-dissolve in 150 μl of n-hexane:isopropanol (95:5, v/v).

(ii)   *High-performance liquid chromatography*

(a)   Transfer to an autosampler.

(b)   Automatic injection and chromatography.

(c)   Automatic collection of individual steroid fractions.

(d)   Evaporate the individual fractions.

(e)   Re-dissolve in appropriate amounts of ethanol:water (50:50 v/v).

(f)   Count the appropriate aliquots for recovery.

(iii)   *Radioimmunoassay*

(a)   50 μl of sample (duplicate) or standard (1600 − 6.25 pg) in triplicate plus 800 μl of γ-globulin buffer containing [^{3}H]steroid (RIA radioactivity) and steroid antiserum.

(b)   Incubate for at least 2 h at 4°C.

(c)   Add 100 μl of charcoal suspension.

(d)   Shake and centrifuge (10 min at 4°C, 3300 g).

(e)   Decant.

(f)   Count for ^{3}H-radioactivity of the bound fraction.

(g)   Calculate the results.

The excretion rates for steroids accord with previous data (*Table 9*). The data reveal the mandatory requirement for RIA of steroids in urine to include a chromatographic step in order to avoid unspecific compounds immunologically reacting in the assays.

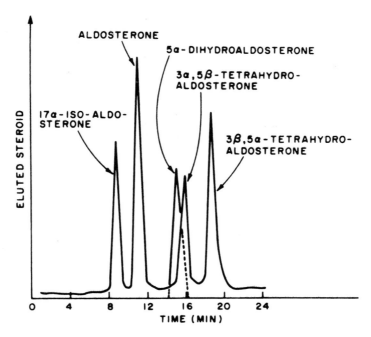

Figure 11. Chromatogram showing the separation of aldosterone, 17 iso-aldosterone and reduced metabolites of aldosterone. A μ-Bondapak C_{18} column 0.4×30 cm is eluted with 50% aqueous methanol; flow-rate 1 ml/min at 35°C.

6.4 Steriods in tissues

6.4.1 *Metabolism and mechanism of action of aldosterone*

Aldosterone plays an important role in electrolyte homeostasis by regulating active sodium transport and potassium excretion in the kidney. The key to the mechanism of the action of aldosterone may rest in the biochemical events that occur during the period after administration before the biological effects are expressed in the kidney — the so-called latent period which lasts 45–90 min. Morris (58) has considered in rats that hepatic and renal metabolism of aldosterone might play an essential role in the mechanism of aldosterone action by production of biologically active products. Following physiological doses of [³H]aldosterone much of the activity in the liver and the kidney is associated with very polar metabolites. New procedures have been developed to isolate, separate and characterize the products.

Aldosterone and its reduced metabolites are removed from plasma, urine or aqueous extracts from tissue by extraction with organic solvents. The neutral metabolites are adequately separated on h.p.l.c. (see *Figure 11*). The polar metabolites are extracted with 10 volumes of acetone:methanol (1:1 v/v) for 18 h at 37°C. Using a method developed at the Karolinska Institute, five fractions of radiometabolites of aldosterone are achieved by chromatography on Sephadex DEAP-LH-20 (*Figure 12*). The fractions represent 'families' of steroid metabolites distinguished by their conjugation pattern. The first fraction contains a group of aldosterone metabolites which are polar neutral products of aldosterone. *Figure 13* compares the patterns obtained by eluting the pre-

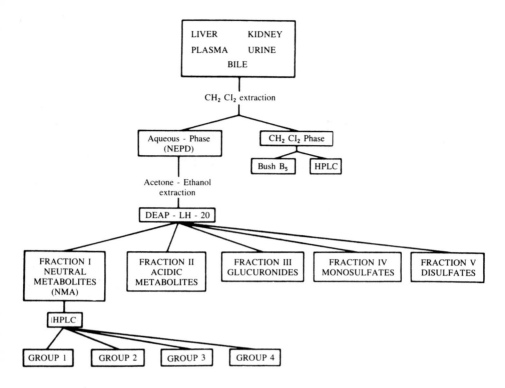

Figure 12. The general scheme of analysis of the radiometabolites of [³H]aldosterone present in the cytosol of the liver and kidney, and in the plasma urine and bile.

viously separated families of steroids from μ-Bondapak C_{18} columns by stepwise elution with increments of methanol – water and acetonitrile – water systems. The chemical structures of all neutral metabolites of aldosterone in tissues or plasma have not been determined with certainty. The peaks of radiometabolites eluted from the h.p.l.c. represent very little mass and must be monitored by their radioactivity. Peaks with retention properties of monohydroxylated metabolites of aldosterone seem to be of importance and their identification and measurement may have significant importance particularly in various clinical disease states, for example hypertension. This aspect is beyond the scope of this chapter.

6.4.2 *Analysis of steroids secreted by cells in monolayer culture*

The fact that a range of steroids can be separated with the use of h.p.l.c. makes the system suited to the identification of steroids secreted by pathological tissues in which significant changes of function have occurred. O'Hare *et al.* (5) have described patterns of steroidogenesis for cultures of adrenal carcinoma and adenoma, hyperplastic adrenals, adrenal tissue tumours secreting aldosterone, the testes of a child with male pseudo-hermaphroditism and a testicular interstitial cell tumour. Cells are incubated with cold and radioactive steroids. Cultured medium samples (2 – 5 ml) are extracted with 10 ml of dichloromethane. The organic phase is washed with 3 ml of 0.1 M NaOH to remove saponifiable lipids which contribute small u.v.-absorbing peaks in the chromatogram.

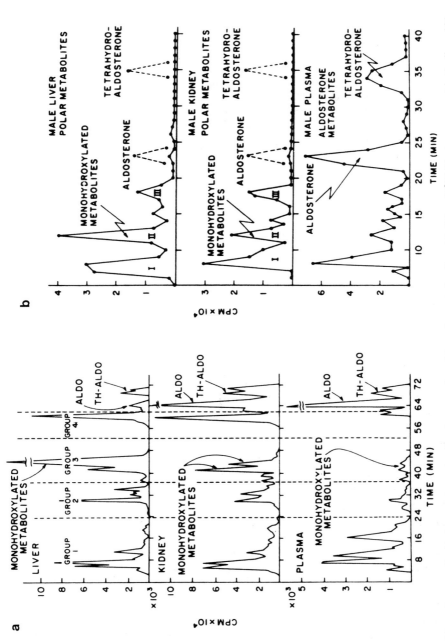

Figure 13. High-performance liquid chromatogram showing the separation of the polar neutral radiometabolites of [³H]aldosterone present in the liver, kidney and plasma of male rats. (**a**) μ-Bondapak C₁₈ column 0.4 × 30 cm; stepwise elution with 15% aqueous methanol, 30% aqueous methanol and 50% aqueous methanol; flow-rate 1 ml/min; temperature 25°C. (**b**) μ-Bondapak C₁₈ column 0.4 × 30 cm; 50% aqueous methanol; flow-rate 0.5 ml/min; temperature 25°C.

153

Table 10. Retention times (min) measured from injection for steroid standards on Zorbax-ODS using three gradient systems.

Steroid	Methanol:water[a] 40 – 100%	Acetonitrile:water[a] 32 – 100%	Dioxane:water[a] 20 – 100%
6β-Hydroxycortisol	3	3.5	4
11-Dehydroaldosterone	8	5	15
17-Isoaldosterone	11	6	15
18-Hydroxy-11-dehydrocorticosterone	11.5	6.5	17.5
Prednisone	12	9	23
Aldosterone	13.5	8	19
Estriol	14	8	25
Cortisone	14	9	25.5
19-Hydroxyandrostenedione	15	11.5	20
7α-Hydroxytestosterone	15.5	9	19.5
18-Hydroxycorticosterone	15.5	7	21
Prednisolone	15.5	9	26.5
Cortisol	16	9	27
Adrenosterone	18	17	28
19-Hydroxytestosterone	19	10	24
16α-Hydroxytestosterone	21	11	27
11-Dehydrocorticosterone	21.5	15	29.5
Dexamethasone	24	13	35
11β-Hydroxyandrostenedione	24	17	32
21-Deoxycortisol	26.5	16	34.5
Corticosterone	31	18	36
11β-Hydroxytestosterone	31	15	33.5
18-Hydroxydeoxycorticosterone	31.5	16	34.5
11-Deoxycortisol	33	20	37.5
6α-Hydroxyprogesterone	34	24.5	38.5
16α-Hydroxyprogesterone	35	24	38
11-ketoprogesterone	37	30	40
Estrone	37	30.5	42.5
11β-Hydroxy-20α-dihydroprogesterone	38	26	39
Androstenedione	39	36	42
6β-Hydroxyprogesterone	39	30	41
Estradiol	40	29	43
11β-Hydroxyprogesterone	41	33	43
11-Deoxycorticosterone	41	36	43.5
17α-Hydroxyprogesterone	41.5	38	45
Testosterone	42	35	43.5
16α-Hydroxy-20α-dihydroprogesterone	42.5	32	42
17α-Hydroxy-20β-dihydroprogesterone	43	32.5	43.5
Dehydroepiandrosterone	44	41	44
Androstenediol	45	38	–
17α-Hydroxypregnenolone	45.5	39	–
5α-Dihydrotestosterone	46.5	42	–
Progesterone	47	45	49
20α-Dihydroprogesterone	47.5	43.5	47.5
20β-Dihydroprogesterone	48.5	46	49.5
Pregnenolone	48.5	47	50
Cholesterone	54	>60	–

[a]Gradient of y = x^3 over 50 min at 45°C with programmed flow-rates.

Dichloromethane extracts are washed with water, dried under nitrogen and the extracts re-dissolved in the primary h.p.l.c. solvent.

A Zorbax-ODS column maintained at 45°C is eluted with one of three solvent systems with a gradient $(y = x^3)$ over 50 min with programmable gradient elution. The retention times of standards in these systems are summarized in *Table 10*. The eluate is monitored continuously for u.v. absorption and fractions are collected for counting of radioactivity.

Human adrenocortical cells have the capacity to metabolize pregnenolone to seven major hormones — cortisol, 11-deoxycortisol, corticosterone, deoxycorticosterone, androstenedione, 11β-hydroxyandrostenenedioine and 16α-hydroxyprogesterone. The metabolites obtained from human testes in culture are testosterone, 17α-hydroxyprogesterone, progesterone, 20-dihydroprogesterone and 17α-hydroxy,20α-dihydroxyprogesterone. Radioactive peaks indicate the present of other polar metabolites. In the analysis of steroids produced by cells in culture it is found that the acetonitrile:water and the methanol:water systems are complementary. Most of the compounds produced can be identified by the use of one or both systems.

Applications of this technique are illustrated by the analysis of aldosterone-containing samples from human adrenocortical tumours and for the characterization of steroidogenesis in cell cultures of human foetal adrenal cortex (59). O'Hare *et al.* have also studied progesterone synthesis, secretion and metabolism by human teratoma-derived cell lines (60).

7. CONCLUSION

H.p.l.c. is now a proven technique for the separation and measurement of steroid hormones. Further improvements in the technology (notably in detection systems) will extend the breadth of information offered by the technique. This chapter has been directed to the analysis of steroids in biological fluids.The clinical relevance of the data necessitates high standards of analytical quality. H.p.l.c is a viable approach to the overall study of steroid biochemistry extending to the purification of steroid receptors which direct the action of steroid hormones in regulatory cellular processes and to the catalytic elements required for the biosynthesis of steroids.

8. ACKNOWLEDGEMENTS

I would like to thank my technical staff, H.Sudan, G.Lovell and H.Patel for their valuable contribution to this research. I would like to express my appreciation to Pratima Shah for her careful typing of the manuscript. Some figures were reproduced from the work of others with the kind permission of the authors and copyright holders.

9. REFERENCES

1. Morris,D.J. (1981) *Endocrine Rev.,* **2**, 234.
2. Monder,C. and Bradlow,H.L. (1977) *J. Steroid Biochem.,* **8**, 897.
3. Honour J.W. (1984) In *Biochemistry of Steroid Hormones,* 2nd edition, Makin,H.L.J. (ed.), Blackwell Scientific Publications, London, p. 382.
4. Shackleton,C.H.L., Taylor,N.F. and Honour,J.W. (1980) *Atlas of Gas Chromatographic Profiles of Neutral Steroids in Health and Disease,* Packard Instrument Co.
5. O'Hare,M.J., Nice,E.C., Magee-Brown,R. and Bullman,H. (1976) *J. Chromatogr.,* **125**, 357.
6. Schoneshofer,M. and Dulce,H.J. (1979) *J. Chromatogr.,* **164**, 17.
7. O'Hare,M.J. and Nice,E.C. (1983) In *Steroid Analysis by HPLC — Recent Applications,* Kautsky,M.P. (ed.), Marcel Dekker Inc., New York, p. 277.

Steroids

8. O'Hare,M.J., Nice,E.C. and Capp,M. (1980) *J. Chromatogr.*, **198**, 23.
9. Hara,S. and Hayashi,S. (1977) *J. Chromatogr.*, **142**, 689.
10. D'Agostino,G., Castagnetta,L., Mitchell,F. and O'Hare,M.J. (1985) *J. Chromatogr.*, **338**, 1.
11. Derks,H.J.G.M. and Drayer,N.M. (1978) *Steroids*, **31**, 289.
12. Tscherne,R.J. and Capitano,G. (1977) *J. Chromatogr.*, **136**, 337.
13. Seki,T. and Yamaguchi,Y. (1984) *J. Chromatogr.*, **305**, 188.
14. Satyaswaroop,P.G., de la Osa,E.L. and Gurpide,E. (1977) *Steroids*, **30**, 139.
15. Watanabe,K. (1985) *J. Chromatogr.*, **337**, 126.
16. Lundmo,P. and Sunde,E. (1984) *J. Chromatogr.*, **308**, 289.
17. Edmonds,C.G., McCloskey,J.A. and Edmonds,V.A. (1983) *Biomed. Mass Spectrom.*, **10**, 237.
18. Fell,A.F., Scott,H.P., Gill,R. and Moffat,A.C. (1983) *J. Chromatogr.*, **282**, 123.
19. Houghton,E., Dumasia,M.C. and Wellby,J.K. (1981) *Biomed. Mass Spectrom.*, **8**, 558.
20. Bradlow,H.L. (1977) *Steroids*, **30**, 581.
21. Shackleton,C.H.L. and Whitney,J.O. (1980) *Clin. Chim. Acta*, **107**, 231.
22. Heikkinen,R., Fotsis,T. and Adlercreutz,H. (1981) *Clin. Chem.*, **27**, 1186.
23. Honour,J.W. and Kent,J. (1982) *Clin. Chim. Acta*, **129**, 229.
24. Kabra,P.M., Tsai,F.H. and Morton,L.J. (1983) *Clin. Chim. Acta*, **128**, 9.
25. Schoneshofer,M., Kage,A. and Weber,B. (1983) *Clin. Chem.*, **29**, 1367.
26. Anderson,S.H.G. and Sjovall,J. (1984) *Anal. Biochem.*, **134**, 309.
27. Novotny,M., Karlsson,K.-E., Konishi,M. and Alasandro,M. (1984) *J. Chromatogr.*, **305**, 159.
28. Kawasaki,T., Maeda,M. and Tsjuji,A. (1982) *J. Chromatogr.*, **233**, 61.
29. Culbreth,P.H. and Sampson,E.J. (1981) *J. Chromatogr.*, **212**, 221.
30. Hofreiter,B.T., Mizera,A.C., Allen,J.P., Masi,A.M. and Hicok,W.C. (1983) *Clin. Chem.*, **29**, 1808.
31. Shimizu,K., Amagaya,S. and Ogihara,Y. (1983) *J. Chromatogr.*, **272**, 170.
32. De Vries,C.B. and De Jong,A.P.J.M. (1980) *J. Steroid Biochem.*, **13**, 387.
33. Imaizumi,N., Morimoto,N., Kigoshi,T., Uchida,K., Hosojima,H. and Yamamoto,I. (1984) *J. Chromatogr.*, **308**, 295.
34. Ojima,M. and Kambegawa,A. (1980) *Tohoku J. Exp. Med.*, **132**, 75.
35. Cochran,R.C., Darney,K.J. and Ewing,L.L. (1979) *J. Chromatogr.*, **173**, 349.
36. Shimada,K., Tanaka,M. and Nambara,T. (1984) *J. Chromatogr.*, **307**, 23.
37. Jawad,M.J., Wilson,E.A. and Vernon,M.W. (1984) *Clin. Chem.*, **30**, 118.
38. von Stetton,O. and Schlett,R. (1983) *J. Chromatogr.*, **254**, 229.
39. Coghlan,J.P., Denton,J.A., Fan,J.S.K., McDougall,J.G. and Scoggins,B.A. (1976) *Nature*, **273**, 608.
40. Das,R. and Kirk,D.N. (1984) *J. Chem. Soc. Perkin. Trans.*, *I*, 1821.
41. Kirk,D.N. and Slade,C.J. (1984) *J. Chem. Soc. Perkin. Trans.*, *I*, 2595.
42. Weisman,Y., Bar,A., Root,A., Spirer,Z. and Golander,A. (1984) *Clin. Chim. Acta*, **139**, 1.
43. Carson,S.W. and Jusko,W.J. (1984) *J. Chromatogr.*, **306**, 345.
44. Smith,M.D. (1983) In *Steroid Analysis by HPLC — Recent Applications*, Kautsky,M.P. (ed.), Marcel Dekker Inc., New York, p. 105.
45. Bjargava,A.S., Seeger,A. and Gunzel,P. (1977) *Steroids*, **30**, 407.
46. Lyons,F. and Shuster,S. (1981) *Clin. Endocrinol.*, **19**, 53.
47. Robinson,D.T., Earnshaw,R.J., Mitchell,R., Poules,R., Andrews,R.S. and Robertson,W.R. (1984) *J. Steroid Biochem.*, **21**, 601.
48. Schoneshofer,M., Fenner,A. and Dulce,H.J. (1981) *J. Steroid Biochem.*, **14**, 377.
49. Stoks,P.G. and Benraad,T.J. (1983) *J. Chromatogr.*, **276**, 408.
50. Nakamura,J. and Yakata,M. (1983) *Clin. Chem.*, **29**, 847.
51. Farhi,R.L. and Monder,C.L. (1978) *Anal. Biochem.*, **90**, 58.
52. de Vries,C.P., Popp-Snijders,C., de Kieviet,W. and Akkerman-Faber,A.C. (1977) *J. Chromatogr.*, **143**, 624.
53. Dixon,P.F., Lukha,P. and Scott,N.R. (1979) *Proc. Anal. Div. Chem. Soc.*, **16**, 302.
54. Musey,P.I., Collins,D.C. and Preedy,J. (1978) *Steroids*, **31**, 583.
55. Seki,T. and Yamaguchi,I.Y. (1983) *J. Liquid Chromatogr.*, **6**, 1131.
56. Winkel,C.A., Milewich,L., Parker,C.R., Gant,N.A., Simpson,E.R. and MacDonald,P.C. (1980) *J. Clin. Invest.*, **66**, 803.
57. Schoneshofer,M. and Weber,B. (1983) *J.Steroid Biochem.*, **18**, 65.
58. Morris,D.J. and Tsai,R. (1980) *Adv. Chromatogr.*, **19**, 261.
59. Simonian,M.H. and Capp,M.W. (1984) *J. Clin. Endocrinol. Metab.*, **59**, 643.
60. O'Hare,M.J., Nice,E.C., McIllinney,R.A.J. and Capp,M.W. (1981) *Steroids*, **38**, 719.

CHAPTER 8

Vitamins

M.J. SHEARER

1. INTRODUCTION

The technique of h.p.l.c. has had a marked impact on the analysis of all vitamins in fields as diverse as nutrition, medicine, biochemistry, food science and pharmaceutics. In the sense that the choice of an analytical method will depend on the precise needs of the analyst and especially the type and nature of the tissue or fluid to be analysed, it is well beyond the scope of this chapter to give 'universal' methods for any of the vitamins. This problem is compounded by the fact that many vitamins possess many molecular forms (vitamers) with biological activity.

In an attempt to reduce the scope and at the same time keep a continuity to this chapter, the author has concentrated on one specific area: this is the analysis of vitamins in the study and diagnosis of disease or for the purpose of assessing the nutriture of the vitamins in individuals or population groups. In most cases the author has selected methods for the measurement of each vitamin in blood; for certain vitamins, however, such as riboflavin and niacin, their assay in urine may assume a greater nutritional importance. For vitamin D the assay of hydroxylated metabolites in blood is of greater clinical significance and importance than the measurement of the parent vitamin. Even within this limited field of study it is evident that the literature contains a large number of different methods in which h.p.l.c. is used to solve a more or less specific problem of analysis. Nevertheless, for each vitamin there are certain broad principles of analysis and it is the author's intention to try and define these principles and illustrate them with specific procedures.

Inevitably the impact of h.p.l.c. has been greater for some vitamins than others. For some such as vitamins A, E and C, h.p.l.c. has provided alternative procedures, which possess a greater specificity and sensitivity of detection, to already well-established chemical methods. For other vitamins such as vitamin D, folic acid and vitamin B_{12} h.p.l.c. has revolutionized the resolution and purification of molecular forms without having had a similar impact on their detection at tissue concentrations. In such cases h.p.l.c. is proving invaluable as a rapid purification technique for the off-line assay of vitamins by competitive protein binding assays, radioimmunoassays or microbiological assays. For one vitamin, vitamin K, h.p.l.c. methods with direct detection techniques have provided the first ever measurements of the vitamin in human plasma by any method.

As a group, vitamins are chemically extremely diverse and are not linked by any common threads in chemical structure. With this variety in both form and biological function, it seems improbable that any one analyst would have had direct experience in the measurement of all the vitamins. This is certainly true for this author whose own speciality lies with the fat-soluble vitamins, particularly vitamin K. Of necessity therefore the author has needed to select procedures for the water-soluble vitamins entirely from the literature. In selecting a particular procedure the author has tried to stress the importance of sample collection, storage, preparation and clean-up procedures which are often as critical, and often more so, than the h.p.l.c. procedures.

The wide difference in chemical structure of vitamins is reflected by the variety of h.p.l.c. procedures used for their analysis. This chapter therefore includes examples of the three most common methods of detection (using spectrophotometric, fluorometric or electrochemical detectors) together with examples of both pre- and post-column derivatization techniques to increase the selectivity and/or sensitivity of detection. In addition, examples will be found for the major modes of separation with analyses based on the principles of normal-phase (NP), reversed-phase (RP), ion-exchange and ion-pair (IP) h.p.l.c.

For reasons of space only brief details of the method of quantification have been given for each assay described. This includes the general method of quantification (e.g. external or internal standardization) and, where appropriate, the use and approximate concentrations of an internal standard. Examples of calibration curves and calculations are not provided but further details are often available in the original texts.

Three vitamins are not included in this chapter. For two, biotin and pantothenic acid, there has been little nutritional or clinical impetus to measure these vitamins and there are few, if any, examples of their measurement by h.p.l.c. in this context. Vitamin B_{12} has been omitted for different reasons which require further explanation. Firstly, there can be no doubt about either the clinical value of plasma measurements of B_{12} or that h.p.l.c. is the most effective chromatographic technique for resolving the variety of naturally occurring cobalamins. On the other hand, serum levels of B_{12} are too low to allow their direct detection by h.p.l.c.; this limits the role of h.p.l.c. to its capability for the rapid and high resolution of cobalamins and their assay in the column fractions by microbiological or radio-assays. H.p.l.c. is here used in much the same way as for the assay of vitamin D metabolites. The difference is that h.p.l.c. is now widely used for plasma analyses of vitamin D metabolites whereas the author can find only one example of a similar use of h.p.l.c. for the analysis of cobalamins in human plasma. Certainly, the existence of well-established assays for vitamin B_{12} using microbiological or isotope dilution techniques, which do not require a chromatographic step, has not provided any incentive to develop h.p.l.c. methods for routine analyses of vitamin B_{12} in human plasma. Besides the lack of methods which lie within the scope of this chapter, another factor which swayed the author to omit this vitamin is the difficulty and current uncertainty that surrounds the procedures used to extract cobalamins from plasma.

2. VITAMIN A AND PROVITAMIN CAROTENOIDS

2.1 Introduction

The parent compound of the vitamin A group is all-*trans* retinol. The chemical structures of this and other naturally occurring vitamin A compounds, including β-carotene, a

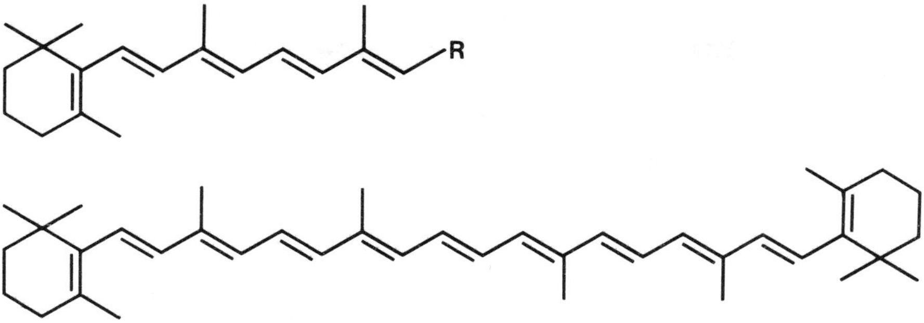

Figure 1. (Top): chemical structure of parent vitamin A compounds. For retinol R = CH$_2$OH; for retinaldehyde R = CHO and for retinoic acid R = COOH. **(Bottom):** structure of β-carotene, a representative of the provitamin A carotenoids.

representative of the wide spectrum of carotenoids which have provitamin A activity, are shown in *Figure 1*.

In the last few years h.p.l.c. has probably become the method of choice for the tissue analysis of both vitamin A and carotenoids replacing in many laboratories older methods based on spectrophotometric, colourimetric or fluorescence techniques. Although traditional assays for vitamin A are sensitive enough, their main shortcomings are interferences from other compounds like β-carotene in colourimetric assays and phytofluene in fluorescence assays (1). By exploiting their unusually long u.v. absorption maxima ($\sim$325 nm) or their natural fluorescence, the sensitive and selective on-line detection of vitamin A compounds by h.p.l.c. is readily accomplished.

H.p.l.c. has also facilitated carotenoid analyses enabling, for the first time, the measurement of individual carotenoids in plasma (2). Again, the absorption of carotenoids in the visible region ($\sim$450 nm) allows a high degree of selectivity to be obtained using a spectrophotometric detector.

Many h.p.l.c. methods, some very similar, have been developed to measure specific vitamin A compounds such as retinol, either alone, or together with other carotenoids and often with vitamin E (α-tocopherol). Multiple assays of this type are being increasingly used in epidemiological studies (3).

2.2 Assay of retinol in plasma

In the post-absorptive state the vitamin A in human blood consists almost wholly of retinol combined in plasma with retinol-binding protein (RBP) at concentrations of around 500 μg/l. Its measurement is often used as an indicator of vitamin A status in individuals and populations.

2.2.1 Sample preparation and extraction

Blood should be collected into heparin. Three anti-coagulants (oxalate, citrate and EDTA) have been reported to cause losses of retinol (4). Since vitamin A compounds and carotenoids are sensitive to oxygen and light, all manipulations should be carried out under minimum light and evaporation steps should be carried out under nitrogen. When bound to RBP in plasma, however, retinol is quite stable when stored in the dark at $-20°$C (1).

Retinol is easily and quantitatively extracted from plasma into non-polar solvents such as hexane after disruption of the retinol−RBP complex by polar solvents such as ethanol. Perchloric acid as a denaturing agent should be avoided since this may cause destruction of retinol (4).

2.2.2 *Design of h.p.l.c. assays*

Both NP and RP systems of h.p.l.c. have been used to measure retinol. NP-h.p.l.c. has the advantage that plasma extracts in non-polar solvents (e.g. hexane) can be injected directly onto the column whereas for injection onto RP columns, hexane extracts need to be evaporated down and re-dissolved in the mobile phase or other compatible solvent. On the other hand, it is more difficult to control retention on silica columns and methods using NP-h.p.l.c. have lacked the convenience of readily available internal standards like short chain retinyl esters which have proved so successful in RP assays. Another advantage of RP systems is that it is possible to measure simultaneously some carotenoids, retinyl esters and vitamin E compounds with no or minimal changes to the composition of the mobile phase. For these reasons RP columns have usually been preferred for the assay of retinol. A useful and recent innovation designed to avoid an evaporation step in RP analyses is to extract plasma with butanol:ethyl acetate (1:1). The assay of retinol based on the direct injection of butanol:ethyl acetate extracts onto an RP column showed excellent peak shapes and precision (4).

To measure retinol in plasma, u.v. detection at 325 nm has sufficient sensitivity and selectivity for most purposes. If the simultaneous measurement of α-tocopherol is required, a compromise wavelength of around 290 nm should be selected since α-tocopherol has practically no absorbance at 325 nm. Alternatively, an u.v. detector capable of monitoring more than one wavelength may be used. H.p.l.c. with fluorescence detection of retinol provides even greater selectivity and a sensitivity about one order of magnitude better than u.v. detection (5). In selecting a detector, however, practical considerations should also be borne in mind; in this respect u.v. detectors are simpler to operate and give a linearity of response over a wider range than fluorescence detectors.

2.2.3 *Rapid micro-assay of retinol in plasma*

In the author's laboratory a rapid micro-assay has been developed to measure retinol in 100 μl of plasma. Such an assay has advantages for epidemiological studies or where the blood volume is limited, as in neonatal studies. The procedure is based on an RP method using hexane extraction and retinyl acetate as an internal standard (6). Retinyl acetate is commercially available, is cheap and, in the author's laboratory, has proved reliable. The same basic method is also suitable for fluorescence detection (5) and for the direct injection of butanol:ethyl acetate (1:1) extracts of plasma (4).

The method described in *Table 1* and illustrated in *Figure 2* uses a short column (thus increasing sample throughput) and, when packed with Spherisorb 5 ODS-2, allows the convenience of using 100% methanol as the mobile phase. An assay of this nature is very suitable for automated sample injection.

2.3 **Assay of retinyl esters in plasma**

After a meal there is a transient appearance in plasma of retinyl esters as they pass

Table 1. Rapid micro-assay of retinol in plasma.

Sample extraction

1. Accurately pipette 100 μl of plasma into a micro-centrifuge tube (polypropylene, 1.5 ml capacity with cap).
2. Accurately add 100 μl of a solution of all-*trans*-retinyl acetate (Sigma) in ethanol (accurately known concentration of ~0.5 μg/ml) as the internal standard and vortex mix for 15 sec.
3. Pipette 200 μl of n-hexane into the tube as the extraction solvent and vortex mix for 30 sec. Transfer the tube to a mechanical shaker (e.g. Eppendorf mixer model 5432) and shake the contents for 10 min.
4. Centrifuge the contents on a micro-centrifuge (e.g. Eppendorf centrifuge model 5414) for 5 min to separate an upper hexane layer from a lower aqueous-ethanolic layer.
5. Transfer the upper hexane layer (containing retinol and retinyl acetate) by pipette to a glass, tapered tube (e.g. Dreyer agglutination tubes) and evaporate to dryness under a stream of nitrogen at 40°C.
6. Immediately before h.p.l.c., reconstitute the lipid residue in 100 μl of ethanol, vortex mix briefly, and inject 20 μl onto the h.p.l.c. column.

H.p.l.c. conditions

1. Column: Spherisorb-ODS 2, dimensions 12.5 cm × 5 mm (i.d.) (5 μm silica chemically bonded with ODS groups and fully capped; from Phase Separations).
2. Mobile phase: 100% methanol.
3. Flow-rate: 1 ml/min.
4. Detector: u.v., variable wavelength absorbance detector set at 325 nm.

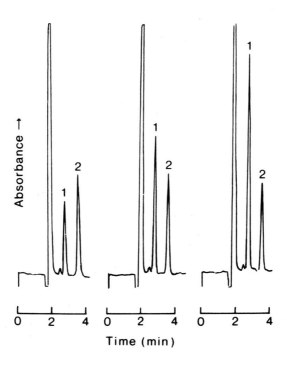

Figure 2. Chromatograms illustrating the rapid micro-assay of retinol in plasma at concentrations (from left to right) of 270, 500 and 890 μg/l, respectively. The chromatographic conditions are as described in *Table 1*. Peaks: **1** = retinol; **2** = retinyl acetate (internal standard).

Table 2. Assay of retinyl esters in plasma[a].

Sample extraction

1. Accurately pipette 200 μl of plasma into a centrifuge tube.
2. Accurately add 0.6 ml of water, 2 ml of a solution of retinyl propionate (AEC, 03600 Commentry, France) in methanol (accurately known concentration of ~0.15 μg/ml) as the internal standard, and 1 ml of chloroform. Mix thoroughly for 1 min and allow to stand for 5 min.
3. Add 1 ml of water and 1 ml of chloroform. Mix gently and centrifuge at 1500 g for 5 min.
4. Transfer the low chloroform phase to a clean tube and evaporate to dryness in a rotary evaporator under reduced pressure or under a stream of nitrogen at 40°C.
5. Immediately before h.p.l.c., reconstitute the lipid residue in 100 μl of methanol:chloroform (4:1, v/v). Sonicate in a ultrasonic bath[b] for 10 min and inject 50 μl of the solution onto the h.p.l.c. column.

H.p.l.c. conditions

1. Column: RSIL C_{18} HL, dimensions 15 cm × 3 mm (i.d.) (10 μm silica chemically bonded with ODS groups and having 18% carbon loading; from RSL, St. Martens-Latem, Belgium).
2. Mobile phase: 100% methanol.
3. Flow-rate: 1 ml/min.
4. Detector: u.v., variable wavelength absorbance detector set at 330 nm.

---

[a]Adapted from ref. 7.
[b]The lipid extract is not completely soluble in the mobile phase (100% methanol). To obtain complete dissolution of the residue 20% chloroform is added and the solution sonicated.

from the intestine to be stored in the liver. Plasma measurements of retinyl esters after an oral dose of vitamin A are sometimes used to assess the absorption of vitamin A and as an indicator of hypervitaminosis A.

In RP assays of retinol (see Section 2.2) retinyl esters are usually not seen because of their low endogenous concentrations, their long retention times and their incomplete extraction by hexane. To completely extract retinyl esters a more exhaustive lipid extraction with methanol:chloroform (2:1) should be used (7). After giving an oral dose of vitamin A, however, esters of vitamin A are easily detected in plasma. Details of a method taken from reference (7) are given in *Table 2*. Three major peaks are seen on the chromatograms, the first representing a minor peak is retinyl linoleate, the second is a composite peak containing retinyl palmitate and retinyl oleate and the third peak is retinyl stearate. As described in *Table 2*, the method is sensitive to plasma levels of retinyl esters down to 100 μg/l when 200 μl of plasma is extracted. As with RP assays for retinol, short chain retinyl esters (retinyl acetate or propionate) make good internal standards and retinol can be measured concomitantly. It would be easily possible to increase the sensitivity of the method by using a fluorescence detector and scaling up the procedure.

2.4 Assay of retinoic acid in plasma

Retinoic acid which has partial vitamin A activity circulates in human plasma at concentrations of less than one-hundreth that of retinol. Its assay in plasma has only recently been achieved by a method in which interfering lipids are first removed by a double-phase extraction technique at different pH values. This is followed by h.p.l.c. on a silica column and u.v. detection at 350 nm (8). Details of the procedure are outlined in *Table 3*.

Table 3. Assay of retinoic acid in plasma[a].

Sample extraction

1. Accurately pipette 3.5 ml of plasma into a centrifuge tube.
2. Accurately add 25 μl of a solution of all-*trans*-13-demethyl retinoic acid (Hoffmann-La Roche Inc, Nutley, NJ, USA) in ethanol (accurately known concentration of ~ 1.8 μg/ml) as the internal standard, 3.5 ml of ethanol and 1.5 ml of 2 M NaOH.
3. Add 7 ml of n-hexane and mix on a rotary mixer for 10 min at 4°C to extract the neutral and basic lipophilic compounds.
4. Centrifuge briefly to separate the two phases. Remove and discard the upper hexane phase.
5. Acidify the aqueous phase with 3 ml of 2 M HCl and re-extract lipids into 7 ml of n-hexane by mixing on a rotary mixer for 10 min at 4°C.
6. Transfer the upper hexane phase to a clean vessel and evaporate to dryness in a rotary evaporator under reduced pressure.
7. Immediately before h.p.l.c., reconstitute the lipid residue in 100 μl of the mobile phase (see h.p.l.c. conditions) and inject 50 μl onto the h.p.l.c. column.

H.p.l.c. conditions

1. Column: RSIL silica, dimensions 15 cm × 3 mm (i.d.) (5 μm silica; from RSL, St. Martens-Latem, Belgium).
2. Mobile phase: 99.5% n-hexane, 0.2% acetonitrile and 0.3% acetic acid (by vol.).
3. Flow-rate: 0.75 ml/min.
4; Detector: u.v., variable wavelength absorbance detector set at 350 nm.

[a]Adapted from ref. 8.

2.5 Assay of provitamin A carotenoids

Although dietary provitamin carotenoids may be oxidatively cleaved to vitamin A within the mucosal cell, in humans an appreciable fraction escapes oxidation and the intact carotenoids may be detected in plasma. Recent interest in the assay of carotenoids in plasma (including those with no provitamin A activity) has focused on their possible protective role against cancer.

Carotenoids represent some of the most non-polar compounds found in nature. As such, excellent separations may be achieved by non-aqueous RP-h.p.l.c. on highly re-tentive octadecylsilyl (ODS) packings such as Zorbax ODS (2). Advantages of non-aqueous RP include an enhanced solubility of lipophilic extracts in the mobile phase thus aiding their injection and protecting against solute precipitation on the column, high column efficiencies and a long-term stability of the column bed. An example of the separation of carotenoids by this technique is shown in *Figure 3*.

To quantify carotenoids in human plasma, hexane extracts may be analysed directly on RP (ODS) columns coupled to a photometric detector operated in the visible region (~ 450 nm). A method of plasma analysis based on the resolution of carotenoids shown in *Figure 3* is described in *Table 4*. This method taken from reference (9) uses another carotenoid, echinenone, as an internal standard. The use of photodiode array detectors capable of programmed multi-wavelength detection has added a new sophistication; such detectors allow the detection of carotenoids, vitamin A compounds and vitamin E compounds in the same run at or near the absorption maximum of each compound. At the same time photodiode array detectors can provide detailed spectral information of peaks as they elute from the column.

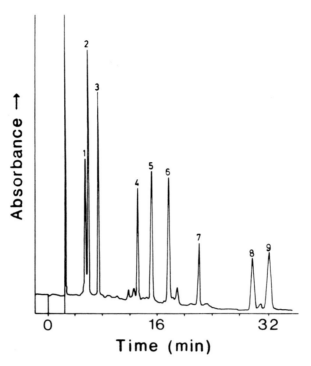

Figure 3. Resolution of carotenoid standards on a column (25 cm × 4.6 mm) of Zorbax ODS with a mobile phase of 70% acetonitrile, 20% dichloromethane and 10% methanol (by vol.), a flow-rate of 1 ml/min and spectrophotometric detection at 450 nm. Peaks: **1** = lutein; **2** = zeaxanthin; **3** = canthaxanthin; **4** = β-cryptoxanthin; **5** = echinenone; **6** = lycopene; **7** = torulene; **8** = α-carotene; **9** = β-carotene. Taken from ref. 2.

Table 4. Assay of provitamin A carotenoids in plasma[a].

Sample extraction

1. Accurately pipette 100 μl of plasma into a micro-centrifuge tube[b].
2. Accurately add 100 μl of echinenone (Hoffmann-La Roche and Co., Basle, Switzerland) in ethanol (accurately known concentration of ~0.2 μg/ml) as the internal standard and vortex mix for 15 sec.
3. Pipette 120 μl of n-hexane into the tube as the extracting solvent and vortex mix for 1 min.
4. Centrifuge the tube contents on a micro-centrifuge[b].
5. Transfer 100 μl of the upper hexane layer to a clean tapered tube[b] and evaporate to dryness under a stream of nitrogen at 50°C.
6. Immediately before h.p.l.c., reconstitute the lipid residue in 100 μl of the mobile phase (see h.p.l.c. conditions), vortex mix briefly, and inject an aliquot (50−90 μl) onto the h.p.l.c. column.

H.p.l.c. conditions

1. Column: Supelcosil LC-18, dimensions 25 cm × 4.6 mm (i.d.) (5 μm silica chemically bonded with ODS groups; from Supelco Inc, Bellefonte, PA, USA).
2. Mobile phase: 70% acetonitrile, 20% dichloromethane and 10% methanol (by vol.).
3. Flow-rate: 1.7 ml/min.
4. Detector: u.v.-visible, discrete multiwavelength absorbance detector (e.g. model 440 from Waters Associates) fitted with a 436 nm filter.

---

[a]Adapted from ref. 9.
[b]See *Table 1* for further details.

3. VITAMIN D

3.1 Introduction

Though vitamin D is now strictly regarded as a prohormone and its dihydroxylated metabolites as hormones, it is included here because of its historical classification as a fat-soluble vitamin. Vitamin D eludes one of the traditional concepts of a 'vitamin' in being synthesized within the skin by u.v. irradiation. This, the major source of vitamin D, is known as cholecalciferol (vitamin D_3). Smaller amounts of cholecalciferol may be obtained through the diet. Another source to modern man is ergocalciferol (vitamin D_2) which is used for the fortification of foods. The chemical structures of vitamin D compounds are shown in *Figure 4*.

Vitamin D is also exceptional among vitamins in that it is clinically more important to be able to measure circulating levels of its hydroxylated metabolites rather than the parent forms. The main metabolites of clinical and analytical interest are 25-hydroxy-vitamin D [25-(OH)D], 1,25-dihydroxyvitamin D [1,25-$(OH)_2$D] and 24,25-dihydroxy-vitamin D [24,25-$(OH)_2$D]. Each of these may exist as their D_2 or D_3 forms though normally the D_3 forms strongly predominate.

The first plasma analyses for the metabolites of vitamin D were carried out using competitive protein binding (CPB) assays which exploited the occurrence in nature of specific proteins (such as those present in plasma, or target cells in the kidney and intestine) which have a high affinity for the metabolites. More recently radioimmuno-assay (RIA) techniques have been introduced. Although both types of assay are very sensitive (capable of detecting picogram amounts) they are not inherently specific and, in addition to the vitamin D metabolite being measured, other metabolites may bind to the binding protein or antibody. A further problem is that other plasma proteins or lipids may interfere non-specifically. To achieve specificity it has been found necessary to introduce additional clean-up steps firstly by lipid extraction and secondly by chromatographic techniques to isolate individual vitamin D metabolites.

In recent years h.p.l.c. has revolutionized the chromatographic separation of vitamin D and its metabolites. In addition to providing a fast and efficient purification procedure before carrying out CPB or RIAs, h.p.l.c. methods now exist to measure those forms

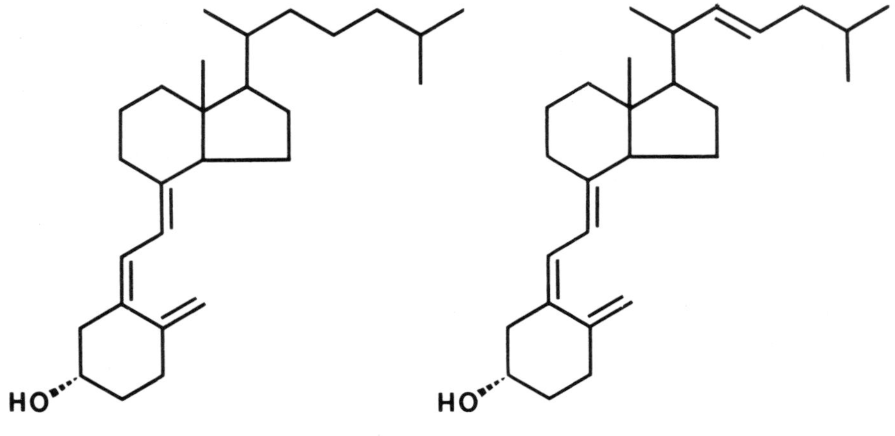

Figure 4. Chemical structures of (left) cholecalciferol and (right) ergocalciferol.

of vitamin D that circulate at sufficiently high concentrations to allow their direct detection by an u.v. photometer. Such assays are commonly used for 25-(OH)D and occasionally also for the parent vitamin and 24,25-(OH)$_2$D.

This section will mainly consider those procedures used in the extraction and h.p.l.c. of vitamin D and its metabolites. Although the appropriate use of CPB or RIAs will be covered, for reasons of scope and space precise experimental details will not be described here; they may be found, however, in an excellent multi-authored book on vitamin D methodology (10).

3.2 Sample preparation and extraction of vitamin D and its metabolites

Vitamin D and its metabolites are reasonably stable in plasma and in the short term may be stored at $-20°C$. In the long term storage at $-70°C$ is preferable; at this temperature in polyethylene tubes the rate of metabolite degradation in 1 year is reportedly 5% or less.

Most plasma assays begin by the incubation of plasma with an appropriate tritium tracer(s) to monitor recovery or act as the tracer in the CPB assays or RIAs (10).

A universally applicable technique in the preparation of plasma samples is that of lipid extraction. Two lipid extraction procedures are widely used. The first and perhaps more reliable is the well known Bligh and Dyer extraction or a modification of this procedure (*Table 5*). In the original method lipids are extracted in a single phase by the addition of methanol:chloroform (2:1). After centrifugation and transfer of the supernatant, the ratio of methanol:chloroform:water is adjusted to give a two-phase system with vitamin D and its metabolites present in the lower chloroform phase. This is a very effective lipid extraction procedure and due to its very exhaustiveness many extraneous interfering lipids are co-extracted. A modification is to substitute the chloroform component with dichloromethane. This has been reported to significantly reduce the amount of interfering lipids without affecting the extraction recovery of vitamin D and its metabolites. The second lipid extraction technique which is generally quicker and more convenient (although more hazardous) is to extract plasma with diethyl ether (*Table 5*). Its obvious advantages are the ease with which the ether phase may be separated and evaporated to dryness. On the other hand, less polar forms such as vitamin D and 25-(OH)D may be incompletely extracted by ether, though excellent recoveries are obtained for the dihydroxylated metabolites. Care must be taken to use peroxide-free ether to avoid oxidation of vitamin D metabolites and to minimize explosion hazards from peroxides when the ether is being evaporated to dryness.

Other solvents and solvent mixtures have inevitably been devised to extract vitamin D and its metabolites but a comparatively recent innovation which deserves attention is the use of commercially available Sep-Pak cartridges (Waters Associates). Their use combines a rapid extraction procedure with a chromatographic clean-up step. They consist simply of short, open-ended, inert plastic tubes pre-packed with either a NP or RP microparticulate packing. Attachment of a syringe with a Luer end fitting to one end of the cartridge allows the sample to be first loaded and then solvents to be rapidly pushed through the cartridge. To extract vitamin D and its metabolites from plasma, Sep-Pak cartridges packed with an RP, ODS-bonded silica (Sep-Pak C$_{18}$) may be used (*Table 6*). Besides providing a simultaneous clean-up step, the use of Sep-Pak cartridges provides savings on time and solvent requirements.

Table 5. Lipid extraction method for vitamin D and metabolites.

Bligh and Dyer method: extraction with methanol:chloroform (2:1 v/v)

1. Pipette a plasma aliquot into a glass-stoppered tube and add 3.75 volumes of methanol:chloroform (2:1 v/v)[a].
2. Shake vigorously by hand, by vortex mixer or by mechanical shaker for 5 min.
3. Centrifuge at 1000−1500 *g* for 10 min to spin down the precipitated protein. Decant the single phase extract into a clean glass tube[b].
4. If necessary, re-extract the protein residue with the same solvent proportions as the first extraction and combine the two extracts.
5. To the extract add further volumes of chloroform and water (or saturated KCl solution[c]) so that the final proportions of methanol:chloroform:water are 1:1:0.9 (by vol.).
6. Centrifuge at 1000−1500 *g* for 10 min to separate the two phases, an upper aqueous-methanol phase and a lower chloroform phase containing vitamin D and metabolites.
7. Remove the upper aqueous-methanol phase, re-extract with a further 0.5 vol. of chloroform and combine chloroform washings with the original chloroform phase.
8. Evaporate the chloroform extract to dryness in a rotary evaporator under reduced pressure or under a stream of nitrogen at 40°C.

Extraction with diethyl ether

1. Pipette a plasma aliquot into a glass-stoppered tube and add 2−3 volumes of peroxide-free diethyl ether.
2. Shake vigorously for 5 min or more gently for 20 min on a horizontal shaker.
3. Either
   (a) centrifuge briefly and with a pipette transfer the upper ether layer to a glass separating funnel; or
   (b) allow to settle for 1−2 min, freeze the bottom aqueous layer in a dry ice−acetone bath and pour off the upper ether layer into a glass separating funnel.
4. Re-extract the lower layer (after thawing, if necessary) twice more and combine all three ether extracts in the separating funnel.
5. Wash the combined ether extracts twice with 40 ml of 0.1 M sodium phosphate buffer, pH 10.5 with gentle mixing. Run off the lower alkaline buffer and discard.
6. Run off the ether layer into a clean vessel and evaporate to dryness in a rotary evaporator under reduced pressure or under a stream of nitrogen at 40°C.

[a]In one modification dichloromethane is used in place of chloroform.
[b]In another modification the single phase extract is not decanted but left to stand for 15−60 min. The appropriate volumes of chloroform (or dichloromethane) and water (optional) are then added to the same tube to obtain, after centrifugation, a two-phase system in which a solid protein interphase is sandwiched between the upper aqueous-methanol layer and the lower chloroform phase.
[c]See ref. 11.

Table 6. Extraction of vitamin D metabolites from plasma using Sep-Pak C_{18} cartridges[a].

1. Pipette 2−3 ml of plasma[b] into a centrifuge tube and add an equal volume of acetonitrile.
2. Vortex mix and centrifuge at 2000 *g* for 5 min.
3. Using a 10-ml glass syringe with a Luer end fitting, pre-wash a Sep-Pak C_{18} cartridge (Waters Associates) with 3 ml of acetonitrile followed by 3 ml of water.
4. Add 1 ml of water to the plasma supernatant and introduce into the glass syringe. Attach the Luer end fitting to the cartridge and push the supernatant through the cartridge to load the extract at the head of the cartridge.
5. Elute the cartridge with 4 ml of methanol:water (7:3, v/v) and discard the eluate.
6. Elute the cartridge with 3 ml of acetonitrile and collect the eluate (containing vitamin D metabolites) into a glass, stoppered, tapered tube.
7. Evaporate the eluate to dryness under a stream of nitrogen at 40°C.

[a]Adapted from ref. 12.
[b]To monitor the analytical recovery it is usual to first incubate the plasma with a radiolabelled tracer of the metabolite to be assayed (see also *Table 7*).

3.3 Assay of vitamin D in plasma

Plasma concentrations of the parent vitamins cholecalciferol (vitamin D_3) and ergo-calciferol (vitamin D_2) are not reliable indices of vitamin D status and their measurement is not often needed in a clinical setting.

Compared with its metabolites, vitamin D is difficult to assay by CPB assays. This is mainly due to its poor solubility in assay media and the fact that there is no known binding protein that has a high affinity for vitamin D. Direct h.p.l.c. assays for vitamin D using u.v. detection have therefore been tried with some success but there may be a problem with detection. The strategy of two procedures (11,13) is similar in that both use NP-h.p.l.c. on a column of Zorbax-SIL (Du Pont Co.) as a semi-preparative stage (D_2 and D_3 eluting as one peak) and RP-h.p.l.c. on a column of Zorbax-ODS (Du Pont) as the analytical stage (D_2 and D_3 separated as two peaks). One method (13) extracts a greater volume (3−5 ml) of plasma and employs two preliminary clean-up steps using open-columns of Sephadex LH-20 (Pharmacia, Co.) and Lipidex 5000 (Packard Instruments, Co.). In the other method (11), in which only 2 ml of plasma are extracted, the detection of vitamin D_2 and D_3 in normal plasma is difficult because of lipid interferences so that a third separation on Zorbax-SIL is usually needed: this then gives a measure of the total vitamin D since both D_2 and D_3 co-elute on NP systems. Both methods, however, give similar values for circulating total vitamin D in normals (~ 2 $\mu g/1$). No further experimental details will be given here but may be found in the original texts (11,13). The principles of direct h.p.l.c. assays for vitamin D, however, are very similar to those for the more important 25-(OH)D metabolite which is considered in more detail in Section 3.4.2.

3.4 Assay of 25-hydroxyvitamin D in plasma

The metabolite 25-(OH)D produced in the liver from vitamin D is the major circulating form of vitamin D and its measurement in plasma serves as an excellent index of vitamin D status. In man, over 80% of the total 25-(OH)D is normally derived from cholecalfiferol (D_3). Absolute plasma levels are around 25 $\mu g/l$, but may vary widely (10−80 $\mu g/l$) depending on the diet and degree of sunlight exposure. There is a characteristic seasonal variation with plasma levels being maximal in late summer and minimal in winter.

3.4.1 *H.p.l.c. in CPB assays or RIAs of 25-hydroxyvitamin D*

The first assays of 25-(OH)D using CPB techniques were developed before the evolution of h.p.l.c. when either open-column chromatography on silicic acid or Sephadex LH-20 gels were usually used to remove interfering compounds. Although open-columns of silicic acid or Sephadex LH-20 are certainly capable of separating 25-(OH)D from vitamin D and 24,25-(OH)$_2$D, the two main cross-reacting and therefore interfering compounds in plasma, there is no doubt that h.p.l.c. is a more efficient procedure for resolving vitamin D metabolites and removing interfering lipid contaminants. In addition, h.p.l.c. provides the best method for resolving the D_2 and D_3 forms of 25-(OH)D so that if required they can be measured separately. This is not a capability of the majority of assays for 25-(OH)D using open-column chromatography.

H.p.l.c. methods which may be used to purify lipid extracts before assay by CPB

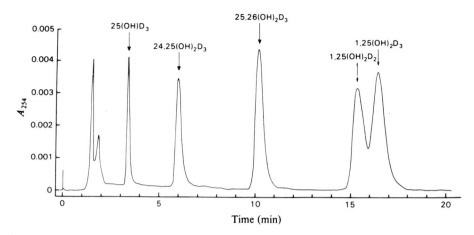

Figure 5. Resolution of vitamin D metabolite standards on a column (25 cm × 4.6 mn) of Zorbax-SIL with a mobile phase of 10% (v/v) propan-2-ol in hexane, a flow-rate of 2 ml/min and u.v. detection at 254 nm. Taken from ref. 13.

or RIA techniques are adaptable but are often based on the microparticulate silica, Zorbax-SIL (Du Pont, Co.). With mixtures of propan-2-ol in hexane, this packing is able to resolve all the major metabolites of vitamin D including the D_2 and D_3 forms (14). A separation suitable for isolating the major vitamin D metabolites for subsequent assay is shown in *Figure 5*. As shown for 1,25-$(OH)_2D$ the D_2 forms of the metabolites elute slightly before their D_3 forms in this system and when assaying total 25-(OH)D the collection of the column eluate should be timed to include both 25-$(OH)D_2$ and 25-$(OH)D_3$. If 25-$(OH)D_2$ and 25-$(OH)D_3$ are to be assayed separately by binding assays then their resolution should be increased by decreasing the proportion of propan-2-ol in hexane. With a Zorbax-SIL column a mobile phase of hexane:propan-2-ol (24:1) at a flow-rate of 2 ml/min gives an excellent resolution of 25-$(OH)D_2$ and 25-$(OH)D_3$ in about 10 min.

Although mixtures of hexane and propan-2-ol usually give good separations of vitamin D metabolites, peak tailing may be encountered when the propan-2-ol concentration is increased beyond 10% and the solvents are anhydrous. The problem may be resolved by incorporating a small percentage of methanol into the mobile phase or by the use of other ternary solvent mixtures (15).

3.4.2 *Direct h.p.l.c. assay of 25-hydroxyvitamin D in plasma*

A number of methods employing h.p.l.c. with u.v. detection are now available for the direct measurement of 25-(OH)D in plasma. These methods, which are superseding CPB assays, differ considerably in experimental design and the number of purification steps.

The problem in evaluating such methods is that only rarely have they been compared with each other or with a well-established physical technique. When they have, as in a recent comparison of direct h.p.l.c. assays with isotope dilution − mass spectrometry (ID − m.s.), the results are revealing (16). They show that the best results are obtained with a combination of NP and RP separations though the sequence in which this is

Table 7. Assay of 25-(OH)D$_2$ and 25-(OH)D$_3$ in plasma[a].

Sample extraction

1. Add 10 μl of an ethanol solution containing $\sim$5000 c.p.m. of radiolabelled[b] 25-(OH)D$_3$ to 2 ml of plasma and incubate at 4°C for 30 min.
2. Extract the lipids by the method of Bligh and Dyer as described in *Table 5*.

<u>Isolation of a 25-(OH)D fraction by NP-h.p.l.c.</u>

H.p.l.c. conditions

1. Column: Zorbax-SIL, dimensions 22 cm $\times$ 6.2 mm (i.d.) (5 μm silica packing; from DuPont and Co., Wilmington, DE, USA).
2. Mobile phase: 5.5% (v/v) propan-2-ol in n-hexane.
3. Flow-rate: 1.5 ml/min.
4. Detector: u.v., fixed wavelength absorbance detector set at 254 nm.

Method

1. Dissolve the total extract ($\sim$20 mg of lipid) in 1 ml of mobile phase (see h.p.l.c. conditions) and filter through a 0.45 μm Teflon membrane filter. Evaporate to dryness under a stream of nitrogen, re-dissolve in 200 μl of mobile phase and inject the total volume onto the silica column.
2. Collect a fraction corresponding to 25-(OH)D (10−14 min) into a clean tapered tube and evaporate to dryness under a stream of nitrogen.

<u>Re-chromatography of 25-(OH)D fraction by RP-h.p.l.c.</u>

H.p.l.c. conditions

1. Column: Zorbax-ODS, dimensions 22 cm $\times$ 6.2 mm (i.d.) (5 μm silica chemically bonded with ODS groups; from DuPont).
2. Mobile phase: 9% (v/v) water in methanol.
3. Flow-rate: 1.5 ml/min.
4. Detector: u.v., fixed wavelength absorbance detector set at 254 nm.

Method

1. Reconstitute the 25-(OH)D$_2$ fraction collected from the NP stage of h.p.l.c. in 100 μl of mobile phase (see h.p.l.c. conditions) and inject the total volume onto the RP column.
2. Detect and measure peaks of 25-(OH)D$_3$ (14 min) and 25-(OH)D$_2$ (15.3 min).
3. Collect the eluate between 13 and 15 min to recover the radiolabelled 25-(OH)D$_3$ added initially. Measure the radioactivity in a scintillation counter to determine the analytical recovery.

---

[a]Adapted from ref. 11.
[b]A suitable radiolabelled tracer is [26,27-^{3}H]25-(OH)D$_3$, specific activity 10−20 Ci/mmol or 130−180 Ci/mmol (Amersham International, Bucks, UK). This is added to monitor the recovery of 25-(OH)D.

carried out does not seem to be important. The most unsatisfactory results are obtained when an open-column purification step (either Sephadex LH-20 or Lipidex 5000) is followed directly by quantification by NP-h.p.l.c.; this method usually gives grossly elevated values. Quantification of 25-(OH)D by NP-h.p.l.c. can be greatly improved by using RP as a second semi-preparative stage after Sephadex LH-20 or by using a Sep-Pak cartridge (*Table 6*) as a purification stage instead of Sephadex LH-20. If quantification by RP-h.p.l.c. is preferred, a purification stage using NP-h.p.l.c. gives satisfactory results. When these precautions are observed it is possible to obtain results which are within 20−30% of the ID−m.s. reference method (16). Whether NP- or RP-h.p.l.c. is chosen as the final analytical stage, both modes are able to resolve 25-(OH)D$_2$ and

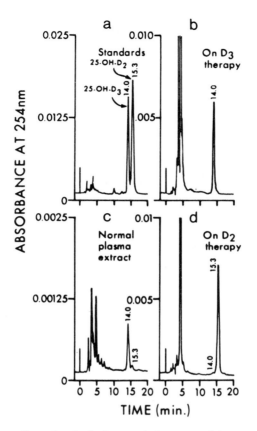

Figure 6. Chromatograms illustrating the final reversed-phase stage of the assay of 24-hydroxyvitamin D in plasma and showing (**a**) standards of 25-(OH)D₃ and 25-(OH)D₂, (**b**) a plasma extract from a subject on vitamin D₃ therapy, (**c**) a plasma extract from a normal subject and (**d**) a plasma extract from a subject on vitamin D₂ therapy. The chromatographic conditions are as described in *Table 7*. Taken from ref. 11.

25-(OH)D₃. This is useful for finding out what proportion of the total plasma 25-(OH)D originated from cholecalciferol and ergocalciferol, respectively.

Many direct h.p.l.c. methods for 25-(OH)D include a preliminary open-column purification step mainly to reduce the amount of lipid and to prevent overloading of the subsequent h.p.l.c. stages. Depending on the volume of plasma extracted, this may not be necessary. It is quite possible to inject lipid extracts from 2 ml of plasma directly onto a 22 cm × 6.2 mm (i.d.) column of microparticulate silica and to collect a sufficiently pure fraction to detect 25-(OH)D₂ and 25-(OH)D₃ after re-analysis by RP-h.p.l.c. (11). A procedure based on only two separations by h.p.l.c. is described in *Table 7* and illustrated in *Figure 6*.

3.5 Assay of 1,25-dihydroxyvitamin D in plasma

1,25-(OH)₂D is synthesized from 25-(OH)D principally by the kidney and is the most active hormonal form of vitamin D. The ability to assay this metabolite in blood is of clinical importance for the diagnosis and study of disorders of vitamin D metabolism in patients with impaired renal function, calculus disease or disorders of bone metab-

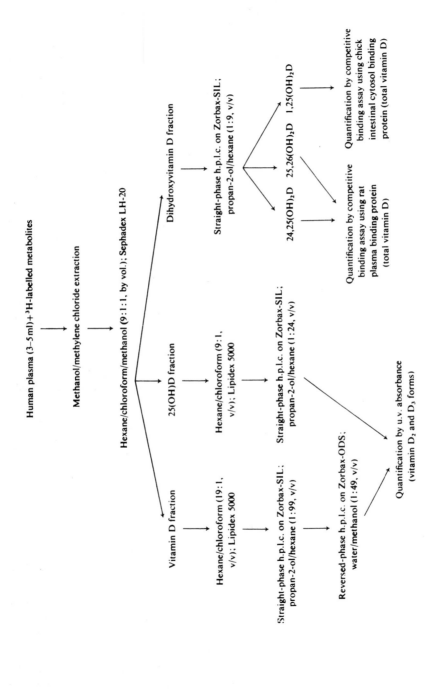

Figure 7. Outline of a multiple assay procedure for the analysis of vitamins D_2 and D_3, 25-(OH)D_2 and 25-(OH)D_3, 24,25-(OH)$_2$D, 25,26-(OH)$_2$D and 1,25-(OH)$_2$D in human plasma. Taken from ref. 13.

olism. Since circulating plasma levels of 1,25-(OH)$_2$D are very low (~ 30 ng/l) they cannot be measured directly by h.p.l.c. with u.v. detection and the hormone is usually assayed by CPB or RIA techniques.

The low plasma levels of 1,25-(OH)$_2$D makes its assay by radio-receptor techniques very vulnerable to interference from other vitamin D metabolites and small amounts of unknown lipid contaminants. A rigorous purification procedure is therefore necessary which should include h.p.l.c. as the final stage. One of the most common separation schemes is to use Sephadex LH-20 followed by NP-h.p.l.c. on Zorbax-SIL. The separation shown in *Figure 5* is suitable for this purpose but ternary solvent mixtures give better peak shapes and are capable of the baseline resolution of 1,25-(OH)$_2$D$_2$ and 1,25(OH)$_2$D$_3$ enabling both to be assayed separately (15).

3.6 Assay of 24,25-dihydroxyvitamin D in plasma

24,25-(OH)$_2$D, another renal metabolite, circulates in plasma at concentrations of around 2 μg/l and, like 1,25-(OH)$_2$D, is usually assayed by protein binding or RIA techniques. Exactly the same lipid purification scheme may be used as described for 1,25-(OH)$_2$D in Section 3.5. 24,25-(OH)$_2$D is particularly susceptible to peak tailing on NP columns with hexane and propan-2-ol mixtures but this may be obviated by ternary solvent mixtures such as hexane:propan-2-ol:methanol (87:10:3) (15).

Plasma concentrations of 24,25-(OH)$_2$D are high enough to be detected directly by h.p.l.c. with u.v. detection. In one method (17) 24,25-(OH)$_2$D is quantified after two sequential separations by NP-h.p.l.c., while in another (18) the metabolite is purified by NP and detected after RP-h.p.l.c. The two methods give comparable values for plasma concentrations of 24,25-(OH)$_2$D.

3.7 Assay for multiple vitamin D metabolites

In studying vitamin D metabolism it may be necessary to measure a number of metabolites in the same sample. For this purpose there exist a variety of multiple assay procedures (10). An outline of a comprehensive strategy to measure vitamin D and all its major metabolites in one sample is given in *Figure 7*.

For the busy clinical laboratory there is much merit in a simple multiple assay procedure to measure 25-(OH)D, 1,25-(OH)$_2$D and possibly 24,25-(OH)$_2$D without resolution into their D$_2$ and D$_3$ forms. Such a procedure is described in *Table 8*.

4. VITAMIN E

4.1 Introduction

As shown in *Figure 8*, compounds with vitamin E activity belong to two groups: all have a 6-chromanol ring structure and a side chain which may be saturated (tocopherols) or unsaturated at positions 3', 7' and 11' (tocotrienols). In each group there are four naturally occurring compounds differing in the number and position of methyl groups in the chromanol ring: these are named α-, β-, γ- and δ-tocopherols and tocotrienols, respectively (*Figure 8*). Tocopherols and tocotrienols are widely but not uniformly distributed in nature. In both animal tissues and foods of animal origin α-tocopherol predominates and is the chemical structure with the highest biological activity. In vegetable oils and cereal grains other tocopherols (especially γ-tocopherol) and tocotrienols are

Table 8. Multiple assay procedure for 25-(OH)D, 1,25-(OH)$_2$D and 24,25-(OH)$_2$D in plasma.

Sample preparation and extraction

1.　Add and incubate appropriate tracer(s) of vitamin D metabolites with ~3 ml of plasma[a].
2.　Extract vitamin D metabolites using a Sep-Pak C$_{18}$ cartridge as described in *Table 6*.

Isolation of metabolite fractions by NP-h.p.l.c.

H.p.l.c. conditions[b]

1.　Column: Zorbax-SIL, dimensions 25 cm × 4 mm (i.d.) (5 μm silica packing; from DuPont).
2.　Mobile phase: 90% n-hexane, 5% methanol and 5% propan-2-ol (by vol.).
3.　Flow-rate: 2 ml/min.
4.　Detection: u.v. absorbance detector set at 265 nm.

Method

1.　Reconstitute vitamin D metabolite fractions from the Sep-Pak procedure in 70 μl of mobile phase (see h.p.l.c. conditions) and inject total onto the Zorbax-SIL column.
2.　Collect individual fractions of 25-(OH)D, 1,25-(OH)$_2$D and 24,25-(OH)$_2$D as required[c].

Assay of 25-(OH)D, 1,25-(OH)$_2$D and 24,25-(OH)$_2$D fractions

1.　Assay the 25-(OH)D fraction by RP-h.p.l.c. and u.v. detection as described in *Table 7*.
2.　Assay the 1,25-(OH)$_2$D and 24,25-(OH)$_2$D fractions individually using appropriate CPB or RIA[d].

[a]For further details see *Tables 6* and *7* and refs. 10, 11 and 13.
[b]These h.p.l.c. conditions are taken from ref. 15.
[c]For further details of collection procedures see ref. 13.
[d]For further details of CPB and RIA see ref. 10.

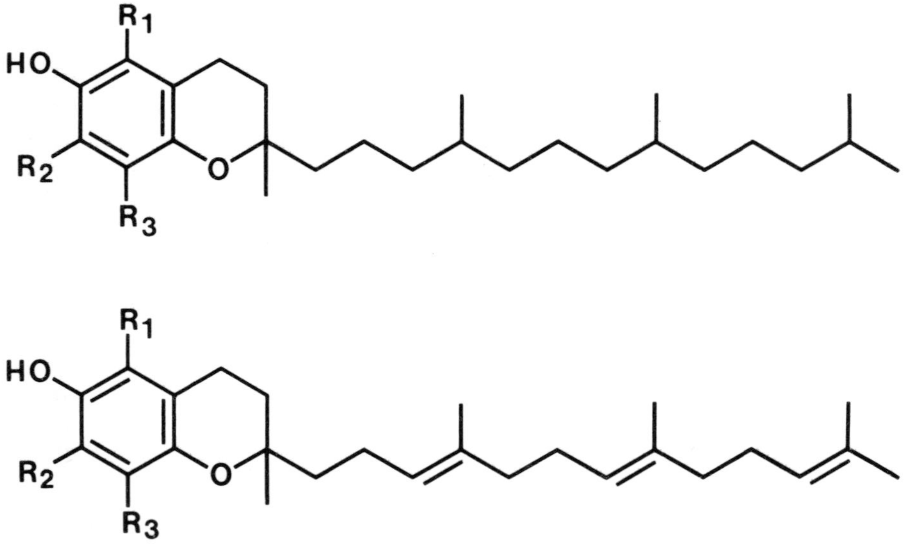

Figure 8. Chemical structures of (**top**) tocol and tocopherol and (**bottom**) tocotrienols. For tocol R$_1$, R$_2$, R$_3$ = H. For α-tocopherol or α-tocotrienol R$_1$, R$_2$, R$_3$ = CH$_3$. For β-tocopherol or β-tocotrienol, R$_1$, R$_3$ = CH$_3$, R$_2$ = H. For γ-tocopherol or γ-tocotrienol R$_1$ = H, R$_2$, R$_3$ = CH$_3$. For δ-tocopherol and δ-tocotrienol R$_1$, R$_2$ = H, R$_3$ = CH$_3$.

widespread and may be the major forms. Tocopherols have three asymmetric carbon atoms at position 2 in the ring and positions 4' and 8' in the side chain; natural α-tocopherol has the RRR configuration while commercially available, synthetic α-tocopherol is *all-rac-α-tocopherol*.

Earlier methods for the analysis of vitamin E in tissues included colourimetry, spectrophotometry, and fluorimetry usually after isolating a pure or vitamin E-rich fraction by saponification (not always necessary), lipid extraction and open-column or thin-layer chromatography (t.l.c.). Tissue analyses for vitamin E based on gas-liquid chromatography (g.l.c.) have been developed but the methods are far from ideal since they either require fairly complex sample preparation procedures to remove interfering lipids (particularly cholesterol) or a long chromatographic analysis time. Another drawback of g.l.c. is the possibility of the degradation of vitamin E compounds at the high temperatures needed for their analysis. H.p.l.c. is a much more versatile technique: the resolution of vitamin E compounds is more readily achieved while their physicochemical properties make them amenable to detection using spectrophotometric, fluorimetric or electrochemical detectors (ECD).

4.2 Assay of tocopherols in blood

Unlike the other fat-soluble vitamins, vitamin E is found in both plasma and cellular elements of blood, the latter including erythrocytes, leucocytes and platelets. The tocopherol content (w/v) of packed erythrocytes represents about 15% of the plasma concentration, is present in the membrane and exchanges with the plasma pool. In human plasma vitamin E is transported in association with lipoproteins; in the fasting state mainly with low density and high density lipoproteins. As in other tissues the predominant form in human plasma is α-tocopherol accounting for about 90% of the total plasma concentration of vitamin E, the remainder mostly comprising γ-tocopherol and β-tocopherol in a ratio of 5:1, respectively. Only traces of δ-tocopherol and tocotrienols are present in human plasma and are not detected by most current h.p.l.c. assays for vitamin E. With plasma concentrations in the range of about $5-15$ mg/l, α-tocopherol has the highest plasma concentration of any of the fat-soluble vitamins. Despite the wide range of plasma concentrations, the measurement of α-tocopherol in plasma is a useful index of vitamin E status and it is generally accepted that individuals with plasma concentration below 5 mg/l are vitamin E deficent.

4.2.1 *Sample preparation and extraction*

Although most anti-coagulants may be used for the collection of blood plasma, the integrity of lipoproteins to which tocopherols are bound is best preserved by EDTA: α-tocopherol in plasma and lipoprotein fractions stored at 4°C in the dark have been reported to be stable for several days. On the other hand tocopherols are sensitive to oxidation and for longer periods of storage plasma samples should be kept at -20°C or below. The oxidation of tocopherols is accelerated by light, heat, alkalis or metal ions but if oxygen is excluded they are stable to heat and alkaline conditions. The stability to alkali in the absence of oxygen is important because a saponification step is often used in the isolation of vitamin E from tissues either before or after the lipid extraction step. In either case saponification is useful in removing triglycerides and in liberating tocopherols from possible esterified forms. For some tissues direct saponification before solvent extraction may increase the efficiency of extraction of vitamin E. If saponification is used, precautions must be taken to prevent the oxidative degradation of tocopherols. This is usually accomplished by the addition of anti-oxidants such as pyrogallol or ascorbic acid and by the exclusion of air from the reaction vessel. For tissues such as plasma and the cellular elements of blood, saponification does not increase the efficiency of extraction and direct extraction methods are therefore safest. Like retinol, the tocopherols and tocotrienols are readily and completely extracted into non-polar solvents such as hexane after the addition of a deproteinizing agent such as ethanol.

4.2.2 *Design of h.p.l.c. assays*

In choosing a method to assay vitamin E in plasma the analyst needs to consider his/her individual requirements and constraints such as the required specificity and sensitivity, ease of operation, analysis time, method of quantification (e.g. possible use of an internal standard) and cost. A major consideration is whether it is necessary to measure and therefore resolve all the tocopherols in plasma since the positional β- and γ-isomers of tocopherol may only be resolved by NP-h.p.l.c. Given that β- and γ-tocopherols together account for only about 10% of the total plasma tocopherol content, their separation may be of academic importance only and this is certainly true for the clinical evaluation of vitamin E deficiency. In this case RP-h.p.l.c. may also be used; on ODS-bonded packings α-tocopherol is typically resolved from a composite peak containing both β- and γ-tocopherol (19). For the routine analysis of a highly lipid-soluble molecule like vitamin E, RP-h.p.l.c. is generally preferable because it is easier to achieve and maintain stable retention times on RP columns than on NP columns. The difficulty of accurately controlling the retention of lipophilic compounds on silica columns is associated on the one hand with the need to deactivate the strong adsorption sites on the silica surface (to prevent peak tailing and obtain high column efficiencies) and on the other hand with the practical problems in achieving this, particularly in controlling the water content of the mobile phase which strongly influences retention when using non-polar solvent mixtures. When using RP-h.p.l.c., however, the relatively non-polar nature of vitamin E compounds affords the opportunity of choosing a highly retentive ODS support in tandem with a non-aqueous mobile phase: the advantages of non-aqueous RP-h.p.l.c. for lipophilic molecules have already been outlined (Section 2.5). A further advantage of RP-h.p.l.c. for the analysis of α-tocopherol in plasma is that a short chain tocopheryl ester may be used as an internal standard; for analyses not involving saponification α-tocopheryl acetate meets all the analytical criteria for an internal standard, is readily available commercially and is inexpensive. α-Tocopheryl acetate is not suitable as an internal standard for analyses using NP-h.p.l.c. since, compared with tocopherols and tocotrienols, all tocopheryl esters are insufficiently retained by silica packings. Instead tocol is a useful internal standard for NP systems but, being more unstable than tocopherols towards alkali, should not be used if a saponification step is included in the extraction procedure. This stricture also applies to the use of α-tocopheryl acetate which would be hydrolysed during saponification.

Though the absorbance of vitamin E in the u.v. region is relatively low (molar extinction coefficient of α-tocopherol is 3500 at 292 nm), the plasma concentrations are sufficiently high to be able to measure α-tocopherol in 100 μl of plasma and β- and γ-tocopherols in 500 μl of plasma (20). Some selectivity in u.v. detection is gained by the relatively long wavelength maximum of α-tocopherol (292 nm); at this wavelength retinol is also detectable and simultaneous assays of α-tocopherol and retinol are possible using RP-h.p.l.c. (6). Tocopherols and tocotrienols possess native fluorescence and this may be exploited to increase the sensitivity and selectivity of vitamin E assays. The minimum detectable amount of α-tocopherol by fluorimetric detection is 10 ng or less (21) and by photometric detection 30 ng (20). For plasma analyses the extra sensitivity of fluorescence measurements may be useful in detecting β-, γ- and δ-tocopherols (21) though a photometric method for measuring β- and γ-tocopherols in plasma is perfectly satisfactory (20).

As easily oxidizable compounds, tocopherols may be readily measured by ECD. At a glassy-carbon electrode (with Ag/AgCl as the reference electrode) the half-wave potential for α-tocopherol determined by hydrodynamic voltammetry is about +0.6 V and, using a thin-layer cell combined with RP-h.p.l.c., as little as 50 pg of α-tocopherol can be detected at a potential of +0.7 V (22). The application of ECD to plasma analyses of vitamin E have not been widely adopted, mainly because such high sensitivities are not normally needed to measure the major vitamin E compounds in plasma. A potential restriction of ECD is that NP systems with non-polar solvents cannot dissolve sufficient supporting electrolyte for direct current measurements, though a possible way around this problem is to use a post-column method of adding the supporting electrolyte.

Two methods described in detail below are chosen to illustrate the rapid analysis of α-tocopherol in small volumes of plasma by RP-h.p.l.c. and the assay of α-, β- and γ-tocopherols by NP-h.p.l.c.. Both methods use photometric detection but for extra sensitivity the NP method may be readily adapted to fluorescence detection. The RP method cannot be directly adapted to fluorescence detection since the internal standard α-tocopheryl acetate, unlike tocol, is not fluorescent.

4.2.3 *Rapid micro-assay of plasma α-tocopherol*

Details of a rapid micro-assay for α-tocopherol in plasma developed in the author's laboratory are given in *Table 9*. The assay is identical in design to that already described for retinol (Section 2.2.3) and is based on the RP method of Bieri *et al.* (6) using α-tocopheryl acetate as an internal standard. Differences from the assay as originally described (6) include the use of a shorter column (10 cm long instead of 30 cm) which allows a lower flow-rate (1.0 ml/min instead of 2.5 ml/min) for a similar analysis time. In addition the use of a more retentive column packing (Spherisorb 5 ODS-2 instead of μ-Bondapak C_{18}) enables a non-aqueous mobile phase to be used (mixtures of dichloromethane and methanol instead of methanol and water) with consequent advantages for sample solubility, column efficiency and long-term stability. Examples of chromatograms obtained by this micro-assay (*Table 9*) are shown in *Figure 9*. Note that the β- and γ-isomers elute as a single peak before α-tocopherol. As with the retinol assay (Section 2.2.3) a short chain ester (α-tocopheryl acetate) is an excellent internal standard not found in nature. Even though synthetic α-tocopheryl acetate is used as a vitamin E supplement and may be present in infant formulas or health foods, this compound is hydrolysed during intestinal absorption but, unlike vitamin A, is not re-esterified before release into the lymphatics, and therefore appears in the plasma as unesterified α-tocopherol.

Table 9. Rapid micro-assay of α-tocopherol in plasma.

Sample extraction

1. Accurately pipette 100 μl of plasma into a micro-centrifuge tube [a].
2. Accurately add 100 μl of a solution of α-tocopheryl acetate (Sigma) in ethanol (accurately known concentration of ~50 μg/ml) as the internal standard and vortex mix for 30 sec.
3. Pipette 200 μl of n-hexane into the tube as the extraction solvent and vortex mix for 30 sec. Transfer the tube to a mechanical shaker[a] and shake the contents for 10 min.
4. Centrifuge the contents on a micro-centrifuge[a] for 5 min to separate an upper hexane layer from a lower aqueous-ethanolic layer.
5. Transfer the upper hexane layer (containing the α-tocopherol and α-tocopheryl acetate) by pipette to a glass, tapered tube[a] and evaporate to dryness under a stream of nitrogen at 40°C.
6. Immediately before h.p.l.c., reconstitute the lipid residue in 100 μl of ethanol, vortex mix briefly, and inject 20 μl onto the h.p.l.c. column.

H.p.l.c. conditions

1. Column: Spherisorb-ODS 2, dimensions 12.5 cm × 5 mm (i.d.)[a].
2. Mobile phase: 7% (v/v) dichloromethane in methanol.
3. Flow-rate: 1 ml/min.
4. Detector: u.v., variable wavelength absorbance detector set at 292 nm.

[a]See *Table 1* for further details.

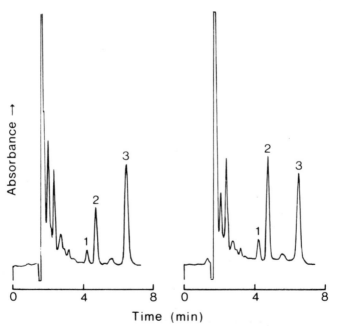

Figure 9. Chromatograms illustrating the rapid micro-assay of α-tocopherol in plasma at concentrations of (**left**) 4.3 mg/l and (**right**) 9.2 mg/l. The chromatographic conditions are as described in *Table 9*. Peaks: **1** = β- and γ-tocopherols; **2** = α-tocopherol; **3** = α-tocopheryl acetate.

The same assay procedure (*Table 9*) can be easily adapted to measure α-tocopherol and retinol simultaneously. In this case both α-tocopheryl acetate and retinyl acetate (in ethanol) should be added as internal standards keeping the ratio of plasma:ethanol:

Table 10. Assay of α-, β- and γ-tocopherols in plasma[a].

Sample extraction for α-tocopherol

1. Accurately pipette 100 μl of plasma into a micro-centrifuge tube[b].
2. Accurately add 100 μl of a solution of tocol (Eisai Research Laboratories, Tokyo, Japan) in ethanol (accurately known concentration of $\sim$20 μg/ml) as the internal standard, and vortex mix for 15 sec.
3. Pipette 500 μl of n-hexane into the tube as the extraction solvent and vortex mix for 4 min or shake for 10 min on a mechanical shaker[b].
4. Centrifuge the contents on a micro-centrifuge[b].
5. Transfer the upper hexane layer (containing tocopherols and tocol) to a glass, tapered tube[b] and evaporate to dryness under a stream of nitrogen at 40°C.
6. Immediately before h.p.l.c., reconstitute the lipid residue in 20 μl of the mobile phase (see h.p.l.c. conditions) and inject onto the h.p.l.c. column.

Sample extraction for β- and γ-tocopherol

1. Accurately pipette 500 μl of plasma into a suitable centrifuge tube.
2. Accurately add 100 μl of a solution of tocol in ethanol (accurately known concentration of $\sim$10 μg/l) as the internal standard, 400 μl of ethanol and vortex mix for 15 sec.
3. Pipette 1.5 ml of n-hexane into the tube as the extraction solvent and vortex mix for 4 min or shake for 10 min on a mechanical shaker.
4. Follow steps 4$-$5 as for the extraction of α-tocopherol.

H.p.l.c. conditions

1. Column: RSIL silica, dimensions 15 cm $\times$ 3 mm (i.d.) (5 μm silica; from RSL, St. Martens-Latem, Belgium).
2. Mobile phase: 0.6% (v/v) propan-2-ol in n-hexane.
3. Flow-rate: 1 ml/min.
4. Temperature: 30°C.
5. Detector: u.v., variable wavelength absorbance detector set at 294 nm.

---

[a]Adapted from ref. 20.
[b]See *Table 1* for further details.

hexane at 1:1:2. As already mentioned (Section 2.2.2) both α-tocopherol and retinol may be detected in plasma near the absorption maximum of α-tocopherol (292 nm).

4.2.4 *Assay of α-, β- and γ-tocopherols in plasma*

A method able to measure α-, β- and γ-tocopherols individually in plasma is described in *Table 10*. To resolve all the tocopherols, NP-h.p.l.c. must be used. Detection may be achieved by u.v. absorption (*Table 10*) or with greater sensitivity by fluorescence measurements (21). For quantification, tocol is a convenient internal standard. With the high concentration of α-tocopherol in plasma relative to other tocopherols, it is better to separate the analysis of α-tocopherol from that of the β- and γ-isomers. The chromatographic conditions are the same for both analyses; the only differences being the volumes of plasma extracted and the amount of tocol added as an internal standard (*Table 10*). The separation of β- and γ-isomers on a column of 5 μm silica (RSL) with propan-2-ol as a moderator (*Table 10*) is illustrated in *Figure 10*. An equally good resolution of tocopherols may be achieved with other microparticulate silicas and other moderators. Diethyl, di-*iso*-propyl and methyl-*t*-butyl ethers have all been used as moderators in hexane but methyl-*t*-butyl ether is preferable because of its greatly reduced tendency to form deleterious (and explosive) peroxides.

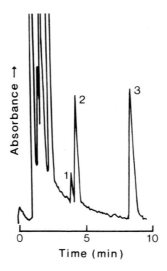

Figure 10. Chromatograms illustrating the assay of β- and γ-tocopherols in plasma. The chromatographic conditions are as described in *Table 10*. Peaks: **1** = β-tocopherol; **2** = γ-tocopherol; **3** = tocol (internal standard). Taken from ref. 20.

5. VITAMIN K

5.1 Introduction

All naturally occurring K vitamins have the same 2-methyl-1,4-naphthoquinone nucleus but differ in the length and degree of saturation of their side chain (*Figure 11*). Phylloquinone (vitamin K_1), synthesized by plants, has a phytyl side chain whereas the multiple series of menaquinones (vitamin K_2), synthesized by bacteria, have multiprenyl side chains; they are designated by the abbreviation MK-n according to the number of prenyl units. A variety of minor forms of the menaquinone series also exist in which one or more of the prenyl units is saturated. In animal tissues K vitamins are present in extremely low concentrations. Whereas open-column and t.l.c. techniques have been used to study, but not accurately quantify, storage forms of vitamin K in human liver (phylloquinone and MKs 6−13) the same techniques are not capable of detecting the low circulating levels in human plasma. It has not yet proved possible to develop radio-receptor assays or RIAs for K vitamins and to date all our information on plasma levels has come from recently developed assays based on h.p.l.c. Only phylloquinone has been measured in human plasma although the levels reported for normal, fasting subjects have varied quite widely with mean values ranging from 0.3 to 2.6 μg/l.

The properties of K vitamins offer several avenues of approach to their detection by h.p.l.c. Firstly, with a molar extinction coefficient of up to 19 000 in the 240−270 nm region, u.v. detection is reasonably sensitive and levels down to 500 pg can be detected with an instrument setting of 0.005 absorption-units full-scale (a.u.f.s.) The reversible reduction of the quinone moiety to the hydroquinone makes ECD an attractive alternative for the detection of K vitamins. H.p.l.c.-linked ECD assays of phylloquinone now exist whereby, under ideal operating conditions, less than 50 pg can be detected. Finally, although K vitamins possess no native fluorescence, they are

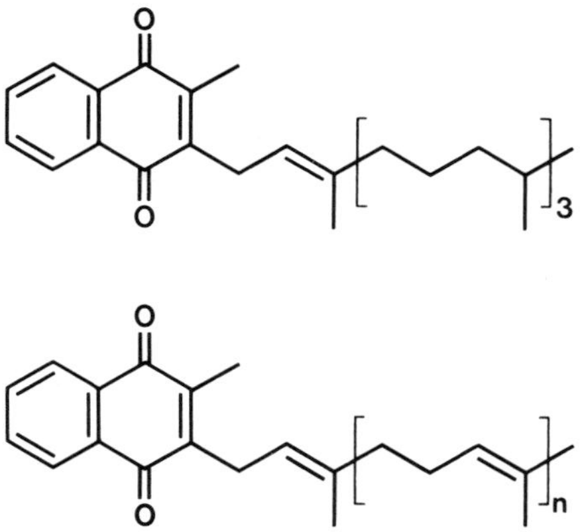

Figure 11. Chemical structures of (**top**) phylloquinone or vitamin K_1 and (**bottom**) menaquinones or vitamins K_2.

readily reduced or degraded to forms that do fluoresce. One such fluorophore is the hydroquinone form and this may be detected fluorometrically after the chemical, photochemical or electrochemical reduction of the corresponding K vitamin. Recently developed h.p.l.c. assays with fluorometric detection can also detect less than 50 pg of phylloquinone.

5.2 **Assay of phylloquinone in plasma**

The assay of phylloquinone in plasma is a comparatively recent achievement and the clinical implications are still being investigated. There is already evidence that the plasma levels of phylloquinone may reflect the nutritional status of vitamin K. Most importantly, plasma assays have provided for the first time the means to study the circulating levels and transport of vitamin K in health and disease. Menaquinones seem to be present in plasma at much lower concentrations than phylloquinone and assays for them are as yet unavailable.

5.2.1 *Sample preparation and extraction*

To obtain plasma, blood may be collected into any anti-coagulant; EDTA and heparin are commonly used in the author's laboratory. Thereafter the main precaution is that the sample should be shielded from strong light. Phylloquinone is stable for months, even years, when stored at $-20°C$. All K vitamins are rapidly destroyed by light and alkali (it is essential to remove all traces of detergents from glassware) but are relatively stable towards heat, oxygen and dilute acids. Since it is now possible to detect picogram amounts of K vitamins, particular care should be taken to prevent contamination of samples with lipids or phylloquinone from extraneous sources such as rubber fittings and lubricants or during h.p.l.c. from syringes and valve injectors (e.g. from phylloquinone standards). Advisable precautions are to rinse glassware with ethanol or acetone before use and to keep separate h.p.l.c. syringes for standard and sample injections.

Phylloquinone circulates in human plasma bound to lipoproteins from which it may

Table 11. Hexane extraction of vitamin K from plasma.

1.	To one volume of plasma in a glass, stoppered centrifuge tube add 2 volumes of ethanol and vortex mix briefly[a].
2.	Add 4 volumes of n-hexane and mix the contents vigorously by alternative hand shaking and vortex mixing for 5 min.
3.	Centrifuge at 1500 *g* for 10 min to separate an upper hexane layer from a lower aqueous-ethanolic layer and precipitated proteins.
4.	Transfer the upper hexane layer with a Pasteur pipette to a glass, stoppered tube.
5.	If necessary (e.g. when not using an internal standard), re-extract the lower layer with a further 4 volumes of hexane and pool with the first hexane extract.
6.	Evaporate the hexane extract to dryness under a stream of nitrogen at 50°C or in a rotary evaporator under reduced pressure.

[a]An internal standard appropriate to the method of detection (see text) is added at this stage. The internal standard should be added in ethanolic solution and a further volume of ethanol added if needed so that the final plasma:ethanol ratio is 1:2 (v/v).

be readily extracted into a non-polar solvent after disruption of the lipoprotein molecules. As with retinol and tocopherols, extraction with hexane after flocculation of proteins with ethanol is a simple and effective extraction method. The extraction procedure used in the author's laboratory is described in *Table 11*. No advantage is gained by a more exhaustive lipid extraction procedure like the Bligh and Dyer extraction used for vitamin D (*Table 5*) and may be actually undesirable since more extraneous polar lipids are also extracted. It is safe to remove solvents at temperatures up to 60°C either in a rotary evaporator or under a stream of nitrogen.

5.2.2 *Design of h.p.l.c. assays*

(i) *Preliminary purification.* Whatever the final detection method, one of the biggest problems in measuring endogenous plasma phylloquinone is to remove co-extracted lipids. The problem is 2-fold. Firstly, bulk lipids need to be removed to enable the sample extract to be dissolved in a small volume of the mobile phase (usually 50 – 100 μl) before analysis by h.p.l.c. Secondly, lipids that interfere with the final detection method must also be removed. Some bulk lipids, such as triglycerides, are easily removed whereas cholesteryl esters, with a similar polarity to vitamin K, are more difficult to remove. In addition, trace amounts of unknown lipids tend to persist during the purification procedure; their removal is a particular problem in assays based on u.v. detection. One preliminary purification procedure previously used in the author's laboratory is open-column chromatography of lipid extracts on columns of silica gel (23). A more rapid procedure, however, is to use Sep-Pak silica cartridges (Waters Associates) and this is described in *Table 12*.

(ii) *H.p.l.c. stages.* Although chromatography on open-columns of silica or on Sep-Pak silica cartridges removes lipids that are both less polar (e.g. hydrocarbons) and more polar (e.g. sterols, glycerides, fatty acids and phospholipids) than vitamin K, many lipids, including cholesteryl esters, remain. Some assay designs therefore include an extra purification stage using NP-h.p.l.c. before a final analytical stage using RP-h.p.l.c. Fractionation of lipid extracts on NP columns effectively removes cholesteryl esters

Table 12. Isolation of a vitamin K fraction from lipid extracts using Sep-Pak silica cartridges.

1.	Using a 10-ml glass syringe with a Luer end fitting, pre-wash a Sep-Pak silica cartridge (Waters Associates) with $10-20$ ml of n-hexane[a].
2.	Dissolve the lipid extract[b] in 2 ml of n-hexane and introduce into the glass syringe. Attach the Luer end fitting to the cartridge and push the hexane solution through the cartridge to load the extract at the head of the cartridge.
3.	Rinse the tube that contained the lipid extract with a further 2 ml of hexane and load onto the cartridge in the same way.
4.	Elute the cartridge with 10 ml of hexane to elute a hydrocarbon fraction and discard the eluate.
5.	Elute the cartridge with 10 ml of 3% (v/v) diethly ether in n-hexane and collect the eluate (containing vitamin K and other lipids) into a glass, stoppered, tapered tube.
6.	Evaporate the eluate to dryness under a stream of nitrogen at 50°C or in a rotary evaporator under reduced pressure.

[a]The pre-washing step with hexane removes u.v.-absorbing material from the cartridge which may otherwise interfere with the assay of phylloquinone based on u.v. detection. For electrochemical detection this step may be omitted.
[b]See *Table 11* for the lipid extraction procedure using hexane. The loading capacity of each Sep-Pak silica cartridge using this procedure is approximately 100 mg of lipid. For plasma samples from normolipaemic subjects, up to 10 ml of plasma may be extracted and prepared using one Sep-Pak silica cartridge.

and other interfering lipids and, by further reducing the lipid bulk, allows the extract to be readily dissolved in small volumes of the mobile phases used for RP-h.p.l.c.

RP-h.p.l.c. is almost universally used for the final analytical stage of phylloquinone assays mainly because this mode is the most effective in separating lipids with closely related polarities and/or structures including the K vitamins themselves. RP-h.p.l.c. is almost a prerequisite for the direct electrochemical detection of K vitamins in the column eluate since only polar mobile phases can dissolve the supporting electrolyte needed to conduct a current. The selection of the RP packing should be made on the basis of the final detection method. For u.v. detection the use of highly retentive ODS-bonded packings with non-aqueous solvents are most suitable; their advantages for carotenoid analysis have already been mentioned (Section 2.5) and for K vitamins are discussed elsewhere (24).

For ECD less retentive packings, such as octyl-bonded phases, are needed so that semi-aqueous mobile phases can be used. The less efficient resolution in semi-aqueous mobile phases is compensated by the extra selectivity of ECD.

(iii) *Detection methods.* The principles of photometric detection are well known and its application to the detection of K vitamins has been reviewed elsewhere (23,24). The limitations of u.v. detection are its relative lack of selectivity and sensitivity. In the author's experience some $5-10$ ml of plasma needs to be extracted and processed to detect endogenous plasma levels of phylloquinone. Nevertheless, the stability of u.v. detectors is good and, combined with the high resolving power of non-aqueous RP-h.p.l.c., reliable results can be obtained. U.v. detection is particularly suitable for measuring raised plasma levels after the administration of pharmacological doses of the vitamin.

The more recent introduction of ECD for h.p.l.c. has provided the opportunity for more sensitive and selective measurements of K vitamins. The first combined h.p.l.c.-ECD measurements of vitamin K used the reductive mode with cells based on a thin-layer design and containing a glassy-carbon working electrode. The principle of this method is as follows. When a sufficiently negative potential is applied to a glassy-carbon electrode over which vitamin K is flowing, the quinone moiety is reduced to the hydroquinone and the flow of electrons from the electrode can be measured as current. The magnitude of the current which is recorded by the detector is proportional to the amount of vitamin K electrolysed at the electrode surface; with thin-layer cells, however, only a small fraction (typically $2-5\%$) of the analyte is reduced. At the high sensitivities needed to detect phylloquinone in plasma, the reductive mode has several practical disadvantages. One of these is interference from oxygen which, if not removed by de-aeration techniques, causes high background currents and baseline instability. When working at high sensitivities even traces of oxygen entering or leaving the system can cause steeply sloping baselines and artifactual peaks when samples are injected. Another problem is the loss in sensitivity due to passivation of the working electrode by species which adsorb to the electrode surface. Such problems restrict the practical utility of reductive ECD but even so this mode is still about three times as sensitive as u.v. detection (25).

The development of a redox method for the ECD of vitamin K eliminates interference from the reduction of oxygen and increases the selectivity of detection (26). In this method the detector is a dual-electrode cell with the electrodes arranged in series: vitamin K is first reduced at the upstream (or generator) electrode to the hydroquinone and this product is then re-oxidized at the downstream (or detector) electrode. Much of the increase in sensitivity and selectivity stems from the use of a relatively low oxidative potential at the downstream electrode which allows the re-oxidation of vitamin K hydroquinone without the concomitant oxidation of other electroactive lipids or species (e.g. peroxide or water which are the products of oxygen reduction at the upstream electrode). A further practical advantage is to be gained from the use of porous, graphite electrodes having a flow-through design; with their high surface areas such electrodes enable a greater proportion of the analyte to be electrolysed and are less easily passivated than thin-layer electrodes. Methods based on dual-electrode ECD are capable of detecting 50 pg or less of phylloquinone in only $1-2$ ml of plasma (27).

A third choice of detection of K vitamins in h.p.l.c. is by the fluorescence exhibited by certain products of reduction or degradation of K vitamins. Methods designed to measure the fluorescence after post-column photochemical reaction or chemical reduction can detect about 150 pg of phylloquinone (28). An alternative approach in which a 'coulometric' detector is used as a post-column reactor to reduce phylloquinone to the fluorescent hydroquinone derivative is capable of detecting 25 pg of phylloquinone (29). As described (29) this method has the practical disadvantage of requiring two expensive detectors in series. In the author's laboratory a method with a similar sensitivity has been developed using a dual-electrode ECD alone. Details of this method together with an earlier method based on the more universally available u.v. detector are given below.

5.2.3 *Assay of phylloquinone in plasma with u.v. detection*

The following two-stage h.p.l.c. assay was developed in the author's laboratory and uses phylloquinone 2,3-epoxide as an internal standard (23,24). One restriction is that phylloquinone epoxide should not be used as an internal standard for plasma analyses in subjects treated with coumarin or indanedione antagonists of vitamin K since these drugs induce the plasma accumulation of phylloquinone epoxide. Normally, however, phylloquinone epoxide is undetectable in plasma.

(i) *Instrumentation.* It is recommended that separate chromatographs be dedicated to the NP and RP stages of the assay, respectively. If only one system is available extreme care should be taken to eliminate all traces of mobile phase from the apparatus when changing over from the RP to the NP system, otherwise the transfer of even traces of methanol to NP columns will result in a loss of retention for vitamin K and a consequent delay in re-equilibration. The specifications of the pump and u.v. detector used for the semi-preparative stage of h.p.l.c. are not critical. For the final analytical stage a combination of a high-performance pump and an u.v. detector giving minimal noise at 270 nm and 0.005 a.u.f.s. should be chosen.

(ii) *Method.*

(1)   Extract $5-10$ ml of plasma with hexane and isolate a non-polar lipid fraction containing vitamin K by chromatography on Sep-Pak silica cartridges as described in *Tables 11* and *12*.

(2)   Further purify the lipid fraction by NP-h.p.l.c. on columns of Partisil-5 (Whatman Inc.) as described in *Table 13*.

Dichloromethane with a controlled water content (50% water-saturated) has been found to be an effective moderator for the chromatography of vitamin K on NP columns (23, 24). Prepare this by mixing equal volumes of dichloromethane kept in a flask under a layer of water (100% water-saturated dichloromethane) with dry dichloromethane (h.p.l.c. grade is usually sufficiently dry but may be dried with calcium chloride if necessary). Use the resulting 50% water-saturated dichloromethane preferably on the day of preparation since on storage in glass vessels the water content will slowly decline due to adsorption of water by the vessel wall. The dichloromethane used in the author's laboratory (Rathburn Chemicals Ltd) also contains 0.1% methanol as stabilizer, thus the final mobile phase (*Table 13*) will contain about 0.02% methanol which will also act as a moderator and significantly influence the retention of non-polar molecules like vitamin K. Experience, however, suggests that these small concentrations of methanol may have a beneficial effect on peak shape. The advantage of using Partisil-5 as the silica support is that, with mixtures of hexane and 50% water-saturated dichloromethane, phylloquinone co-elutes with the phylloquinone epoxide internal standard. This minimizes the risk of the differential loss of phylloquinone and phylloquinone epoxide when collecting the vitamin K fraction. The precise location and collection of the fraction of eluate which contains phylloquinone and phylloquinone epoxide is a critical part of the assay. At this stage both compounds are masked by other u.v.-absorbing lipids and their retention time must first be determined by injecting standards. One practical problem is that the retention of phylloquinone may slowly change during the day but this can usually be detected from changes in the retention of other u.v.-absorbing peaks which are characteristic of the sample under analysis. The 'fingerprint' pattern produced by u.v.-absorbing peaks also helps to locate the fraction of eluate which contains phyllo-

Table 13. Isolation of a phylloquinone fraction by NP-h.p.l.c.

H.p.l.c. conditions

1. Column: either Partisil-5 silica (5 μm irregular silica; from Whatman) when the final analytical stage is by u.v.-detection or Spherisorb-5 nitrile (5 μm silica chemically bonded with cyano propyl silyl groups; from Phase Separations) when the final analytical stage is by dual-electrode ECD. The dimensions of both columns are 25 cm $\times$ 5 mm (i.d.).
2. Mobile phase: mixtures of 50% water-saturated[a] dichloromethane in n-hexane. The concentration of dichloromethane is either in the range of 15−22% (v/v) or 3−6% (v/v) for columns of Partisil-5 silica and Spherisorb-5 nitrile, respectively.
3. Flow-rate: 1 ml/min.
4. Detection: u.v., fixed or variable wavelength absorbance detectors set at 254 or 270 nm.

Method

1. Adjust the mobile phase composition so that the retention of a phylloquinone standard is about 8−10 min at a flow-rate of 1 ml/min. Equilibrate the column by allowing the mobile phase to flow through the column until the retention time of a phylloquinone standard[b] injected at periodic intervals is constant[c].
2. Thoroughly wash the valve injector[d] with mobile phase and inject a solvent blank to ensure that no standard is carried over with the sample injection.
3. Dissolve the vitamin K fraction isolated by the Sep-Pak procedure (*Table 12*) in 70 μl of mobile phase, vortex mix briefly to dissolve the lipid and inject the total volume onto the h.p.l.c. column.
4. Collect the eluate fraction which encloses phylloquinone and, where added, the appropriate internal standard into a glass, stoppered, tapered tube and evaporate to dryness under a stream of nitrogen at 50°C.

---

[a]See text for further details of the water-saturation procedure.
[b]Depending on the method of detection in the final analytical stage (*Table 14*) the solution of phylloquinone standard may also include an appropriate internal standard (see text).
[c]The equilibration of Partisil-5 is much slower than for Spherisorb-5 nitrile.
[d]A suitable valve injector is the model 7125 syringe loading sample injector from Rheodyne, Cotati, CA, USA. This should be fitted with a 100 μl loop.

quinone and the internal standard (23,24).

Details of the final analytical stage of the photometric assay are given in *Table 14*. The appearance of the chromatograms (*Figure 12*) may vary slightly according to the separation achieved at the semi-preparative stage. In the author's experience highly retentive packings such as Hypersil ODS (Shandon Ltd) or Zorbax ODS (Du Pont Co.) are most suitable. The choice of mobile phase may also be important. For columns of Hypersil ODS and Zorbax ODS, non-aqueous mixtures of dichloromethane in methanol usually give good resolution of phylloquinone and phylloquinone epoxide from interfering u.v.-absorbing compounds; the selectivity with this solvent pair being generally superior for plasma analyses than other solvent pairs such as dichloromethane in acetonitrile. After injecting a plasma extract it may be necessary to wait for several minutes to allow for the elution of u.v.-absorbing compounds which are more strongly retained than phylloquinone and may interfere with subsequent injections; the removal of these late-eluting compounds may be speeded up by increasing the flow-rate.

5.2.4 *Assay of phylloquinone in plasma with ECD*

The assay described is that currently used in the author's laboratory and is based on the detection of phylloquinone with a dual-electrode ECD using the redox mode (26,

Table 14. Final analytical stage of the assay of phylloquinone in plasma.

Assay with u.v. detection

H.p.l.c. conditions

1. Column: ODS Hypersil, dimensions 25 cm × 5 mm (i.d.) (5 μm silica chemically bonded with ODS groups; from Shandon Southern).
2. Mobile phase: 15% (v/v) dichloromethane in methanol.
3. Flow-rate: 1 ml/min.
4. Detector: u.v., variable wavelength absorbance detector set at 270 nm and 0.005 A.U.F.S.

Method

1. Dissolve the phylloquinone fraction isolated by NP-h.p.l.c. (*Table 13*) in mobile phase (70−100 μl) and vortex mix briefly to dissolve the lipid.
2. Inject up to 70 μl onto the column via a valve injector (100 μl loop).
3. Detect and measure the chromatographic peaks of phylloquinone epoxide added as the internal standard (retention time 7−8 min), and phylloquinone (retention time 9−10 min).
4. Allow time for late eluting peaks before injecting further samples.
5. Inject standard solutions to obtain a calibration graph relating peak height ratios of phylloquinone/ phylloquinone epoxide to weight ratios.

Assay with dual-electrode ECD

H.p.l.c. conditions

1. Column: Spherisorb-5 octyl, dimensions 25 cm × 5 mm (i.d.) (5 μm silica chemically bonded with octyl silyl groups; from Phase Separations).
2. Mobile phase: 3−6% (v/v) 0.05 M acetate buffer (pH 3.0) in methanol and containing 0.1 mM EDTA.
3. Flow-rate: 1 ml/min.
4. Detector: dual-electrode ECD[a] with the upstream (generator) electrode set at −1.3 V and the downstream (detector) electrode set at 0 V.

Method

1. Dissolve the phylloquinone fraction isolated by NP-h.p.l.c. (*Table 13*) in ethanol (50−100 μl) and vortex mix briefly to dissolve the lipid.
2. Inject up to 20 μl onto the column via a valve injector (20 μl loop).
3. Detect and measure the chromatographic peak of phylloquinone (retention time ~10 min) and the appropriate internal standard (either 2,3-dihydrophylloquinone or menaquinone-6 both eluting after phylloquinone).
4. Inject standard solutions to obtain a calibration graph relating peak height ratios of phylloquinone/ internal standard to weight ratios.

---

[a]See text (Section 5.2.4) for further details of the ECD.

27). The internal standards for the analysis of plasma samples are either 2,3-dihydro-phylloquinone [$K_1(I-H_2)$] or menaquinone-6 (MK-6). Of the two compounds, $K_1(I-H_2)$ has the widest applicability being neither suspected nor detectable in human tissues. MK-6, on the other hand, is a naturally occurring vitamer which, though undetectable in normal human plasma (under the conditions of the present assay), is occasionally detectable in patients with hyperlipoproteinaemia who also have abnormally raised plasma levels of phylloquinone.

The ECD method has the same two-stage h.p.l.c. design as the u.v. method described in Section 5.2.3.

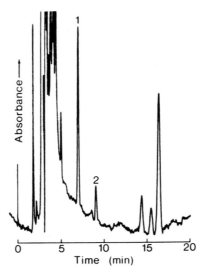

Figure 12. Chromatogram illustrating the final analytical stage of the assay of phylloquinone in plasma at a concentration of 0.43 μg/l with u.v. detection at 270 nm. The chromatographic conditions are as described in *Table 14*. Peaks: **1** = phylloquinone 2,3-epoxide (internal standard); **2** = phylloquinone.

(i) *Instrumentation.* The assay is designed for a specific detector, the Model 5100A Coulochem detector equipped with a model 5011 dual-electrode analytical cell containing two porous graphite electrodes in series (Environmental Sciences Associates, Inc.). In addition, though not essential, a conditioning cell (model 5021 from E.S.A. Inc.) placed in line between the column and the analytical cell may be found useful. One use of the conditioning cell is to serve as an extra electrode surface for the reduction of phylloquinone to phylloquinol. A stringent requirement for this detector is that the solvent delivery should be as pulse-free as possible. In the author's laboratory a model 300 h.p.l.c. pump from Applied Chromatography Systems Ltd. meets these requirements.

(ii) *Method.* The initial extraction and purification steps are identical to those described for the u.v. method (Section 5.2.3 and *Tables 11, 12* and *13*) except that 0.5−2.0 ml of plasma should be processed instead of 5−10 ml. As with the u.v. method a semi-preparative stage using NP-h.p.l.c. serves to remove interfering lipids and reduces the lipid bulk. However, the removal of electroactive interfering lipids is not so critical as for u.v. detection and the final chromatograms obtained with the redox mode of ECD are relatively unaffected by the width of the collection window used to collect the vitamin K fraction at the semi-preparative h.p.l.c. stage. This is useful because although both $K_1(I-H_2)$ and MK-6 are separated from phylloquinone on NP columns, the possible introduction of error due to the incomplete collection of analyte and internal standard is offset by the larger volume of eluate that may be collected. Unlike the u.v. method (Section 5.2.3) there is no special advantage in using Partisil-5 as the column support for the semi-preparative h.p.l.c. stage. Instead cyano-bonded phases such as Spherisorb-5 nitrile (Phase Separations Ltd.) are preferable because of their rapid equilibration with mobile phases, stability of retention and long column life. The chromatographic behaviour of K vitamins on cyano-bonded phases is identical to silica columns except that lower concentrations of moderators in hexane are required for the same retention (24). Thus the concentration of 50% water-saturated dichloromethane required for the semi-preparative stage is 15−22% (v/v) for Partisil-5 and 3−6% for Spherisorb-5 nitrile columns, respectively (*Table 13*).

The chromatographic and ECD conditions used for the final stage of the assay are given in *Table 14*. RP packings bonded with octylsilyl groups (C_8) are recommended because they are less retentive towards K vitamins than ODS packings (C_{18}) and allow a greater proportion of an aqueous buffer (acting as the supporting electrolyte) to be used in the mobile phase. The choice of a mixture of 0.05 M acetate buffer (pH 3.0) in methanol as the mobile phase was made on the basis of the favourable electrochemical response of K vitamins in this electrolyte (25,27). The precise percentage of acetate buffer in methanol should be adjusted to give a retention for phylloquinone of about 8−10 min; for a flow-rate of 1 ml/min this is usually within the range of 3−6%. The optimal applied potentials (*Table 14*) are based on the hydrodynamic voltammograms for the reduction of phylloquinone at the generator (upstream) electrode and the re-oxidation of phylloquinol at the detector (downstream) electrode but also take account of the chromatographic selectivity obtained at different potentials (27). For the chromatographic conditions of *Table 14*, the maximum current for phylloquinone is usually obtained when potentials of −1.3 V and +0.2 V are applied to the generator and detector electrodes, respectively, but a greater selectivity is obtained by reducing the potential of the detector electrode to 0 V. Examples of chromatograms illustrating the measurement of phylloquinone in plasma with $K_1(I-H_2)$ or MK-6 as internal standards are shown in *Figure 13*. As with the u.v. method, late eluting peaks may interfere with subsequent

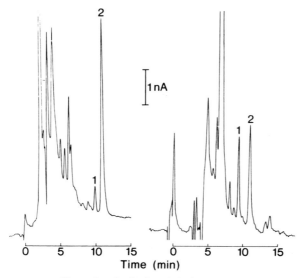

Figure 13. Chromatograms illustrating the final analytical stage of the assay of phylloquinone in plasma with dual-electrode ECD. The chromatographic conditions are as described in *Table 14*. (**Left**): analysis of phylloquinone (**peak 1**) at a plasma concentration of 0.12 µg/l using 2,3-dihydrophylloquinone (**peak 2**) as internal standard and 5% acetate buffer in methanol for the mobile phase. (**Right**): analysis of phylloquinone (**peak 1**) at a plasma concentration of 1.27 µg/l using menaquinone-6 (**peak 2**) as internal standard and 3% acetate buffer in methanol for the mobile phase.

injections; for plasma samples this problem is much less evident when the detector potential is set at 0 V than when working at higher positive potentials such as +0.2 V.

One problem with ECD is that the sensitivity may decrease quite dramatically due to passivation of the electrode by species which become adsorbed to the electrode surface. With their high surface area, the 'coulometric' cells used in this assay usually maintain their sensitivity over several days' continued use. In the author's laboratory it has recently become apparent that a major contribution to electrode passivation in this assay derives not from adsorbed lipids but from the reduction of metal ions at the generator electrode; this process is readily prevented by the addition of 0.1 mM EDTA to the mobile phase. To regain sensitivity one of two procedures can be adopted. The first is to reverse the polarity of the generator electrode to +1.3 V while continuing to run or recycle the mobile phase (often overnight). At the same time the potential of the detector electrode may be set to a negative potential either −0.5 V or −1.0 V. If this 'burn-off' procedure is ineffective the cells should be detached from the instrument and washed sequentially with methanol, dichloromethane, tetrahydrofuran, water, 2 M sodium hydroxide (20 min), water, 6 M nitric acid (20 min), water and finally methanol.

6. VITAMIN C

6.1 Introduction

From the point of view of human nutrition, there are two naturally occurring compounds with vitamin C activity: these are the parent vitamin, L-ascorbic acid and its oxidation product L-dehydroascorbic acid (*Figure 14*). In human tissues, ascorbic acid is the predominant form of the vitamin.

For many years it has been possible to measure vitamin C in tissues by a variety of chemical procedures (30). Since ascorbic acid and dehydroascorbic acid are readily interconvertible by oxidation−reduction reactions, methods of analysis based on chemical reactions of either compound may be used. If a reaction of ascorbic acid is chosen, total vitamin C may be determined by first reducing any dehydroascorbic acid present. Alternatively, the two vitamers may be estimated separately by carrying out two determinations, one before and one after the reduction of dehydroascorbic acid. A similar strategy may be used for reactions of dehydroascorbic acid except that here an oxidation step is incorporated into the assay. The most well known chemical method for the determination of ascorbic acid is the indicator−dye reduction method with 2,6-dichloro-

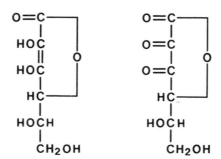

Figure 14. Chemical structures of (**left**) L-ascorbic acid and (**right**) L-dehydroascrobic acid.

phenol-indophenol. Many variants of this assay exist using different oxidants and methods for determining the end-point of the oxidative titration. The main reaction used to measure dehydroascorbic acid is a condensation reaction with *o*-phenylenediamine (OPD) to produce a quinoxalinyl lactone which is highly fluorescent.

The growth of h.p.l.c. has seen many applications of this technique to vitamin C analysis. While the resolving power of h.p.l.c. solves many problems of interfering compounds, the detection of dehydroascorbic acid is difficult without a derivatization step. By failing to account for the presence of dehydroascorbic acid in human tissues many published h.p.l.c. procedures fall short of the ideal. In addition, many authors give no details of the stability of the vitamin during sample preparation. The extreme lability of vitamin C means that stabilization of the vitamin is of crucial importance from the moment the tissue is sampled.

6.2 Assay of vitamin C in blood

The lowering of tissue concentrations of vitamin C which may eventually lead to the clinical symptoms of scurvy are accompanied by a reduced vitamin C concentration in blood plasma, leucocytes and erythrocytes. Blood concentrations of vitamin C in healthy populations may vary widely, these variations often reflecting the dietary availability and intake of vitamin C at different times of the year. It is therefore difficult to define a normal range but plasma levels of the order of $4-14$ mg/l may be expected, whole blood levels being slightly higher. Plasma levels which fall below 1 mg/l for any length of time will lead to the symptoms of scurvy. The concentration of vitamin C is rapidly affected by changes in dietary intake and may not reflect the true tissue reserves (31). The high vitamin C content of leucocytes is thought to reflect tissue concentrations more accurately but techniques for the preparation of a pure leucocyte fraction can be tedious. As a compromise, the analysis of the vitamin C content of whole blood is often used to assess the vitamin C status.

6.2.1 *Sample preparation and extraction*

The instability of ascorbic acid is due to the ready oxidation of the enediol groups at the second and third carbon atoms to produce dehydroascorbic acid which may be further degraded irreversibly to other products via 2,3-diketogulonic acid. A particular problem with blood analyses is that ascorbic acid may be oxidized to dehydroascorbic acid during the deproteinization of blood when oxygen is released from oxyhaemoglobin. Obviously, this is less of a problem when an oxidation step is incorporated into the assay procedure; nevertheless, dehydroascorbic acid is itself unstable and it is therefore desirable to prevent any uncontrolled oxidation. A stabilizing agent shown to be effective for the storage of whole blood samples is a mixture of 0.24 M ethyleneglycolbis-(β-aminoethyl ether)-N,N,N',N'-tetraacetic acid (EGTA) and 0.2 M glutathione (32). The oxidation of ascorbic acid in solution is accelerated by metal ions such as iron and copper and by alkalis. The vitamin is most stable at pH values between 4 and 6, at higher pH values the lactone ring is increasingly labile to hydrolysis. Precautions should always be taken to exclude strong light and any rise in temperature during the analysis.

A variety of agents have been used to extract vitamin C. Most are aqueous solutions of acids often including additives such as EDTA to restrict losses of the vitamin (30).

The classical extracting solutions are metaphosphoric and trichloroacetic acids at concentrations of $3-6\%$. These reagents have the added advantage of precipitating proteins, a step which is always necessary before injecting samples onto h.p.l.c. columns. On the other hand, with their high acidity and ionic strength, solutions of metaphosphoric acid, when injected directly, may cause a decrease in retention of ascorbic acid particularly on anion-exchange columns (33). 50 mM perchloric acid has proved a satisfactory alternative extractant and diluent which may be injected directly onto the chromatographic column (33).

6.2.2 *Design of h.p.l.c. assays*

In the mildly acidic solutions in which ascorbic acid is most stable, the vitamin exists as an anion and is therefore readily retained by anion-exchange packings. Although strong anion exchangers are very successful when used in conjunction with a highly selective method of detection such as amperometric measurements (33), chromatography on weak anion exchangers such as amino-bonded phases are reported to give a superior resolution of ascorbic acid from contaminating components in plasma when using a less selective method of detection such as u.v. absorbance (34). In its ionic form ascorbic acid is not well retained by non-polar, RP packings but excellent retention and resolution may be achieved by the expedient of adding an IP reagent such as tetrabutylammonium phosphate to the mobile phase.

A particular problem with the detection of vitamin C compounds is that the two biologically active compounds, ascorbic acid and dehydroascorbic acid, do not share the same detection properties. Thus, only ascorbic acid may be readily detected with a u.v. spectrophotometric detector since the loss of the ring double bond in dehydroascorbic acid is accompanied by the loss of u.v. absorption at the usual wavelength maxima for ascorbic acid (245 nm in acid solution and 265 nm in neutral solution). It is possible to detect dehydroascorbic acid at 210 nm but the sensitivity and selectivity is usually too poor to be of practical use for the analysis of most biological materials. Some chemical reactions of dehydroascorbic acid, however, may be exploited to produce u.v.-absorbing derivatives. Useful derivatives are those obtained after reaction with 2,4-dinitrophenylhydrazine or OPD. With OPD the quinoxaline derivative thus formed is highly fluorescent and this property may also be used as the basis of even more selective and sensitive assays by h.p.l.c. coupled to a fluorimetric detector (32). The ease of oxidation of ascorbic acid is ideally suited to ECD at carbon electrodes using a potential of about $+0.7$ V (versus Ag/AgCl) (33). Amperometric detection with conventional thin-layer cells is about five times more sensitive than u.v. detection for the detection of ascorbic acid but, again, has the drawback of not allowing the simultaneous detection of dehydroascorbic acid.

In view of the above limitations, it is difficult to select from the literature a single ideal method for the analysis of vitamin C in blood. The assay described in detail in Section 6.2.3 below, though not particularly simple, does have the merit of placing special importance on sample preparation and the stability of the vitamin. It is also a good illustration of how a pre-column derivatization step can be used to increase the sensitivity and selectivity of an assay.

6.2.3 *Assay of total vitamin C in whole blood by RP-h.p.l.c. with pre-column derivatization*

The assay is based on the enzymic oxidation of ascorbic acid to dehydroascorbic acid and the condensation of the latter with OPD to form 3-(1,2-dihydroxyethyl)furo[3,4-*b*]-quinoxaline-1-one (DFQ). This quinoxaline derivative is then chromatographed by RP-h.p.l.c. and detected fluorimetrically (32). The assay may be performed with a conventional h.p.l.c. pump and fluorescence detector. Details of the procedure are given in *Table 15*. Whole blood samples collected into the EGTA−glutathione solution are stable for a period of 8 days when stored in the dark at −20°C, though only for a few hours at room temperature. The reaction times given in *Table 15* for the enzymic oxidation of ascorbic acid (5 min) and the condensation reaction with OPD (30 min) are based on separate experiments to determine the optimum reaction times for standard solutions and blood samples, respectively (32). After carrying out the derivatization step, the sample could be safely stored in the dark at 4°C for h.p.l.c. analysis of DFQ within 24 h. The highly selective nature of this fluorimetric method is illustrated by the clean separation of DFQ and the lack of interfering compounds in the chromatograms of whole blood extracts (*Figure 15*).

Table 15. Assay of total vitamin C in whole blood[a].

Sample extraction and derivatization

1. Collect blood directly into 5-ml plastic tubes containing 0.1 ml of EGTA−glutathione solution[b].
2. Slowly transfer, while vortex mixing vigorously, 1 ml of whole blood into a 10-ml plastic tube containing 4 ml of 0.3 M TCA. Allow the tube to stand for about 20 min in the dark at 4°C, mixing once after 10 min.
3. Centrifuge the contents of the tube at 2000 *g* and 4°C for 10 min.
4. Transfer an aliquot (1.5 ml) of the supernatant to a 5-ml plastic tube, add 0.2 ml of 4.5 M sodium acetate buffer, pH 6.2 and an ascorbic acid oxidase spatula (Boehringer). Incubate the tube contents at 37°C for 5 min, mixing once after 2 min. Remove the enzyme-carrying spatula.
5. Add 0.25 ml of a freshly prepared 0.1% (w/v) solution of OPD. Mix well, and incubate at 37°C in the dark for 30 min. Store the tube in the dark at 4°C and analyse by h.p.l.c. within 24 h.
6. To aliquots of 1 ml of working standard solutions of ascorbic acid, add 4 ml of 0.3 M TCA and 1.2 ml of 4.5 M sodium acetate buffer, pH 6.2. Oxidize with ascorbate oxidase as described in step 4 and react with 0.5 ml of OPD solution as described in step 5.

H.p.l. conditions

1. Column: ODS Hypersil, dimensions 8 cm × 4.6 mm (i.d.) (3 *μ*m silica chemically bonded with ODS groups; from Shandon Southern).
2. Mobile phase: 20% (v/v) methanol in 0.08 M potassium dihydrogen phosphate, pH 7.8.
3. Flow-rate: 1.0 ml/min.
4. Detector: fluorescence detector set for an excitation maximum of 355 nm and an emission maximum of 425 nm.

Method

1. Inject 20 *μ*l of the derivatized sample extract onto the h.p.l.c. column.
2. Inject 20 *μ*l of the derivatized standards of ascorbic acid to obtain a calibration graph of peak heights versus the concentrations of the solutions injected.

[a]Adapted from ref. 32.
[b]See text (Section 6.2.1) for details of sample stabilization.

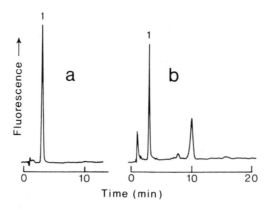

Figure 15. Chromatograms illustrating the assay of total vitamin C in whole blood showing analyses of quinoxaline derivatives **(peak 1)** for **(a)** an ascorbic acid standard and **(b)** an extract of whole blood. Chromatographic conditions are as described in *Table 15*. Taken from ref. 32.

7. THIAMIN (VITAMIN B₁)

7.1 Introduction

The chemical structure of the water-soluble vitamin thiamin (vitamin B_1) features a pyrimidine moiety and a thiazole moiety joined by a methylene bridge (*Figure 16*). The concentration of the parent molecule in animal tissues is low and thiamin is chiefly found (80−90%) as the phosphorylated form thiamin pyrophosphate (TPP) which is the co-enzyme form of the vitamin. Smaller amounts of thiamin monophosphate (TMP) and thiamin triphosphate (TTP) also occur in tissues with the triphosphate predominating (about 10−20% of total thiamin). The biochemical function and many chemical properties of thiamin are dominated by the ready dissociation of the hydrogen atom at position C2 of the thiazole ring.

In the past, thiamin nutriture has been most commonly assessed by measuring the activity of erythrocyte transketolase before and after *in vitro* stimulation with TPP. The direct measurement in tissues of thiamin vitamers has been greatly facilitated by their alkaline oxidation by ferricyanide or other oxidizing agents to fluorescent derivatives called thiochromes. Nearly all methods of chemical analysis rely on this important reaction to increase the sensitivity and selectivity of detection; many modifications exist but a chromatographic step is usually required to remove interferences. The same reaction is easily adapted to h.p.l.c. analyses whereby free thiamin or its phosphorylated forms are detected as thiochromes using either pre- or post-column derivatization techniques.

7.2 Assay of thiamin in blood

As in other tissues, the principal forms of thiamin in blood are the co-enzyme form TPP followed by TTP, both these vitamers being located in the erythrocytes. The very much smaller amounts of TMP and thiamin are only detectable in plasma (35). Human erythrocytes contain approximately 80% of the total blood thiamin. Current evidence suggests that blood levels of thiamin in individuals (normally around 35 µg/l) do reflect

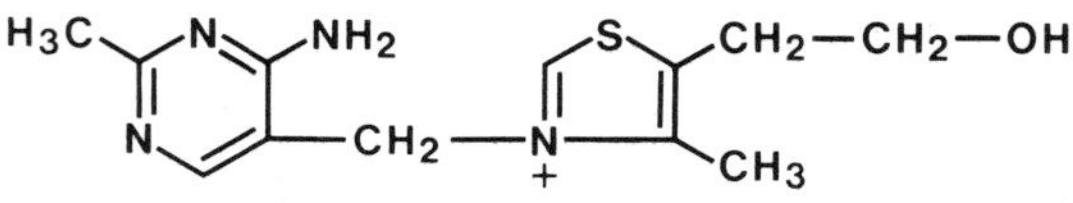

Figure 16. Chemical structure of thiamin.

their thiamin status and are reduced, though not dramatically so, in nutritional deficiency. The ability to measure thiamin in blood by h.p.l.c. methods has given a new impetus to studies of the thiamin metabolism in human nutrition and disease. It is now possible to measure thiamin vitamers in as little as 100 μl of human blood (35,36).

7.2.1 *Sample preparation and extraction*

Samples of whole blood and serum may be stored at $-20°C$ for several weeks without significant changes in thiamin content. At $4°C$ the vitamin slowly decomposes; losses of about 20% in the total thiamin content of whole blood may be expected over a 10-day period (37).

Thiamin is most often extracted from blood with trichloroacetic acid (TCA) though some workers recommend perchloric acid (PCA) (37). Acidic deproteinizing and extracting reagents also have beneficial stabilizing properties since thiamin is most stable at pH values between 2 and 4. The vitamin is less stable at neutral pH and is rapidly destroyed at pH values of 8 and above.

Most methods of thiamin analysis currently available, with or without h.p.l.c., only measure total thiamin and to do this a hydrolysis step is included in which the three phosphorylated forms of thiamin are converted to free thiamin. The liberation of thiamin is carried out enzymatically, often with Taka-diastase (a lyophilized preparation of *Aspergillus oryzae* containing mainly α-amylase, phosphatase and protease activities). In blood analyses this hydrolysis step is usually carried out in buffered solution after extraction with the deproteinizing agent.

7.2.2 *Design of h.p.l.c. assays*

Since maximum stability of thiamin is obtained at acidic pH values, it is sensible to carry out h.p.l.c. using an acidic mobile phase bearing in mind that for maximum long-term stability of most column packings, the pH should be maintained above pH 2. Electrophoretic studies show that, in acetate buffer at pH 3.8, TTP is negatively charged, TPP is electroneutral or weakly positively charged while TMP and thiamin have a positive charge. Thiamin compounds have been successfully analysed using a variety of column packings, but RP separations have gained the greatest popularity for clinical applications. The pK_{a1} of thiamin is 4.8 and therefore mobile phases with pH values below this are very suitable for the RP mode of retention (with or without the addition of an IP counter-ion). A good separation of TTP, TPP, TMP and thiamin in this order of elution may be obtained on a μ-Bondapak C_{18} packing (Waters Associates) using phosphate buffer (pH 4.3) as the mobile phase (38). A refinement to RP methods is to add an IP reagent to the mobile phase. Using the same μ-Bondapak support, good results are obtained by using a methanol/citrate mobile phase (pH 4.0) to which sodium

1-octanesulphonate is added as the counter-ion (37). The order of elution of thiamin compounds on RP packings from the triphosphate through to free thiamin is the same at low pH values whether or not an IP reagent has been added. The same order of elution is also obtained by conventional chromatography on a Sephadex (Pharmacia) cation-exchange resin but the use of modern h.p.l.c. ion-exchange packings has not found wide application for the analysis of tissue samples, presumably because equivalent or superior chromatography can be obtained on the more popular and easier to use RP packings using ion-suppression or IP techniques.

Although thiamin compounds may be detected spectrophotometrically at 254 nm, the limit of detection (~ 30 ng) and specificity is insufficient to allow the measurement of thiamin vitamers in animal tissues. Instead, a fluorometric method of detection is almost invariably used in which thiamin and thiamin phosphate esters are quantitatively converted to thiochrome or thiochrome phosphate esters, a reaction that can be carried out without hydrolysis of the phosphate bond. This reaction may be adapted to h.p.l.c. analyses using two different approaches. The first approach is to directly chromatograph the sample containing thiamin compounds (with or without hydrolysis of thiamin phosphates to thiamin) and to add the appropriate reagents for thiochrome formation to the column eluate (i.e. post-column derivatization) (35 − 38). The second method is to perform the thiochrome reaction before chromatography (i.e. pre-column derivatization) and to chromatograph the thiochrome derivatives themselves (39). Obviously, the chromatographic behaviour of the thiochromes will differ considerably from the parent thiamin compounds so that methods must be designed to achieve the required separation of these derivatives; again, RP-h.p.l.c. is often used. An important difference is that, unlike thiamin compounds, thiochrome and thiochrome phosphates are stable in alkaline solutions. The alkaline oxidation to thiochrome is usually achieved with potassium ferricyanide though the more hazardous cyanogen bromide is sometimes preferred. To detect thiochromes, the excitation wavelength of the fluorimeter should be set near to 375 nm and the emission wavelength in the range of 425 − 450 nm. The limit of detection of thiamin hydrochloride by h.p.l.c. with fluorescence detection is of the order of 30 pg (0.1 pmol) which is approximately three orders of magnitude better than is possible by spectrophotometric detection.

Until recently, the only methods available were those which gave a measure of the total thiamin content of blood; these have the advantage of simplicity and are readily adaptable to automated h.p.l.c. It is now feasible, however, to measure individual thiamin vitamers in blood and the information that this gives may well be desirable for certain applications. To take account of these different requirements, two methods are given in detail. The first is a well validated method for measuring total thiamin and gives detailed information on aspects such as chromatographic optimization, precision and reference values for thiamin in human blood (37). The second method, although not yet well validated, has the important feature of being able to separate and detect individual thiamin vitamers in blood (35).

7.2.3 *Assay of total thiamin in blood by RP-IP h.p.l.c. and post-column derivatization*

This assay is based on the post-column derivatization of thiamin to thiochrome after hydrolysis of phosphate esters to thiamin by acid phosphatase (37).

Table 16. Assay of total thiamin in blood[a].

Sample preparation and extraction

1. Collect blood samples into heparin or EDTA. To extract whole blood freeze the sample without centrifugation, thaw and homogenize. Slowly transfer, while vortex mixing vigorously, a 2-ml haemolysed sample into a plastic tube containing 2 ml of a 10% (w/v) solution of cold PCA. To extract the plasma, mix vigorously a 2-ml sample with 0.5 ml of a 25% (w/v) solution of cold PCA. Allow blood and plasma extracts to stand at 0°C for 15 min.

2. Centrifuge the contents of the tube at 2000 *g* and 4°C for 20 min.

3. Transfer 1 ml of the supernatant to a tube, mix with 0.5 ml of internal standard solution[b] and add 0.1 ml of acid phosphatase solution[c]. Incubate overnight at 37°C[d].

4. Filter through a 0.45 μm membrane filter and inject a 20 μl aliquot via a valve injector into the h.p.l.c. column.

H.p.l.c. conditions

1. Column: μ-Bondapak C_{18}, dimensions 30 cm × 3.9 mm (i.d.) (10 μm silica chemically bonded with ODS groups; from Waters Associates).

2. Mobile phase: 45% (v/v) methanol in 0.05 M sodium citrate buffer, pH 4.0 containing 10 mM sodium 1-octanesulphonae. Degas the mobile phase.

3. Flow-rate: 1.2 ml/min.

4. Post-column derivatization: set the post-column reactor[e] to deliver an aqueous mixture of 2.5 mM $K_3Fe(CN)_6$ and 3 M NaOH to the column effluent at a flow-rate of 0.3 ml/min.

5. Detector: fluorescence detector with the excitation wavelength set at 367 nm and the emission wavelength at 435 nm.

[a]Adapted from ref. 37.
[b]The internal standard solution is an aqueous mixture of 15 μM salicylamide (2-hydroxybenzamide from Sigma), 0.6 M NaOH and 1.8 M sodium acetate.
[c]A solution of lyophilized acid phosphatase from potatoes (type II, activity 0.4 units/mg from Sigma) is prepared in 0.9% (w/v) NaCl at a concentration of 10 mg/ml.
[d]After incubation, prepared samples were stable for 15 h at room temperature.
[e]See text (Section 7.2.3) and ref. 37 for details of the post-column reactor and the optimization of the derivatization conditions.

(i) *Instrumentation.* Conventional h.p.l.c. equipment may be used but details may be mentioned for the post-column reactor. This consists of a stainless steel, zero-dead-volume tee piece (bore 0.25 mm i.d., Valco Instruments) and a Teflon capillary (0.75 mm i.d., 1.8 mm o.d., 90 cm long) wound to a spiral tubular reactor (6.5 mm o.d.) and shielded from light. Under the conditions of the post-column reaction, the authors showed that the thiochrome reaction was complete within 15 sec and that the 90 cm length of Teflon capillary, corresponding to a residence time of 16 sec, was optimal. A peristaltic pump delivered the oxidizing reagent to the reactor at 0.3 ml/min through a 1 m length of silicon tubing which served as a pulse damper.

(ii) *Method.* Details of the method are given in *Table 16.* The RP-IP mode of separation allowed the separation of thiamin and thiamin phosphate esters. The high proportion of methanol (45% v/v) in the mobile phase has the advantage of enhancing the fluorescence intensity of thiochrome.

The combination of PCA as a deproteinizing-extracting reagent and acid phosphatase to hydrolyse thiamin phosphate esters is unusual but gives reliable results and much cleaner chromatograms than the more commonly used pair of TCA and Taka-diastase. In addition, Taka-diastase preparations may have the disadvantage of containing small

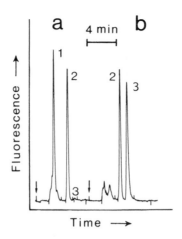

Figure 17. Chromatograms illustrating the assay of total thiamin in whole blood **(a)** before and **(b)** after enzymic hydrolysis with acid phosphatase by which thiamin phosphate esters (e.g. thiamin pyrophosphate) are hydrolysed to free thiamin. Chromatographic conditions are as described in *Table 16*. Thiamin is detected by post-column derivatization of thiamin to thiochrome and fluorimetric detection. Peaks: **1** = thiamin pyrophosphate (TPP); **2** = salicylamide (internal standard); **3** = thiamin. Taken from ref. 37.

Table 17. Assay of individual vitamers of thiamin in blood[a].

Sample preparation and extraction

1. To 0.2 ml aliquots of whole blood or plasma in a 1.5 ml capacity polyethylene centrifuge tube, add 0.2 ml of a 10% (w/v) solution of TCA and vortex mix vigorously.
2. Centrifuge the contents of the tube at 35 000 g for 5 min and inject 100 μl of the supernatant onto the h.p.l.c. column.

H.p.l.c. conditions

1. Column: μ-Bondapak C_{18}, dimensions 30 cm × 4 mm (i.d.) (10 μm silica chemically bonded with ODS groups; from Waters Associates).
2. Mobile phase: 0.3% (v/v) acetonitrile in 0.2 M NaH_2PO_4.
3. Flow-rate: 1.0 ml/min.
4. Post-column derivatization: add a solution of 0.01% (w/v) $K_3Fe(CN)_6$ in 15% (w/v) NaOH to the column effluent at a flow-rate of 0.5 ml/min.
5. Detector: fluorescence detector with the excitation wavelength set at 375 nm and the emission wavelength at 450 nm.

---

[a]Adapted from ref. 35.

amounts of thiamin. Salicylamide is a suitable internal standard to correct for chromatographic losses, but should not be added until after the extraction step since it becomes partially bound to denatured proteins. Examples of chromatograms for an extract of whole blood before and after enzymatic hydrolysis of thiamin phosphate esters are shown in *Figure 17*. Before hydrolysis only the major vitamer TPP is discernible. After treatment with acid phosphatase the TPP peak (which may include smaller amounts of TTP and TMP) disappears and a single peak of thiamin is seen.

7.2.4 Assay of individual vitamers of thiamin in blood by RP-h.p.l.c. and post-column derivatization

Only brief details of this method are given (*Table 17*). The principle of the post-column derivatization is similar to that described in Section 7.2.3. The important feature is that no hydrolysis step is included and the phosphate esters are separated by h.p.l.c. and detected individually. The chromatographic separation on a C_{18} packing is achieved with a 0.2 M solution of NaH_2PO_4 as the mobile phase and adjustment of the retention by the addition of a small amount (3 g/l) of acetonitrile (35).

8. RIBOFLAVIN (VITAMIN B_2)

8.1 Introduction

Riboflavin, formerly known as vitamin B_2, has the chemical structure 7,8-dimethyl-10-(1'-D-ribityl)isoalloxazine (*Figure 18*). In tissues riboflavin exists primarily as the co-enzyme forms riboflavin 5'-phosphate (flavin mononucleotide, FMN) and flavin— adenine dinucleotide (FAD).

Traditionally riboflavin compounds have been measured by microbiological or fluorometric assays: the latter are direct assays without a chromatographic stage and are usually based on fluorescence measurements before and after quenching with sodium hydrosulphite. With their reasonable chemical stability and intense fluorescence, flavins are well suited to analysis by h.p.l.c. but established h.p.l.c. methods for the measurement of flavins in biological samples are still few and far between, presumably reflecting the relative lack of interest in the nutriture of this vitamin.

8.2 Assay of riboflavin in blood and urine

The most widely used method for assessing the nutritional status of riboflavin is a stimulation assay of the FAD-containing enzyme, glutathione reductase, in erythrocytes. There have been relatively few attempts to relate riboflavin status in humans to direct blood measurement of riboflavin vitamers and apparently none using h.p.l.c. Instead, more extensive studies in human populations have been made using the urinary excretion of riboflavin as an indicator of riboflavin status. Methods now exist whereby urine concentrations of riboflavin may be reliably and simply determined by the direct injection of urine samples onto an h.p.l.c. column.

8.2.1 Sample preparation and extraction

In blood, riboflavin and riboflavin co-enzymes may exist in the free form, but the major

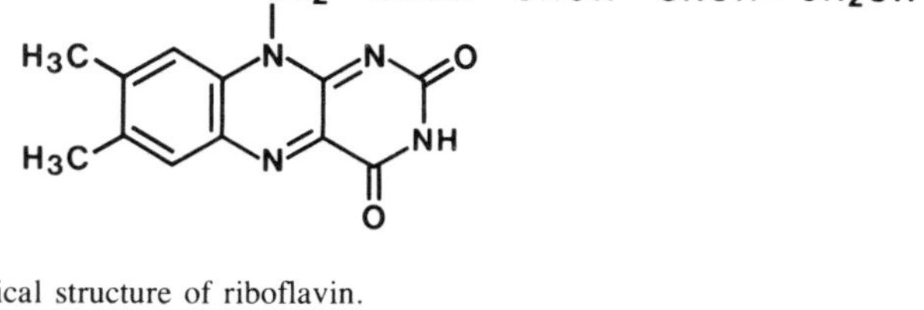

Figure 18. Chemical structure of riboflavin.

fraction is bound to proteins, primarily albumin. Although the kidney can excrete both riboflavin and FMN, the latter is dephosphorylated in the bladder and only free riboflavin is excreted in the urine.

Flavins are relatively heat stable but are extremely sensitive to photodegradation and stringent precautions need to be taken to ensure the protection of samples from light during their analysis. As with other vitamins the sample preparation and extraction procedure needs to be tailored to the particular tissue and the precise needs of the analyst. With the exception of urine analyses, the first decision is whether to measure total riboflavin by first hydrolysing FMN and FAD to riboflavin. This can be done chemically with dilute (0.1 M) inorganic acids or enzymically with phosphatase and nucleotidase preparations. To measure all three major forms of riboflavin individually, the sample may be extracted with $5-10\%$ (w/v) TCA but precautions need to be taken to minimize hydrolysis of the co-enzyme forms. Extractions should therefore be performed with ice-cold reagents and completed within $15-20$ min.

The h.p.l.c. analysis of riboflavin in urine requires no sample pre-treatment except for low-speed centrifugation and the advisability of filtering samples through a 0.45 μm membrane. To prevent bacterial growth, urine should be collected into a preservative; dilute HCl or oxalic acid dihydrate have been shown not to affect the analysis of riboflavin (40). Acid preservatives have the double advantage of providing the low pH values at which riboflavin is most stable. Riboflavin in urine, if protected from the light, is stable for at least 24 h at room temperature and for at least 2 weeks at 5°C (41).

8.2.2 *Design of h.p.l.c. assays*

Little has been published on the h.p.l.c. analysis of flavins with respect to mammalian tissue or fluid analyses. The isocractic resolution within 10 min of FAD, FMN and riboflavin in this elution order is readily achieved by simple RP-h.p.l.c. on a μ-Bondapak (10 μm) C_{18} column (Waters Associates) with a mobile phase of ammonium phosphate buffer (pH 5.5) in acetonitrile (42). This method was designed to study the hydrolysis of riboflavin nucleotides added to plasma and the u.v. detector used is not sensitive enough to detect endogenous plasma levels. With mobile phases of methanol/water or methanol/phosphate buffer, the resolution of riboflavin compounds on μ-Bondapak C_{18} columns is less efficient; riboflavin is still resolved but the co-enzyme forms, FMN and FAD, co-elute. Such systems are suitable for the measurement of riboflavin in urine (40,41).

Oxidized forms of flavins absorb in the u.v. and visible regions of the spectrum but to detect endogenous concentrations fluorescence detection must be used. Riboflavin and the co-enzyme forms all emit fluorescence at around 530 nm when excited at $440-500$ nm.

8.2.3 *Assay of riboflavin in urine by RP-h.p.l.c. and fluorometric detection*

The method chosen is a simple and rapid RP method which allows the direct measurement of riboflavin using an isocratic methanol/water mobile phase and detection of the native fluorescence of riboflavin (40). Details of the method are given in *Table 18*. Since urine samples are injected directly, it is essential to protect the analytical column with a guard column packed with a pellicular C_{18} packing such as Bondapak C_{18}/Cor-

Table 18. Assay of riboflavin in urine[a].

Sample preparation

1. Collect 24 h urines into containers which have been masked to exclude all light[b] and to which 5 g of oxalic acid dihydrate has been added as a preservative. Refrigerate the urine during and after the collection period.
2. Measure the urine volume and keep a 20-ml aliquot for analyses.
3. Centrifuge the urine aliquot at 2000 g for 10 min and transfer to a clean plastic tube. It is advisable to filter the supernatant through a 0.45 μm filter.
4. Inject $20-100$ μl of urine directly onto the h.p.l.c. columns followed by a series of injections of the working standard (accurately known concentration of ~ 5 mg/l).

H.p.l.c. conditions

1. Column: μ-Bondapak C_{18}, dimensions 30 cm $\times$ 3.9 mm (i.d.) (10 μm silica chemically bonded with ODS groups; from Waters Associates) and fitted with a guard column[c] of Bondapak C_{18}/Corasil, dimensions 2.5 cm $\times$ 3.9 mm (i.d.) ($37-53$ μm pellicular ODS packing; from Waters Associates).
2. Mobile phase: 34% (v/v) methanol in water.
3. Flow-rate: 1 ml/min.
4. Detector: fluorescence detector with the excitation wavelength set at 450 nm and the emission wavelength at 530 nm.

[a]Adapted from ref. 40.
[b]It is important to exclude light at all stages of the assay.
[c]A guard column is essential to protect the analytical column.

asil ($37-53$ μm from Waters Associates). When chromatographic performance deteriorates (after ~ 100 injections) the packing in the guard column may simply be replaced using a dry packing technique. Chromatograms of urine samples show only a single chromatographic peak of riboflavin (retention ~ 6 min) and the concentration may be accurately determined by the method of external standardization. The chromatographic resolution, together with the high selectivity of fluorescence detection, is sufficient to prevent interferences from other flavins incuding possible degradation products of riboflavin (e.g. alloxazine, lumichrome and lumiflavin). Certain natural compounds and drugs with similar fluorescence characteristics to riboflavin also give no interfering peaks (see Chapter 10, Section 4.5.4 and ref.40).

9. NICOTINIC ACID AND NICOTINAMIDE (NIACIN)

9.1 Introduction

The generic term niacin includes two major compounds, nicotinic acid and nicotinamide (*Figure 19*). The term niacin, however, is also sometimes used as an alternative specific name for nicotinic acid with niacinamide an alternative name for nicotinamide. Both compounds, together with tryptophan, may be converted into the co-enzyme forms nicotinamide adenine dinucleotide (NAD^+) and nicotinamide adenine dinucleotide phosphate ($NADP^+$).

The most widely used and sensitive assays for nicotinic acid and nicotinamide are microbiological assays using organisms that need niacin for growth; a requirement which may be either very specific or relatively non-specific for different vitamers or their metabolic products. Chemical assays for niacin are less sensitive and are based on the

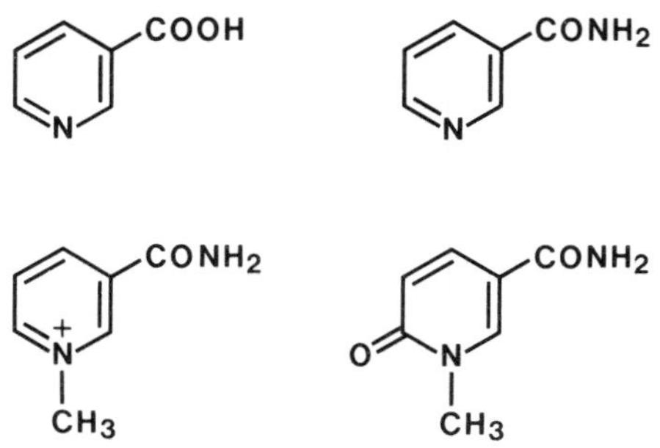

Figure 19. Chemical structures of niacin and two urinary metabolites. (**Top left**): nicotinic acid. (**Top right**): nicotinamide. (**Bottom left**): N'-methylnicotinamide. (**Bottom right**): N-methyl-2-pyridone-5-carboxylamide.

reaction of substituted pyridines with cyanogen bromide to form pyridinium derivatives; as this reaction is not specific to niacin, chemical methods may suffer from the presence of interfering compounds. As with other vitamins, h.p.l.c. is being increasingly used to achieve specific and sensitive measurements of niacin compounds in tissues and fluids.

Aside from its status as an essential nutrient, niacin compounds have a non-vitamin role in medicine, a role which is owed to various pharmacological activities of niacin when given in doses which are massive compared with physiological requirements.

9.2 Assay of nicotinic acid and nicotinamide in plasma

Current interest in the measurement of plasma levels of niacin lies, in the main, with pharmacological studies. Endogenous concentrations of nicotinic acid and nicotinamide in plasma are relatively low (< 50 μg/l) and cannot be measured by available h.p.l.c. methods which were designed to monitor pharmacological plasma levels in the range of $100-400$ μg/l or above.

9.2.1 Sample preparation and extraction of plasma

Blood samples may be collected into heparin and, after centrifugation, plasma samples stored at $-20°$C. One problem in extracting nicotinic acid and nicotinamide from plasma is that their chemical properties are sufficiently different that a method for extracting one vitamer may not necessarily be satisfactory for extracting the other. Thus nicotinamide has a greater solubility in organic solvents and, unlike nicotinic acid, may be extracted from aqueous solution with diethy ether. Nicotinic acid is amphoteric with pK_a values of 4.9 and 2.1 and forms salts with acids and bases. Nicotinamide has no acidic properties. Nicotinamide is extraordinarily stable to high temperatures but is hydrolysed to nicotinic acid by both alkalis and acids. Nicotinic acid is also stable but will be decarboxylated in alkaline solution if heated to high temperatures.

Most methods of extraction for subsequent h.p.l.c. analyses derive from pharmacological studies in which only nicotinic acid or only nicotinamide was measured. A widely used method of extracting nicotinic acid from plasma is to precipitate proteins with acetone or aqueous acetone and, after centrifugation, to extract the supernatant with chloroform to remove interfering lipids (43–45). Further interferences may be removed by evaporating the water from the supernatant (by allowing to stand overnight under reduced pressure in a desiccator containing a molecular sieve and silica gel) and re-

Table 19. Assay of pharmacological levels of nicotinamide in plasma[a].

Sample preparation and extraction

1.   To 1 ml of plasma add 10 μl of internal standard solution[b], and 10 μl of water. Vortex mix for 30 min.
2.   Using a syringe with a Luer end fitting, pre-wash a Sep-Pak C_{18} cartridge (Waters Associates) with 2 ml of methanol and 5 ml of water.
3.   Introduce the plasma sample into a syringe. Attach the Luer end fitting to the cartridge and slowly push the plasma through the cartridge.
4.   Elute the cartridge with 0.5 ml of water and discard the eluate.
5.   Elute the cartridge with 1.5 ml of the h.p.l.c. mobile phase (see h.p.l.c. conditions) and collect the eluate (containing nicotinamide and the internal standard) into a centrifuge tube.
6.   Centrifuge briefly ($\sim$2 min), filter through a 0.4 μm membrane and inject an aliquot of 25 – 150 μl onto the h.p.l.c. column.

H.p.l.c. conditions

1.   Column: μ-Bondapak C_{18} (Waters Associates), dimensions 30 cm × 4 mm (i.d.) or LiChrosorb RP-18 (Merck), dimensions 25 cm × 4 mm (i.d.). (Both packings are 10 μm silica chemically bonded with ODS groups.) To protect the analytical column connect in line a guard column of Bondapak C_{18}/Corasil (Waters Associates), dimensions 2.5 cm × 4 mm (i.d.) (37 – 53 μm pellicular ODS packing).
2.   Mobile phase: 42% (w/v) methanol in water, the latter component containing 0.3% (w/v) of sodium dioctylsulphosuccinate at a pH of 2.5 (adjusted with formic acid)[c].
3.   Flow-rate: 2.0 ml/min.
4.   Detector: u.v., fixed or variable wavelength absorbance detector set at 254 nm or 260 nm.

---

[a]Adapted from ref. 46.
[b]The internal standard is an aqueous solution of isonicotinamide with an accurately known concentration of approximately 400 mg/l.
[c]To prepare the mobile phase dissolve 4.446 g of sodium dioctylsulphosuccinate in 1450 ml of water, adjust the pH to 2.5 with formic acid and mix with 1050 ml of methanol. Filter and degas before use.

dissolving in methanol (43). An alternative clean-up procedure is to acidify the supernatant with 0.1 M HCl, evaporate to dryness in a centrifugal evaporator, re-dissolve in methanol, evaporate to dryness once again and finally dissolve in acetone. This allows the solubilization of nicotinic acid but not some interfering compounds which may be removed by centrifugation (44). A simple and effective procdure for extracting nicotinamide from plasma (although not nicotinic acid) is to use Sep-Pak C_{18} cartridges (Waters Associates) and a two-step elution procedure (46). This is described in *Table 19*.

9.2.2 *Design of h.p.l.c. assays for plasma analyses*

In keeping with the acidic and basic properties of nicotinic acid and the basic properties of nicotinamide the analysis of these compounds may be achieved by ion-exchange or IP-h.p.l.c. Pharmacological plasma levels of nicotinic acid and the metabolite nicotinuric acid may be resolved from plasma constituents by ion-exchange h.p.l.c. using a strong cation-exchange packing (44). In the same system the plasma peak of nicotinamide is obscured by an interfering peak but can be measured in a separate run by a slight modification to the mobile phase composition. Niacin compounds are not well retained by RP packings with mixtures of methanol or acetonitrile with water or buffers and although the separation of pure standards is possible the retention is insufficient to resolve them from u.v.-absorbing interferences in plasma samples (43). The addition of a quaternary amine such as tetrabutylammonium phosphate, however, increases the retention of acidic compounds such as nicotinic acid or nicotinuric acid by an IP mechanism and allows them to be resolved and measured in plasma (43). To increase the retention of nicotinamide, an opposite counter-ion such as sodium dioctylsulphosuccinate may be added at a low pH. This results in the selective retention of nicotinamide and its ready resolution from plasma constituents (46).

Pharmacological plasma levels of nicotinic acid and nicotinamide may easily be detected by an u.v. detector; the optimum wavelength of detection is 260 nm but detectors with a fixed wavelength of 254 nm are also suitable. A novel detection method for nicotinic acid is based on the reaction of the aromatic carboxyl group to form the highly fluorescent 4-hydroxymethyl-7-methoxycoumarin ester derivative which may be detected in plasma by RP-h.p.l.c. (45).

Most of the methods mentioned in this section are suitable for either the plasma measurement of nicotinic acid (43−45), its metabolite nicotinuric acid (43,44) or nicotinamide (46). An example of one of these methods for nicotinamide which is suitable for pharmacokinetic studies is described in Section 9.2.3 below.

9.2.3 *Assay of nicotinamide in plasma by RP-IP h.p.l.c. and u.v. detection*

This method combines a rapid extraction technique using Sep-Pak C_{18} cartridges with a good chromatographic resolution by RP-IP h.p.l.c. (46). The assay may be carried out with a conventional h.p.l.c. pump and u.v. absorbance detector. Details of the method are described in *Table 19*. Although the Sep-Pak extraction procedure gives a recovery of better than 90% for nicotinamide and the internal standard isonicotinamide, the recovery of nicotinic acid is only about 30% and therefore its simultaneous assay is not feasible. The method yields clean chromatograms with base line separation of nicotinamide and isonicotinamide at about 4 and 6 min, respectively; it is possible to process some 30−40 samples per day.

9.3 **Assay of urinary metabolites of niacin**

While plasma measurements of nicotinic acid and/or nicotinamide are useful for pharmacological studies, they cannot be used to assess niacin status in humans. This can be done by measuring urinary metabolites of niacin, commonly N^1-methylnicotinamide (N^1-MN) and N-methyl-2-pyridone-5-carboxylamide (2-pyridone). The ratio of 2-pyridone to N^1-MN is a particularly useful index of niacin nutriture and both metabolites can now be measured accurately by h.p.l.c. methods with u.v. detection. Because of the lack of selectivity of u.v. detection, most methods require a preliminary clean-up of urine samples. A successful pre-purification of urine is achieved by conventional ion-exchange chromatography (47). This purification is based on the principle that whereas 70−80% of u.v.-absorbing (240−270 nm) compounds in urine are anionic in character and at neutral pH are retained by an anion-exchange resin, the metabolites N^1-MN and 2-pyridone are cationic and neutral in character, respectively, and are not retained. Elution of the anion-exchange column with water enables both metabolites to be quantitatively recovered. Details of this clean-up procedure together with a subsequent h.p.l.c. procedure for the assay of N^1-MN and 2-pyridone metabolites are given in *Table 20* and illustrated in *Figure 20*. This method uses the same RP column but two different

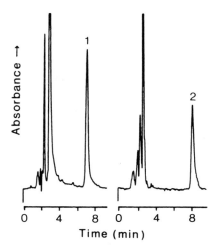

Figure 20. Chromatograms illustrating the assay of **(left)** N-methyl-2-pyridone-5-carboxylamide **(peak 1)** and **(right)** N′-methylnicotinamide **(peak 2)** metabolites of niacin in urine. The chromatographic conditions are as described in *Table 20*. Taken from ref. 47.

Table 20. Assay of urinary metabolites of niacin[a].

Anion-exchange clean-up procedure

1. Convert Dowex 1- × 8 anion-exchange resin (100−200 mesh, chloride form; Bio-Rad Laboratories) to the hydroxide form by passing 20 vols of 1 M NaOH through 1 vol of resin followed by distilled water until the pH of the eluant is less than 8. Store in this form at 4°C in the dark for no more than 1 week.
2. Pour 4 ml of resin into small custom-made columns[b] plugged with glass wool.
3. Place under each column a 50-ml volumetric flask containing 1 ml of 0.5 M K_2HPO_4 buffer (pH 7) and 0.25 M 1-octanesulphonate.
4. Depending on the urine concentration, pipette an aliquot of 1−8 ml of urine into a tube containing 0.5 ml of 0.5 M K_2HPO_4 buffer (pH 7) and 0.5 ml of water. Mix well.
5. Load the buffered urine sample onto the Dowex column under nitrogen pressure so that the flow-rate is 6−12 drops/min.
6. Elute the column with distilled water until the volume of eluate in the volumetric flask is approximately 48 ml. Adjust the pH to 7 (pH paper) with 3−5 drops of phosphoric acid and make up to 50 ml with distilled water.

H.p.l.c. conditions

1. Column: Ultrasphere IP or ODS, dimensions 25 cm × 4 mm (i.d.) (5 μm silica chemically bonded with ODS groups; from Beckman Instruments Inc) and fitted with a 3 cm RP-18 Spheri-5 guard column (also 5 μm ODS packing; from Brownlee Laboratories Inc, Santa Clara, USA).
2. Mobile phase: either 10% (v/v) acetonitrile in 10 mM K_2HPO_4 buffer and 5 mM 1-octanesulphonate, pH 7 (adjusted with phosphoric acid) for analyses of N^1-MN or 2% (v/v) acetonitrile in 10 mM K_2HPO_4 buffer, pH 7 for analyses of 2-pyridone.
3. Flow-rate: 1.5 ml/min.
4. Inject aliquots of prepared standards and obtain a calibration graph of peak areas versus the concentration of the 2-pyridone metabolite.

[a]Adapted from ref. 47.
[b]For further details of custom-made columns see ref. 47.

mobile phases to analyse N^1-MN and 2-pyridone individually in separate chromatographic runs (47). In the first chromatographic system the cationic character of the metabolite N^1-MN is utilized to form an IP using 5 mM sodium 1-octanesulphonate as an anionic counter-ion. In the second system the neutral metabolite 2-pyridone is chromatographed by simple RP-h.p.l.c. without addition of a counter-ion. If desired, the analysis of these metabolites could be carried out in a single chromatographic run by addition to the mobile phase of 1-octanesulphonate counter-ion used for 2-pyridone analysis. Under these conditions the 2-pyridone metabolite elutes with the same retention (~ 7 min) while the retention of N^1-MN is increased from near the solvent front without the counter-ion to about 30 min after the addition of 1-octanesulphonate. This difference in retention, however, is such that the overall analysis time using two chromatographic runs is shorter than for a single chromatographic run (47). A modification to this method allows the assay of N^1-MN by the direct injection of human urine samples (48). This is accomplished by simply doubling the counter-ion concentration from 5 mM to 10 mM and reducing the acetonitrile concentration from 10% to 8% (v/v). Similar attempts to eliminate the clean-up step for the assay of the 2-pyridone metabolite, however, were not successful (48).

10. VITAMIN B$_6$

10.1 Introduction

Vitamin B$_6$ is the generic name for six naturally occurring and biologically active vitamers which are all derivatives of 2-methyl-3-hydroxy pyridine. The parent compounds pyridoxine or pyridoxol (PN), pyridoxal (PL) and pyridoxamine (PM) have alcohol, aldehyde and amine groups at the 4-position of the pyridine ring, respectively (*Figure 21*). In addition, all three vitamers are found as their respective 5′-phosphate esters: pyridoxine phosphate (PNP), pyridoxal phosphate (PLP) and pyridoxamine phosphate (PMP) of which PLP and PMP are the major co-enzyme and storage forms in mammalian tissues. All the B$_6$ vitamers are readily interconvertible by tissue enzymes and there is only one major excretory product, 4-pyridoxic acid (4-PA).

Early assays for vitamin B$_6$ were based on animal bioassays or microbiological assays. Apart from their well known practical disadvantages, such assays give no information on the tissue composition of individual B$_6$ vitamers. Assays based on the stimulation of selected enzymes that require vitamin B$_6$ as a co-enzyme are both reliable and sensitive but their very specificity for the co-enzyme form PLP remains their major shortcoming. Recent interest has focused on the possibility of developing chromatographic assays to resolve and detect individual B$_6$ vitamers. Much progress has been made in this direction and h.p.l.c. is fast becoming the method of choice for the analysis of vitamin B$_6$ in tissues.

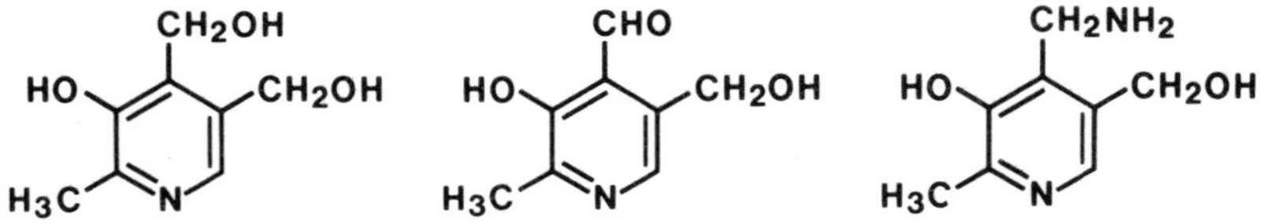

Figure 21. Chemical structures of parent compounds of vitamin B$_6$. (**Left**): pyridoxine or pyridoxol, (**middle**): pyridoxal, (**right**): pyridoxamine.

10.2 **Assay of B₆ vitamers in plasma**

All forms of vitamin B_6 have been detected in human plasma with the exception of PNP. There is as yet no general agreement as to the vitamin B_6 composition of human plasma although the weight of evidence suggests that PLP is the principal form with plasma concentrations normally about $5-10$ $\mu g/l$ (49). The degree of binding of vitamin B_6 to plasma proteins varies for individual vitamers; PLP is tightly bound, primarily to plasma albumin, whereas the non-phosphorylated PL is bound less avidly, and PN seems to have little or no protein binding. The excretion product 4-PA is also present in plasma at similar concentrations to PLP. The vitamin B_6 composition of whole blood differs significantly from plasma: this is mainly due to a higher concentration in erythrocytes and other cellular elements of the mainly intracellular vitamer PMP. In nutritional and metabolic studies, however, vitamin B_6 is usually only measured in plasma samples. Many investigators consider that plasma PLP measurements are a sensitive and reliable index of the nutritional status of vitamin B_6 in man. With h.p.l.c. it is now becoming feasible to assess the nutriture of vitamin B_6 by measuring all the five vitamers that occur in plasma together with the metabolite 4-PA.

10.2.1 *Sample preparation and extraction*

In collecting serum or plasma care should be taken to avoid haemolysis and therefore possible contamination with B_6 forms derived from cellular elements of blood. To obtain plasma, the anti-coagulants citrate, EDTA or heparin are commonly used. The addition of 0.55 mg of Na_2HPO_4 and 0.60 mg of NaH_2PO_4 per ml of blood is sometimes recommended to inhibit phosphatase activity which may hydrolyse the phosphorylated forms of vitamin B_6 (50).

All forms of vitamin B_6 are unstable to light and excessive heat; all procedures should therefore be carried out in subdued or red light at temperatures below about 40°C. All B_6 vitamers are quite stable in dilute acids but PL and PLP are destroyed by alkalis. Even at neutral pH, solutions of PLP, particularly with concentrations in the low ng/ml range, will slowly degrade over 24 h unless the solutions are degassed and kept at 4°C or below. Although PLP in whole blood has been reported to be stable for several months when stored at -20°C, over half of this vitamer may be lost within a week from plasma stored at -20°C.

When analysing tissue samples the analyst needs to be aware of the possibility of both enzymic and non-enzymic transamination reactions by which, for instance, PL and PLP may be converted to PM and PMP; such reactions can alter the vitamer composition without a loss of total vitamin content. Another problem in vitamin B_6 analyses is the possible reaction between either pyridoxal (PL or PLP) and amino acids or between pyridoxamine (PM or PMP) and keto acids to form a Schiff's base. With native proteins, PLP has a tendency to form a Schiff's base with the ϵ-amino group of lysine residues, a linkage that is hydrolysed by acid.

The extraction of both free and protein-bound forms of vitamin B_6 from plasma does not seem to be as difficult a problem as with some other mammalian tissues and is usually achieved by the addition of TCA, PCA, tungstic, metaphosphoric or sulphosalicylic acids at concentrations around $5-10\%$ (w/v). For the h.p.l.c. analyses the sample should be centrifuged and filtered. PCA may be removed as the potassium salt while TCA may be removed by extracting with diethyl ether or diethyl ether containing 2% trioctylamine. A simple extracting procedure using TCA is as follows.

(i)   Slowly add a solution of 20% (w/v) TCA to an equal volume of plasma with constant and vigorous mixing.

(ii) Centrifuge and extract the supernatant with water-saturated peroxide-free diethyl ether until the pH of the supernatant is at least 4.5

(iii) Filter the aqueous phase through a 0.45 μm membrane.

Dropwise addition of the extracting reagent is advisable to minimize the occlusion of the vitamin with precipitated protein; up to 5−10% may be lost in this way and can only be recovered by further washing of the precipitate. The addition of a suitable internal standard which is equally occluded is useful in correcting for such losses. The techniques used for sample preparation and extraction are of crucial importance to vitamin B_6 analyses. Major potential sources of error lie either in the incomplete recovery, losses or interconversions of vitamin B_6, together with the possibility of chromatographic artifacts from the extracting reagents.

10.2.2 *Design of h.p.l.c. assays*

The simultaneous measurement of a possible six forms of vitamin B_6 together with 4-PA at the concentrations found in plasma is a complex analytical problem. Attempts to solve this problem by RP-h.p.l.c., with or without IP, have not been successful. While it is possible to resolve standard mixtures of B_6 vitamers on RP packings the analysis of plasma samples has been hampered by the inability to obtain adequate resolution from fluorescent interferences (51). Two h.p.l.c. methods which have shown promise for plasma analyses are based on ion-exchange principles with either anion-exchange (50) or cation-exchange (51) packings. A method based on anion-exchange h.p.l.c. (50) can resolve and detect all plasma forms of vitamin B_6 and 4-PA but has the disadvantages of requiring the use of two columns with a column-switching step together with a sophisticated fluorimeter capable of programmed wavelength changes during a rather lengthy chromatographic run ($\sim$ 70 min). H.p.l.c. methods based on cation-exchange chromatography seem more promising. Conventional cation-exchange chromatography on open-columns with stepwise solvent changes had previously provided the first detailed analysis of the vitamer composition of human plasma (52): with h.p.l.c. and gradient elution a complete separation of vitamin B_6 compounds can be obtained on a single cation-exchange column in about 50 min (51).

The detection of B_6 vitamers in plasma is possible with fluorescence detection, but not with spectrophotometric detection. Although vitamin B_6 compounds possess native fluorescence, the optimal excitation and emission wavelengths vary for different vitamers and are dependent on solvent, ionic strength and pH. With some microprocessor-controlled fluorimeters it is now feasible to optimize the excitation and emission wavelengths for each B_6 vitamer as it elutes from the column (50) but such instruments are expensive. An alternative approach is to enhance the fluorescence of vitamin B_6 compounds by derivatization but this is usually only selective for a pair of vitamers (phosphorylated and non-phosphorylated) having the same group at the 4-position of the pyridine ring. Common reactions that have been used in h.p.l.c. analyses are those of PL and PLP with semicarbazide or cyanide to give the highly fluorescent semicarbazide or cyanohydrin derivatives, respectively (53). If the chromatography is carried out with an acidic mobile phase, as in cation-exchange separations of B_6 vitamers, it may be necessary to adjust the pH of the column eluate (by post-column addition) to a range at which the fluorescence of all the vitamers is optimized (51).

H.p.l.c. methods for the analysis of B_6 vitamers in human plasma are still in their infancy and there is as yet no general consensus on the plasma concentrations of individual vitamers. The two methods using ion-exchange h.p.l.c. (50,51) give good agreement for plasma concentrations of PLP but the anion-exchange method (50) gave 10-fold higher values for PN concentrations. It is not clear whether this major difference lies in the different extraction reagents used (sulphosalicylic acid in the anion-exchange and TCA in the cation-exchange method) or the chromatographic resolution but it is possible that the high plasma PN values obtained by the anion-exchange method are artifactual. In view of the present uncertainty of plasma values, it is difficult to select an ideal procedure. The cation-exchange method of Coburn and Mahuren (51) described in detail in Section 10.2.3 is the simplest and has the great merit of having been favourably evaluated by other investigators (49).

Table 21. Assay of B_6 vitamers in plasma[a].

Sample extraction

1. Extract 2 ml of plasma with 20% (w/v) TCA as described in the text (Section 10.2.1).
2. To 1 ml of sample extract and immediately before h.p.l.c. analysis, accurately add 5 μl of a solution of 2-amino-5-chlorobenzoic acid (Aldrich Chemicals) in water (accurately known concentration of ~2 μg/ml) as the internal standard and inject 500 μl onto the h.p.l.c. column.

H.p.l.c. conditions

1. Column: Vydac 401 TP-B (cation-exchange), dimensions 30 cm $\times$ 4.6 mm (i.d.) (10 μm silica chemically bonded with sulphonic acid groups; from Separations Group, Hesperia, CA, USA) and fitted with a guard column, dimensions 5 cm $\times$ 4.5 mm (i.d.) also containing Vydac 401 TP-B.
2. Mobile phase: prepare three solvents as follows.
    A = 0.02 M HCl
    B = 0.1 M NaH_2PO_4 (adjusted to pH 3.3 with 0.1 M H_3PO_4)
    C = 0.5 M NaH_2PO_4 (adjusted to pH 5.9 with 0.5 M NaOH)
    A typical program is as follows:
    (i) 100% A from 0 to 13 min.
    (ii) 100% B from 13 to 17 min.
    (iii) Linear gradient from 100% B to 88% (v/v) B in C from 17 to 25 min.
    (iv) Linear gradient from 88% (v/v) B in C to 100% C from 25 to 30 min.
    (v) 100% C from 30 to 40 min.
    (vi) Re-equilibrate with solvent A for 10 min.
3. Flow-rate: 1.5 ml/min.
4. Post-column derivatization: set the post-column reactor to deliver a freshly prepared 0.1% (w/v) solution of sodium bisulphite in 1 M Na_2HPO_4 (adjusted to pH 7.5 with 1 M NaH_2PO_4) at a flow-rate of 4.5 ml/h.
5. Detector: fluorescence detector with the excitation wavelength set at 330 nm and the emission wavelength at 400 nm.

[a]Adapted from ref. 51.

10.2.3 *Assay of* B_6 *vitamers in plasma by cation-exchange h.p.l.c. with fluorescence detection*

In this assay the B_6 vitamers in plasma are resolved by gradient elution on a cation-exchange packing (Vydac 401TP-B) and detected with a fluorimeter after the post-column addition of a phosphate buffer and sodium bisulphite (51).

(i) *Instrumentation.* An h.p.l.c. pump capable of ternary gradient formation and a post-column pump capable of pulse-free flow at very low flow-rates (i.e. 4.5 ml/h) should be used. The detector is a fluorimeter with the excitation wavelength set to 330 nm and the emission wavelength set to 400 nm.

(ii) *Method.* Extract plasma samples with TCA as described in Section 10.2.1. Details of the h.p.l.c. procedure are described in *Table 21* and a typical separation shown in *Figure 22*. Up to 500 µl of sample extracts can be injected without significant effect on the chromatographic resolution. An ideal internal standard has not been found but the compound 2-amino-5-chlorobenzoic acid, added just before sample injection, and

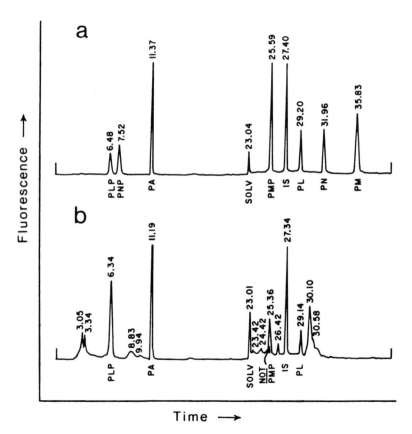

Figure 22. Chromatograms illustrating the assay of vitamin B_6 vitamers in plasma showing analyses of **(a)** a standard mixture containing 2 ng each of PLP, PNP, 4-PA, PMP, PL, PN and PM and **(b)** a plasma extract. Chromatographic conditions are as described in *Table 21*. Taken from ref. 49.

not allowed to stand for any length of time, serves to monitor chromatographic recovery. The gradient program listed in *Table 21* is typical only and may need to be adjusted slightly to account for the gradual decrease in retention as the column ages. It is likely that linear gradient segments after elution with 0.02 M HCl could be replaced by a single exponential gradient (51).

Of three reagents tested (semicarbazide, cyanide and bisulphite), the post-column addition of bisulphite provides the most selective enhancement of the fluorescence of PLP. The fluorescence is also enhanced by combining the bisulphite with a phosphate buffer to increase the pH of the column effluent to 7.5 while keeping the dilution to about 5%.

This method has been found by others (49) to give comparable values with a method (52) also based on cation-exchange chromatography but with an open-column and with off-line fluorimetric measurements of each vitamer. Especially good correlations were obtained for the major vitamer PLP. For the low plasma levels of PMP, PM and PN the h.p.l.c. method tended to give lower values than the open-column method suggesting a higher specificity for h.p.l.c.

11. FOLIC ACID (FOLATE, FOLACIN)

11.1 Introduction

Of all the vitamins, folic acid perhaps poses the greatest challenge to the analyst: this is due to the occurrence in nature of a large family of folates (some of which differ only slightly in chemical structure), their low concentrations in tissues and the problems associated with preventing the interconversion or degradation of folates during their isolation. The structure of the parent compound, folic acid or pteroylglutamic acid (*Figure 23*) is composed of three elements: a double-ringed structure, known as the pteridine ring, is linked to a *p*-aminobenzoic acid moiety (to form pteroic acid) and this in turn is linked to a single glutamic acid residue. Naturally occurring folates, including the co-enzyme forms, may differ structurally in:

(i)   the state of oxidation of the pteridine ring;
(ii)   the nature of the one-carbon substituents at the N5 and N10 positions;
(iii)   the number of glutamic acid residues which are linked one to another via γ-glutamyl linkages to form an oligo-γ-glutamyl chain.

The vitamer composition may differ substantially between different tissues and between extracellular and intracellular locations. The polyglutamate forms are found preferentially within cells, they do not cross cell membranes, and appear to be the preferred folate substrates for enzymes involved in one-carbon metabolism.

The first methods for measuring folate in tissues were microbiological assays with organisms such as *Lactobacillus casei*. Microbiological assays respond equally to mono-

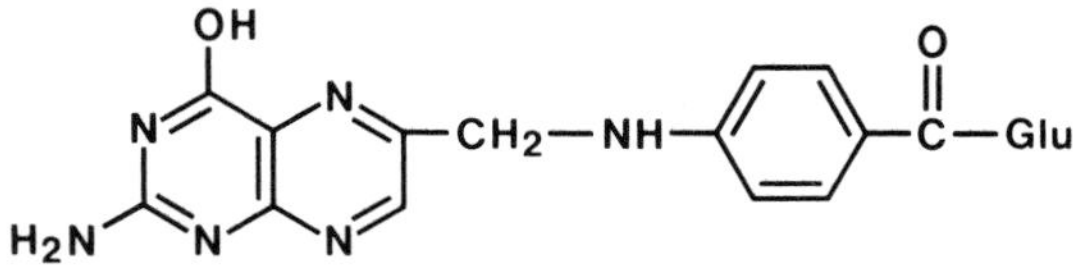

Figure 23. Chemical structure of folic acid or pteroylglutamic acid. Glu = glutamic acid.

glutamates but poorly to polyglutamates. Although they are time-consuming and tedious, and may suffer from interference from antibiotics or anti-folate drugs, microbiological assays do allow the accurate assay of 'total folate' provided that polyglutamates are converted to monoglutamates (by folate conjugase enzymes) before assay. More recently, radioassays based on the principles of competitive protein binding have been developed. Although radioassays are much more rapid and convenient than microbiological assays, a major problem is their differential response, not only between monoglutamates and polyglutamates but between monoglutamates which differ in their oxidation states and one-carbon substituent groups. This limits their use and makes them unsuited to the assay of the mixture of folates (even after conjugase treatment) that is normally encountered in tissues.

There are two main areas in which h.p.l.c. is proving invaluable to folate analyses. The first is in providing a rapid separation of folates in tissues which may then be quantified off-line by microbiological assay. The second and more exciting development is that it is now becoming feasible to use h.p.l.c. for both the resolution and direct detection of monoglutamate forms of folate in tissues.

11.2 Assay of folates in blood

It is fortuitous for the analyst that dietary folates after absorption and metabolism are transported in plasma as monoglutamates, predominately as 5-methyltetrahydrofolate. This makes the task of analysing the folate content of plasma a good deal simpler than for tissues such as liver. Although normal ranges differ considerably, both with the type of assay and between different centres, plasma concentrations in the range of $3-25$ μg/l may be encountered in a healthy population (54). Plasma measurements are frequently used as an aid to the assessment of the nutritional status of folic acid and as a diagnostic test for investigating the cause of megaloblastic anaemias. The measurement of folate in erythrocytes is also used in this context, though less frequently. The finding of a low level of folate in erythrocytes is a better indicator of folate deficiency than a low plasma level (54). The folate in erythrocytes differs from that in plasma in being largely composed of folate polyglutamates (in man predominantly pentaglutamate with lesser amounts of tetra- and hexaglutamates). The total folate content of erythrocytes is much higher than in plasma and calues from 150 to 600 μg/l of packed erythrocytes may be expected in healthy adults (54).

11.2.1 Sample preparation and extraction

With the wide variety of biological forms the procedures used to prepare and extract folates from tissues may be extremely complex. The method adopted will therefore need to take account of the tissue analysed, the nature of the final assay (i.e. microbiological, isotopic or h.p.l.c.) and the scope of the assay in terms of the number and nature of the molecular forms to be measured. In practice, the assignment of the glutamyl chain length of folates is carried out by separate methods and chromatographic procedures from those used to isolate the folate monoglutamates. Since for clinical and nutritional purposes it is usual to hydrolyse the γ-glutamyl side chain before analysis, methods used to determine the structure of native polyglutamate forms will not be considered in detail in this chapter.

Whatever the tissue, a number of general properties and precautions need to be emphasized. Biologically active folates exist in tissues in a reduced state (H_2 or H_4) and these are susceptible to oxidation. The use of an anti-oxidant such as ascorbate is therefore essential for any extended sample preparation and extraction procedure. Folates are also susceptible to photodegradation and all procedures need to be carried out under minimal lighting conditions. Folates in tissues are generally bound to proteins. In plasma endogenous folate appears to be weakly and non-specifically bound to a variety of proteins from which it can be readily removed by a stronger binding agent such as activated charcoal. Two commonly used methods to liberate protein-bound folates (after first adding $1-2\%$ ascorbate) are simple heating (up to 100°C) or the addition of an acid deproteinizing agent.

The analysis of plasma or serum represents a special case of folate analysis because only one form, 5-methyltetrahydrofolate, predominates. For prolonged storage of plasma (collected into heparin) ascorbic acid may be added at a concentration of 5 mg/ml (55). Where plasma 5-methyltetrahydrofolate is to be measured directly by h.p.l.c., the extraction and purification procedure adopted depends largely on the sensitivity and selectivity of the detector. For u.v. detection, a rather extensive sample preparation was found to be necessary which included two conventional chromatographic steps (56). Even with ECD which is generally much more selective than u.v. detection, a two-step concentration and purification procedure was needed (57); in this method, however, plasma extracts are purified entirely by h.p.l.c., first on an RP C_8 column and secondly on a strong anion-exchange column. With fluorescence detection it is claimed (55) that low levels of 5-methyltetrahydrofolate may be detected in plasma using an extremely simple extraction procedure as follows.

(i)   To 0.3 ml of plasma add 4 μl of 1 M Na_2CO_3.
(ii)   Stir the mixture and heat in a boiling water bath for 5 min.
(iii)   Break the protein precipitate with a stainless steel needle and centrifuge on a micro-centrifuge for 5 min.

The supernatant thus obtained is then ready for injection onto the chromatograph.

The assay of folate in erythrocytes poses different problems. First the haemolysis of whole blood (by freezing and thawing) leads to the exposure of the polyglutamate forms to plasma conjugase enzymes which at an optimal pH of 4.5 would be completely converted to their monoglutamates in a matter of seconds. For the assay of folate monoglutamates a hydrolysis step with endogenous or exogenous conjugase is a necessary part of the assay procedure. On the other hand, haemolysates will also contain active folate-interconverting enzymes that can alter the one-carbon moiety of the native folates. To prevent such changes in folate composition, the tissue extract is often heated rapidly to about 95°C in a solution of 1% ascorbate at pH 6 (human conjugases are inactive above pH 5.5). An alkaline pH should be avoided since the combined effects of heat and alkali render the C9−N10 bond unstable and liable to cleavage.

It is clear that methods used to release protein-bound folates are imperfect and both the addition of acid reagents to lower the pH or heating may lead to folate interconversions and losses through destruction or co-precipitation of folates with the denatured proteins. The addition of ascorbate as an anti-oxidant may itself present problems. It has been reported that heating tissues to high temperatures in ascorbate solutions may lead to several folate interconversions due to the generation of formaldehyde from ascorbate; this may, however, be prevented by the addition of 0.2 M 2-mercaptoethanol and buffering the folate tissue extract [in 2% (w/v) ascorbate] to pH 7.85 (58).

11.2.2 *Design of h.p.l.c. assays*

Even with h.p.l.c. it has not yet proved possible to resolve all the naturally occurring folates in one chromatographic system and in practice the analysis of folate polyglutamates is usually considered separately from the analysis of folate monoglutamates.

The separation of folate polyglutamates by h.p.l.c. may be achieved on a strong anion-exchange packing such as Partisil-10 SAX (Whatman Inc) using gradient elution; the retention of folate polyglutamates is governed by the interaction of the glutamate carboxylic groups and therefore retention increases with the length of the polyglutamate chain. Folate polyglutamates may also be resolved on RP packings by gradient elution with increasing concentrations of acetonitrile in acetate buffer; in this case the elution order is reversed with the longer-chain forms eluting first. These and other related methods are useful for identifying the polyglutamate chain length of tissue folates but further details of these methods are outside the scope of this chapter.

The resolution of folate monoglutamates is most commonly achieved by RP-h.p.l.c. with or without the addition of an IP reagent. With tetrabutylammonium phosphate as the counter-ion and using a methanol/water mobile phase, a total of eight monoglutamate forms of folate have been separated by isocratic elution on a μ-Bondapak C$_{18}$ column (Waters Associates) (59). This system (59) and a similar one (58) are suitable for the analysis of tissues using off-line measurements of individual vitamers by microbiological assay. Folate monoglutamates may also be separated by RP methods using a μ-Bondapak phenyl packing (Waters Associates) with mobile phase mixtures of acetonitrile in sodium phosphate buffer; this system has been shown to be suitable for the direct fluorimetric

Table 22. Assay of 5-methyltetrahydrofolate in whole blood with u.v. detection[a].

Sample preparation and extraction

1. Collect blood into heparin. Slowly add 4 ml of whole blood to 36 ml of 1% (w/v) ascorbate solution, sonicate, vortex mix and adjust the pH to 4.5
2. Incubate at 37°C for 90 min and centrifuge.
3. Purify the supernatant on a 4 g column of non-polar polystyrene adsorbent (Bio-Beads SM-2, 20−50 mesh from Bio-Rad Laboratories)[b].
4. Further purify the eluant from step 3 on a 0.3 g column of DEAE (Cellex D from Bio-Rad Laboratories)[b].
5. Filter the folate-containing fraction from step 4 (total volume 10 ml) through a 0.45 μm membrane filter and inject aliquots of 100−200 μl onto the h.p.l.c. column.

H.p.l.c. conditions

1. Column: μ-Bondapak C$_{18}$, dimensions 30 cm × 3.9 mm (i.d.) (10 μm silica chemically bonded with ODS groups; from Waters Associates).
2. Mobile phase: linear gradient from 0.1 M acetate buffer, pH 5.5 to 34% (v/v) acetonitrile in 0.1 M acetate buffer, pH 5.5 in 30 min.
3. Flow-rate: 0.5 ml/min.
4. Detector: u.v., fixed or variable wavelength absorbance detector set at 280 nm.

---

[a]Adapted from ref. 56.
[b]See ref. 56 for further details.

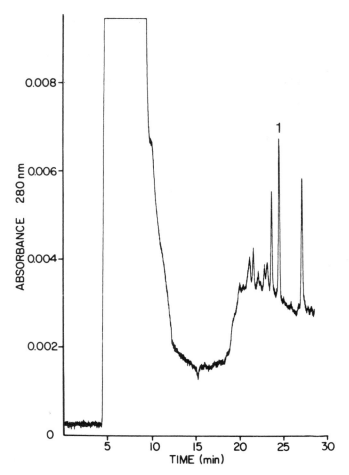

Figure 24. Chromatogram illustrating the assay of 5-methyltetrahydrofolate (**peak 1**) in whole blood. Chromatographic conditions are as described in *Table 22*. Taken from ref. 56.

detection of folate monoglutamates after extraction from tissues (60).

The detection of folates after h.p.l.c. has been achieved with u.v. absorption, fluorimetric detectors or ECD though few practical applications of ECD have been published. The u.v. absorption spectra of folates is owed to the pterin and *p*-aminobenzoic acid components of their structure; the nature of the spectrum and the wavelength maxima being dependent on the state of oxidation and the pH. Generally the most useful wavelengths for the detection of folates by h.p.l.c. lie in the 250−290 nm range, with 280 nm most commonly selected. The main disadvantage of u.v. detection for the direct analysis of folates in tissues is its relatively poor sensitivity and, even for plasma which contains only one predominant vitamer, some 20 ml of plasma must be extracted to detect the peak of 5-methyltetrahydrofolate (56). Many folates are naturally fluorescent and their detection with fluorimetric detectors presents an attractive alternative to u.v. detection. The major plasma folate 5-methyltetrahydrofolate is highly fluorescent and plasma concentrations down to 1 ng/ml are readily detectable (55). Other folates which do not

Table 23. Assay of 5-methyltetrahydrofolate in plasma with fluorescence detection.

Method using RP-IP h.p.l.c.[a]

Sample preparation and extraction

1. Collect blood into heparin and centrifuge. Remove the plasma and add 5 mg/ml of ascorbic acid. Mix well.
2. Extract 0.3 ml of plasma with 4 μl of 1 M Na_2CO_3 as described in Section 11.2.1, filter and inject aliquots of $10-50$ μl onto the h.p.l.c. column.

H.p.l.c. conditions

1. Column: LiChrosorb RP-18, dimensions 25 cm $\times$ 4 mm (i.d.) (5 μm silica chemically bonded with ODS groups; from Merck).
2. Mobile phase: 20% (v/v) methanol in 0.1 M sodium phosphate buffer, pH 4.5 containing 5 mM tetrabutylammonium phosphate[b].
3. Flow-rate: 1 ml/min.
4. Detector: fluorescence detector with the excitation wavelength set at 295 nm and the emission wavelength at 350 nm.

Method using RP (phenyl) h.p.l.c.[c]

Sample preparation and extraction

1. See text, Section 11.2.4.

H.p.l.c. conditions

1. Column: μ-Bondapak phenyl, dimensions 30 cm $\times$ 3.9 mm (i.d.) (10 μm silica chemically bonded with phenyl groups; from Waters Associates).
2. Mobile phase: 15% (v/v) linear gradient from 7.2% to 11.3% (v/v) of acetonitrile in 0.033 M sodium phosphate, pH 2.3 in 15 min.
3. Flow-rate: 1 ml/min.
4. Detector: high sensitivity fluorescence detector[d] with the excitation wavelength set at 295 nm and the emission wavelength at 356 nm.

[a]Adapted from ref. 55.
[b]Prepare mobile phase as follows: filter a 25 mM solution of tetrabutylammonium phosphate in methanol through a 0.2 μm filter. To 200 ml of the filtrate add 0.1 mol of H_3PO_4 and 680 ml of glass-distilled water. Adjust the pH to 4.5 with 1 M NaOH and dilute to 1 l with water. Filter again and degas.
[c]Adapted from ref. 60.
[e]e.g. Perkin-Elmer model LS-5 spectrophotofluorometer.

fluoresce may be easily converted to fluorescent derivatives by post-column oxidation reactions. The electrochemical oxidation of 5-methyltetrahydrofolate at a glassy-carbon electrode also forms the basis of a sensitive detection method for this compound (57).

11.2.3 *Assay of 5-methyltetrahydrofolate in whole blood with u.v. detection*

This direct h.p.l.c. method for the assay of 5-methyltetrahydrofolate in whole blood is chosen for two main reasons: firstly, the u.v. detector is still the most widely used detector and, secondly, this method, although cumbersome, has been shown to give good agreement with a microbiological assay using *Lactobacillus casei* (56). An outline of the method is given in *Table 22*. The adjustment of the haemolysate to pH 4.5 and incubation at 37°C allows the endogenous plasma conjugases to hydrolyse polyglutamate forms of 5-methyltetrahydrofolate to the monoglutamate form (see Section 11.2.1). The haemolysate must then be purified by a time-consuming, but successful, two-step procedure; firstly by chromatography on a neutral, non-polar, polystyrene adsorbent and, secondly, by ion-exchange chromatography. Details of these procedures are not given here but may be found in the original text (56). The h.p.l.c. procedure is also lengthy, requiring gradient elution but the peak of 5-methyltetrahydrofolate is sharp and well separated from u.v. interferences (*Figure 24*). It is also possible to measure 5-methyltetrahydrofolate in plasma by the same method but this is rather impractical since 20 ml of plasma needs to be extracted (56).

11.2.4 *Assay of 5-methyltetrahydrofolate in plasma with fluorescence detection*

With the increased sensitivity and selectivity of fluorescence detectors for measuring 5-methyltetrahydrofolate, it is now becoming possible to assay this folate by direct h.p.l.c. assay in relatively small volumes of plasma. Again, such methods are not yet in wide use and further developmental work is still needed, especially to compare the values obtained with traditional folate assays. Two methods are given in *Table 23*. The first using IP-h.p.l.c. is cited because of the simple extraction method and the potential of this method for rapid sample throughput, though neither chromatograms of plasma analyses nor any evaluation with another method were presented by the authors (55). The second method uses RP-h.p.l.c. on a phenyl-bonded phase; this assay is well documented for the analysis of several tissues and the chromatographic procedure is very sensitive and well suited to the detection of other minor monoglutamate forms of folate present in tissues (60). The authors of this method gave no examples of plasma analyses but stated that the method is suitable for the assay of 5-methyltetrahydrofolate in human plasma. Since their extraction and purification procedures were designed for the more complex and simultaneous assay of several folates in tissues, further details are not given here; it is likely, however, that plasma analyses of 5-methyltetrahydrofolate could be carried out with a much simpler extraction procedure than that needed for other other tissues. Again, the use of a gradient in their h.p.l.c. method (*Table 23*) was introduced simply to avoid interference from ascorbate which tends to quench the fluorescence of an early eluting folate. With further development it should be feasible to use isocratic elution for the plasma assay of 5-methyltetrahydrofolate.

12. ACKNOWLEDGEMENTS

The author wishes to acknowledge and thank Mr P.T.McCarthy for his help in the development of h.p.l.c. assays for retinol and α-tocopherol. The development of the dual-electrode electrochemical assay for vitamin K was carried out in collaboration with Dr J.Hart and the expert help of Mr P.T.McCarthy and Mr O.Crampton. Special thanks are also due to Dr Y.Haroon for his part in the development of the assay of vitamin K with u.v. detection and advice on the dual-electrode electrochemical detection of vitamin K, to Dr J.Hart for many helpful discussions on electrochemistry and vitamin B_6, to Mr C.Turner for his advice on the assay of vitamin D and to Mrs V.Cichy for typing the manuscript. The author acknowledges the support of an MRC project grant (No. G8220270 SA) for work on vitamin K.

13. REFERENCES

1. Olson,J.A. (1984) In *Handbook of Vitamins, Nutritional, Biochemical and Clinical Aspects*. Machlin,L.J. (ed.), Marcel Dekker Inc., New York and Basel, p. 1.
2. Nelis,H.J.C.F. and De Leenheer,A.P. (1983) *Anal. Chem.*, **55**, 270.
3. Miller,K.W. and Yang,C.S. (1985) *Anal. Biochem.*, **145**, 21.
4. Nierenberg,D.W. (1984) *J. Chromatogr.*, **311**, 239.
5. Collins,C.A. and Chow,C.K. (1984) *J. Chromatogr.*, **317**, 349.
6. Bieri,J.G., Tolliver,T.J. and Catignani,G.L. (1979) *Am. J. Clin. Nutr.*, **32**, 2143.
7. De Ruyter,M.G.M. and De Leenheer,A.P. (1978) *Clin. Chem.*, **24**, 1920.
8. De Leenheer,A.P., Lambert,W.E. and Claeys,I. (1982) *J. Lipid Res.*, **23**, 1362.
9. Bieri,J.G., Brown,E.D. and Smith,J.C., Jr. (1985) *J. Liquid Chromatogr.*, **8**, 473.
10. Bikle,D.D., ed. (1983) *Assay of Calcium-regulating Hormones*. Springer-Verlag, New York, Berlin, Heidelberg and Tokyo.
11. Jones,G. (1978) *Clin. Chem.*, **24**, 287.
12. O'Riordan,J.L.H., Adami,S., Sandler,L.M., Clemens,T.L. and Fraher,L.J. (1982) In *Vitamin D: Chemical, Biochemical and Clinical Endocrinology of Calcium Metabolism*. Norman,A.W., Schaefer,K., Herrath,D.V. and Grigoleit,H.G. (eds), Walter de Gruyter, Berlin and New York, p. 751.
13. Shepard,R.M., Horst,R.L., Hamstra,A.J. and DeLuca,H.F. (1979) *Biochem. J.*, **182**, 55.
14. Jones,G. and DeLuca,H.F. (1975) *J. Lipid Res.*, **16**, 448.
15. Jones,G. (1980) *J. Chromatogr.*, **221**, 27.
16. Holmberg,I., Kristiansen,T. and Sturen,K. (1984) *Scand. J. Clin. Lab. Invest.*, **44**, 275.
17. Dreyer,B.E. and Goodman,D.B.P. (1981) *Anal. Biochem.*, **114**, 37.
18. Korhonen,R.T., Savolainen,K.E. and Mäenpää,P.H. (1983) *J. Chromatogr.*, **275**, 418.
19. De Leenheer,A.P., De Bevere,V.O., Cruyl,A.E. and Claeys,A.E. (1978) *Clin. Chem.*, **24**, 585.
20. De Leenheer,A.P., De Bevere,V.O.R.C. and Claeys,A.E. (1979) *Clin. Chem.*, **25**, 425.
21. Piironen,V., Varo,P., Syväoja,E.L., Salminen,K. nd Koivistoinen,P. (1984) *Int. J. Vit. Nutr. Res.*, **53**, 35.
22. Ikenoya,S., Abe,K., Tsuda,T., Yamano,Y., Hiroshima,O., Ohmae,M. and Kawabe,K. (1979) *Chem. Pharm. Bull.*, **27**, 1237.
23. Shearer,K.J. (1986) In *Methods in Enzymology*. Chytil,F. and McCormick,D.M. (eds), Academic Press Inc., Orlando. Vol. **123**, p. 235.
24. Shearer,M.J. (1983) In *Advances in Chromatography*. Giddings,J.C., Grushka,E., Cazes,J. and Brown, P.R. (eds), Marcel Dekker Inc., New York and Basel, Vol. **21**, p. 243.
25. Hart,J.P., Shearer,M.J., McCarthy,P.T. and Rahim,S. (1984) *Analyst*, **109**, 477.
26. Haroon,Y., Schubert,C.A.W. and Hauschka,P.V. (1984) *J. Chromatogr. Sci.*, **22**, 89.
27. Hart,J.P., Shearer,M.J. and McCarthy,P.T. (1985) *Analyst*, **110**, 1181.
28. Lefevere,M.F., Frei,R.W., Scholten,A.H.M.T. and Brinkman,U.A.T. (1982) *Chromatographia*, **15**, 459.
29. Langenberg,J.P. and Tjaden,U.R. (1984) *J. Chromatogr.*, **305**, 61.
30. Cooke,J.R. and Moxon,R.E.D. (1981) In *Vitamin C (Ascorbic Acid)*. Counsell,J.N. and Hornig,D.H. (eds), Applied Science Publishers, London and New Jersey, p. 167.
31. Schorah,C.J. (1981) In *Vitamin C (Ascorbic Acid)*. Counsell,J.N. and Hornig,D.H. (eds), Applied Science Publishers, London and New Jersey, p. 23.
32. Speek,A.J., Schrijver,J. and Schreurs,W.H.P. (1984) *J. Chromatogr.*, **305**, 53.
33. Pachla,L.A. and Kissinger,P.T. (1979) In *Methods in Enzymology*. McCormick,D.B. and Wright,L.D. (eds), Academic Press Inc., New York and London, Vol. **62**, p. 15.
34. Johnsen,H., Ringvold,A. and Blika,S. (1985) *Acta Ophthalmol.*, **63**, 31.
35. Kimura,M. and Itokawa,Y. (1983) *Clin. Chem.*, **29**, 2073.
36. Kimura,M., Fujita,T. and Itokawa,Y. (1982) *Clin. Chem.*, **28**, 29.
37. Wielders,J.P.M. and Mink,C.J.K. (1983) *J. Chromatogr.*, **277**, 145.
38. Kimura,M., Panijpan,B. and Itokawa,Y. (1982) *J. Chromatogr.*, **245**, 141.
39. Bontemps,J., Philipe,P., Bettendorff,L., Lombet,J., Dandrifosse,G., Schoffeniels,E. and Crommen,J. (1984) *J. Chromatogr.*, **307**, 283.
40. Gatautis,V.J. and Naito,H.K. (1981) *Clin. Chem.*, **27**, 1672.
41. Smith,M.D. (1980) *J. Chromatogr.*, **182**, 285.
42. Pietta,P. and Calatroni,A. (1982) *J. Chromatogr.*, **229**, 445.
43. Hengen,N., Seiberth,V. and Hengen,M. (1978) *Clin. Chem.*, **24**, 1740.
44. Takikawa,K., Miyazaki,K. and Arita,T. (1982) *J. Chromatogr.*, **233**, 343.
45. Tsuruta,Y., Kohashi,K., Ishida,S. and Ohkura,Y. (1984) *J. Chromatogr.*, **309**, 309.
46. De Vries,J.X., Günthert,W. and Ding,R. (1980) *J. Chromatogr.*, **221**, 161.

47. Carter,E.G.A. (1982) *Am. J. Clin. Nutr.*, **36**, 926.
48. Kutnink,M.A., Vannucchi,H. and Sauberlich,H.E. (1984) *J. Liquid Chromatogr.*, **7**, 969.
49. Lui,A., Lumeng,L. and Li,T.-K. (1985) *Am. J. Clin. Nutr.*, **41**, 1236.
50. Vanderslice,J.T., Maire,C.E. and Beecher,G.R. (1981) In *Methods in Vitamin B-6 Nutrition.* Leklem,J.E. and Reynolds,R.D. (eds), Plenum Press, New York, p. 123.
51. Coburn,S.P. and Mahuren,D. (1983) *Anal. Biochem.*, **129**, 310.
52. Lumeng,L., Lui,A. and Li,T.-K. (1980) *J. Clin. Invest.*, **66**, 688.
53. Dakshinamurti,K. and Chauhan,M.S. (1981) In *Methods in Vitamin B-6 Nutrition.* Leklem,J.F. and Reynolds,R.D. (eds), Plenum Press, New York, p. 99.
54. Chanarin,I. (1980) In *Vitamins in Medicine.* Barker,B.M. and Bender,D.A. (eds), William Heinemann, London, Vol. **1**, p. 247.
55. Giulidori,P., Galli-Kienle,M. and Stramentinoli,G. (1981) *Clin. Chem.*, **27**, 2041.
56. Hoppner,K. and Lampi,B. (1983) *Nutr. Rep. Int.*, **27**, 911.
57. Lankelma,J., van der Kleijn,E. and Jansen,M.J.T. (1980) *J. Chromatogr.*, **182**, 35.
58. Wilson,S.D. and Horne,D.W. (1984) *Anal. Biochem.*, **142**, 529.
59. McMartin,K.E., Virayotha,V. and Tephly,T.R. (1981) *Arch. Biochem. Biophys.*, **209**, 127.
60. Gregory,J.F., Sartain,D.B. and Day,B.P.F. (1984) *J. Nutr.*, **114**, 341.

CHAPTER 9

Nucleotides, nucleosides and bases

DAVID PERRETT

1. INTRODUCTION

1.1 Historical development

The separation of nucleotides, nucleosides and bases has occupied a central role in the development of modern h.p.l.c.. It features among the first applications of liquid column chromatography following the development of analytical grades of ion-exchange resins. In 1949 Waldo Cohn and co-workers (1) at Oak Ridge were able to separate a variety of nucleoside monophosphates or bases on ion-exchangers but analysis times by present day standards were very long, for example 20 h for four bases. This type of separation was subsequently refined, improved and applied to a variety of biochemical and clinical problems by many researchers. It was to these same compounds that the first applications of modern h.p.l.c were made in 1967 when Horvath et al. (2) developed pellicular ion-exchange packings, the first high efficiency stationary phases. Substantial improvements in speed followed the application of microparticulate ion-exchange packing materials to the separation of nucleotides (3). Although nucleosides were originally separated on ion-exchange pellicular packings, reversed-phase (RP) microparticulate phases were soon widely employed. A simple methanol/buffer gradient was found to give excellent separations (4) even with physiological fluids.

Although RP separation of nucleosides has continued unchallenged, various other approaches to the chromatography of the more polar nucleotides have been developed. Their separation on RP systems, RP with ion-pairing (IP), both isocratically and with gradient elution, and RP with zwitterion-pairing are now attractive alternatives.

The impetus for much of this interest lies in the central role of the nucleotides in metabolism and the variety of such compounds that can be found in nature. There are five purine and pyrimidine bases of predominant importance: adenine, guanine, uracil, cytosine and thymidine. These give rise to both catabolic products and related nucleosides and ribo- and deoxyribonucleotides. Even at the simplest level this means that they form some 50 important compounds; although in nature the amounts of these compounds vary considerably. The complexity is in fact even greater; anion-exchange separations of urine reveal at least 150 nucleic acid-like compounds and high resolution chromatography of tissue extracts separates over 40 nucleotide peaks.

There are a wide variety of approaches to the analysis of nucleic acid components. Many rely upon the characteristic u.v. spectra of the compounds and although sensitivities are reasonable the level of discrimination is low. Similar sensitivities but increased specificity can be achieved using a number of standard enzymatic procedures. The highest sensitivities are found with the firefly luminescent methods for ATP and the radioimmunoassay procedures for cAMP and cGMP. Recently, the use of ^{31}P n.m.r. to semi-quantitate levels of free ATP, ADP and AMP within intact tissue has become available.

The complexity and diversity of nucleotides, etc. to be found in tissues and body fluids almost certainly means a chromatographic approach to their analysis is necessary. The classical ion-exchange techniques were very slow and this encouraged the development of both t.l.c. and electrophoretic separations. Today h.p.l.c. is the almost obligatory approach for both qualitative screening and quantitative analysis.

1.2 **Fields of application**

The fundamental importance of nucleic acids and related compounds to the living organism means that their quantitative and qualitative analysis is of importance in a wide number of fields, e.g. energy metabolism, purine biosynthesis, pharmacology and cyclic nucleotides. Some areas of clinical interest where h.p.l.c. has been applied are metabolic errors (gout, Lesch−Nyhan syndrome, severe combined immunodeficiency), oncology (anti-metabolites), physiology (smooth muscle metabolism, energy metabolism), haematology (blood cell preservation, platelet aggregation) and monitoring ischaemic damage during organ transplants.

Much work has been focused on providing patterns or chromatographic fingerprints of samples such as the nucleotides in various tissues in the same animal or the same tissue in different species. Comparisons of the patterns of u.v.-absorbing compounds in normal urine and specimens obtained in various disease states have been made. Interest in the clinical importance of purine metabolism for a long time centred on disorders of the purine salvage pathways such as gout and the Lesch−Nyhan syndrome but, more recently, h.p.l.c. of nucleotides has proved valuable in the understanding of the severe combined immunodeficiency diseases (SCID) associated with the absence of adenosine deaminase or purine nucleoside phosphorylase in the red cells and other cells of patients with these disorders. In such cases abnormal levels of deoxynucleotides have been found to accumulate in the red cells. It is beyond the brief of this chapter to discuss the full and complex field of purine and pyrimidine metabolism in biomedicine.

In pharmacology a number of drugs, particularly some used in the treatment of various cancers, have structures based on the purine ring, for example 6-mercaptopurine and allopurinol. The recently introduced anti-viral agents such as acyclovir also possess a purine ring. The same base structure is also found in a number of central nervous system drugs such as caffeine, theophylline and theobromine. Although their analysis is usually considered along with other pharmacological compounds in h.p.l.c. texts their separation is in fact only a specific method derived from the more general approaches to be discussed in this chapter. Outside the area of animal biochemistry the h.p.l.c. of nucleotides can still have application. For instance the nucleotide content of seeds may indicate the vigour and viability of the crop, a useful means of testing the seeds.

2. THE STRUCTURE AND PHYSICAL PROPERTIES OF BASES AND RELATED COMPOUNDS

The physical and chemical properties of the common purine and pyrimidine bases are fully documented in other more comprehensive sources (5) and only brief but relevant details will be given here.

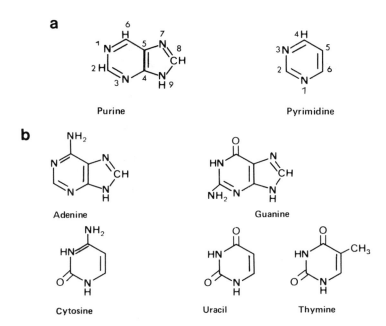

Figure 1. (**a**) Structure and numbering scheme of the purine and pyrimidine rings. (**b**) Structures of the common purine and pyrimidine bases.

Figure 1a shows the structural forms and the ring numbering scheme of the two basic compounds, pyrimidine and purine. In the three pyrimidine compounds, uracil, thymine and cytosine, and the two purine compounds, adenine and guanine, which form the major nitrogenous bases of RNA and DNA, the ring structures are substituted as shown in *Figure 1b*. There are a large number of other purine and pyrimidine compounds. Some such as 6-methylguanine occur naturally in some nucleic acids but only to a small extent. Another major group of modified derivatives have been synthesized in anti-cancer studies and some of these now have therapeutic application, e.g. 6-mercaptopurine.

The bases can combine with ribose or deoxyribose to form ribonucleosides and deoxy-ribonucleosides, respectively. The pentose can then be further bonded via an ester link usually onto carbon atom 5 with one, two or three phosphate groups to form nucleotides. These arrangements are shown in *Figure 2a* and *b*. In addition, other nucleotide forms can exist. Cyclic nucleotides, which are important regulators in many biochemical and physiological mechanisms, contain 3′,5′-cyclic phosphates. Ribonucleotide 3′-phosphates can be released from certain RNA linkages. It is the presence of these highly negatively charged phosphate groups which dictates the differences in the approaches to the chromatographic analysis of nucleotides compared with nucleosides and bases.

3. SEPARATION OF NUCLEIC ACID COMPOUNDS

The heterocyclic ring structure of purines and pyrimidines confers a high degree of hydrophobicity to these compounds. This hydrophobicity is in turn modified by the

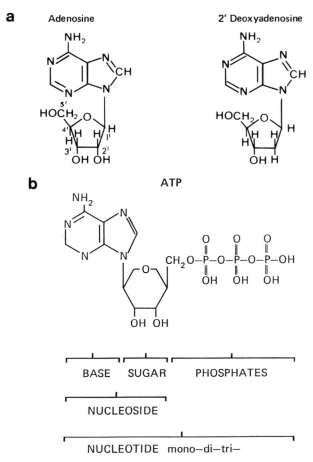

Figure 2. (**a**) Structure and numbering scheme of ribo- and deoxyribonucleotides. (**b**) Structure of a nucleotide. Example: adenosine triphosphate (ATP).

various substituent groups attached to the ring in physiological nucleotides and bases. In the case of nucleotides the dominant modification is the addition of the strongly ionic phosphates. It is clear therefore that a wide range of h.p.l.c. separation mechanisms can be applied to the resolution of these classes of compounds. In the last 40 years just about every available mode has been employed with varying degrees of success. Most of the early methods used polystryene-based or Sephadex type ion-exchangers or crude solid absorbents such as silica.

Table 1 summarizes the various chromatographic approaches using h.p.l.c. grade packing materials that can be employed to resolve mixtures of nucleic acid components. Additionally it gives some indication of the degree of usefulness of the methods for complex physiological extracts. Of course such a list cannot be definitive and must act only as a guide in selecting the final approach. The choice of separation procedure will be a compromise that is dependent on a number of factors other than the compound to be determined, some of which are sample dependent such as nature of the sample, number of components to be separated and volume to be injected. Others are equipment

Table 1. Common chromatographic approaches for nucleic acid components.

| Mode | Normal | Ion-exchange | | | Reversed-phase | | | |
| | | Anion | | Cation | ODS | | Ion-pair | |
Isocratic/gradient	Iso	Iso	Grad	Iso	Iso	Grad	Iso	Grad
Bases	a	a	a	a	b	c	d	d
Nucleosides	e	a	b	a	b	c	b	b
Nucleotides	e	b	c	a	a	a	c	c

[a]Separations possible under extreme conditions.
[b]Good separations particularly of simple mixtures.
[c]Excellent separations of complex mixtures.
[d]Not normally necessary since other modes much better.
[e]Poor resolution of even simple mixtures.

limited; for instance separations can be strongly influenced by the make, even the batch, of packing material (a perennial h.p.l.c. bug bear!) or perhaps only an isocratic h.p.l.c. system without a column heater is available. In general, for complex samples the use of a gradient system will be found to be almost essential.

3.1 Nucleotides

3.1.1 *Ion-exchange chromatography*

Because of their phosphate ester linkages, nucleotides are highly charged in the pH range $2-7$, the useful pH range for silica-based stationary phases. Over the pH range $1-5$ the charge directly increases with the number of phosphate residues, e.g. AMP $<$ ADP $<$ ATP. Additionally this gross level of charge is apparently modified by the substituent groups on the ring such that the following order of elution from an anion-exchange column is observed: CTP $<$ ATP $<$ UTP $<$ ITP $<$ GTP, but this order is very pH dependent. Ion-exchange chromatography has therefore provided a very satisfactory approach to the resolution of nucleotides in complex mixtures. Elution from anion-exchange resins using increasing salt gradients has been employed since the very earliest days of column chromatography. The speed of analysis has been substantially improved by the use of h.p.l.c. technologies and the separation of at least 23 nucleotides can now be achieved in less than 15 min (6).

Nucleotides can be separated on all the available silica-based microparticulate anion-exchangers. These can be of the weak -NH_2 variety, e.g. aminopropylsilane (Si-CH_2-CH_2-CH_2-NH_2, APS) or the strong quaternary (SAX) variety, e.g. trimethylaminopropyl [Si-CH_2-CH_2-CH_2-$N^+(CH_3)$ Cl^-]. In a weak anion-exchanger the amine groups are only fully charged over a limited pH range, e.g. $1-7$, whereas for strong ion-exchangers the useable range extends from 1 to 12. In practice the use of silica packings at pH values above 7 is not recommended due to dissolution of the silica matrix in the eluent.

A variety of column lengths have been employed ranging from 10 to 30 cm but most workers have used columns of the standard internal diameter 0.46 cm. Few separations on micro-bore columns have been described. Radial compression columns packed with a SAX packing have also been employed by workers using Waters equipment but the separations are no different to those obtained on conventional columns. The particle size most often used is 10 μm only because the most popular packing, Partisil-SAX, was until recently of that diameter. Other smaller sizes are now available, e.g. 3 μm and 5 μm APS−Hypersil. Packings with the same nominal surface modifier can be prepared by different chemistries to give varying degrees of surface coverages: some are commercially available, e.g. APS−Hypersil 1 and 2. Ion-exchange materials are characterized by their ion-exchange capacity. This ranges from 0.4−0.9 mEq/g for silica-based packings to 1.8 mEq/g for traditional styrene−divinylbenzene resins.

Isocratic ion-exchange chromatography is characterized by the elution of charged bound species with eluents of appropriate ion concentration and pH. For nucleotides very rapid separations but with little selectivity can be achieved with isocratic elution from anion-exchange columns. k' decreases with increasing molarity and column temperature and increases with lowering the pH of the buffer. Smaller changes in k' and useful variations in selectivity are often achieved by changing the nature of the eluting counter-ion. Incorporation of a few percent of organic modifier into the eluent can also dramatically change the selectivity. To avoid damage to the h.p.l.c. remember that many buffer salts are only poorly soluble in water containing more than a few percent of solvents such as methanol. The reasons for these selectivity effects are complex and poorly understood. To some degree the organic solvent will effect the ionization of both the ion-exchanger and the nucleotides as well as changing the solubility of the nucleotides. As with most h.p.l.c. separations it is unlikely that a unique separation mechanism is involved although one may predominate and the final chromatogram is the result of an interplay of a number of mechanisms. Therefore although nucleotides are, in the main, resolved by ion-exchange interactions, some of the detail of the separation may result from other mechanisms such as RP interactions of the purine ring and the surface coating. Overall it is found that ion-exchange columns functioning as ion-exchangers (since they can also be used as a normal phase) are not as efficient as RP columns of the same dimensions. Typical efficiencies are 4000−5000 plates/10 cm for a 5 μm packing compared with 6000−7000 for a similar octadecylsilyl (ODS) material.

Groups of nucleotides, e.g. the monophosphate nucleotides or the nucleotides of a particular base, can be separated in minutes at high sensitivities. An example of such a rapid anion-exchange separation is shown in *Figure 3a*. Separations of this type, although chromatographically interesting, are unlikely to be of much practical value due to their low selectivity range and only mixtures of related compounds can be satisfactorily resolved. These are most often employed to evaluate a newly bought or newly packed column to determine its chromatographic efficiency. Isocratic systems can be run at much higher sensitivity than gradient systems and can therefore be useful in quantitating trace levels of nucleotides provided a suitable separation can be achieved. Such systems have been used for measuring cAMP and dGTP in biological extracts (*Figure 3b*).

For complex biological extracts suitable resolution on an ion-exchange column can only be achieved using gradient elution. In practice, gradient ion-exchange chromatography acts like frontal displacement chromatography. The charged species is absorbed by the top layer(s) of the column bed and remain at that site until the ionic strength of the eluent is such that the bound species is displaced by the counter-ions

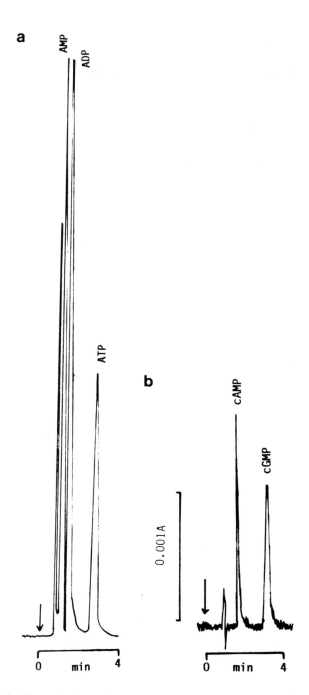

Figure 3. Optimized isocratic anion-exchange separations for nucleotides. Chromatographic details common for both; column, 4.6×100 mm 5 μm APS−Hypersil (Shandon); detector, Cecil CE212 254 nm; flow, 1 ml/min, pressure 700 p.s.i.; temperature, ambient; injector, 25 μl loop. **(a)** High speed separation of three adenosine nucleotides in 3 min. 1 nmol of each injected. Eluent, 0.8 mol/l KH_2PO_4 pH 2.6. Sensitivity, 0.1 A full scale. **(b)** High sensitivity analysis of cyclic nucleotide standards (50 pmol). Eluent, 0.08 mol/l KH_2PO_4 pH 2.8.

in the eluent. The displaced compounds are then eluted from the column with little further interaction with the packing. At a fixed pH the strength of the interaction of the species with the column packing and therefore the concentration of the eluent is dependent on the charge of the species and the ion-exchange capacity of the packing. This mechanism has been supported by observations on a wide variety of column materials and a number of practical considerations in setting up an h.p.l.c separation result.

Since relatively little chromatographic separation takes place along the length of the column following release of the bound species, the resolution achieved by the separation is effectively independent of the length of the column. Short columns (5−10 cm) can give efficiencies equivalent to that of long columns (25−30 cm) and the separation of over 20 nucleotides in less than 15 min is easily attained (*Figure 4*). Resolution is

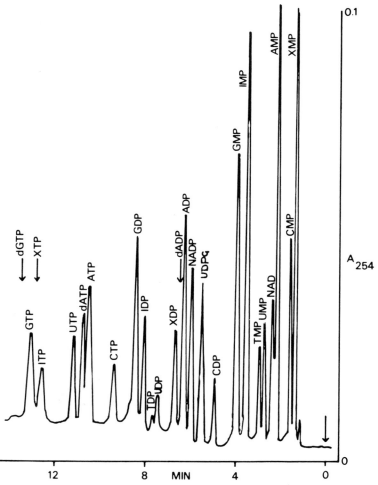

Figure 4. Anion-exchange gradient separation of 23 nucleotides in 13 min. Chromatographic details: column, 4.6 × 100 mm 5 μm APS−Hypersil (Shandon); detector, Cecil CE212 254 nm; eluent, linear gradient generated on low pressure side of pump 0.04 mol/l KH_2PO_4 pH 2.8 to 0.5 mol/l KH_2PO_4 + 0.8 mol/l KCl pH 2.7; flow, 1 ml/min; pressure, 400−500 p.s.i.; temperature, ambient; sample, 1 nmol of each standard nucleotide. Injector, 25 μl loop.

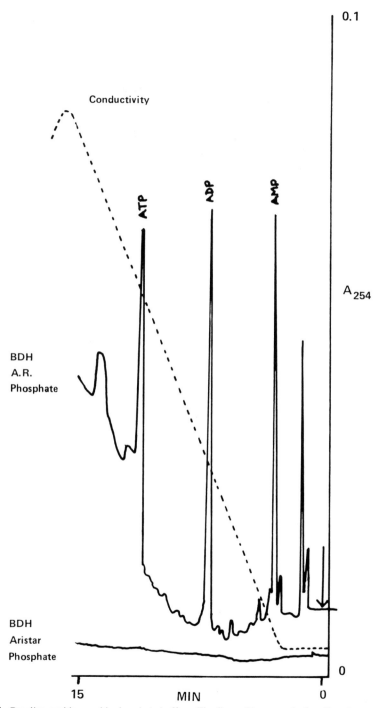

Figure 5. Baseline problems with phosphate buffers. The figure illustrates the baseline rise occurring during the chromatography of a simple nucleotide sample using AR grade buffer salts compared with the baseline obtained for Aristar phosphate and A.R. KCl. Chromatographic conditions are as in *Figure 4*. Dashed line indicates conductivity of eluent, i.e. shape of actual gradient.

Table 2. Baseline rise depends on phosphate and water.

Supplier	Grade	Water	Maximum rise in baseline absorbance 254 nm
Merck	Optipure	Distilled + de-ionized	0.016
	AR	Distilled + de-ionized	0.015
M & B	Proanal	Distilled + de-ionized	0.019
BDH	GPR	Distilled + de-ionized	0.021
	A.R	Distilled + de-ionized	0.035
	Aristar	Distilled + de-ionized	0.001
	Aristar	Distilled only	0.012
	Aristar	De-ionized only	0.009
Fisons	H.p.l.c.	Distilled + de-ionized	0.002

in the main a function of gradient slope and flow-rate; that is the rate of change of ion strength and/or pH at the top of the column. As with all gradient separations a suitable period of pumping the first eluent is necessary to re-equilibrate the column. This is particularly so for nucleotides because the separation of some groups of nucleotides, e.g. ATP and GTP, is influenced by the pH of both buffers (6).

A disadvantage of an ion-exchange separation is that during use many of the surface ion-exchange sites are irreversibly blocked by chemical reaction with impurities in the buffers but the resolution of the column does not decrease provided the concentration of the high concentration buffer is lowered in proportion. Increasing the strength of the ionic interactions by the use of strong rather than weak anion-exchangers means that either more concentrated eluents must be employed or a larger volume of the same eluent must pass down the column to elute the highly retained nucleoside triphosphates Increasing the number of ion-exchange sites in the column by either increasing the surface coverage of the silica or decreasing the particle size requires similar increases to the buffer or gradient composition. A disadvantage of these changes is that the use of more concentrated eluents can be detrimental to performance due to baseline artifacts.

In most published methods the column is eluted with a phosphate gradient, usually KH_2PO_4 although a number of other salts have been used. The final eluent is about 50-fold the molarity of the initial buffer, the exact concentrations are dependent on the type of column packing employed and the use the column has received. Typical values are given in the legend to *Figure 4*. Unfortunately there is a considerable amount of an unknown u.v.-absorbing impurity in most commercial phosphates. This impurity is first adsorbed onto the column and then eluted off later in the gradient giving rise to a significant baseline rise (*Figure 5*). In order to avoid this rise it is necessary to screen the available buffer salts and then use the one giving the smallest baseline rise. Examples of the dependence of the rise on the quality of the reagents is given in *Table 2*. Replacing half the concentration of phosphate in the final buffer with potassium chloride will reduce the rise. The quality of the water used is also vital and only freshly distilled and de-ionized water has been found suitable in this laboratory. With such precautions the baseline rise can be limited but never entirely eliminated. Other workers using ammonium phosphates have found the same problems.

3.1.2 *Reversed-phase ion-suppression chromatography*

Due to their strong ionic character, nucleotides (excepting cyclic nucleotides) are not well resolved on RP packings such as C_{18}. Their retention by such packings can be improved by ion-suppression, i.e. selection of a low pH mobile phase in order to suppress the secondary ionization of the phosphate groups. Solvents such as methanol can be employed to modify retention without effecting the resolution. Under such chromatographic conditions the elution order is given by triphosphate < diphosphate < monophosphate but the difficulties of resolving nucleotide mixtures are indicated by the following k' values obtained with ODS$-$Hypersil: ATP (1.6), ADP (2.4), AMP (3.6), GTP (2.2) and GMP (3.8). Anomalous behaviour has been reported for 2' and 3' ribonucleotides when chromatographed on C_8 columns in concentrated buffers, i.e. 0.6 M at pH 3. Under such conditions nucleoside monophosphates are well retained and excellent separations are possible on standard mixtures. In view of the need for very concentrated eluents it seems likely that this is not a simple ion-suppression mechanism but is in fact a form of IP. With all these RP techniques not only are there problems in adequately resolving nucleotide mixtures but, in biological extracts, other compounds such as nucleosides and bases also elute with low k' values.

3.1.3 *Reversed-phase ion-paired (RP-IP) separations*

The strongly ionic nature of the phosphate esters means that nucleotides are able to interact with a variety of cationic IP agents. In the presence of low concentrations of such pairing agents nucleotides are well retained by C_{18} columns and excellent separations

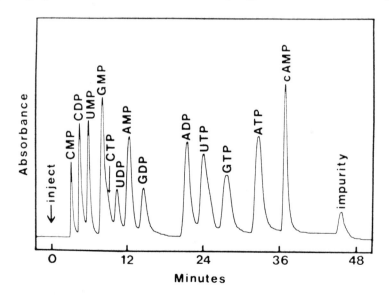

Figure 6. Gradient RP$-$liquid chromatography with ion pairing of nucleotide. Chromatographic details: column, 4.6 × 250 mm 5 μm Spherisorb ODS; detector, Waters 254 nm 0.16 a.u.f.s.; eluent, concave gradient (Waters curve 8) over 40 min from 25 mmol/l tetrabutylammonium hydrogen sulphate (TBAHS) in 0.05 mol/l KH_2PO_4, NH_4Cl buffer pH 3.9 to 0.05 mol/l TBAHS in 0.1 mol/l KH_2PO_4 NH_4Cl buffer pH 3.4 + 30% MeOH; flow, 1 ml/min; pressure, 400$-$50 p.s.i.; temperature, ambient. Chromatogram reproduced with permission from ref. 7.

have been reported by a number of investigators. A variety of possible mechanisms have been proposed to explain this improvement in retention in the presence of solvophobic ions. Whether the mechanism is one of dynamic ion-exchanger formation or retention of IP the general finding is that at suitable pH the k' values for most nucleotides can be increased by 3- or 4-fold by the inclusion of approximately $1-5$ mmol/l of an IP reagent.

Hoffman and Liao (7), employing tetra-n-butylammonium hydrogen sulphate (TBAHS) as the IP agent, were the first to report the separation of some 14 nucleotides by chromatography on a C_{18} column. The order of elution was reversed from that achieved by ion-suppression and was similar to that found with anion-exchange, except that cytidine nucleotides were poorly retained. Again because of the increasing ionic charge on the nucleotides it was necessary to use a gradient from 0 to 30% methanol. A typical RP-IP separation is shown in *Figure 6* and the full chromatographic details are given in the legend.

Only recently has this successful approach been rigorously investigated. Perrone and Brown (8) have examined some of the variables involved in the IP of a wide variety of nucleotides and presented a number of rules. As expected, the increase in k' was a direct function of the hydrophobicity of the ion-pair's backbone, i.e. tetrabutyl > tetraethyl > tetramethyl. None of these pairing agents significantly retained cytidine compounds whereas the effects were most dramatic for the thymidines. The optimum concentration of TBAHS, between 10 and 25 μmol/l, was also less than that required with the other pairing agents. Retention of the IP was greater at pH 5.7 than pH 3, the only pH values studied. In most cases the elution order was mono < di < triphosphates. The relationship of pH to k' for a series of nucleotides on ODS$-$Hypersil is shown in *Figure 7*. At pH 5.7 the nucleotide-ion pairs behaved like their corresponding bases and their elution order was C < U < G < I < A < T (see Section 3.3 for further details). Unlike the RP separation of nucleosides and bases the IP chromatography of nucleotides is markedly influenced by the concentration of buffer salts in the eluent since these too will compete for the IP agent. For example increasing the concentration of KH_2PO_4 from 50 to 200 mmol/l halves the k' of the adenosine nucleotides, the effect being approximately linear.

For preparative RP-h.p.l.c., a useful volatile buffer can be made using triethylamine/ammonium bicarbonate buffers. The IP agent can be made in solution by bubbling CO_2 through solutions of triethylamine (100 mM) in water or ethanol until the pH is 6.7 (9). These two buffers can then form the extremes of the gradient.

3.1.4 *Zwitterion chromatography*

A novel form of IP called zwitterion chromatography was introduced and characterized by Knox and Jurand (10). Here a zwitterion-pairing agent such as 11-amino undecanoic acid (C11AA) forms a quadrupolar IP with, among other classes of compounds, nucleotides and these IP can be separated by RP-h.p.l.c. The optimum concentration of C11AA is $1-2$ mmol/l and methanol may be used to control the retention time. The C11AA is absorbed onto the RP packing material and therefore the column must be equilibrated with the IP agent before use. The k' of the nucleotides and to some extent the selectivity is very pH dependent. k' increases as the pH is reduced from 6 to 4; in fact the useful

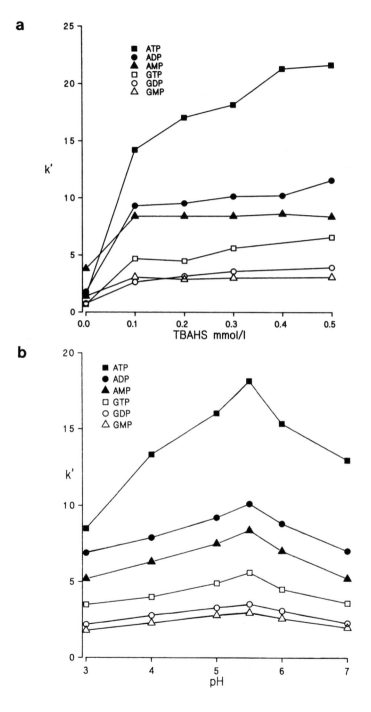

Figure 7. Variation of the k' for nucleotides on IP−liquid chromatography on ODS−Hypersil with (**a**) concentration of TBAHS in 0.2 mol/l KH_2PO_4 pH 5.5 buffer:MeOH (96:4) and (**b**) pH at constant TBAHS concentration (0.3 mmol/l) otherwise as in (**a**).

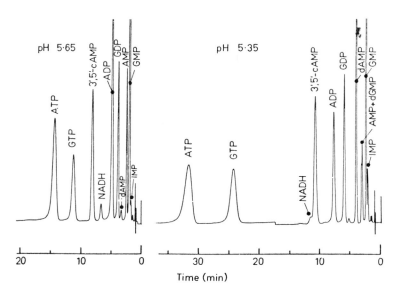

Figure 8. Effect of pH on zwitterion chromatography of nucleotides. Chromatographic details: column, 4.6 × 100 mm 5 μm ODS−Hypersil (Shandon); detector, 254 nm; eluent, water/methanol (88:12, v/v) 75 mmol/l in phosphate buffer and 1.25 mmol/l in C11AA. Reproduced with permission from ref. 10.

range is only pH 5.2−5.7 approximately. Unlike the RP-IP systems this system does not necessarily require a gradient. Excellent separations of at least 10 nucleotides can be achieved isocratically but it has received little attention for the separation of complex biological extracts (*Figure 8*).

3.1.5 *Metal chelate chromatography*

As an alternative to RP-IP separation a number of methods utilize the interaction between nucleotides and metal ions to achieve resolution. These methods typically employ immobilized bidentate ligands such as dithiocarbamate−cobalt(III) complexes or dithiocarbamate alone and elution with mobile phases containing Mg(II) or a similar metal ion. Reasonably good separations of up to 10 nucleotides, nucleosides and bases have been achieved (11). The elution order is similar to that for RP alone. Without Mg(II) k' values could be very long, suggesting strong interactions. Retention times could be reduced by addition of Mg(II) up to 2 mM and by increasing the pH. Folley *et al.* (12) combined metal chelate chromatography and IP chromatography. Nucleotides were eluted from ODS columns by a gradient from 0 to 5 mmol/l Mg(II) in the presence of 30 mmol/l triethylamine and without an organic modifier.

3.2 **Cyclic nucleotides**

Cyclic nucleotides are in many respects anomalous since they have chromatographic characteristics of both nucleotides and nucleosides. On anion-exchange columns their retention time is intermediate between their associated mono- and di-phosphates. Selectivity of the various nucleotides is excellent and rapid isocratic group separations can be achieved. Unlike other nucleotides they are particularly well retained on RP

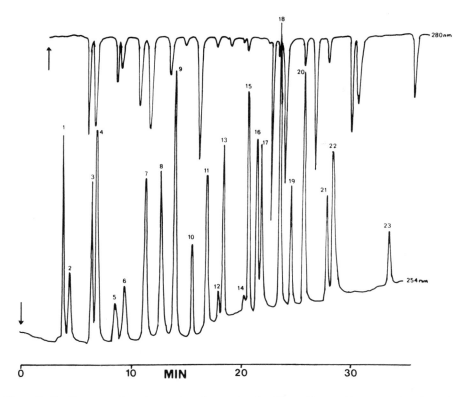

Figure 9. Gradient separation of a complex mixture of nucleosides and bases with two wavelength monitoring. Chromatographic details: column, 4.9 × 250 mm 5 µm Spherisorb ODS; temperature, ambient; detector, Waters 440 254/280 nm; range, 0.04 a.u.f.s.; eluents, A: 40 mmol/l ammonium acetate pH 5:MeOH (99:1), B: MeOH:acetonitrile:THF (80:10:10); gradient, 0−30% B in 30 min; flow, 1 ml/min. Peak identity: **1**, orotic acid; **2**, orotidine; **3**, pseudouridine; **4**, uracil; **5**, tyrosine; **6**, uric acid; **7**, uridine; **8**, hypoxanthine; **9**, xanthine; **10**, oxypurinol; **11**, allopurinol; **12**, oxipurinol riboside; **13**, allopurinol riboside; **14**, 4-pyridone carboxamide; **15**, 7-methylguanine; **16**, adenine; **17**, tryptophan; **18**, adenosine; **19**, theobromine; **20**, deoxyadenosine; **21**, theophylline; **22**, N^6-methyladenosine; **23**, caffeine. Chromatogram kindly supplied by George Morris Purine Laboratory, Guys Hospital, London SE1.

packings such as C_{18} without the addition of IP agents. Retention differences are such that to achieve group separations the use of a shallow methanol gradient may be required (13). The order of elution is the same as that for the corresponding nucleosides (see Section 3.3).

3.3 Separation of nucleosides and bases

Although cation-exchange chromatography using either traditional resins or, later, pellicular h.p.l.c. packing was originally the method of choice for the separation of nucleosides and bases few workers now use such systems. The introduction of bonded RP silicas in the mid-1970s led to the development of rapid chromatographic methods for these compounds which are now almost universally employed (4).

Since they lack the charged phosphates of the nucleotides, nucleosides and bases are excellent candidates for RP chromatography on C_{18} packings. Given the large number of divergent compounds in the group it is not surprising that considerable differences

Table 3. Structure—retention rules for purines and pyrimidines on RP-h.p.l.c..

1.	Any substituent in a compound causing charge formation decreases k', e.g. methyl nucleosides.
2.	Any substituent that causes the compound to exist mainly as the lactam or amine tautomers decreases k'.
3.	Both type of group and its position on the ring affect k', the order being OH < H < NH_2 < NHR. A methyl group approximately doubles the k'.
4.	The ribosyl group of nucleosides doubles the k' of the base.
5.	Deoxyribonucleotides are better retained than the corresponding ribonucleotide.
6.	The linear phosphate esters of nucleotides dramatically reduce the k'.
7.	Cyclic phosphate esters, e.g. cAMP, have increased retention over the corresponding nucleoside.

in the retention characteristics are observed. This means that although suitable concentrations of organic modifier can be found which would allow isocratic elution of certain mixtures particularly useful for drug analyses, for complex physiological samples gradient elution is almost essential (*Figure 9*). The retention behaviour of the common nucleosides and bases has been rationalized following the investigations of Brown and Grushka (14). They employed a model based on the phenomenon of stacking of nitrogenous bases in aqueous solution. Stacking refers to a vertical association between overlapping rings of either homogeneous or heterogeneous aromatic compounds possessing heteroatoms. Unlike the base pairing of DNA or RNA, this stacking is thought to be a hydrophobic interaction which is disrupted by the presence of organic solvents. From both theory and observation, Brown and Grushka derived a series of rules, which are summarized in *Table 3*.

Control of the retention times on the ODS systems can be achieved as usual by variations in the composition of the column eluent. In RP chromatography the pH of the buffer will influence the retention time in a manner dependent on the pK of the bases. Since the pKs of most of the bases are outside the usual operating range of silica packing, i.e. pH 2−7, the pH effects are small; only for adenine with a pK_b of 4.15 is the retention time significantly increased by a pH change from 4 to 6. Again for nucleosides which are usually better retained than the corresponding base, pH does not significantly affect retention. Two exceptions are adenosine when the pH increases from 3 to 5 there is a dramatic increase in retention time whereas for xanthosine the reverse is the case. The role of organic modifiers is as one would expect. Increasing concentrations of methanol decrease k' but cause only minor variations in selectivity. Similarly the ionic strength of the eluent is not critical but should be kept as low as possible to reduce baseline noise. Increasing the column temperature reduces the k' and has some effects on the selectivity. Because the separation obtainable with simple RP systems is so good there is little need to employ either tertiary solvent mixtures such as water/methanol/tetrahydrofuran or IP for nucleosides and bases. Even so heptanesulphonate (1 mmol/l) in phosphate buffer (pH 5.6) has been used to modify the separation of some standard mixtures. It may be that inclusion of a similar IP agent may be useful in attempts to resolve particularly difficult peaks or drug metabolites. Such problem pairs are hypoxanthine—guanine and hypoxanthine—xanthine. In order to achieve baseline separation it is necessary not only to carefully adjust the composition of the eluent but also possibly to try different batches of the column packing material.

In most of the published applications using either 5 or 10 μm ODS packings, gradients have been employed to separate the large numbers of u.v.-absorbing peaks (not all of which are purine or pyridimine compounds in biological fluids). Gradients from 0 to 60% methanol in 0.01 M phosphate pH 5.5 buffers are typical and run times of about 30 min will allow the resolution of most of the important physiological nucleotides and bases (*Figure 9*). With such a gradient at least 28 u.v.-absorbing compounds can be

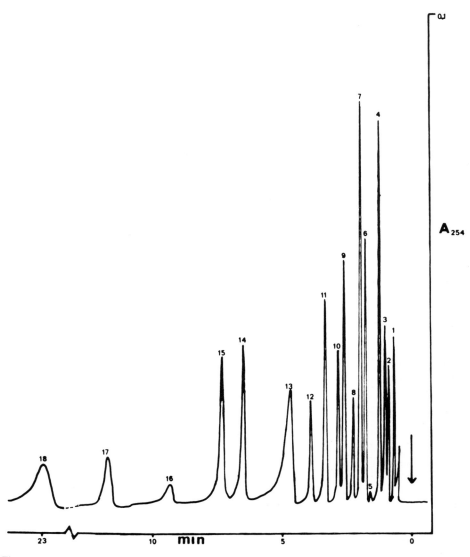

Figure 10. Isocratic separation of a complex mixture of nucleosides, bases and related compounds. Chromatographic details: column, 4.6 × 100 mm 3 μm ODS−Hypersil (Shandon); detector, Cecil CE2012 254 nm; flow, 2.5 ml/min; pressure, 2000 p.s.i.; eluent, 0.004 mol/l KH_2PO_4 pH 5.8 + MeOH (99:1); temperature, ambient; sample, 1 nM of each standard except adenine 2 mM (20 μl loop). Peak identity: **1**, orotic acid; **2**, uric acid; **3**, cytosine; **4**, uracil; **5**, tyrosine; **6**, cytidine; **7**, hypoxanthine; **8**, xanthine; **9**, uridine; **10**, oxypurinol; **11**, allopurinol; **12**, xanthosine; **13**, adenine; **14**, inosine; **15**, guanosine; **16**, tryptophan; **17**, thymidine; **18**, adenosine.

resolved. Provided h.p.l.c. grades of buffer materials are employed the baseline rise should not exceed 0.01 A at 254 nm. Even so this level of useable sensitivity (0.05 a.u.f.s.) may not be sufficient to quantitate some trace nucleosides and bases in physiological fluids such as plasma. With the arrival of the newer stationary phases with 3 μm diameter, silica columns with higher efficiencies can be packed. With these columns separations almost equivalent to those obtainable with gradient elution can be achieved isocratically (15). The use of isocratic elution means that the system is simpler and able to operate at higher sensitivity (e.g. 0.005 a.u.f.s.) without undue baseline noise. Since there is no re-equilibration necessary the system should have a higher throughput. Isocratic elution is also particularly valuable when either very high sensitivity is required for relatively simple separations or electrochemical detection is employed (*Figure 10*).

4. DETECTION OF NUCLEIC ACID COMPONENTS

4.1 **U.v. detection**

Nucleic acid components possess strong chromophores, which absorb in the u.v. spectrum between 240 and 270 nm (*Table 4*). These coincide with the intense line at 253.7 nm in the mercury spectrum. Because the earliest h.p.l.c. detectors were fixed wavelength detectors equipped with mercury lamps and suitable filters, 254 nm has been almost universally applied to the detection of nucleotides, etc. This fortunate coincidence also explains why nucleic acid components were frequently the compounds on which advances in h.p.l.c. equipment were made. With the present generation of u.v. monitors this wavelength permits the measurement of the majority of unmodified nucleotides, nucleosides and bases with good sensitivity (approximately 50 pmol injected). This level of sensitivity is adequate for the quantitation of nucleotides in most tissue extracts but may not be sufficient for many nucleosides and bases in similar extracts. It is also insufficient for the determination of cyclic nucleotides in physiological fluids when the relative concentration of nucleotides in samples, i.e. ATP = cAMP $\times$ 10^3, can also make resolution difficult.

With variable wavelength h.p.l.c. detectors compounds can be monitored at their absorbance maxima and therefore at highest sensitivity. The spectra of some selected compounds are shown in *Figure 11*. Variable wavelength is obviously important for the sensitive and selective detection of compounds which possess maximal absorption at different wavelengths, such as 6-mercaptopurine at 330 nm and uric acid at 292 nm.

Table 4. U.v. characteristics of nucleotides, nucleosides and bases.

	pH	Max nm[b]	E $\times$ 10^{-3}	Ratio[a] 254/270	254/220
ATP	2	257	14.7	1.77	3.05
GTP	1	256	12.4	1.81	3.80
CTP	2	280	13.0	0.52	1.03
UTP	2	262	10.0	1.40	33.1

[a]For Cecil 212 detectors areas determined with SP4270.
[b]Max and E are very similar for NDP, NMP, nucleoside and base.

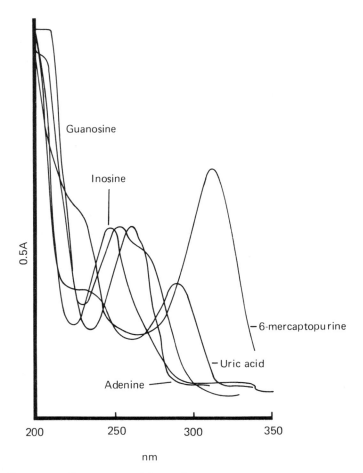

Figure 11. U.v. spectra of some representative purines.

It is particularly useful for those studying energy metabolism to monitor in the region 206−210 nm; at this wavelength not only are the adenosine nucleotides detected but also the important metabolites creatine and creatine phosphate. Following many design improvements, the factors which originally favoured the fixed wavelength detectors, such a lower price and higher sensitivity, apply less and less. Variable wavelength monitors with maximum sensitivities of 0.001 a.u.f.s. are now available. Even so 254 nm is still most commonly employed since it offers a good compromise for the most common compounds in biological samples and it also allows easy comparison with older published data.

Variable and dual wavelength h.p.l.c. detectors have recently proved popular in determining wavelength ratios as an aid to peak identification in complex extracts of physiological fluids. At present few workers have employed photodiode array detectors for these compounds. Yet for complex biological separations they could prove particularly valuable in identifying peaks and testing the homogeneity of eluted peaks.

4.2 **Fluorescent detection**

Even though high sensitivity can be achieved with present day u.v. detectors there is a need for a more sensitive means of detecting nucleic acid components, but to date no universal procedure for increasing detection limits has been described. For many types of compounds improvements in detection limits and specificity can often be attained by using fluorescent and electrochemical detectors (ECD).

Over the pH range normally associated with column eluates the majority of purine bases, etc. do not fluoresce. The only naturally fluorescent compound in extracts of plasma analysed for nucleosides and bases is in fact an amino acid, tryptophan (ex 280 nm, em, 360 nm). Using a post-column reactor to adjust the eluate to either pH 1−2 or 10−12 an increased number of purines and pyrimidines will fluoresce. In particular some methyl guanines can be determined at picomole quantities with fluorimeter settings of 295 nm (ex) and 370 nm (em) cut-off filter.

Pre- and post-column derivatization can be employed to introduce fluorophores into suitable molecules. The side chains of various modified purines have been derivatized, for example 6-mercaptopurine has been measured in plasma following reaction of the -SH group and the separation of the resulting products by RP-h.p.l.c. Direct derivatization of the purine or pyrimidine ring would yield a more useful product but no general reagent has been described. Derivatization of the ring has been used to measure some modified compounds such as fluorouracil (16) and thioguanine (17).

Fluorescent derivatives of adenine and cytidine compounds can be formed by reaction with haloacetaldehyde. Following pre-column derivatization the fluorescent derivatives of adenine, adenosine, AMP and cAMP can be separated by RP-h.p.l.c. (see Section 8.2 for details).

4.3 **Electrochemical detection**

The other h.p.l.c. detector capable of high sensitivity is the ECD. A number of lines of evidence point to the potential usefulness of this detector with purines, etc. H.p.l.c.-ECD methods for uric acid (18), theophylline and caffeine (19), both of which possess purine rings, have been described. The mechanism of oxidation of the simple purines at the pyrolytic graphite electrode was studied some years ago (for review see ref. 20). In one early study the eluate from a Sephadex column was monitored with a voltammetric detector and the four bases plus GMP were detected in an 8 h run. More up to date applications to h.p.l.c. are very few. However recent work has shown that h.p.l.c.-ECD can have much wider application to the determination of purines, etc.

Using a flow injection system the electrochemical oxidation at a variety of electrode surfaces, e.g. glassy carbon, gold, platinum, of a number of purine and pyrimidine compounds, can be readily determined (21). The electrochemical activity of these compounds at pH 4, 7 and 9 is summarized in *Table 5* and some typical voltammograms are shown in *Figure 12*. Since the response of the detector was dependent on both the preparation of the surface and the material of the electrode and independent of the chromatography, *Table 5* should only be taken as a rough guide to electrochemical activity. Guanine, xanthine and their nucleosides and nucleotides are electrochemically active at working potentials greater than 0.9 V vs Ag/AgCl on a glassy carbon electrode at all pH values. Adenine, adenosine and hypoxanthine are most reactive at pH 7 and

9. Uracil was weakly reactive over the same pH range. Other purines and pyrimidines tested so far could not be detected. The optimum working potentials are in general greater than 1 V and are, to some extent, affected by the pH of the carrier buffer. Quantitatively guanine and its related compounds gave the highest electrochemical response and single picomoles could be detected. Commercially available amperometric ECDs (e.g., Bioanalytical Systems and EDT Research) equipped with glassy carbon electrodes can be employed and, presumably, coulometric detectors (e.g. ESA Coulochem) with flow through carbon polymer electrodes will also work. Thiopurines are different in that their detection is based on the electrochemical oxidation of the -SH group rather than the purine ring itself and occurs at a lower potential.

4.4 **Dual detection**

Since the u.v. absorption spectra of most purine compounds is fairly broad it is possible to monitor most of the compounds at a variety of wavelengths. Using two detectors in series, i.e. with their flow cells connected together by a short piece of narrow bore

Table 5. Survey of electrochemical activity of bases, nucleosides and nucleotides using flow injection with detector at 1.1 V[a], vs Ag/AgCl.

	pH	Base	Nucleoside	NMP	NDP	NTP	cNMP
Adenine	4	b	b	e	e	e	e
	7	c	c	e	e	e	e
	9	c	c	e	e	e	e
Guanine	4	d	b	c	c	c	b
	7	d	b	c	c	c	b
	9	d	b	b	b	b	b
Xanthine	4	c	b	c	c	c	b
	7	c	b	c	c	c	b
	9	c	b	b	b	b	b
Uracil	4	b	f	e	f	e	e
	7	b	f	e	f	e	e
	9	b	f	e	f	e	e
Hypoxanthine	4	b	e	e	f	f	e
	7	c	e	e	f	f	e
	9	c	e	e	f	f	e
Cytosine	4	e	e	e	e	e	e
	7	e	e	e	e	e	e
	9	e	e	e	e	e	e
Thymine	4	f	e	f	f	f	f
	7	f	e	f	f	f	f
	9	f	e	f	f	f	f

[a]Electrochemical activity was surveyed by flow injection analysis using an EDT LCA4 detector equipped with a glassy carbon electrode.
[b]Weakly electroactive.
[c]Moderately electroactive.
[d]Strongly electroactive.
[e]Not electroactive.
[f]Not tested.

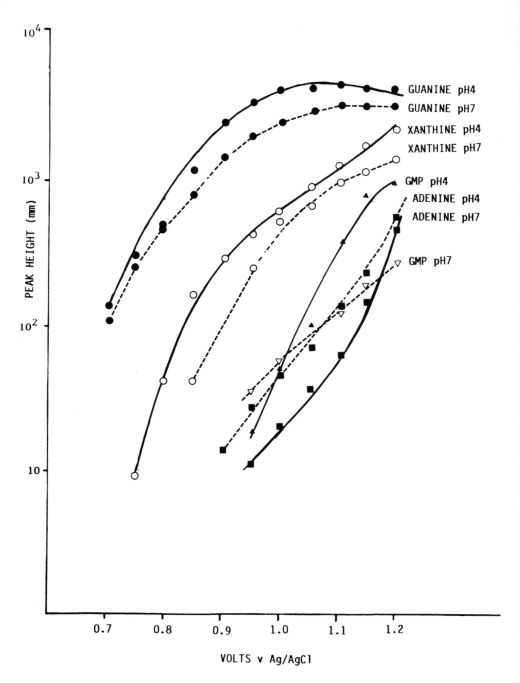

Figure 12. Voltammograms of some electrochemically active bases, etc. Profiles were determined by flow injection analysis at a Bioanalytical Systems glassy carbon electrode using 0.05 mol/l phosphate buffer of the pH indicated containing 10% methanol. 2 nmol of each standard injected.

Teflon tubing, a dual output can be achieved. The wavelength ratio so determined can provide a significant amount of additional information about the identity of the peak and/or its purity. The usual wavelengths employed are 254 nm and 280 nm since both can be generated from mercury lamps. Variable wavelength detectors allow any combination of wavelengths to be employed. Since, for the mercury lamp, the spectral lines are well defined, the ratios are reasonably constant from one system to another. This is not necessarily so with variable wavelength detectors since they employ a variety of bandwidths which will provide non-standard ratios. Even so the wavelength ratios are very reproducible in any one system (*Table 4*).

U.v. detection being non-destructive can also be coupled in series with other detectors such as fluorimeters, or destructive detectors such as ECD and post-column reaction systems. It has already been mentioned that few natural compounds that are naturally fluorescent elute along with the bases and nucleosides and the fluorimetric detector has little to offer the analysis in this mode.

Using a dual u.v.−ECD detection system it is possible to detect a wide variety of compounds in physiological extracts (*Figure 11*). The chromatographic system should preferably be isocratic, so RP or IP separations are ideal. In the case of guanine-related compounds the ECD is significantly more sensitive than the u.v. detector. In the same manner as two u.v. wavelengths can be used to give a ratio which is characteristic of a u.v.-absorbing peak, an ECD/u.v. ratio can be obtained. This ratio can differ by orders of magnitude and is a very useful guide to the identification of components. Even more so than with u.v. ratios, the ECD/u.v. ratio is dependent on the actual chromatographic system. Although peak broadening caused by a u.v. cell placed before the ECD cell should be minimal the variations in response of the individual glassy carbon electron surfaces may vary widely.

5. EXTRACTION PROCEDURES

5.1 **Choice of extractant**

Nucleotides are rapidly degraded by intracellular enzymes including 5′-nucleotidases to lower order nucleotides, then to nucleosides and finally, bases. These, in turn, may be salvaged and re-formed into nucleotides, e.g. hypoxanthine may be converted to IMP by hypoxanthine-guanine phosphoribosyl transferase (HGPRTase). It is important, therefore, to block such interconversions in the time between sampling and extracting the nucleotides for analysis. Since this degradation is in the main biochemical, the rate is tissue dependent. For example, substantial degradation of liver nucleotides occurs within seconds at 37°C whereas human red cell nucleotides are relatively stable over several hours. The extraction techniques employed will therefore reflect these differences. The final procedure, like all extraction methods suitable for use with h.p.l.c., should fulfil a number of additional requirements. In particular, the method should be simple, reliable, reproducible and compatible with h.p.l.c. The extraction of nucleotides has recently been reviewed by Perrett (22) and the extraction of nucleosides has been covered by Brown (23).

Nucleotides are released by acid extractants from mammalian cells. The most popular methods are perchloric acid (PCA) extraction followed by neutralization with potassium hydroxide and removal of the potassium perchlorate precipitate, and trichloroacetic acid (TCA) followed by extraction of the excess TCA with water-saturated diethyl ether. Modifications include direct injection of the acid extracts or neutralization of the extract with tris(hydroxymethyl)aminomethane (Tris). These methods are unacceptable since nucleotides are unstable on storage in acid solution and injection of concentrated Tris solutions disturbs the chromatography. Although TCA and PCA give comparable extraction efficiencies, the PCA/KOH procedure leaves a saturated solution of $KClO_4$ and more precipitate tends to form on storing the sample at $-20°C$. Losses of nucleotides of up to 10% by absorption onto this precipitate can occur. Whichever precipitant is chosen various parameters, such as extractant to tissue ratio, extractant concentration and final volume, govern the final extraction efficiency. For any one procedure these should be optimized and the outlines given in this section should only be taken as guides.

Excess TCA is removed by multiple extractions (minimum 3×4 volumes) with water-saturated diethyl ether and PCA is precipitated with KOH. Both methods are extremely simple but it is easy to make errors, for example adding excess KOH. To overcome such errors Khym (24) introduced a combined solvent extraction-cum-neutralization procedure, whereby excess acid was removed by extracting with a water-insoluble amine dissolved in a water-immiscible solvent. The amino−solvent pair can be 0.5 M Alamine 336 or tri-N-octylamine dissolved in Freon-TF which is mixed with the aqueous extract for 3−4 min. The concentration of amine must be controlled and it must be freshly prepared. The procedure was optimized by Van Haverbeke and Brown (25) who concluded that the TCA concentration must be at least 9% (w/v) and that the exact amount of amine to neutralize the solution (determined by titration) is required. Excess amine could reduce recovery of ATP from erythrocytes by 30%. The consensus of opinion is that, at least with mammalian cells, TCA is the most efficient protein precipitating agent and that there may be advantages in using an amine/immiscible solvent neutralization scheme.

5.2 Extraction methods

5.2.1 *Whole tissues*

The most studied sources of nucleotides are animal tissues, particularly rat liver and the formed elements of human blood such as red cells. The techniques necessary to achieve satisfactory preparations are a direct function of the metabolic activity of the tissue. It has been known for many years that the ATP concentration of tissues can drop many fold during the dissection of liver. With the application of h.p.l.c. analysis it has become clear that equally large changes in the concentration of other nucleotides also occur in ischaemic tissues.

In order to minimize changes in nucleotide composition due to warm ischaemia it is necessary to stop enzyme action by rapidly freezing the tissue. Freezing the sample is preferably performed *in situ* with the live animal under light anaesthesia. The frozen tissue can then be homogenized in a cold solution of protein precipitant without further changing the nucleotide content. Since the changes are time dependent it is essential to perform all the operations in the minimum possible time. Light ether or Nembutal anaesthesia produces only slight changes in the adenosine nucleotides and ATP/ADP ratio. No studies on the effect of anaesthesia on the complete nucleotide pattern studied by h.p.l.c. has been reported. Care must be taken not to significantly traumatize the animal since stress can also cause some degree of change.

Freeze-clamping *in situ* is best performed using metal tongs as described by Wollenberger (26). The dimensions of the tongs should be appropriate to the tissue being sampled. Small thick copper jaws are needed for sampling from mice and rats whilst larger jaws are suitable for larger animals or tougher tissue. Typically the jaws should clamp between 50 and 200 mg of wet tissue.

(i)   Place the jaws of the tongs in liquid nitrogen ($-196°C$) or liquid air contained in a Dewar vessel until they attain the temperature of the bath. The handles of the tongs must be well insulated.

(ii)   Expose the tissue to be clamped and gently ease aside the surrounding skin and organs.

(iii) In one movement raise the tongs from the Dewar and squeeze the tissue rapidly between the flat jaws. In this way the tongs rapidly freeze the tissue preventing metabolic changes and, if applied with a rapid action and moderate force, they mechanically fracture the tissue.

(iv)   Following freeze clamping crudely free the frozen tissue using a sharp strong scalpel and lift clear the frozen pellet still held by the tongs.

(v)   Cut away all material not between the jaws before easing the pellet off the jaws onto a cold weighing boat and rapidly weighing.

(vi)   Add the weighed frozen tissue to a homogenizer tube containing an appropriate volume of ice-cold protein precipitant. 1 ml of 10% w/v TCA per 100 mg wet weight of tissue is usually sufficient but the optimum proportion should be determined for each tissue.

(vii) Perform homogenization immediately and continue until the mixture appears uniform in colour and texture. The time required is dependent on the mass and type of tissue and the type of homogenizer but it is usually less than 30 sec. Both a motor-driven homogenizer of the pestle and tube (Potter-Elvehjem) variety and the enclosed blade (Turax) type are suitable.

(viii) Separate nucleotide-containing acid supernatant by centrifugation. Immediately remove the excess acid using one of the techniques described in Section 5.1.

To standardize the results collect a small sample ($10-20$ mg) of frozen tissue into a pre-weighed tube and then dry or freeze-dry to a constant weight so as to determine the wet weight:dry weight ratio of the original. If required the protein or DNA concentration of the sample can be determined using standard techniques in either a sample of the final homogenate or by solubilizing the TCA precipitate.

5.2.2 *Blood cells*

Red blood cells should be obtained from fresh heparinized blood by immediate centrifugation at about 2000 *g* for 10 min and preferably at 4°C. The plasma and buffy coat are removed and, if required, the cells can be washed with 1 volume of ice-cold saline. The packed red cells (1 vol) are slowly added to ice-cold 10% TCA (2 vol) or other protein precipitant and vortexed. The precipitate is removed by centrifugation and the nucleotide-containing supernatant transferred to a glass tube. Excess TCA is then removed as already described. An aliquot of the packed cells is retained for determination of their haematocrit, haemoglobin or total protein concentration to which the final concentration of nucleotides will be referred. When rapid sampling is required it is possible to extract whole blood and the values obtained will approximate to those for red cells alone. In order to allow for the plasma water, the volume and strength of the TCA used should be adjusted accordingly.

Platelets and other white cells can be obtained by standard methods such as Ficol − Hypaque fractionation. Because these techniques are relatively slow and the cells are more metabolically active than red cells, measureable degradation of nucleotides will occur. After the final wash of the isolation procedure, centrifuge to remove as much as possible of the washings and, while vortexing, add 10% TCA (100 μl per 10^6 cells). It is often necessary to sonicate or homogenize the mixture to completely disintegrate the cells.

5.2.3 *Other cells*

Compared with blood cells, bacterial and tissue culture cells are significantly more metabolically active and nucleotides degrade at faster rates during isolation. Few detailed studies on extraction methods have been published but a number of differences in approach are obvious [see ref. (22) for review]. Usually cells are harvested by either centrifugation or filtration prior to acid extraction. Payne and Ames (27) investigated both isolation procedures and concluded that consistent and reproducible results were achieved only by vacuum filtration through membranes. Nucleotides were immediately extracted either *in situ* or by placing the filter in 1 M formic acid for 30 min. In contrast to workers with animal tissues, researchers with these cells have traditionally, but not exclusively, used formic or acetic acids to release intracellular metabolites. Lundin and Thore (28) compared 10 methods for extracting nucleotides from a variety of bacteria including *Escherichia coli* prior to a firefly assay. Methods tested included various acid and/or solvent extraction procedures. The results were compared using total nucleotide concentrations and energy charge (EC). The lowest EC was obtained with formic acid and chloroform whilst TCA gave the highest values. Their findings however do not agree with the recent study of Olempska and Freeze (29). Similar procedures should be employed to harvest tissue culture cells and rapid filtration is possibly the best isolation technique. Workers have tended to use the more familiar mammalian extractants such as TCA. Nucleotides can also be isolated from plant tissues by homogenizing the tissue or seed in TCA as has been used for animal tissue. The procedure also releases a large number of nucleotide sugars such as uridine 5′-diphosphoglucose (UDPG) which complicate the chromatogram (30).

It is clear therefore that the most important factor in isolating nucleotides is to fully evaluate the available procedures with regard to a particular tissue or cell type before embarking on a major study. The criteria for a successful extraction procedure are outlined in the following section.

5.3 **Validation of extraction techniques**

The quality of the extraction of nucleotides is assessed in the usual manner by calculating the overall recovery and reproducibility but also by determining any changes that may have occurred in the *in vivo* concentration of nucleotides during extraction. This is assessed by either the ATP/ADP ratio or the EC of the cell.

$$EC = \frac{ATP + 1/2\ ADP}{ATP + ADP + AMP}$$

EC can be considered to be a quantitative estimate of the energy status of the cell. Its value should approach unity in a cell with maximum energy status and fall to zero in a fully depleted cell. In well prepared tissue extracts the EC is generally between 0.85 and 0.95.

Both the EC and the ATP/ADP ratio are conveniently determined using h.p.l.c. since the necessary values are measured simultaneously and errors are minimal. For red cells with a 'true' ATP/ADP ratio of 14, a 2% breakdown of ATP to ADP can change the ATP/ADP ratio by 24% and the ADP level, provided there is no breakdown to AMP, increases by 28%. Since the analytical errors were very small the ATP/ADP ratio is an extremely sensitive measure of both the energy status of the cell and the rate of enzymatic and chemical degradation of the intracellular nucleotides. Changes in the ATP/ADP ratio are paralleled by changes in other triphosphate/diphosphate pairs. It is not uncommon to find that, with practice at isolating and extracting a tissue, the ATP/ADP ratios increase dramatically. The first extractions of some organs such as liver often give values below 1, whereas an experienced worker can consistently achieve ratios as high as 7. Such variability is also unfortunately reflected in the published literature.

5.4 Internal standards

With complex extraction procedures such as those for nucleotides it is preferable to use an internal standard to correct for both recovery and analytical variability. Since it is not easy to add a marker inside a cell before extraction it is usual to add a known amount of a standard nucleotide that does not occur in the cells along with the acid precipitant. The internal standard will now correct mainly for the dilution and sampling errors. The amount of internal standard added should be such that, allowing for dilution, it will give a prominent well-resolved peak with a height of about 80% full scale in the typical chromatogram. Various nucleotides such as CMP, XMP and XDP have been used as internal standards (*Table 6*) but they all have disadvantages. CMP can be difficult to resolve from a number of frontally eluting compounds when an ion-exchange system is used. Nucleoside di- and tri-phosphates can degrade too readily. In the author's laboratory cyclic nucleotides, e.g. cXMP, although relatively expensive, are considered better since they have good chemical stability, occur only in trace

Table 6. Internal standards.

Nucleotides	Bases/nucleosides
CMP	Theophylline
XMP	Cyclic nucleotides
XDP	
Polynucleotides	
Cyclic nucleotides	
Radiolabelled bases	Radiolabelled bases

amounts in most tissues and elute in the middle of many chromatographic systems. When no suitable internal standard is available, a radiolabelled marker can be employed. We have used [^{14}C]guanine or [^{14}C]inosine since with ion-exchange separations bases are frontally eluted and it is easy to collect the frontal peak in order to determine its radioactive content and calculate the recovery.

5.5 Stability of nucleotide extracts

Nucleotides are readily hydrolysed in acidic solutions but are relatively stable between pH 5 and 8. It is for this reason that PCA and TCA extracts are processed to completely remove the excess acid so that they can be stored at neutral pH. In frozen unneutralized TCA extracts the ATP content can drop by up to 36% per week whereas a neutralized solution is stable even after 6 months at $-20°C$. Provided the samples are neutralized, nucleotide extracts can be kept at room temperature during analysis. This is particularly important when auto-injectors are being used and samples may wait for many hours before being injected.

5.6 Sources of error in nucleotide determinations

Without doubt the major source of error in nucleotide determinations is incorrect sample preparation leading to degradation of nucleotides due to warm ischaemia. Other errors can be caused by chemical impurities and poor sampling.

The sensitivity and resolution of h.p.l.c. often detects impurities and/or breakdown products in standard materials. This is particularly so for easily hydrolysed compounds like nucleoside triphosphates. In this laboratory commercial adenine and guanine nucleotides are usually found to contain trace amounts of their degradation products, but with pyrimidine nucleotides these can in some cases exceed 10% of the total. Ribonucleotides can also be contaminated with deoxyribonucleotides and vice versa. U.v.-absorbing impurities also arise from other chemicals in either the eluent or the extraction procedure. The problem of the phosphate gradient used to elute anion-exchange columns has already been discussed. Both Ficoll−Hypaque and EDTA may contaminate blood cells with u.v.-absorbing impurities. Some non-nucleotides are also observed, for example, ascorbic acid elutes close to CMP on the ion-exchange system and can even be quantified in lymphocytes.

For meaningful estimates of intracellular nucleotides, the sample must be homogeneous. The percentage contamination of blood cell preparations can be easily determined but it is almost impossible to freeze clamp uniform areas of tissues. The best approach is to use tongs with the smallest heads compatible with the tissue and the analytical system. Tissues such as liver and kidney when freeze-clamped can contain substantial amounts of blood, and mathematical corrections for the trapped erythrocytes can be applied. Platelet preparations usually contain some red cells and Goday *et al.* (31) have shown that the presence of platelets in lymphocyte preparations can give false results. In all cases though one must balance the advantages of preparing a more homogeneous sample against the nucleotide degradation which may occur in the time taken to achieve a significant improvement in the sample.

6. ISOLATION OF NUCLEOSIDES FROM BIOLOGICAL MATERIALS

The two most studied sources of nucleosides and bases are plasma (or serum) and urine. Although they occur intracellularly, metabolism ensures that, at least in the healthy, well-oxygenated cell, the predominant form is the nucleotide, and nucleoside and base levels are very low. The nucleosides and bases in cells contribute towards the frontal peak in the ion-exchange chromatography of nucleotides and such fractions can be collected and re-run on an RP system to quantitate cellular nucleosides.

6.1 Plasma

In order to avoid extraneous u.v.-absorbing peaks that can be derived from EDTA and acid − citrate − dextrose-treated plasma it is preferable to use heparinized plasma or serum. The plasma should be separated from the red cells within 10 min to avoid changes in compounds such as hypoxanthine. Prior to h.p.l.c. the protein matrix must be removed but since, in plasma, some compounds such as uric acid occur, both free and protein-bound, differing approaches may be necessary. The total (free plus bound) nucleoside content can be determined by protein precipitation with strong acids such as PCA and TCA which release the bound compounds during the precipitation process. In order to obtain maximum recovery it is important to optimize the ratio of volume and strength of the acid and the volume of plasma. Recoveries of both endogenous and added compounds should be maximized. The highest analytical accuracy will be obtained if a suitable internal standard is used. A number of drugs, for example theophylline, can be used for internal standards (*Table 6*). As a guide we find that 1 vol of plasma should be mixed with about 4 vol of 10% TCA for high and reproducible extractions of some typical nucleosides. The excess acid should be removed as described for nucleotides, not so much because the compounds are unstable in the extract but since at the higher detector sensitivities used the presence of the acids causes a large frontal peak. The amine − Freon method must not be used. Hartwick *et al.* (32) in a study of the isolation of serum nucleosides for h.p.l.c. observed losses of up to 20% caused by the solubility of nucleosides in the Freon.

Free nucleoside concentrations or the total levels of non-protein-bound compounds can be obtained by centrifugation through a suitable ultrafiltration cone (e.g. Amicon type CF25). 1 ml of plasma is pipetted into the cone and centrifuged at 500 r.p.m. for about 15 min to yield about 300 − 400 μl of ultrafiltrate which can then be directly injected. Care must be taken in the selection of the cone and its pore size and it may be necessary to pre-wash the cone with buffered saline to prevent adsorption onto the membrane. Changes in pH during centrifugation may also effect the absolute measurement of moderately protein-bound molecules such as tryptophan. Advantages of the method are simplicity, the lack of addition of foreign chemicals and no dilution of the sample.

Organic solvents are often used to precipitate plasma protein prior to drug assays. The variables in this technique have been optimized by Blanchard (33) and the procedures compared with those using acid precipitants. Approximately 4-fold the volume of an organic solvent is necessary to completely deproteinize plasma compared with TCA. The direct use of organic solvents to precipitate proteins is of little use with nucleosides and bases since many of these compounds have low solubility in organic systems.

Such solvents can therefore be usefully employed in pre-column extraction using off-line adsorption onto small quantities of bonded phase such as in the Sep-Pak or Bond Elut systems. 1 or 2 ml of plasma is loaded onto a ODS cartridge and, following a brief wash with 0.5 ml of 2% MeOH in water to remove the proteins, the nucleosides are eluted with 100% MeOH. The eluate should be freeze dried and reconstituted in column buffer for chromatography. The method will only normally measure the free components in plasma and some poorly retained compounds may be lost with the washings.

Nucleosides and bases are stable in neutral aqueous solution at $-20°C$ for at least 6 months prior to anlaysis.

6.2 **Urine and related fluids**

For most practical purposes urine is protein-free and could be injected directly onto the h.p.l.c. column, but unfortunately it contains a vast number of u.v.-absorbing compounds. Their chromatographic appearance both qualitatively and quantitatively varies considerably even in a normal healthy individual; suggesting that many of them are dietary in origin, e.g. caffeine metabolites. In order therefore to undertake serious studies on say disease profiles it is advisable to standardize dietary requirements and try to reduce some of the endogenous sources of purines, such as chocolate, coffee and beer-type drinks as well as to selectively pre-separate the nucleotides, etc.

Urine may be pre-concentrated and selected fractions prepared for chromatography using RP cartridges and eluents of differing methanol content. Group-specific isolation procedures such as the use of boronate gels can also be usefully employed. Boronate forms an anionic complex with the 2',3'-hydroxyls of ribonucleosides in alkaline pH. Davis and co-workers (33) found that bases, deoxyribonucleosides, deoxyribonucleotides and a variety of miscellaneous interferences were not retained by a phenylboronate gel column, whereas compounds such as adenosine and guanosine were and could be eluted by a suitable pH change.

7. IDENTIFICATION OF PEAKS

Because of the complex chromatograms which result from the analysis of biological extracts for nucleotides and bases, rigid procedures are necessary in order to identify peaks and confirm the homogeneity of peaks. Although the usual criteria such as retention time and co-chromatography are useful for the initial identification of peaks and are acceptable during routine analysis of well-defined samples, a number of more definitive identification procedures have been devised particularly for use with nucleic acid components. These are summarized in *Table 7*; the majority are self explanatory but a few are discussed in more detail below.

With the routine analysis of a complex mixture the operator plays an important role in both the quality control of the separation and in observing changes in the qualitative and quantitative appearance of the chromatogram. Even with the present generation of integrators a visual inspection of the chromatogram is still found to be mandatory to check that the correct peak designations have been made and the concentrations calculated are sensible. Visual inspection can also help to identify peaks; for example on the RP separation of nucleosides the adenine peak tends to have a distinct tail com-

Table 7. Identification of h.p.l.c. peaks.

1.	Peak parameters	Retention time against standards
		Peak shape
		Relative peak size − pattern recognition.
2.	Co-chromatography with authentic compounds.	
3.	Vary chromatography (e.g. buffer pH, column) and repeat 1 and 2.	
4.	Spectral characterization	Absorbance maximum
		Absorbance ratio − dual u.v. detectors
		Scan in flowcell
		Photodiode array detection
		Determine spectral derivatives.
5.	Enzymatic shift.	
6.	Other detection modes	Fluorescence
		Electrochemical
		U.v./F or U.v./ECD ratios
		On-line mass spectrometry.
7.	O t h e r s	Chemical derivatization
		Collect fractions for chemical identification
		Radioactive labelling.

Table 8. Some enzyme peak shifts.

Peak	Enzyme	Reaction pH	Product
Adenosine	Adenosine deaminase	7.5	Inosine
Inosine	hydrolase	7.4	Hypoxanthine, urate
Uric acid	Uricase	8.5	Allantoin
NMP	5′-Nucleotidase	7.4	Nucleoside
Tryptophan	Tryptophanase	8.3	Indole
cAMP	Phosphodiesterase cAMP	7.5	AMP

pared with other bases.

The use of dual wavelength detection and dual detectors to obtain 280 nm/254 nm or u.v./ECD ratios for determining peak identity and homogeneity has already been referred to. The ratios so determined are reproducible for any pair of detectors. Therefore, not only will the ratio help in peak identification but if a slight contaminant is present in the peak the ratio may be substantially changed. Stop-flow or diode array detection should be particularly valuable in suggesting peak identities. U.v. spectra can be obtained in the flow cell and, after correcting for eluent background, the resulting spectra can be compared with standards either obtained in the h.p.l.c. or taken from published sources. Diode array detectors with suitable software can also be used to obtain first and second order derivatives of the u.v. spectra which are a powerful means of determining peak homogeneity, however the cost of such systems is high.

A particularly useful means of identifying peaks of biochemical origin and one which is very popular for nucleosides and bases is that of enzyme peak shifting. If on the basis of retention time and co-chromatography a peak can be tentatively identified and a specific enzyme exists that can metabolize that peak then incubation of the original sample with the enzyme should cause the peak to disappear and possibly its metabolite(s) to appear elsewhere on the chromatogram. Examples of some peak shifts are given in *Table 8*.

8. HIGH SPECIFICITY ANALYSES

Although u.v. monitoring is a universal detector for nucleic acid compounds for many applications it is limited by both its sensitivity (approximately $10-50$ pmol injected) and its poor selectivity, which may mean that gradient elution is necessary in order to resolve a particular compound. This in turn will reduce the sensitivity further. The need exists for systems able to measure selected groups of compounds at high sensitivity and with a short analysis time.

Pre- and post-column derivatization can be employed to introduce stronger chromophores, electrophores and most commonly fluorophores into suitable molecules to increase sensitivity. Since nucleic acid components are already strong chromophores, the first option offers few advantages. A modification of this routine may be useful to change the detection wavelength as happens when 6-mercaptopurine is coupled to N-ethylmaleimide. The side chains of various modified purines can be derivatized prior to chromatography but these are not generally useful reactions. Direct derivatization of the purine or pyrimidine ring to yield fluorescent products has been used to measure some modified bases but the methods are specific and no general derivatization reagent has been described. Although no general high sensitivity derivatization method has been described, some very useful specific methods have been developed.

8.1 Cyclic nucleotides

Although anion-exchange h.p.l.c. is well suited to the separation of cyclic nucleotide mixtures, in practice and using u.v. detection it is not applicable to crude acid extracts of tissues. This situation is due to the overwhelming concentrations of non-cyclic nucleotides, which prevent the identification of the cyclic nucleotide peaks. The cyclic nucleotides are extracted from tissues, etc. by procedures similar to those previously described. In order to measure cAMP, it is necessary to remove the majority of ribonucleotides. This can be done by adsorbing the non-cyclic nucleotides onto the precipitate of barium sulphate formed by adding $Ba(OH)_2$ and $ZnSO_4$ to the sample. In that way it is possible to detect as little as 1 pmol of cAMP using current equipment and microparticulate column packings.

Since on RP columns cyclic nucleotides are well retained, whereas the other nucleotides particularly ATP elute near the front, direct assay of cAMP in tissue extracts is possible. Krstulovic *et al.* (13) were able to determine cAMP in brain tissue using a simple isocratic separation on an ODS column of a crude PCA/KOH extract (*Figure 13*). The assigned peak was shown to be very pure and sensitivities approached 50 pmol injected. With today's improved u.v. detectors a 10-fold increase in sensitivity should be possible. Because of the difficulties of resolving the cyclic nucleotides from other bases and nucleosides it is unlikely that such a simple assay could be applied to plasma or urine without some preliminary fractionation and for such fluids the advantages of a derivatization assay which improves both specificity and sensitivity are clear.

8.2 1,N^6-Etheno derivatives of adenine compounds

Recently interest has refocused on the 1,N[6]-etheno derivatives of adenine compounds. Haloacetaldehydes react with adenine- and cytidine-containing compounds to form

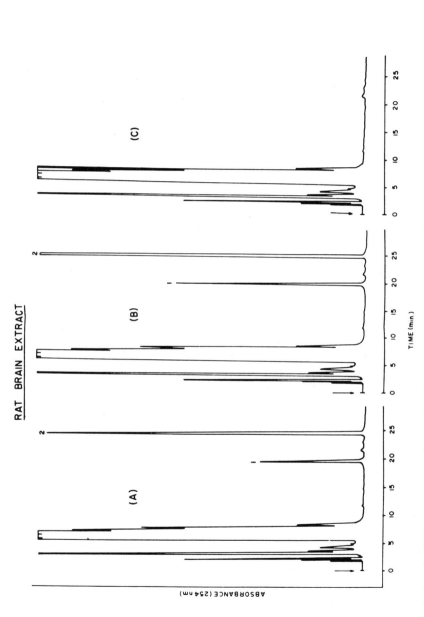

Figure 13. Determination of cAMP in tissue extracts by u.v. detection. Chromatographic details: column, 4.6 × 300 mm, μ-Bondapak; detector, Schoeffel FS770 254 nm; sensitivity, 0.04 a.u.f.s.; eluent, 0.02 mol/l KH_2PO_4 pH 3.7 and MeOH:water (3:2) linear gradient from 0 to 25% in 30 min; flow, 1.5 ml/min; temperature, ambient. Samples: **A**, perchloric extract of rat brain equivalent to 3 mg of tissue; **B**, same sample co-injected with cGMP and cAMP; **C**, same sample after 10 min incubation with cyclic nucleotide phosphodiesterase. Chromatogram reproduced with permission from ref. 13.

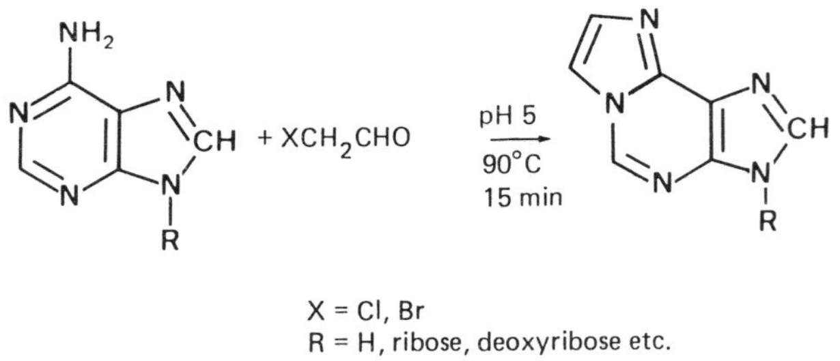

X = Cl, Br
R = H, ribose, deoxyribose etc.

Figure 14. Reaction of adenine compounds with haloacetaldehydes.

1,N⁶-etheno derivatives. The reaction with chloroacetaldehyde (*Figure 14*) has been studied in detail and the products were shown to be highly fluorescent (35). A few workers published methods involving pre-column derivatization and separation of the fluorescent derivatives of adenine, adenosine and cAMP by h.p.l.c. These simple systems for the bases demonstrated that the method is extremely sensitive, being able to determine less than 50 fmol of the derivatives. Since the reaction can be specific for adenine compounds it was soon shown to be possible to determine cAMP directly in plasma and urine.

With the introduction of improved column packing materials it became feasible to resolve the 1,N⁶-etheno derivatives of the adenosine nucleotides by RP-h.p.l.c. Since the derivatization procedure does not affect the phosphate side chain, the products remain ionic and the chromatography of nucleotides is, as already described, not totally satisfactory on RP packings. They can, of course, also be separated by anion-exchange chromatography. In the author's laboratory a good separation of a mixture of adenosine compounds containing bases, ribonucleotides and deoxyribonucleotides and cAMP by RP-h.p.l.c. in the presence of tetrabutylammonium ion has been achieved. The pH, IP and methanol concentrations must be carefully adjusted in order to separate the ribonucleotide derivatives from adenine and adenosine, particularly when deoxyribonucleotides and nicotinamide nucleotides are also present (*Figure 15*). Recently it has been reported (35) that bromoacetaldehyde can replace chloroacetaldehyde in the reaction and gives a 20% improvement in the yield of the nucleotide derivatives since it reacts faster and hence acid hydrolysis of the nucleotides is reduced. For either reagent the derivatization procedure is simple and reproducible.

Chloroacetaldehyde can be obtained either as the free compound (Fluka) or by distillation from 5% sulphuric acid of the more readily available dimethyl acetal derivative. Chloroacetaldehyde distils over at 85−87°C and should be diluted with water to a final concentration of 1 M. Bromoacetaldehyde is not at present commercially available. 100 μl aliquots of solutions containing adenosine compounds in a stoppered glass tube are buffered to pH 4.5 with 1 M acetate buffer (approximately 20 μl) and 10 μl of 1 M chloroacetaldehyde added. The tube is then heated at 90°C for 10 min. Since some hydrolysis of ATP can occur it may be preferable to derivatize at a low temperature and for a short period of time for the most accurate determination of that compound. The exact conditions for any particular sample should be determined. The less extreme derivatization conditions with bromoacetaldehyde may be advantageous here. The resultant derivatives are stable for weeks at 4°C and can be injected directly onto RP columns.

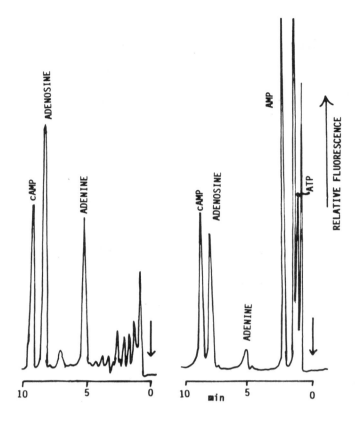

Figure 15. Separation of various adenosine nucleotides, etc. following chloroacetaldehyde derivatization. Chromatographic details: column, 4.6 × 100 mm 3 μm ODS − Hypersil (Shandon); detector, Schoeffel FS970 ex 234 nm, em >380 nm band pass filter; flow, 1.2 ml/min; pressure, 1500 p.s.i.; eluent, 0.05 mol/l ammonium acetate pH 5:MeOH (250:20); temperature, ambient. Sample A, 4 pmol of each standard; injector, 20 μl loop; B, normal urine (diluted × 10).

8.3 **Electrochemical detection of guanine and related compounds**

As already mentioned ECD in the oxidative mode can be used to determine some purine and pyrimidine compounds. The method is most sensitive towards compounds containing the guanine ring but to date most published applications have been concerned with the metabolic oxidation product, uric acid, and a number of h.p.l.c.-ECD assays have been published. Kissinger and co-workers developed a specific method (8) for the measurement of uric acid in serum. Protein-free plasma or serum was injected onto a cation-exchange column and eluted with 0.1 M pH 5.25 acetate buffer. The urate peak eluted at 4 min and was detected by a carbon paste electrode maintained at +0.625 V vs Ag/AgCl reference electrode. Their method has been modified by others, for example see ref. 37, to use a glassy carbon working electrode and RP chromatography with ion-suppression. With these procedures uric acid can be accurately determined in as little as 10 μl of plasma with an absolute sensitivity of less than 1 pmol.

A recent publication (38) reported the determination of guanosine nucleotides by h.p.l.c. with dual ECD. The nucleotides including cGMP were resolved on a μ-Bondapak

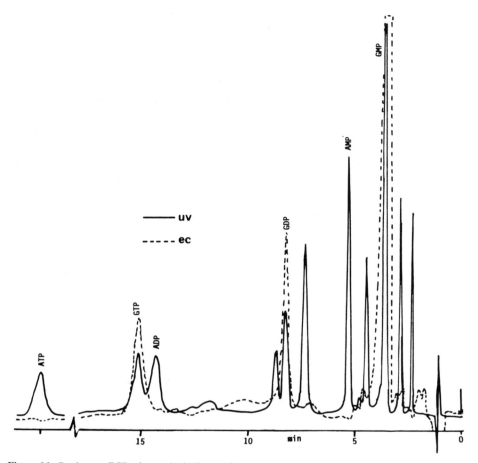

Figure 16. Dual u.v. −ECD of a standard mixture of guanine and adenine nucleotides, nucleosides and bases. Chromatographic details: column, 10 × 0.46 cm ODS−Hypersil; eluent, 0.05 mol/l ammonium acetate pH 5.5 containing 2.5 mmol/l tetrabutylammonium chloride:MeOH (90:10); flow, 1.2 ml/min; pressure, 1500 p.s.i.; sample, 0.5 nmol each standard (20 μl); detectors, BAS glassy carbon electrode + 1.1 V vs Ag/AgCl 100 nA fsd; Cecil CE2012 at 254 nm 0.05 a.u.f.s. in series.

C_{18} column using a mobile phase of 0.05 M phosphate buffer in the presence of 2.5 mmol/l TBAHS and 8% methanol. The first electrode was held at +0.95 V and the second at +0.70 V vs Ag/AgCl. The reasons for this combination were unclear since no additional peak identification was achieved unlike the use of dual electrodes in a combined oxidation/reduction sequence. At the first electrode it was possible to measure the guanosine nucleotides including cGMP over the range 1−1000 pmol injected and the assay was applied to brain extracts. The same level of sensitivity can be achieved with a simpler single electrode system (21) (*Figure 16*).

8.4 Deoxynucleotides

Deoxynucleotides can be isolated from cells by the same procedures and with the same precautions as the ribonucleotides. Deoxynucleotides are less acid stable than ribonucleotides but no information on their relative biochemical stability is available. The major problems are analytical since, although they elute close to their respective ribonucleotides and can be readily resolved by a variety of systems, they are usually present in very low concentrations. To overcome this difference in relative concentration, methods involving the selective degradation of ribonucleotides prior to h.p.l.c. have been devised.

Periodate reacts selectively with the 2',3'-*cis* diol of ribonucleotides and the reaction products are readily resolved from the unreacted deoxynucleotides following the removal of excess periodate with rhamnose. An additional step involves the addition of methylamine to cleave the N-glycosidic bond thereby forming the free base, and the resultant mixture can be injected directly onto an anion-exchange column. Recently Tanaka *et al.* (39) have optimized this procedure. In outline their final procedure is as follows.

(i)   Add 20 μl of 20 mM deoxyguanosine and 20 μl of 0.2 M NaIO$_4$ to 80 μl of cell extract.

(ii)   Vortex the mixture and centrifuge for 20 sec followed by incubation at 37°C for 2 min.

(iii)   Add 2 μl of rhamnose followed by 30 μl of 4 M methylamine (neutralized to pH 6.5 with phosphoric acid).

(iv)   Mix, centrifuge for 20 sec and incubate at 37°C for 30 min then cool on ice.

(v)   Inject final reaction mixture onto a strong anion-exchange column and detect the resolved nucleotides at 254 nm.

The sensitivity of this procedure is about 30 pmol injected. It is possible to combine periodate oxidation with derivatization with a haloacetaldehyde to give a very sensitive methodology for deoxynucleotides.

Other methods for selectively measuring the deoxynucleotides involve anion-exchange fractionation of nucleotide pairs, followed by conversion to nucleoside pairs using acid phosphatase. The deoxynucleotide and the ribonucleoside of both purine and pyridines are then separated by RP-h.p.l.c.

8.5 *Purine-containing drugs*

The majority of the assays of drugs which include a purine ring are simply optimized isocratic versions of the general gradient approach to separating nucleosides and bases. Because of the low specificity of the detection principle for assays of physiological fluids it is usually necessary not only to carefully optimize the chromatography but also to devise some form of selective extraction. For clinical drug assays RP-h.p.l.c. is by far the most popular approach.

Theophylline determination by h.p.l.c. is an extremely well known example having been much publicized by h.p.l.c. manufacturers in their literature. Its determination in plasma, urine and saliva may be used as a model for other similar purine-type drugs. It can be detected with sufficient sensitivity using either u.v. detection (E$_{max}$ = 276 nm) or ECD (V = 1.1 V vs Ag/AgCl). A protocol taken from a recent publication (40) is as follows.

(i)   Extract plasma, to which has been added an internal standard such as proxyphylline, with chloroform/isopropanol (85:15).

(ii)   Evaporate to dryness and reconstitute in column eluent.

(iii)   Apply the sample to an RP column and elute with an acetonitrile/tetrahydrofuran/50 mM acetate buffer pH 4 (4:1:95 by vol) and detect at 280 nm.

The newly developed anti-viral agents such as Acyclovir can also be quantitated in clinical specimens by RP-h.p.l.c. (41)

The thiol-containing anti-metabolites such as 6-mercaptopurine and 6-thioguanine are unusual in possessing marked u.v. absorption at 320−340 nm and RP-h.p.l.c. with u.v. detection can be very specific although the sensitivity may be lacking for some applications. Unfortunately their chromatography on ODS columns is poor and unusual effects due to their absorption onto the stationary phase followed by subsequent displacement by naturally ocurring thiols in the samples can give erroneous results. A more satisfactory approach is to derivatize the -SH group prior to chromatography with, for example, monobromobimane to give a stable fluorescent product that can be resolved by RP-h.p.l.c. (42). Presumably derivatization of other substituents on the purine ring is possible although the ring structure often protects groups such as amino groups from undergoing their most common chemical reactions and few pre-column applications have been published.

9. FUTURE DIRECTIONS

In such a long established field of application for h.p.l.c. it is difficult to envisage what fresh developments could benefit the separation and determination of nucleic acid components. Clearly h.p.l.c. with u.v. detection suits most researchers most of the time. Identification rather than separation is a continuing problem for those working with complex physiological mixtures and, in this respect, it is likely that scanning diode array detectors will prove of value provided suitable software becomes available.

A column system able to resolve nucleotides, nucleosides and bases in one single run can be envisaged and work towards the goal is being performed (43,44). Such systems are usually slow buffered gradient separations on RP columns. To date they are only able to separate a limited number of nucleotides. Possibly, if combined with a suitable IP agent, a combination of column and buffer parameters could be found to allow a more complete chromatogram. Although such a separation is potentially interesting for normal tissue and plasma extracts, its application may be limited by the wide differences in concentration that exist between nucleotides and bases. It may well be that the technology of column packings will return full circle and small particle polymeric packings, which are more rigid than the earlier anion-exchangers, may regain their importance. Complete separations of limited resolving power have been demonstrated on ion-exchange packings (45) but to our knowledge RP separations on the new polymeric materials have not been reported.

In some fields of application, where either levels are very low or the amount of sample is very small, the sensitivity of the u.v. detector is insufficient. Some alternative detection methods have been given in this chapter but to date few workers are making serious use of them. A general derivatization method that could couple a fluorescent label to both adenine and guanine compounds would be a major additional technique. Combining a pre-column derivatization and RP chromatograhy with chemiluminescent detection offers the possibility of detecting nucleic acid components at sub-femtomole levels. These sensitivities would be equivalent to firefly luminescence for ATP and radioimmunoassay for cAMP but the resolving power of h.p.l.c. would make an established and powerful technique even more versatile.

10. REFERENCES

1. Cohn,W.E. (1949) *Science,* **109**, 377.
2. Horvath,C.G., Preiss,B.A. and Lipsky,S.R. (1967) *Anal. Chem.,* **39**, 1422.
3. Hartwick,R.A. and Brown,P.R. (1975) *J. Chromatogr.,* **112**, 651.
4. Hartwick,R.A. and Brown,P.R. (1976) *J. Chromatogr.,* **126**, 679.
5. Jones,W. (1970) *Nucleic Acids – Their Chemical Properties and Physiological Conduct.* 2nd Edition, Longman Green, New York.
6. Perrett,D. (1982) *Chromatographia,* **16**, 211.
7. Hoffman,N.E. and Liao,J.C. (1977) *Anal. Chem.,* **49**, 2231.
8. Perrone,P.A. and Brown,P.R. (1984) *J. Chromatogr.,* **317**, 301.
9. Mahoney,C.W. and Yount,R.G. (1984) *Anal. Biochem.,* **138**, 246.
10. Knox,J.H. and Jurand,J. (1981) *J. Chromatogr.,* **203**, 85.
11. Chow,F.K. and Grushka,E. (1979) *J. Chromatogr.,* **185**, 361.
12. Folley,L.S., Power,S.D. and Poyton,R.O. (1983) *J. Chromatogr.,* **281**, 199.
13. Krstulovic,A.M., Hartwick,R.A. and Brown,P.R. (1979) *Clin. Chem.,* **25**, 235.
14. Brown,P.R. and Grushka,E. (1980) *Anal. Chem.,* **52**, 1210.
15. Simmonds,R.J. and Harkness,R.A. (1981) *J. Chromatogr.,* **226**, 369.
16. Iwamoto,M., Yoshida,S. and Hirose,S. (1984) *J. Chromatogr.,* **310**, 151.
17. Herbert,B.H., Drake,S. and Nelson,J.A. (1982) *J. Liquid Chromatogr.,* **5**, 2095.
18. Pachla,L.A. and Kissinger,P.T. (1979) *Clin. Chem.,* **25**, 1847.
19. Lewis,E.C. and Johnson,D.C. (1978) *Clin. Chem.,* **24**, 1711.
20. Dryhurst,G. (1972) *Fortschr. Chem. Forsch.,* **34**, 47.
21. Perrett,D. (1985) *Biochem. Soc. Trans.,* **13**, 1067.
22. Perrett,D. (1986) In *Handbook of Chromatography of Nucleotides, Nucleosides and Bases.* Krustolvic,A. (ed.), C.R.C. Press, Boca Raton, FL, in press.
23. Brown,P.R. (1984) In *HPLC in Nucleic Acid Research.* Brown,P.R. (ed.), Marcel Dekker, New York, p. 31.
24. Khym,J.X. (1975) *Clin. Chem.,* **21**, 1245.
25. Van Haverbeke,D.A and Brown,P.R. (1978) *J. Liquid Chromatogr.,* **1**, 507.
26. Wollenberger,A., Ristau,O. and Schoffa,G. (1960) *Pfluger Arch.,* **270**, 399.
27. Payne,S.M. and Ames,B.N. (1982) *Anal. Biochem.,* **123**, 151.
28. Lundin,A. and Thore,A. (1975) *Appl. Microbiol.,* **30**, 713.
29. Olempska-Beer,Z. and Freese,E.B. (1984) *Anal. Biochem.,* **140**, 236.
30. Standard,S.A., Perrett,D. and Bray,C.M. (1983) *J. Exp. Bot.,* **34**, 1047.
31. Goday,A., Simmonds,H.A., Webster,D.R., Levinsky,R.J., Watson,A.R. and Hoffbrand,A.V. (1983) *Clin. Sci.,* **65**, 635.
32. Hartwick,R.A., Van Haverbeke,D., McKeag,M. and Brown,P.R. (1979) *J. Liquid Chromatogr.,* **2**, 725.
33. Blanchard,J. (1981) *J. Chromatogr.,* **226**, 455.
34. Davis,G.E., Suits,R.D., Kuo,K.C., Gehrke,C.W., Waalkes,T.P. and Borek,E. (1977) *Clin. Chem,* **23**, 1427.
35. Secrist,J.A., Barrio,J.R., Leonard,N.J. and Weber,G. (1972) *Biochemistry,* **11**, 3499.
36. Yoshioka,M., Nishidate,K., Iizuka,H., Nakamura,A., El-Merzabani,M.M., Tamura,Z. and Miyazaki,T. (1984) *J. Chromatogr.,* **309**, 63.
37. Iriyama,K., Yoshiura,M., Iwamoto,T., Hosoya,T., Kono,H. and Miyahara,T. (1983) *J. Liquid Chromatogr.,* **6**, 2739.
38. Yamamoto,T., Shimizu,H., Kato,T. and Nagatsu,T. (1984) *Anal. Biochem.,* **142**, 395.
39. Tanaka,K., Yoshika,A., Tanaka,S. and Wataya,Y. (1984) *Anal. Biochem.,* **139**, 35.
40. Scott,N.R., Chakraborty,J. and Marks,V. (1984) *Ann. Clin. Biochem.,* **21**, 120.
41. Bouquet,S., Regnier,B., Quehen,S., Brisson,A.M., Courtois,Ph. and Fourtillan,J.B. (1985) *J. Liquid Chromatogr.,* **8**, 1663.
42. Burton,N.K., Aherne,G.W. and Marks,V. (1984) *J. Chromatogr.,* **309**, 409.
43. Wynants,J. and Van Belle,H. (1985) *Anal. Biochem.,* **144**, 258.
44. Stocchi,V., Cucchiari,L., Magnani,M., Chiarantini,L., Palma,P. and Crescentini,G. (1985) *Anal. Biochem.,* **146** 118.
45. Nissinen,E. (1980) *Anal. Biochem.,* **106**, 497.

CHAPTER 10

Porphyrins

ENRICO ROSSI and DAVID H.CURNOW

1. INTRODUCTION

Porphyrins consist of a nucleus of four pyrrole rings linked by four methylene bridges to form a cyclic tetrapyrrole in which the four pyrrole rings may be designated A, B, C and D (*Figure 1*). This planar structure allows eight side chains to be affixed at positions 1−8. The pattern of side chain substitution determines the physical and chemical properties of each individual porphyrin. *Table 1* shows the side chain substitution pattern for most of the porphyrins normally found in biological systems.

The source of porphyrins is the haem biosynthetic pathway, a pathway which plays a crucial role in all living systems. One of the intermediates of the pathway, uroporphyrinogen III, is the natural precursor for haem, chlorophyll and vitamin B_{12}. The porphyrin nucleus is incorporated in the key materials for respiration, electron transport and photosynthesis. The biological intermediates in the haem biosynthetic pathway are not porphyrins (with the sole exception of protoporphyrin) but porphyrinogens, in which all four methylene bridges are in the reduced form.

The first and rate-controlling step of the haem biosynthetic pathway is the condensation of succinate and glycine to form δ-aminolaevulinic acid (ALA). This reaction is catalysed by a mitochondrial enzyme, ALA synthase. The next four enzymes of the pathway are in the cytosol. The first of these, ALA dehydrase, catalyses the condensation of two molecules of ALA to form the monopyrrole porphobilinogen (PBG). The first tetrapyrrolic intermediate, uroporphyrinogen III, is derived from the condensation of four molecules of PBG in a two-stage reaction catalysed by two enzymes. Hydroxymethylbilane synthase catalyses the first step which is the conversion of prophobilinogen into the unstable intermediate hydroxymethylbilane. Uroporphyrinogen III synthase then catalyses the conversion of hydroxymethylbilane into uroporphyrinogen III.

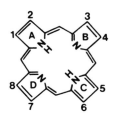

Figure 1. Porphyrin nucleus. *Table 1* shows the side chains at positions 1−8 for most of the porphryins normally found in biological systems.

Table 1. Structures of porphryins[a].

Porphyrins	Side-chain substitution pattern[b]							
	1	*2*	*3*	*4*	*5*	*6*	*7*	*8*
Uroporphyrin I	AcH	PrH	AcH	PrH	AcH	PrH	AcH	PrH
Uroporphyrin III	AcH	PrH	AcH	PrH	AcH	PrH	PrH	AcH
Heptacarboxylic porphyrin I	AcH	PrH	AcH	PrH	AcH	PrH	Me	PrH
Heptacarboxylic porphyrin III[c]	AcH	PrH	AcH	PrH	AcH	PrH	PrH	Me
Hexacarboxylic porphyrin I[c]	Me	PrH	AcH	PrH	AcH	PrH	Me	PrH
Hexacarboxylic porphyrin III[c]	Me	PrH	AcH	PrH	AcH	PrH	PrH	Me
Pentacarboxylic porphyrin I	Me	PrH	Me	PrH	AcH	PrH	Me	PrH
Pentacarboxylic porphyrin III[c]	Me	PrH	Me	PrH	AcH	PrH	PrH	Me
Coproporphyrin I	Me	PrH	Me	PrH	Me	PrH	Me	PrH
Coproporphyrin III	Me	PrH	Me	PrH	Me	PrH	PrH	Me
Deethylisocoproporphyrin	Me	H	Me	PrH	AcH	PrH	PrH	Me
Isocoproporphyrin	Me	Et	Me	PrH	AcH	PrH	PrH	Me
Mesoporphyrin	Me	Et	Me	Et	Me	PrH	PrH	Me
Protoporphyrin	Me	V	Me	V	Me	PrH	PrH	Me

[a]From ref. 1 with permission.
[b]Side-chain abbreviations: Me, methyl; Et, ethyl; V, vinyl; PrH, CH_2CH_2COOH; AcH, CH_2COOH.
[c]Only one isomeric form is shown.

A series of decarboxylation and oxidations then follow, resulting in the formation of protoporphyrin. Uroporphyrinogen decarboxylase catalyses the conversion of the octacarboxylic uroporphyrinogen III to the tetracarboxylic coproporphyrinogen III. All the remaining enzyme reactions take place inside the mitochondrion. The next step is the conversion of coproporphyrinogen III to protophyrinogen catalysed by copro-porphyrinogen oxidase. The next enzyme, protoporphyrinogen oxidase catalyses the oxidation of protoporphyrinogen to protoporphyrin. The final step in the pathway is catalysed by ferrochelatase which incorporates ferrous iron into protoporphyrin to form haem.

The h.p.l.c. separation of porphyrins includes a variety of applications ranging from pure organic chemistry to the determination of the enzymes of the haem biosynthetic pathway. We have not attempted to present all the applications of the recent advances in the h.p.l.c. of porphyrins and have concentrated on the importance of h.p.l.c. in the diagnosis and study of the porphyrias. Porphyrin analysis by h.p.l.c. has advanced significantly since the demonstration in 1977 of the value of porphyrin profiles in the diagnosis of porphyria, one of the important advances being the development of rapid h.p.l.c. methods for the separation of type I and type III porphyrin isomers.

This chapter describes practical applications of methods for the extraction of porphyrins from biological materials, particularly those applicable to the subsequent h.p.l.c. of porphyrins as free acids. Methods for the h.p.l.c. separation of porphyrins as methyl esters have been included because of the availability of extraction methods which yield methyl esters and the occasional necessity to revert to methyl ester preparation to remove interfering substances or to isolate individual porphyrins. Emphasis has been given to the h.p.l.c. systems for free acid porphyrins which provide simultaneous separation of type I and type III isomers because of the importance of potential applications. The availability of these rapid h.p.l.c. methods has led to development of the improved methods for the determination of the haem biosynthetic enzymes described in the final section.

2. EXTRACTION OF PORPHYRINS FROM BIOLOGICAL MATERIALS

2.1 Urine

The most widely used technique for concentrating urine prophyrins is adsorption onto talc. Most experience has accumulated from workers adsorbing the porphyrins onto talc prior to methyl esterification and although talc has been used for the analysis and isolation of urinary porphyrins since at least 1950, very few quantitative studies have been published.

With (2) found that 100 mg of talc adsorbed 200 μg of uroporphyrin or coproporphyrin with less than 1% remaining in the supernatant. These findings are as expected from the extensive use of long wavelength (400−410 nm) u.v. monitoring of supernatant solutions remaining from talc adsorption, where the addition of talc is sometimes continued as a batch-wise process until none of the characteristic red fluorescence of porphyrins remains.

Procedures utilizing talc generally contain the following steps.

(i)   A pH adjustment to the isoelectric point of porphyrins, where they have minimum solubility. The pH used is generally within the range 3−5, some workers preferring to adjust to pH 3−4 and others to pH 4−5.

(ii)   Adsorption onto talc. Some prefer to add stepwise batches of talc until red fluorescence of the supernatant under u.v. light ceases, while others use a preliminary screening test of the urine to assess the quantity of talc to be added.

(iii) An optional washing step, usually with distilled water. The talc may either be dried or left wet for the subsequent addition of a combined eluting−methyl esterification reagent.

(iv)   If free porphyrin acids are reqired, elution with acetone: 1 M HCl (9:1 v/v) may be used. The acetone can be removed by evaporation at 45°C under a stream of nitrogen, leaving the porphyrin free acids in the remaining acid solution.

2.1.1 *Talc adsorption for methyl ester preparation*

With the advent of reversed-phase (RP) h.p.l.c. systems for the separation of porphyrin free acids and the simultaneous separation of type I and type III isomers we no longer recommend preparation of methyl esters except in unusual cases where direct injection of urine shows spurious peaks which make identification or quantification of the porphyrins difficult.

Formation of methyl esters and elution of the talc-bound porphyrins are often combined in a single step by adding esterification reagent directly to the talc (3−5). However, With (2) has shown that elution with methanol−sulphuric acid (95:5 v/v) of known quantities of porphyrin adsorbed onto talc is only 85−95% complete. Even if elution is continued until the eluate becomes colourless under u.v. light some red fluorescence often remains on the talc. Irreversible binding appears to affect polycarboxylic porphyrins, especially uroporphyrin, so that significant differential losses can occur. For example, Wilson *et al.* (6) found poor recoveries of urinary porphyrins with talc

Table 2. Talc adsorption for preparation of porphyrin methyl esters.

1.	Adjust the pH of 50 ml of urine to 3.5 with glacial acetic acid. Add talc (~ 1 g) and mix thoroughly. Adsorption is complete in $2-3$ min. Remove the urine by centrifugation and careful suction.
2.	Transfer the talc to a centrifuge tube with de-ionized water. Wash the talc twice with 10 ml of de-ionized water. Remove the water by centrifugation and suction.
3.	Add 10 ml of methanol−sulphuric acid (95:5 v/v) and resuspend the talc. Allow to stand overnight in the dark at room temperature or for at least 12 h. Alternatively, if the talc is first dried at $40-60°C$, the esterification can be completed in 1 h at $37°C$.
4.	Add 3 ml of chloroform to the talc, mix thoroughly and centrifuge. Remove the supernatant to a separate tube.
5.	Elute remaining porphyrins off the talc with $1-3$ washings of 2 ml of chloroform, checking with a u.v. lamp for residual red fluorescence on the talc. Combine the chloroform washings with the original supernatant.
6.	Prepare a 50 ml separating funnel containing about 30 ml of de-ionized water and a dry test tube containing about 200 mg of potassium carbonate. Pour the chloroform mixture into the water in the separating funnel.
7.	Follow the method for isolation of porphyrin methyl esters shown in *Table 8*.

Table 3. Talc adsorption for preparation of porphyrin free acids.

1.	Adjust the pH of 50 ml of urine to 3.5 with glacial acetic acid. Add about 1 g of talc and mix thoroughly. Adsorption is complete in $2-3$ min.
2.	Collect the talc by filtration in a small (5 cm) Buchner funnel and wash with 2×10 ml of de-ionized water.
3.	Elute the porphyrin from the talc in the funnel with 2×5 ml of acetone−1 M HCl (9:1 v/v).
4.	Evaporate the acetone at $45°C$ under a stream of nitrogen. The remaining HCl contains the porphyrin free acids ready for analysis by the RP-h.p.l.c. system described in *Table 15*.

and Day and Eales (7) commented that talc and fluorosil were known to irreversibly adsorb a high proportion of uroporphyrin. Despite these shortcomings, talc is still used for concentrating urine porphyrins.

The use of adsorbents can be avoided if the h.p.l.c. detector is sensitive enough to detect the porphyrin methyl esters prepared by reacting urine directly with the methylating reagent as shown in *Table 8*. Our experience with fluorescence detection is that urines with total porphyrins as low as 50 nmol/l can be measured.

However, if u.v. detection is used, some form of concentrating the urinary porphyrins becomes necessary if the total urinary porphyrin is below about 500 nmol/l. In these cases, the porphyrins in $50-100$ ml of urine may be adsorbed onto about $0.5-1.0$ g of talc using the procedure in *Table 2*.

2.1.2 *Talc adsorption for free acid preparation*

The separation of porphyrin free acids has the advantage of avoiding the derivatization and extraction steps used for methyl ester preparation. If u.v. detection is used urines with total porphyrins of less than about 500 nmol/l can be talc adsorbed using the method in *Table 3*. Acetone−HCl achieves complete elution, without the need for u.v. monitoring. The final HCl is ready for h.p.l.c. analysis using the conditions described in *Table 15*.

2.2 **Faeces**

2.2.1 *Direct esterification*

The direct reaction of unprocessed faecal material with methylating agents to obtain porphyrin methyl esters was described for t.l.c. techniques (8). Several groups have applied similar extraction methods for separation by h.p.l.c. (3,5,9).

The h.p.l.c. separation of porphyrin esters prepared by this simple technique was a significant improvement on the traditional fractional HCl − ether extraction methods which gave contaminated fractions with up to 30% of the protoporphyrin in the coproto-porphyrin extract (10). However, we recommend an acid extraction method which offers further advantages.

2.2.2 *Acid extraction method*

A method for the extraction of porphyrin free acids from faeces giving a residue-free acid extract suitable for spectrophotometric quantitation of total porphyrin and for separation by h.p.l.c. has been developed (11). The extract is suitable for direct injection into the RP-h.p.l.c. system described in Section 4.6.

HCl is used to quantitatively extract the faecal porphyrins in the presence of ether. The porphyrins remain in the acid layer and interfering chlorophyll and carotenoid pigments are extracted and removed by the ether. The traditional solvent extraction methods for faecal porphyrins (10) extract only ether-soluble porphyrins, mainly dicarboxylic porphyrins and coproporphyrin. The acid extract obtained with the present method contains these ether-soluble porphyrins as well as the ether-insoluble porphyrins (heptacarboxylic porphyrin and uroporphyrin) seen in faeces from porphyria cutanea tarda patients. The total faecal porphyrin value can be calculated from an absorbance scan of the aqueous acid layer and many normal specimens can be excluded from further investigation. The method is shown in *Table 4*.

2.2.3 *Derivation of conversion factor*

The choice of factor for the conversion of the absorbance to concentration is a compromise, since any faecal sample contains several different porphyrins. Dicarboxylic porphyrins form the main fraction of normal excretion. These include metabolic protoporphyrin and a complex mixture of deuteroporphyrin, mesoporphyrin and other related porphyrins derived from haem by the action of gut flora. The haem is of dietary origin (e.g., red meat) and the normal blood loss into the gut of about 2−3 ml per day. The factors for converting the corrected absorbance to concentration in μM are 5.00 for protoporphyrin and 3.05 for coproporphyrin with mesoporphyrin and deuteroporphyrin only slightly higher than the coproporphyrin factor (11). A composite factor of 3.3 was based on the composition of normal faeces.

2.2.4 *Reference range*

A reference range was established by testing faecal specimens from 106 hospital outpatients (65 males and 41 females) who were on unrestricted diets. The distribution of the data was non-Gaussian and could not be easily transformed to a normal

Table 4. Extraction and quantitation of total faecal porphyrins[a].

Equipment

For the quantitation, a recording spectrophotometer capable of producing an absorbance scan in the visible region of the wavelengths between 390 and 425 nm is required.

Method

1. Weigh 25–50 mg of faeces into a graduated centrifuge tube for analysis and a larger sample (~250 mg) into a vessel suitable for drying. Dry the larger sample in a vacuum desiccator, hot air oven or freeze dryer.
2. Add 1 ml of concentrated HCl to the centrifuge tube and vortex mix until the particles disintegrate. Leave to stand for 5 min with occasional vortexing.
3. Add 3 ml of ether (peroxide-free) and thoroughly mix by vortex to give an emulsion. Now add 3 ml of water and mix again. To avoid undue alteration of protoporphyrin, add the water within 10 min of adding the acid to the faeces.
4. Centrifuge the mixture to give an ether layer, a pad of insoluble material at the interface and a layer of aqueous acid. Chlorophyll derivatives and carotenoid pigments partition into the ether phase and the faecal porphyrins remain in the lower aqueous acid layer.
5. Record the volume (v) of the aqueous acid layer (usually 4.5 ml) and using a Pasteur pipette remove sufficient for spectrophotometry to a 1 cm cuvette.
6. Scan the absorbance between 390 and 425 nm. The corrected absorbance (ΔA) required is obtained graphically. Draw a line on the absorbance scan joining the absorption at 390 nm to that at 425 nm. Draw the tangent to the curve of the scan parallel to this line. Measure the vertical height between the two lines to obtain the corrected absorbance. The graphical construction is illustrated in *Figure 2*.
7. Calculate the total faecal porphyrin as follows:

$$\Delta A \times 3.3 \times \frac{v}{t} \times \frac{ww}{dw} \text{ nM/g dry weight}$$

where ΔA is the corrected absorbance, 3.3 is the factor converting absorbance to concentration in μM, v is the volume (ml) of acid extract, t is the weight (g) of faeces taken for analysis, ww is the wet weight (g) of the larger sample, dw is the dry weight (g) of the larger sample.

8. Following scanning, conserve the aqueous acid extract for h.p.l.c. separation. The extract may be injected directly into the RP-h.p.l.c system described in Section 4.6.

[a]From ref. 11.

distribution. These results probably reflect the highly diet-dependent nature of faecal porphyrin excretion. A reference range of less than 200 nM/g dry weight was adopted (11).

2.2.5 *Preparation of methyl esters*

If it is desired to concentrate the porphyrins further before esterification, the free acids in the aqueous extract may be adsorbed onto talc in a similar fashion to urine samples (Section 2.1). Take the aqueous extract (~3 ml) and adjust the pH to between 3.8 and 4.0 with 50 g/100 ml of sodium acetate trihydrate. Now add talc (100–200 mg) and continue as described in *Table 2*. Alternatively the aqueous acid extract may be reacted directly with methanol–sulphuric acid (95:5 v/v) as described in *Table 8*.

2.2.6 *Comparison with direct esterification*

We made methyl ester preparations of eight normal faecal samples by direct esterification of bulk faecal material (9) and by esterification of the acid extract as described in *Table*

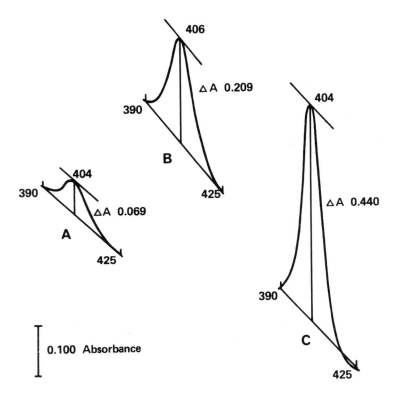

Figure 2. Spectrophotometric scans of absorbance against wavelength in three acid extracts **A**, **B** and **C**. The absorbance difference required is shown as ΔA. Each scan shows wavelengths in nm.

8. We found that the proportion of spurious non-protoporphyrin dicarboxylic porphyrins was reduced from a mean of 67% of the total peak area of the chromatogram in the direct esterification method to 22% using the present method. The reduction in spurious peaks makes the interpretation easier and the peak due to metabolic protoporphyrin is more readily identified.

2.3 Red blood cells

2.3.1 Direct methylation

The extraction and esterification of red blood cell (RBC) porphyrins by direct reaction with methanol−sulphuric acid has been described for quantitative t.l.c. (12). The final chloroform extract contains brown haemin esters derived from haemoglobin which remain near the origin for t.l.c. but are not satisfactory for h.p.l.c. because of their potential to bind strongly to the column. In addition this procedure does not determine zinc protoporphyrin due to the acid-catalysed removal of zinc.

The final product of most of the fluorescent methods in common use for the determination of total RBC porphyrin is a haemin-free HCl extract (13). The disadvantages for h.p.l.c. use are the loss of zinc from zinc protoporphyrin and the acid-catalysed conversion of protoporphyrin to haematoporphyrin.

2.3.2 *Extraction of RBC porphyrins*

An ideal extraction method for red cell porphyrins should have the following characteristics.

(i)   Quantitative extraction of protoporphyrin and of zinc protoporphyrin without loss of zinc.

(ii)   Production of an extract free of haemoglobin, which quenches fluorescence by absorbing light at the excitation maxima of both protoporphyrin (409 nm) and zinc protoporphyrin (417 nm).

(iii)   Production of an extract with low absorbance at the fluorescence excitation wavelength proposed (usually between 400 and 410 nm). If mixtures containing acetic acid are used, the main interfering pigment is haemin.

(iv)   Production of an extract which is protein free and suitable for h.p.l.c. injection.

A method fulfilling all these requirements may not yet be available. *Table 5* summarizes three pubished extraction methods.

The ethyl acetate−acetic acid method probably gives the best extraction of protoporphyrin from blood. Unfortunately the extract contains haemin which can cause rapid deterioration of RP-h.p.l.c. columns.

Red cell porphyrin methods are difficult to assess for complete extraction of zinc and free protoporphyrin because protoporphyrin presents problems in recovery experiments when added to blood. If it is dissolved in organic solvents (e.g. chloroform or ethanol) or in acid and then added to blood the added porphyrin is not present as part of the blood cells.

An alternative assessment of extraction methods of the type shown in *Table 5* is to re-extract the protein pellet using an established method for total RBC porphyrins (13). Hart and Piomelli (15) assessed their acetone−water method with this technique and found that the extraction was 87% complete. Because of the incomplete extraction the authors advise that their method is not suitable for the quantitation of RBC protoporphyrin but only for determining the ratio of zinc protoporphyrin and free protoporphyrin.

Table 5. RBC porphyrin extraction method.

Ethyl acetate−acetic acid extraction[a]
1.   Add 300 μl of ethyl acetate−acetic acid (3:1, v/v) containing internal standard mesoporphyrin to 100 μl whole blood.
2.   Vortex for 30 sec.
3.   Centrifuge and recover the supernatant.

Acetone−water extraction[b]
1.   Add 20 μl of whole blood to a 300 μl suspension of celite (5 g/l in isotonic saline with detergent).
2.   Add 5 ml of acetone−water (4:1, v/v).
3.   Vortex for 10 sec.
4.   Centrifuge and recover the supernatant.

Ethanol extraction[c]
1.   Add 50 μl of whole blood to 200 μl of water. Take 50 μl of this dilution.
2.   Add 1 ml of 95% ethanol.
3.   Vortex for 10 sec.
4.   Centrifuge and recover the supernatant.

---

[a]From ref. 14; [b]from ref. 15; [c]from ref. 16.

Table 6. Ethanol extraction of RBC porphyrins.

1.	Work in subdued light (red safety light is ideal) as protoporphyrin is very light sensitive. Pipette 50 μl of well-mixed anti-coagulated whole blood into a 10 ml centrifuge tube. Heparin or EDTA anti-coagulants are satisfactory.
2.	Add 150 μl of distilled water. This lyses cells and gives maximum recovery of protoporphyrin.
3.	While vortex mixing the tube, add 1 ml of absolute ethanol (AR grade).
4.	Centrifuge for 10 min at 2000 g to pack the protein precipitate.
5.	Recover the ethanol supernatant, ready for injection into the h.p.l.c. system described in *Table 17*.

Table 7. Extraction of plasma porphyrins.

1.	Work in subdued light, especially if plasma from an erythrohepatic protoporphyria patient is being tested. Pipette 0.5 ml of plasma into a 15 ml centrifuge tube.
2.	Add 5 ml of ether−acetic acid (4:1 v/v) with vigorous vortex mixing during the addition and for a further 30 sec.
3.	Centrifuge for 10 min at 2000 g to pack the protein precipitate and pour the supernatant into a test tube.
4.	Add 3 ml of 2.7 M HCl and vortex mix for 30 sec.
5.	Remove the lower acid layer using a Pasteur pipette.
6.	If the h.p.l.c. detection is by fluorescence and the total plasma porphyrin is over 40 nmol/l the acid extract may be injected directly into the h.p.l.c. system described in Section 4.
7.	If the plasma porphyrin is below about 40 nmol/l, concentrate the porphyrins by using talc adsorption. Take the aqueous extract (~ 4 ml) and adjust the pH to between 3.8 and 4.0 with sodium acetate trihydrate (50 g/100 ml). Add talc (100−200 mg) and continue as described in *Table 3*.

We have used an ethanol extraction method with preliminary lysis of whole blood in water and have placed the same restriction on its use. The method is shown in *Table 6*. The ethanol extract is injected into the h.p.l.c. system described in *Table 17* to determine the ratio of zinc protoporphyrin to free protoporphyrin. To quantitate absolute amounts the h.p.l.c. results are combined with a quantitative method for total RBC protoporphyrin (13).

2.4 **Plasma**

2.4.1 *Extraction methods*

Although the extraction and methylation of plasma porphyrins by direct reaction with methanol−sulphuric acid has been reported (12) some workers have extracted plasma porphyrins with acidified organic solvents. For example, Poh-Fitzpatrick *et al.* (17) quantitated plasma porphyrins by diluting plasma in saline containing diatomaceous earth and extracting with ethyl acetate−acetic acid (4:1 v/v). The porphyrins in the ethyl acetate−acetic acid were then extracted into 1.5 M HCl for fluorimetric quantitation. These authors assessed their extraction method by re-extracting the protein pellet and found that 90% of the total porphyrins in porphyria cutanea tarda or erythrohepatic protoporphyria plasma had been recovered. The porphyrins found in variegate porphyria plasma have proven difficult to completely extract and have not yet been fully identified.

We have used a similar extraction method, shown in *Table 7*, based on the total RBC porphyrin method used in our laboratory (13).

2.4.2 *Extraction efficiency*

The porphyrin content of the HCl extract may be quantitated by fluorescence using a uroporphyrin standard (13). We assessed our extraction method by quantitating the plasma porphyrin fluorimetrically and then re-extracting the protein pellet with a further application of the method and reading of the fluorescence. By using plasma from a dialysed renal failure patient who had clinical and biochemical porphyria cutanea tarda and diluting with a normal plasma we were able to cover the range from 2 to 830 nmol/l (reference range $0-10$ nmol/l). The method extracted $87-90\%$ of the total plasma porphyrin over the entire range of concentrations up to 830 nmol/l. These figures were obtained using a plasma which was 68% uroporphyrin and 32% heptacarboxylic porphyrin. The method was developed for the extraction of protoporphyrin from red cells and works equally well for plasma samples containing protoporphyrin.

2.5 **Other biological materials**

Free acid porphyrins can usually be extracted by applying the principles described for urine, faeces, red cells or plasma. Liquid samples can be adjusted to pH 3.5 and the porphyrin free acids adsorbed onto talc and eluted as described in *Table 3*.

Solid or semi-solid materials can be extracted with HCl as described for faeces in *Table 4*. For example, concentrated gall bladder bile was extracted using this method and the acid extract injected into the h.p.l.c. system described in *Table 16*. If the porphyrins in the resulting acid extract need to be concentrated for h.p.l.c. detection, the pH can be adjusted and the porphyrins adsorbed onto talc as described in *Table 7*.

3. SEPARATION OF PORPHYRINS AS ESTERS

3.1 **Preparation of porphyrin methyl esters**

The usual procedure for preparing porphyrin methyl esters from biological materials (urine, faeces, red cells, bile, plasma) is to esterify the whole mixture. Unlike the free carboxylic acids, the porphyrin methyl esters differ only slightly in their solubility. Thus all the porphyrins with two to eight methyl ester groups can easily be extracted quantitatively from a methanol−sulphuric acid−water mixture by chloroform or dichloromethane.

The most widely used esterification reagent is methanol−sulphuric acid (95:5 v/v). Although the reagent has been used (6) with more sulphuric acid (methanol:sulphuric acid, 90:10 v/v), this is not recommended for protoporphyrin as some oxidation of the vinyl groups can occur. Borontrifluoride in methanol has also been used (3). The procedure for isolation of porphyrin methyl esters using methanol−sulphuric acid is described in *Table 8*.

3.2 **H.p.l.c. conditions for methyl esters**

The well-known behaviour of methyl esters in t.l.c. systems led to the development of similar h.p.l.c. systems.

Methyl esters were separated by normal-phase adsorption chromatography using a polar column (5 or 10 μm silica) and organic solvents (e.g. methylacetate−heptane) for elution. Isocratic elution was found to give good separation of the porphyrin esters

Table 8. Isolation of porphyrin methyl esters.

Urines are reacted directly with methanol−sulphuric acid. HCl extracts are made of faecal or plasma samples according to the methods described in *Tables 4* and *7*.

Method

1. Mix 1 ml of urine or 1 ml of aqueous acid extract with 9 ml of methanol−sulphuric acid (95:5 v/v) and leave to stand overnight in the dark at room temperature.
2. Prepare a 50 ml separating funnel containing about 30 ml of de-ionized water and a dry test tube containing 200 mg of potassium carbonate. Add 3 ml of chloroform to the incubated samples and mix. Pour this mixture into the water in the separating funnel.
3. Allow the chloroform to settle at the base of the funnel and then run it onto the potassium carbonate. Vortex mix thoroughly to remove traces of sulphuric acid which can cause de-esterification.
4. Prepare a second 50 ml separating funnel containing 10−15 ml of de-ionized water. Decant the chloroform off the potassium carbonate into the funnel. Wash the chloroform by gently shaking for 2−3 min. Release any pressure build up via the stopper, so that the stem of the funnel remains dry. Allow to stand at least 10 min for good phase separation.
5. Run the chloroform into a clean dry graduated glass tube. Using a 80−100°C hot bath (preferably oil or glycol rather than water) carefully evaporate the chloroform to dryness. Water is removed as a chloroforom−water azeotrope boiling at 56°C (pure chloroform boils at 61°C).
6. Dissolve the methyl esters in chloroform (0.5 ml or less) ready for h.p.l.c. injection.

Table 9. Isocratic h.p.l.c. conditions for porphyrin methyl esters.

Column:	Silica, 5 or 10 μm, 25 cm × 4.6 mm.
Elution solvent:	n-Heptane−methyl acetate (3:2 v/v).
Flow-rate:	1.5 ml/min.
Detection:	U.v. absorption at 400 nm or fluorescence with activation wavelength 400 nm and emission wavelength 620 nm.

with the retention times increasing as the number of ester side chains increased but with some broadening of the latter peaks, notably uroporphyrin. Detection was by u.v. absorption at 404 nm. This system was used to obtain diagnostically distinctive faecal and urinary porphyrin profiles for each of the porphyrias (9). H.p.l.c. units which cannot perform gradient elution can successfully use this single solvent (isocractic) system which is described in *Table 9*.

This system was modified and used with success in the authors' laboratory. The availability of a h.p.l.c. system with two pumps allowed the development of a gradient elution system which gave complete resolution of porphyrins containing two to eight methyl ester groups within 15 min. The use of fluorescence detection rather than u.v. adsorption allowed the detection and quantitation of normal urine and faecal porphyrins without preliminary talc adsorption. The h.p.l.c. conditions for gradient elution are described in *Table 10*.

3.3 Preparation of standards

We have prepared quantitative standard mixtures for calibrating the h.p.l.c. conditions described in *Table 10*. The methyl esters of protoporphyrin IX, coproporphyrin I and uroporphyrin I were separately dissolved in chloroform and their concentrations measured. The following published extinction coefficients (1 g/100 ml solutions in chloroform for a 1 cm pathlength) were used: protoporphyrin ester, 2.89×10^3 at 407.5 nm, coproporphyrin ester, 2.53×10^3 at 399.5 nm and uroporphyrin ester,

Table 10. Gradient h.p.l.c. conditions for porphyrin methyl esters.

Column:	Silica, 5 or 10 μm, 25 cm $\times$ 4.6 mm.
Elution solvents:	n-Heptane and ethyl acetate.
Flow-rate:	1.5 ml/min.
Gradient:	1. Equilibrate the column with 35:65 (v/v) ethyl acetate−heptane and inject the sample.
	2. Run a 6 min linear gradient up to 45:55 (v/v) ethyl acetate−heptane.
	3. From 6 to 12 min run a further linear gradient up to 85:15 (v/v) ethyl acetate−heptane.
	4. Run 85:15 (v/v) ethyl acetate−heptane to the end of the run at 18 min.
Detection:	U.v. absorption at 400 nm or fluorescence with activation wavelength 400 nm and emission wavelength 620 nm.
Equipment:	These conditions were developed on a dual pump 1084B h.p.l.c. (Hewlett-Packard) equipped with electronic peak area integration and a FS970 fluorescence detector (Schoeffel Instruments). The detector was operated with a deuterium lamp output and excitation wavelength 400 nm with a 580 nm cut-off filter for the emission.

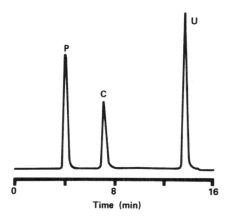

Figure 3. H.p.l.c. of a standard mixture of porphyrin methyl esters. H.p.l.c. conditions as in *Table 10*. P, protoporphyrin, 215 nmol/l; C, coproporphyrin, 170 nmol/l; U, uroporphyrin, 235 nmol/l.

2.30×10^3 at 405.5 nm.

Standard solutions were prepared by mixing known volumes of the three solutions, covering a range of concentration up to 400 nmol/l. The standards were separated using the h.p.l.c. conditions described in *Table 10* and the areas under the fluorescence peaks calculated by electronic integration. Standard curves were obtained by plotting peak areas against molar concentrations. The h.p.l.c. separation for a typical standard is shown in *Figure 3*.

3.4 Specimen requirements

Our procedure for the investigation of patients referred for the evaluation of porphyrin metabolism is to obtain random collections of unpreserved urine and faeces, and a heparinized whole blood sample. Random urine samples are convenient for out-patients and can be obtained without delay, important for PBG estimation. As the concentration of random samples varies widely, correction for concentration is essential for the interpretation of the porphyrin result. We correct by measuring urinary creatinine (mM),

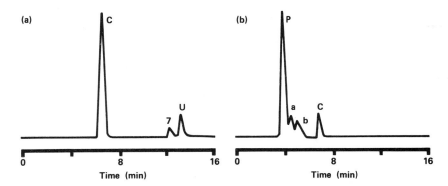

Figure 4. Normal subject. H.p.l.c. conditions as in *Table 10*. (**a**) H.p.l.c. of urine porphyrin methyl esters. Total urine porphyrins: 150 nmol/l (reference range <300 nmol/l) or 9 nM/mM creatinine (reference range <25 nM/mM). C, coproporphyrin; 7, heptacarboxylic porphyrin; U, uroporphyrin. (**b**) H.p.l.c. of faecal porphyrin methyl esters. Total faecal porphyrins: 50 nM/g dry weight (reference range <200 nM/g). P, protoporphyrin; a,b, unidentified dicarboxylic porphyrins; C, coproporphyrin.

using a reference range of less than 25 nM of total porphyrin per mM of creatinine.

Total urine porphyrins are measured by direct spectrofluorimetry of a 50-fold dilution of urine in 0.28 M HCl (18). Urine PBG is measured by anion-exchange chromatography as described by Mauzerall and Granick (19). Total faecal porphyrins are measured by extracting the faecal porphyrins with HCl followed by spectrophotometric scanning (11) as shown in *Table 4*. Total RBC porphyrins are measured by a spectrofluorimetric method (13).

3.5 Methyl ester porphyrin profiles

3.5.1 *Normal subject*

The results of total urine and faecal porphyrin estimations and h.p.l.c. profiles for a normal subject are shown in *Figure 4a* and *b*, respectively. The faecal porphyrin h.p.l.c. trace illustrates the presence of non-protoporphyrin dicarboxylic porphyrins. These are a complex mixture of deuteroporphyrin, mesoporphyrin and related porphyrins derived from bacterial action of the gut flora on haem and protoporphyrin. The haem is of dietary origin or from the normal 2−3 ml per day blood loss into the gut.

3.5.2 *Porphyrias*

(i) *Acute intermittent porphyria (AIP)*. This is one of the three acute porphyrias which are characterized by episodic acute attacks. Biochemically these are characterized by the excretion of excess porphyrin precursors of ALA and PBG in the urine. The urine porphyrins seen in an acute attack (*Figure 5*) are mostly derived from PBG by non-enzymic condensation. The urine porphyrins and occasionally the PBG can be normal during remission. The total faecal porphyrin is almost always normal and h.p.l.c. separation does not give a diagnostically significant profile.

(ii) *Variegate porphyria (VP)*. This is one of the acute porphyrias in which the urine porphyrins and the h.p.l.c. profile are often normal during periods of remission. Acute attacks may occur only rarely during the patient's lifetime. The urine h.p.l.c. profile

273

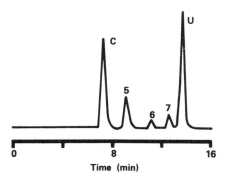

Figure 5. Acute intermittent porphyria, patient in acute attack. H.p.l.c. of urine porphyrin methyl esters. H.p.l.c. conditions as in *Table 10*. Urine PBG: 9.5 μM/mM creatinine (reference range <0.7 μM/mM). Total porphyrins: 12 100 nmol/l or 795 nM/mM creatinine. C, coproporphyrin; 5, pentacarboxylic porphyrin; 6, hexacarboxylic porphyrin; 7, heptacarboxylic porphyrin; U, uroporphyrin.

is not diagnostic and the faeces should always be tested as about 33% of patients with VP are observed with skin symptoms only and not acute attacks. The total feacal porphyrin is invariably elevated, with the protoporphyrin always more than coproporphyrin, both in attack and remission stages and the h.p.l.c. profile allows clear differentiation of VP from porphyria cutanea tarda (PCT), in which the skin symptoms are identical.

(iii) *Hereditary coproporphyria (HCP).* In HCP the urine porphyrins and h.p.l.c. profile are usually normal during periods of remission. As with VP, acute attacks may occur only rarely during the patient's lifetime. During an acute attack urine PBG and porphyrins are elevated and the urine h.p.l.c. profile shows predominantly coproporphyrin., The faecal porphyrins are elevated in both attack and remission and the porphyrin profile shows that faecal coproporphyrin always exceeds faecal protoporphyrin.

(iv) *Erythrohepatic protoporphyria (EHP).* This condition presents with skin symptoms due to photosensitivity. The total urine porphyrin and h.p.l.c. profile are normal, except in the rare patient with severe liver damage. The faecal porphyrins are frequently only marginally elevated and the h.p.l.c. trace is not diagnostic as similar traces are found in normal subjects on a diet with a high meat content. However, the presence of protoporphyrin in the plasma usually confirms EHP, although some cases of sideroblastic anaemia have been reported with the biochemical features of EHP.

(v) *Porphyria cutanea tarda (PCT).* This condition presents with skin symptoms. The urine and plasma porphyrins are both elevatd. The h.p.l.c. profiles for urine and plasma from the same patient are shown in *Figure 6a* and *b*. The urine h.p.l.c. profile is typical but not diagnostic for PCT. In our experience the plasma h.p.l.c. profile typically shows hexa- and heptacarboxylic porphyrins as well as uroporphyrin. However we always confirm PCT by obtaining the diagnostic faecal h.p.l.c. profile (*Figure 6c*) showing heptacarboxylic porphyrin and isocoproporphyrin.

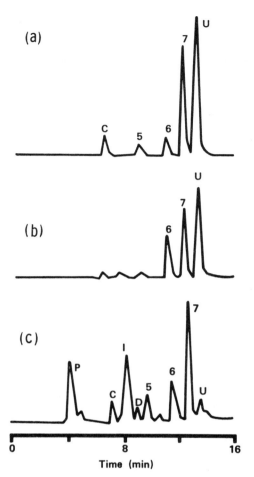

Figure 6. Porphyria cutanea tarda. H.p.l.c. conditions as in *Table 10*. (a) H.p.l.c. of urine porphyrin methyl esters. Urine total porphyrins: 6520 nmol/l or 460 nM/mM creatinine. (b) H.p.l.c. of plasma porphyrin methyl esters. Plasma total porphyrins: 225 nmol/l (reference range < 10 nmol/l). (c) H.p.l.c. of faecal porphyrin methyl esters. Faecal total porphyrins: 1870 nM/g dry weight. P, protoporphyrin; C, coproporphyrin; I, isocoproporphyrin; D, deethylisocoproporphyrin; 5, pentacarboxylic porphyrin; 6, hexacarboxylic porphyrin; 7, heptacarboxylic porphyrin; U, uroporphyrin.

3.6 **Disadvantages of methyl ester h.p.l.c.**

3.6.1 *Mixed esters*

The presence of ethanol in solvents used during the standard preparation of porphyrin methyl esters can be sufficient for the synthesis of significant amounts of mixed methyl−ethyl esters (20). The addition of ethanol as a stabilizer to chloroform is probably the most widespread source. The mixed ester appears as an unidentified peak on h.p.l.c. and can lead to errors in identification or quantitation. The problem can be overcome by either substituting dichloromethane for chloroform or by removing the ethanol from the chloroform prior to use.

3.6.2 *Partial esters*

If esterification is incomplete, partial esters can be recovered in the chloroform fraction and injected into the h.p.l.c. Polycarboxylic porphyrins such as uroporphyrin are particularly prone to the formation of partial esters. With t.l.c. partial esters remain near the point of application and can be identified and re-esterified if necessary. However with h.p.l.c. they remain bound to the column and remain undetected. This problem is overcome by adopting RP-h.p.l.c. of free acids as described in Section 4.

3.6.3 *Metal chelates*

The formation of metal chelates can occur during the isolation of the methyl esters. If copper chelates are formed double peaks appear on the h.p.l.c. trace with u.v. detection (21). The copper chelates are missed if fluorescence detection is used as they do not show the usual fluorescence emission in the visible red wavelengths. Some workers have deliberately converted the methyl esters to copper chelates and used u.v. detection (21).

3.6.4 *Unextracted porphyrins*

In the preparation of methyl esters, only those porphyrins which form chloroform-soluble methyl esters will be extracted. Unesterified porphyrins, sub-uroporphyrin fractions (those running below uroporphyrin on t.l.c.) and the porphyrin − peptide conjugates seen in VP are not extracted into chloroform and will therefore be missed. The use of RP-h.p.l.c. of free acid porphyrins will help the further study of these porphyrins, some of which are unidentified.

4. SEPARATION OF PORPHYRINS AS FREE ACIDS

4.1 **Reversed-phase ion-pair chromatography**

Porphyrin free acids can be separated on RP-h.p.l.c. columns, usually octadecylsilyl (ODS)-bonded silica with ion-pairing reagents, ionic substances which retain some solubility in non-polar organic solvents. For example, tetrabutylammonium phosphate forms neutral ion-pairs with the porphyrin carboxylic acid side chains, thus solubilizing the free acids in the mobile phase and providing a rapid equilibrium with the non-polar support phase.

The more polar porphyrin, uroporphyrin is eluted first, followed by the hepta-, hexa-, penta-carboxylic acid porphyrins and coproporphyrin. For the dicarboxylic porphyrins which follow, the elution order is deuteroporphyrin, mesoporphyrin and protoporphyrin last. Methods have been described for the analysis of free acid porphyrins from urine and faeces (22,23). One of the limitations of ion-pairing reagents is that separation of type I and type III isomers usually only occurs for coproporphyrin. A further limitation is that some investigations (22) have reported the necessity of lengthy re-equilibration of the column with the initial solvent conditions between analyses. Aqueous buffer − organic modifier systems have been developed as alternatives to ion-pairing systems.

4.2 **Buffered reversed-phase systems**

Several groups have reported the use of mixtures of aqueous buffer and organic modifier for RP-h.p.l.c. of free acid porphyrins on ODS columns (24,25). For example, Schreiber *et al.* (24) used a pH 3.0 phosphate buffer − methanol mixture to separate the porphyrins found in urine. This system is limited by the necessity of lengthy re-equilibration with the starting solvent between analyses and a time-consuming specimen preparation procedure to remove interfering substances from urine. These systems also do not achieve separation of type I and type III isomers, with the possible exception of coproporphyrin.

The ammonium − acetate buffer systems described in the following sections do not require long re-equilibration and give separation of all of the type I and type III porphyrin isomers.

4.3 **Ammonium acetate buffer systems**

4.3.1 *Introduction*

The application of ammonium acetate buffer − organic modifier systems to the RP separation of free acid porphyrins has been systematically examined by Lim and co-workers (26 − 28). The effects of buffer concentration, pH and proportion of organic modifier on the resolution have been established for most of the important porphyrins. In particular, the use of ammonium acetate has allowed the separation of all the diagnostically important type I and type III isomers in a single run using a linear gradient of ammonium acetate buffer in organic modifier (28). The application of isocratic ammonium acetate systems to the isomer separation of individual groups of porphyrins (26,27) will be described, followed by a description of gradient systems developed for the separation of porphyrin mixtures (28).

4.3.2 *Advantages of ammonium acetate*

Ammonium acetate has many properties which make it particularly attractive as a buffer for porphyrin separations (1).

(i)   It is fully ionized and a good buffering agent at the pH necessary for porphyrin separation.

(ii)   It is highly soluble in aqueous methanol and acetonitrile, allowing high molar concentrations to be used and thus acid extracts can be injected without damaging the RP columns.

(iii)   It accelerates rates of proton equilibrium, important for the chromatography of porphyrins.

(iv)   It is a good masking agent for residual silanol groups on RP columns.

(v)   It allows the prediction of the retention behaviour of unknown porphyrins from the relative hydrophobicity of the side chain substituents.

(vi)   It is relatively volatile and easily removed if subsequent mass spectrometry is desired.

4.3.3 *Retention behaviour*

Lim's group has established that the main retention mechanism is hydrophobic interaction between the porphyrin side-chain substitutents and the non-polar hydrocarbon chains on the surface of the stationary phase (26). The most hydrophobic side-chain substituent studied was the ethyl group and the least hydrophobic was the acetic acid group. The order of decreasing hydrophobicity is ethyl, methyl, hydrogen, propionic acid and acetic acid. The retention increases with increasing numbers of alkyl side-chain substituents, and the following order of elution is observed: uroporphyrin, hepta-, hexa-, pentacarboxylic porphyrin, coproporphyrin and isocoproporphyrin.

The application of individual isocratic systems to separate the isomers of uroporphyrin, pentacarboxylic porphyrin, coproporphyrin (26) and dicarboxylic porphyrins (27) will be considered in the following sections.

4.3.4 *Uroporphyrin isomers*

The structures of uroporphyrin I and III are shown in *Table 1*. Since neither compound has an alkyl side-chain substituent the relative retention is determined by the propionic acid group which is more hydrophobic than the acetic acid group. Uroporphyrin III has two adjacent propionic acid groups which gives a stronger hydrophobic interaction with the column than uroporphyrin I which has no adjacent proprionic acid groups. Uroporphyrin III should therefore be retained longer and this is observed in the h.p.l.c.

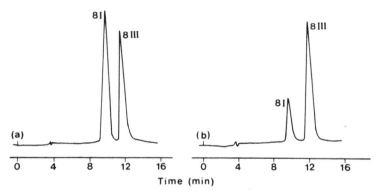

Figure 7. Separation of uroporphyrin I and III isomers. H.p.l.c. conditions as in *Table 11*. From ref. 26 with permission.

Table 11. Isocratic h.p.l.c. conditions for isomers of uroporphyrin and decarboxylation products[a].

Column:	Spherisorb-ODS, 10 cm × 5 mm (Phase Separations), Hypersil-ODS, 25 cm × 5 mm (Shandon Southern)
Mobile phases:	The proportion of acetonitrile in the 1 M ammonium acetate buffer pH 5.16 is given for each group of porphyrins.
	Uroporphyrin : 13:87 (v/v)
	Heptacarboxylic porphyrin : 15:85 (v/v)
	Hexacarboxlic prophyrin : 16:84 (v/v)
	Pentacarboxylic prophyrin : 20:80 (v/v)
	Coproporphyrins : 31:69 (v/v)
Flow-rate:	1 ml/min
Detector:	LS-3 fluorescence detector (Perkin-Elmer). Excitation wavelength 404 nm, emission wavelength 618 nm.
H.p.l.c.:	Model PU 4010 (Pye-Unicam).

[a]From ref. 26.

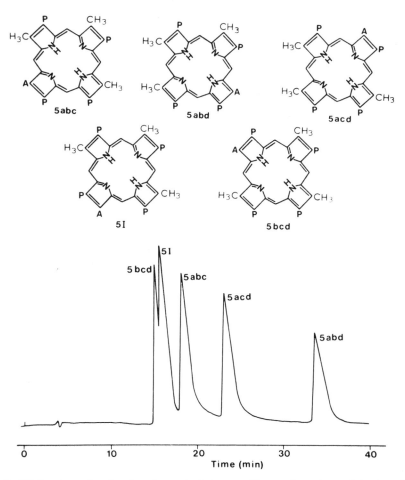

Figure 8. (A) Structures of pentacarboxylic porphyrin isomers. The notation a, b, c and d refer to the four pyrrole rings with ring a on the top left. 5abc refers to the pentacarboxylic porphyrin with methyl groups on rings a, b and c. 5I is the structure of the only possible series I isomer. (b) Separation of pentacarboxylic porphyrin isomers in a standard mixture. H.p.l.c. conditions as in *Table 11*. From ref. 26 with permission.

traces (26) of a standard mixture (*Figure 7*). The isocratic h.p.l.c. conditions developed by Lim *et al.* (26) for the separation of uroporphyrin isomers (and of the decarboxylation products) are shown in *Table 11*.

4.3.5 *Pentacarboxylic porphyrin isomers*

The type I and III pentacarboxylic porphyrins prepared by decarboxylation of uroporphyrin I and III respectively, have been studied by Lim *et al.* (26).

Decarboxylation yields all the four possible type III and one type I pentacarboxylic porphyrin shown in *Figure 8a*. The notation a, b, c and d refers to the rings in which the acetic acid residue has been decarboxylated to methyl, thus 5abc refers to the methyl groups present in rings a, b and c, with ring a on the top left hand side. The relative retention of the pentacarboxylic porphyrins is dominated by the three methyl groups,

279

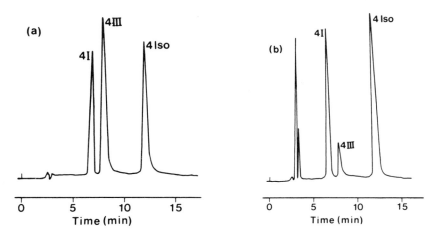

Figure 9. Separation of coproporphyrin isomers. (**a**) Standard mixture, (**b**) from the faeces of a porphyria cutanea tarda patient. H.p.l.c. conditions as in *Table 11*. From ref. 26 with permission.

and the elution order can be predicted by counting the number of bonds between the methyl groups. Of the possible ways of counting the bonds the shorter distance is used. The closer the methyl groups, the stronger the hydrophobic interaction possible with the ODS groups on the column and the longer is the retention time. Of the four type III isomers shown in *Figure 8a*, 5abd has the closest methyl groups (longest retention) followed by 5acd, 5abc and 5bcd. The h.p.l.c. trace shown in *Figure 8b* shows that the elution order is as predicted.

4.3.6 *Coproporphyrin*

The three most important porphyrins with four carboxylic acid residues (*Table 1*) have been separated by isocratic RP-h.p.l.c. (26). The presence of an ethyl group in isocoproporphyrin, especially close to the methyl groups, results in the strongest interaction with the ODS groups on the column and the longest retention time. The adjacent methyl groups of coproporphyrin III gives it a longer retention time than the type I isomer. The separation of these compounds is shown in *Figure 9*.

4.3.7. *Dicarboxylic porphyrins*

The retention behaviour of the main dicarboxylic porphyrins, haematoporphyrin, deuteroporphyrin, mesoporphyrin and protoporphyrin, together with metalloporphyrin derivatives of mesoporphyrin and protoporphyrin have been systematically studied by Lim *et al.* (27). The best selectivity, efficiency and resolution was given by an ammonium acetate−methanol buffer system with a RP column. The structures of the main dicarboxylic porphyrins are shown in *Figure 10a*. Protoporphyrin, with two strongly hydrophobic vinyl groups is the last to be eluted and haematoporphyrin, with two relatively hydrophilic hydroxyethyl groups is the first to elute, as shown in *Figure 10b*. The isocratic h.p.l.c. conditions developed for this separation (27) are shown in *Table 12*.

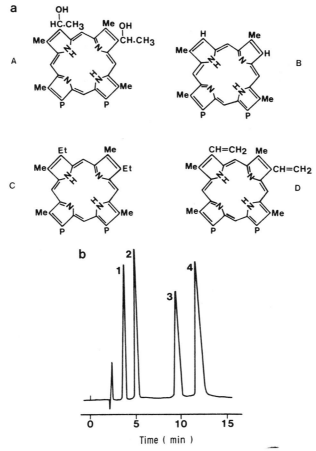

Figure 10. (a) Structures of dicarboxylic porphyrins. **(A)** Haematoporphyrin, **(B)** deuteroporphyrin, **(C)** mesoporphyrin and **(D)** protoporphyrin. P = CH$_2$CH$_2$COOH, Me = CH$_3$, ET = CH$_2$CH$_3$. **(b)** Separation of dicarboxylic porphyrins. H.p.l.c. conditions as in *Table 12*. Peaks; **1** = haematoporphyrin, **2** = deuteroporphyrin, **3** = mesoporphyrin, **4** = protoporphyrin. From ref. 27 with permission.

Table 12. Isocratic h.p.l.c. conditions for dicarboxylic porphyrins[a].

Column:	SAS-Hypersil, 15 cm × 5 mm
Mobile phase:	70:30 (v/v) methanol−1 M ammonium acetate buffer, pH 5.16.
Flow-rate:	1 ml/min
Detector:	U.v.-100 detector, 404 nm (Varian Associates)
H.p.l.c.:	Model 5000 (Varian Associates)

[a]From ref. 27.

4.4. Ammonium acetate gradient systems

4.4.1 Complete porphyrin profile

A RP system giving a complete porphyrin profile, including the simultaneous separation of type I and type III isomers, has been developed by Lim (28). Free acid porphyrins with from eight to two carboxylic acid groups were eluted from a RP column with

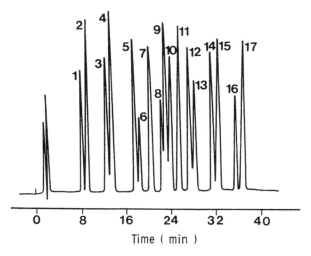

Figure 11. Separation of porphyrins and porphyrin isomers. H.p.l.c. conditions peak identification are given in *Table 13*.

Table 13. H.p.l.c. conditions and peak identification for complete porphyrin profile[a].

Column:	SAS-Hypersil, 15 cm x 5 mm.
Elution solvents:	Solvent A: 10:90 (v/v) acetonitrile − 1 M ammonium acetate buffer, pH 5.16.
	Solvent B: 10:90 (v/v) acetonitrile − methanol.
Flow-rate:	1.0 ml/min
Gradient:	1. Equilibrate the column with 100% solvent A (0% B) and inject the sample.
	2. Run a linear gradient from 0% B to 65% B.
	3. Run 65% B for a further 10 min to the end of the run at 40 min.
Detector:	U.v.-50 detector, 404 nm (Varian Associates).
H.p.l.c.:	Model 5000 (Varian Associates)
Peaks:	1, uroporphyrin I; 2, uroporphyrin III; 3, heptacarboxylic porphyrin I; 4, heptacarboxylic porphyrin III; 5, 6, hexacarboxylic porphyrins I and III; 7, hexacarboxylic porphyrin III (rings A and D decarboxylated); 8, pentacarboxylic porphyrin III (rings B, C and D decarboxylated); 9, pentacarboxylic porphyrin III (rings A, B and C decarboxylated) and pentacarboxylic porphyrin I; 10, pentacarboxylic porphyrin III (rings A, C and D decarboxylated); 11, pentacarboxylic porphyrin III (rings A, B and D decarboxylated); 12, coproporphyrin I; 13, coproporphyrin III; 14, deethylisocoproporphyrin; 15, isocoproporphyrin; 16, mesoporphyrin; 17, protoporphyrin.

[a]From ref. 28.

a gradient of acetonitrile − methanol in acetonitrile − ammonium acetate buffer. The separation of a standard mixture of these 17 porphyrins takes place in less than 40 min, as shown in *Figure 11*. The h.p.l.c. conditions and the peak indentification are shown in *Table 13*.

4.5 Urine porphyrin separation

4.5.1 *H.p.l.c. conditions*

The h.p.l.c. conditions used in the authors' laboratory for the separation of urine porphyrins are shown in *Table 14*. Good separations of type I and III uroporphyrin and coproporphyrin are obtained and with fluorescence detection urines with normal porphyrins can be injected directly.

Table 14. H.p.l.c. conditions for urines.

Column:	ODS-Hypersil, 25 cm x 5 mm.
Elution solvents:	Solvent A: 10:90 (v/v) acetonitrile − 1 M ammonium acetate buffer, pH 5.16.
	Solvent B: 10:90 (v/v) acetonitrile − methanol.
Flow-rate:	1.5 ml/min
Gradient:	1. Equilibrate the column with 100% solvent A (0% B) and inject the sample.
	2. Run a linear gradient from 0% B to 70% B in 25 min.
	3. Run 70% B for a further 3 min to the end of the run at 28 min.
	4. If a standard mixture containing a dicarboxylic porphyrin (e.g. mesoporphyrin) is injected, run 100% B until it elutes (~32 min on our system).
Detector:	FS-970 fluorescence detector (Schoeffel).
	Excitation wavelength 395 nm, 580 nm cut-off filter for the emission.
H.p.l.c.:	Model 1084B dual pump with electronic peak area integration (Hewlett-Packard).

4.5.2 *Standard type I porphyrins*

A mixture of type I uroporphyrin, heptacarboxylic porphyrin, hexacarboxylic porphyrin, pentacarboxylic porphyrin, coproporphyrin and mesoporphyrin (10 nM of each porphyrin per vial) was obtained from Porphyrin Products. Each vial was reconstituted with 0.27 M HCl to give a final concentration of 200 nmol/l of each porphyrin. The h.p.l.c. trace obtained by injecting 50 μl of this mixed standard is shown in *Figure 12a*. Mesoporphyrin is not shown as it requires over 30 min for elution. Using the h.p.l.c. conditions shown in *Table 14* we found that coproporphyrin gave maximal fluorescence emission with excitation at 392 nm (25) and uroporphyrin at 397 nm. An excitation wavelength of 395 nm was used because it gave equal fluorescence emission peak areas for equimolar quantitites of coproporphyrin and uroporphyrin. An excitation wavelength of 404 nm gave significantly reduced fluorescence for both coproporphyrin and uroporphyrin.

4.5.3 *Standard type I and III porphyrins*

A further standard mixture was used to assess the separation of type I and type III uroporphyrin as this separation requires accurate pH adjustment of the ammonium acetate buffer. We found separation was best when the buffer was adjusted to pH 5.16 in the presence of acetonitrile, as described in *Table 13*. The ability of the h.p.l.c. unit to form the gradient described in *Table 14* at a flow-rate of 1.0 ml/min should also be considered. We found that our h.p.l.c. required a flow-rate of 1.5 ml/min.

A standard mixture of type I and type III uroporphyrin and coproporphyrin can be prepared as follows. The methyl esters of each porphyrin can be obtained from Porphyrin Products.

(i) Hydrolyse about 0.5 mg of each porphyrin in 2.7 M HCl for 72 h at room temperature in the dark.

(ii) Spectrophotometrically scan each solution from 390 nm to 425 nm to obtain the corrected absorbances as shown in *Figure 2*.

(iii) Calculate the concentration of each porphyrin solution in μmol/l by multiplying the corrected absorbance with the following factors: 3.05 for coproporphyrin I and III and 2.46 for uroporphyrin I and III (ref. 11).

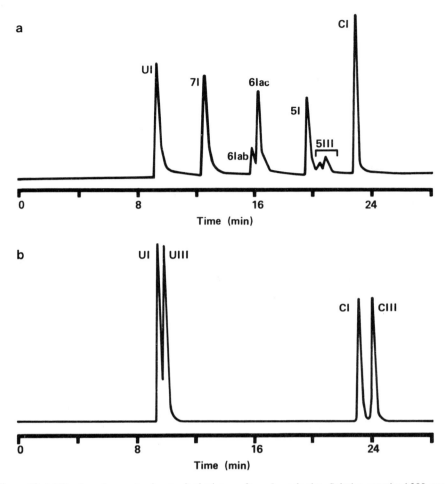

Figure 12. (a) H.p.l.c. of an equimolar standard mixture of type I porphyrins. Solution contained 200 nmol/l of each porphyrin in 0.27 M HCl. H.p.l.c. conditions as in *Table 14*. UI, uroporphyrin I (21% of total peak area); 7I, heptacarboxylic porphyrin I (20%); 6Iab, hexacarboxylic porphyrin I rings a and b decarboxylated (4%); 6Iac, hexacarboxylic porphyrin I rings A and C decarboxylated (16%); 5I, pentacarboxylic porphyrin I (13%); 5III, pentacarboxylic porphyrins III (3%); CI, coproporphyrin I (23%). (b) H.p.l.c. of a standard mixture of type I and type III uroporpnyrins (80 nmol/l each) and type I and type III coproporphyrins (56 nmol/l each) in 0.27 M HCl. H.p.l.c. conditions as in *Table 14*. UI, uroporphyrin I (29% of total peak area); UIII, uroporphyrin III (18%); CI, coproporphyrin I (22%); CIII, coproporphyrin III (21%).

(iv)   Mix the four porphyrin solutions and make a 10-fold dilution with water to give the final quantitative standard mixture in 0.27 M HCl.

The h.p.l.c. trace of our standard mixture is shown in *Figure 12b*.

4.5.4 *Separation of riboflavin*

Almost all of the urines injected gave a fluorescence peak eluting close to uroporphyrin. We identified the peak as riboflavin by using an authentic sample of this water-soluble B-group vitamin. Careful control of the pH of the ammonium acetate buffer was necessary to ensure riboflavin did not co-elute with uroporphyrin. We found that

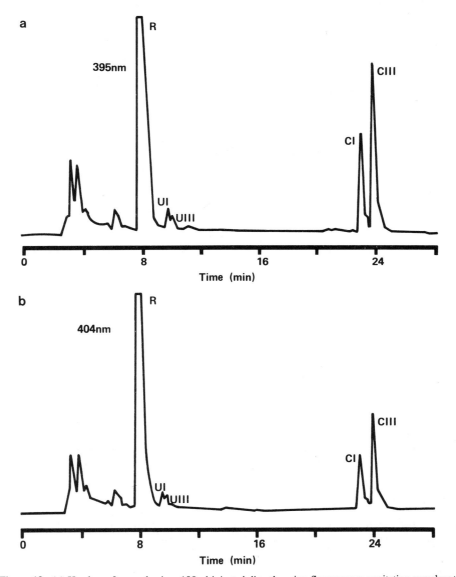

Figure 13. (a) H.p.l.c. of normal urine, 100 μl injected directly using fluorescence excitation wavelength 395 nm. H.pl.c. conditions as in *Table 14.* Total porphyrins: 170 nmol/l or 21 nM/mM creatinine. R, riboflavin; UI, uroporphyrin I; UIII, uroporphyrin III; CI, coproporphyrin I; CIII, coproporphyrin III. Total porphyrin peak area: 99 units. (b) H.p.l.c. of the same normal urine, 100 μl injected directly using fluorescence excitation wavelength 404 nm. Total porphyrin peak area: 56 units.

riboflavin separated best at pH 5.16 adjusted in the presence of acetonitrile as described in *Table 13*. At higher pH values the riboflavin interferes with the separation of type I and type III uroporphyrin.

4.5.5 *Preparation of urine samples*

The h.p.l.c. conditions shown in *Table 14* allow the direct injection of urine without preliminary purification procedures.

(i) *Normal urine porphyrins*. Urines with total porphyrins less than 300 nmol/l are first acidified to dissolve any precipitated calcium salts. The precipitates which often form in stored urines (especially at less than 10°C) include calcium phosphate and can adsorb urine porphyrins. We add 0.2 ml of concentrated HCl to 5 ml of urine, mix until the precipitate redissolves and then inject the specimen. *Figure 13a* shows the h.p.l.c. trace of 100 μl of normal urine (total porphyrin 170 nmol/l) obtained using fluorescence detection with an excitation wavelength of 395 nm. The total peak area due to porphyrins was 99 arbitrary area units. *Figure 13b* shows the h.p.l.c. trace of the same urine with an excitation wavelength of 404 nm, giving a total peak area due to porphyrins of only 56 area units. We used an excitation wavelength of 395 nm for all subsequent urine h.p.l.c. profiles.

(ii) *Elevated urine porphyrins*. If the urine total porphyrin is over 500 nmol/l the sample is diluted with 0.27 M HCl to give a total porphyrin of between 300 and 500 nmol/l. The acidified specimen is mixed until any precipitate present redissolves and is then injected into the h.p.l.c.

4.5.6 *Interference with urine porphyrin h.p.l.c.*

Occasional urine specimens gave h.p.l.c. traces which could not be interpreted due to the presence of spurious fluorescence peaks. Unidentified fluorescence peaks have been seen in several abnormally pigmented urines submitted to the laboratory for pigment identification. Although these urines may have normal urine porphyrins they frequently give interfering peaks on h.p.l.c. separation. We have had success in eliminating the unknown peaks by isolating the porphyrin methyl esters using the method shown in *Table 8* and chromatographing the acid hydrolysate. Alternatively, talc adsorption of free acid porphyrins (*Table 3*) may be sufficient to remove the interfering substances. Occasional urine samples without abnormal pigmentation but with unidentified fluorescence peaks are also chromatographed following isolation of methyl esters.

4.6 **Faecal porphyrin separation**

4.6.1 *H.p.l.c. conditions*

Most of the faecal porphyrins in normal samples are dicarboxylic porphyrins derived by bacterial action on haem. Dicarboxylic porphyrins interact strongly with the hydrophobic groups on the column and the elution gradient was modified by increasing the proportion of organic modifier to speed up the elution, as shown in *Table 15*.

Table 15 H.p.l.c. conditions for faecal extracts.

Column:	ODS-Hypersil, 25 cm x 5 mm.
Elution solvents:	Solvent A: 10:90 (v/v) acetonitrile − 1 M ammonium acetate buffer, pH 5.16.
	Solvent B: 10:90 (v/v) acetonitrile − methanol.
Flow-rate:	1.5 ml/min.
Gradient:	1. Equilbrate the column with 100% solvent A (0% B) and inject the sample.
	2. Run a linear gradient from 0% B to 90% B in 20 min.
	3. Run 90% B for a further 7 min to the end of the run at 27 min.
Detector:	FS-970 fluorescence detector (Schoeffel).
	Excitation wavelength 395 nm, 580 nm cut-off filter for the emission.
H.p.l.c.:	Model 1084B dual pump with electronic peak area integration (Hewlett − Parkard).

The other h.p.l.c. conditions remain the same as those used for urine porphyrin separation.

4.6.2 *Preparation of faecal samples*

Faecal samples are subjected to the acid extraction method shown in *Table 4*, allowing quantitation of faecal total porphyrin and yielding a residue-free extract suitable for h.p.l.c. separation (11). The resulting aqueous acid extract may be injected into the RP-h.p.l.c. system as the 1 M ammonium acetate buffer protects the chemically-bonded hydrophobic groups on the column from hydrolysis.

4.6.3 *Normal faecal porphyrins*

A typical faecal porphyrin profile is shown in *Figure 14a*, where the dicarboxylic fraction is 85% of the total porphyrin with coproporphyrins type I and type III making up the remaining 15%. The predominant dicarboxylic porphyrins in faeces are deuteroporphyrin, monoethyl and monovinyl deuteroporphyrins and protoporphyrin. Small amounts of mesoporphyrin and what is probably monohydroxyethyl deuteroporphyrins are also present.

The occasional subjects we have observed on vegetarian diets have low faecal total porphyrins. *Figure 14b* shows an example. Contrary to the usual normal faecal specimen, coproporphyrins I and III account for 66% of the porphyrin, and the dicarboxylic fraction was only 34% of the total. We found coproporphyrin type I exceeded type III in all normal faecal specimens examined. The faecal dicarboxylic porphyrins found in subjects on a vegetarian diet may derive from the normal blood loss of $2-3$ ml per day into the gut.

All of the faecal extracts examined included a porphyrin eluting in the dicarboxyic fraction between deuteroporphyrin and protoporphyrin. This is probably a mixture of dicarboxylic porphyrins arising from bacterial action on the two vinyl groups of protoporphyrin. The vinyl groups appear to be either completely removed, producing deuteroporphyrin, or partially removed and hydrogenated, producing a mixture of monovinyl and monoethyl deuteroporphyrins. This peak has not been positively identified and is marked 'EV' on the faecal porphyrin chromatograms.

4.7 **Red blood cell porphyrins**

4.7.1 *Preparation of standards*

Protoporphyrin suitable for use as a chromatographic marker can be conveniently prepared by means of mild reduction to remove iron from haemin. We have successfully used the ferrous sulphate method (29) in which the reduction of ferric iron in haemin occurs at the same time as ferrous iron is removed. Zinc protoporphyrin was prepared from protoporphyrin using zinc acetate (30). Both protoporphyrin and zinc protoporphyrin were taken up in ethanol ready for subsequent standardization and h.p.l.c. injection. Standardization was performed by diluting each sample in 2.7 M HCl, thereby converting zinc protoporphyrin to free protoporphyrin and leaving protoporphyrin unchanged for the short time required to obtain an absorbance scan. The absorbances of the acid solutions were scanned between 390 and 425 nm and the corrected absorbance obtained graphically as shown in *Figure 2*. The factor for converting corrected

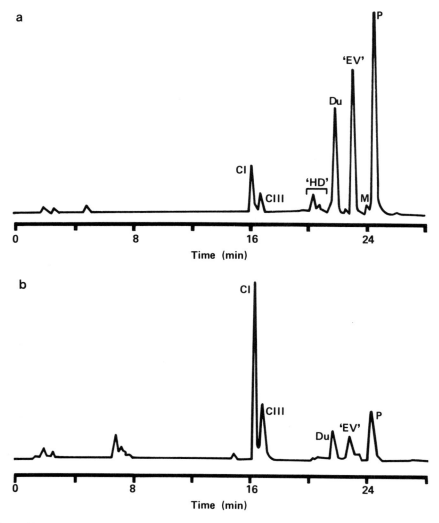

Figure 14. (a) H.p.l.c. of faecal porphyrins form a normal subject on a diet containing meat. H.p.l.c. conditions as in *Table 15*. Total porphyrins: 150 nM/g dry weight. CI, coproporphyrin I, CIII, coproporphyrin III; 'HD', probably monohydroxyethyl deuteroporphyrins; DU, deuteroporphyrin; 'EV', probably monoethyl deuteroporphyrins and monovinyl deuteroporphyrins; M, mesoporphyrin P, protoporphyrin. Total dicarboxylic fraction ('HD', Du, 'EV', M, P): 85% of total peak area. (b) H.p.l.c. of faecal porphyrins from a normal subject on a vegetarian diet. Total porphyrins: 40 nM/g dry weight. Total dicarboxylic fraction (Du, 'EV', P): 34% of total peak area.

absorbance to concentration of protoporphyrin in μM is 5.00 (ref. 11). Equimolar solutions of protoporphyrin and zinc protoporphyrin in ethanol (110 nmol/l) were prepared for use as h.p.l.c standards.

4.7.2 *H.p.l.c. conditions*

The h.p.l.c. conditions were designed for the separation of protoporphyrin and zinc protoporphyrin in ethanol extracts of blood samples (see *Table 6*). The proportion of

Table 16. H.p.l.c. conditions for RBC extracts.

Column:	ODS-Hypersil, 25 cm x 5 mm.
Elution solvents:	Solvent A: 10:90 (v/v) acetonitrile − 1 M ammonium acetate buffer, pH 5.16.
	Solvent B: 10:90 (v/v) acetonitrile − methanol.
Flow-rate:	1.5 ml/min.
Gradient:	1. Equlibrate the column with 100% sovlent A (0% B) and inject the sample.
	2. Run a linear gradient from 0% B to 90% B in 10 min.
	3. Run 90% B for a further 8 min to the end of the run at 18 min.
Detector:	FS-970 fluorescence detector (Schoeffel).
	Excitation wavelength 404 nm, 580 nm cut-off filter for the emission.
H.p.l.c.:	Model 1084B dual pump with electronic peak area integration (Hewlett − Parkard).

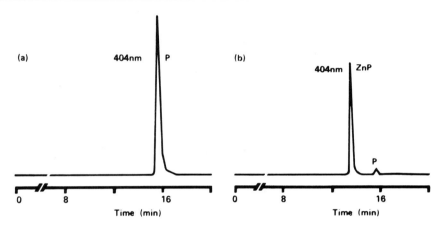

Figure 15. (a) H.p.l.c. of freshly prepared standard free acid protoporphyrin, 110 nmol/l. Fluorescence excitation wavelength 404 nm. H.p.l.c. conditions as in *Table 16*. P, protoporphyrin: peak area 24.5 units. **(b)** H.p.l.c. of freshly prepared standard zinc protoporphyrin, equimolar to the protoporphyrin, 110 nM. ZnP, zinc protoporphyrin: peak area 13.6 units: P, protoporphyrin: <1% of total peak area. The molar fluorescence ratio of protoporphyrin to zinc protoporphyrin is the ratio of the peak areas, i.e. 1.80.

organic modifier was increased to allow the elution of both porphyrins within 20 min. The excitation wavelength on the fluorescence detector was set to 404 nm. The h.p.l.c. conditions are shown in *Table 16*.

4.7.3 *H.p.l.c. calibration of standards*

The h.p.l.c. traces for equimolar solutions of protoporphyrin (*Figure 15a*) and zinc protoporphyrin (*Figure 15b*) in ethanol were obtained using the h.p.l.c. conditions shown in *Table 16*. The peak areas computed by the electronic integrator were 24.5 units for protoporphyrin and 13.6 units for zinc protoporphyrin. The molar fluorescence ratio of protoporphyrin to zinc protoporphyrin is the ratio of the peak areas, i.e. 1.80. This ratio may be dependent on the optical characteristics of different fluorescence detectors and should be individually determined for each instrument. Detectors equipped with a monochromator for the emission wavelength and a photomultiplier tube sensitive to wavelengths up to 650 nm will show that the zinc complex fluoresces at 590 nm and 640 nm while free protoporphyrin fluoresces at 634 nm only.

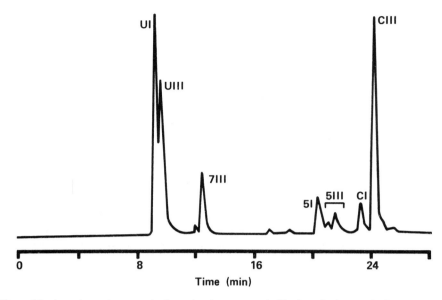

Figure 16. Acute intermittent porphyria, patient in acute attack. H.p.l.c. of urine porphyrins. H.p.l.c. conditions as in *Table 14*. Porphobilinogen: 8.5 μM/mM creatinine. Total porphyrins: 4670 nmol/l or 210 nM/mM creatinine. UI, uroporphyrin I; UIII, uroporphyrin III; 7III, heptacarboxylic porphyrin III; 5I, pentacarboxylic porphyrin I; 5III, mixture of pentacarboxylic porphyrins III; CI, coproporphyrin I; CIII, coproporphyrin III.

4.8 Porphyrin profiles

4.8.1 *Acute intermittent porphyria (AIP)*

Urine samples obtained during an acute attack contain elevated urine porphyrins (*Figure 16*), but most of the uroporphyrin is derived from PBG by spontaneous condensation. PBG is present in much larger molar quantity and even if about 50% of the PBG condenses to amorphous pigments such as porphobilin, the fraction condensing to uroporphyrin forms a significant proportion of the total urine porphyrin. More work is required to determine pre-formed urine porphyrins in fresh samples obtained under carefully controlled conditions.

We have observed normal urine porphyrin profiles in an AIP patient during the remission stage, so that urine h.p.l.c profiles may be used only during acute attacks. Occasional patients also excrete normal quantities of PBG during remission. The total faecal porphyrin is usualy normal and the faecal h.p.l.c. profile should not be used for the diagnosis of AIP.

4.8.2 *Variegate porphyria (VP)*

The urine porphyrins and h.p.l.c. profile are often normal during periods of remission. During acute attacks both urine PBG and porphyrins are elevated. The urine porphyrin profile is not diagnostic for VP. As in AIP, the profile obtained depends on the extent of spontaneous condensation of PBG to uroporphyrins.

Diagnosis of VP is made by the analysis of faecal porphyrins, as the total faecal porphyrin is invariably elevated, both in attack and remission stages and the h.p.l.c. pro-

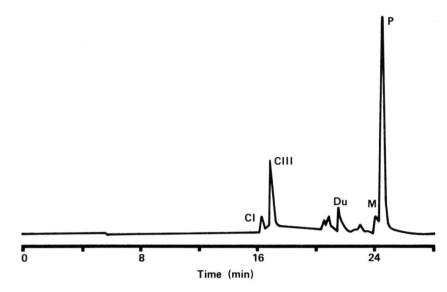

Figure 17. Variegate porphyria, patient in remission. H.p.l.c. of faecal porphyrins. H.p.l.c. conditions as in *Table 15*. Total porphyrins: 2000 nM/g dry weight. CI, coproporphyrin I; CIII, coproporphyrin III; Du, deuteroporphyrin; M, mesoporphyrin; P, protoporphyrin.

file is diagnostic. *Figure 17* shows that the main porphyrin is protoporphyrin with the bacterial degradation products prominent in normal faeces forming a much decreased proportion of the total porphyrin. Coproporphyrin III exceeds coproporphyrin I whereas the reverse is true of all normal faeces so far examined. The analysis of faecal porphyrins is especially important for the differentiation of VP from PCT, in which the skin symptoms are identical. Urine porphyrin analysis alone cannot reliably differentiate these two conditions.

4.8.3 *Hereditary coproporphyria (HCP)*

In HCP the urine porphyrins and the h.p.l.c. profile are usually normal during periods of remission. As with VP, acute attacks may occur only rarely during a patient's lifetime. *Figure 18a* shows the urine h.p.l.c profile of an HCP patient recovering from an acute attack. The urine porphyrin typically shows elevated coproporphyrin III.

Analysis of faecal porphyrins is diagnostic as the total porphyrin is elevated in both attack and remission. *Figure 18b* shows the diagnostic faecal porphyrin profile with coproporphyrin III predominating.

4.8.4 *Porphyria cutanea tarda (PCT)*

This porphyria presents with skin symptoms and elevated urine porphyrins consisting almost entirely of uroporphyrin and heptacarboxylic porphyrins (*Figure 19a*). Typically, the ratio of uroporphyrin to heptacarboxylic porphyrins is less than 2.0. However, this should not be used for diagnosis as we have observed higher ratios in PCT.

The diagnosis of PCT should always be confirmed by the analysis of a faecal specimen which gives a diagnostic h.p.l.c. profile (*Figure 19b*). The most important features

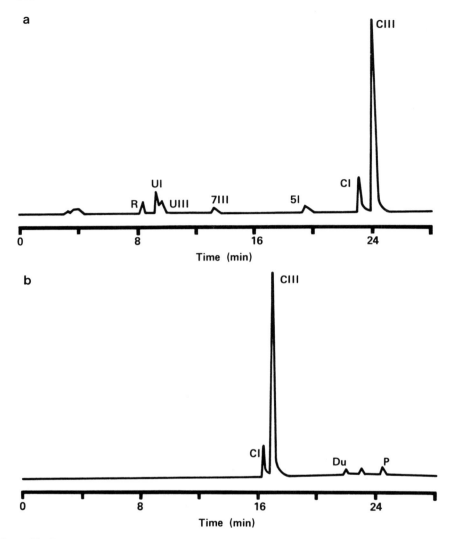

Figure 18. Hereditary coproporphyria. (**a**) Patient recovering from an acute attack. H.p.l.c. of urine porphyrins. H.p.l.c. conditions as in *Table 14*. Porphobilinogen: 0.6 μM/mM creatinine. Total porphyrins: 3500 nmol/l or 150 nM/mM creatinine. R, riboflavin; UI, uroporphyrin I; UIII, uroporphyrin III; 7III, heptacarboxylic porphyrin III; 5I, pentacarboxylic porphyrin I; CI, coproporphyrin I; CIII, coproporphyrin III. (**b**) Patient in remission. H.p.l.c. of faecal porphyrins. H.p.l.c. conditions as in *Table 16*. Total porphyrins: 4200 nM/g dry weight. CI, coproporphyrin I; CIII, coproporphyrin III; Du, deuteroporphyrin; P, protoporphyrin.

of the faecal porphyrin profile are the presence of heptacarboxylic porphyrin III and isocoproporphyrin, both of which are diagnostic for PCT. Penta- and hexacarboxylic porphyrins are also seen. The dicarboxylic porphyrins found in normal faeces are also present.

4.8.5. *Erythrohepatic protoporphyria (EHP)*

The photosensitive skin symptoms observed in EHP are due to elevated RBC free pro-

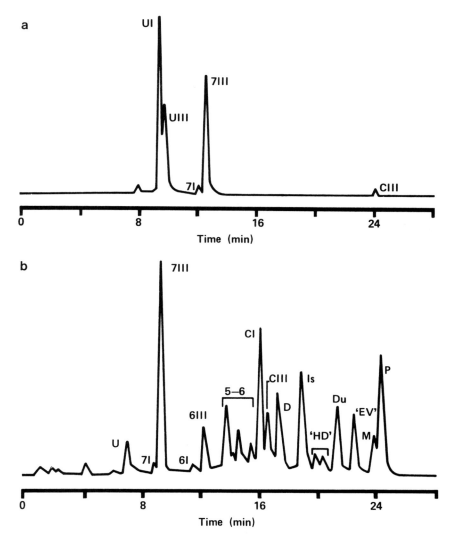

Figure 19. Porphyria cutanea tarda. (**a**) H.p.l.c. of urine porphyrins, patient CF. H.p.l.c. conditions as in *Table 14*. Total porphyrins: 32 100 nmol/l or 1290 nM/mM creatinine. UI, uroporphyrin I (33% of total peak area); UIII, uroporphyrin III (25%); 7I, heptacarboxylic porphyrin I (1%); 7III, heptacarboxylic porphyrin III (38%); CIII, coproporphyrin III (2%). Ratio of (UI + UIII) to (7I + 7III) = 1.5. (**b**) H.p.l.c. of faecal porphyrins. H.p.l.c. conditions as in *Table 15*. Total porphyrins: 660 nM/g dry weight. U, uroporphyrin I and III; 7I, heptacarboxylic porphyrin I; 7III, heptacarboxylic porphyrin III; 6I, hexacarboxylic porphyrin I; 6III, hexacarboxylic porphyrin III; 5-6, pentacarboxylic porphyrin isomers; CI, coproporphyrin I; CIII, coproporphyrin III; D, deethylisocoproporphyrin; Is, isocoproporphyrin; 'HD', probably monohydroxyethyl deuteroporphyrins; Du, deuteroporphyrin; 'EV', probably monoethyl deuteroporphyrins and monovinyl deuteroporphyrins; M, mesoporphyrin; P, protoporphyrin.

toporphyrin. The total urine porphyrins and h.p.l.c. profile are normal, except in the rare patient who develops liver failure. Faecal porphyrin analysis is not diagnostic as the total porphyrin is often only marginally elevated and the h.p.l.c. profile is similar to that found in normal subjects on haem-containing diets.

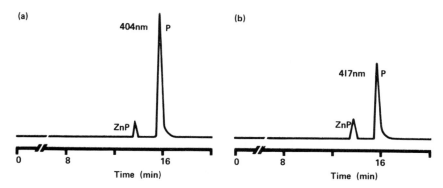

Figure 20. Erythrohepatic protoporphyria. H.p.l.c. conditions as in *Table 16*. (**a**) H.p.l.c. of an ethanol extract of RBC. Fluorescence excitation wavelength: 404 nm, total RBC protoporphyrin: 11.6 μmol/l RBC (reference range <1.5 μmol/l). ZnP, zinc protoporphyrin: 2.6 area units (normally 5% of total); P, protoporphyrin: 48.7 area units (nominally 95% of total). As protoporphyrin fluoresces 1.8 times an equimolar quantity of zinc protoporphyrin correction of the peak areas gives: zinc protoporphyrin, 9% of total porphyrin and protoporphyrin, 91%. (**b**) H.p.l.c. of the same extract with fluorescence activation wavelength 417 nm showing the expected increase in the zinc protoporphyrin signal and decrease in the protoporphyrin signal.

The total RBC porphyrins are invariably elevated and free protoporphyrin always exceeds zinc protoporphyrin. *Figure 20a* shows the h.p.l.c. trace for an ethanol extract (*Table 6*) of EHP red blood cells. Injection of equimolar ethanol solutions of free protoporphyrin and zinc protoporphyrin (*Figure 15*) using the h.p.l.c. conditions in *Table 17* showed that protoporphyrin fluoresces 1.80 times an equimolar amount of zinc protoporphyrin. Correction of the peak areas (see *Figure 20a*) gave a free protoporphyrin of 91% of the total RBC porphyrin. The maximal fluorescence signal for free protoporphyrin is given by an excitation wavelength of 404 nm while zinc protoporphyrin emits maximally at 417 nm. Repeating the injection at excitation 417 nm (*Figure 20b*) shows the increased zinc protoporphyrin signal and decreased free protoporphyrin signal.

4.8.6 *Lead exposure*

Elevated RBC porphyrins are a feature of occupational lead exposure and can be used for monitoring progress as they provide a long-term (2−3 month) index of exposure. Zinc protoporphyrin is the predominant red cell porphyrin in lead exposure, iron deficiency and in chronic infection, inflammatory disease or malignancy. Thus the elevated RBC porphyrin often seen in these conditions can be clearly distinguished from EHP by the h.p.l.c. separation of protoporphyrin and zinc protoporphyrin.

Figure 21a shows the h.p.l.c. trace of an ethanol extract of RBC from a lead-exposed patient. Correction of the peak areas shows that zinc protoporphyrin is 92% of the total RBC porphyrin. Repeating the injection at the maximal excitation wavelength (417 nm) for zinc protoporphyrin (*Figure 21b*) shows the expected increased fluorescence signal.

4.8.7 *Congenital erythropoietic porphyria (CEP)*

This rare porphyria is usually a severe disorder in which marked skin photosensitivity begins soon after birth. CEP is characterised by the overproduction of type I porphyrin

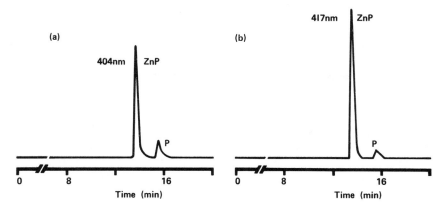

Figure 21. Lead exposure. H.p.l.c. conditions as in *Table 16*. (**a**) H.p.l.c. of an ethanol extract of RBC. Fluorescence activation wavelength: 404 nm, total RBC protoporphyrin: 19.5 μmol/l RBC. RBC lead: 7.9 μmol/l RBC (reference range <3.0 μmol/l). ZnP, zinc protoporphyrin: 16.7 area units (nominally 87% of total); P, protoporphyrin: 2.4 area units (nominally 13% of total). As protoporphyrin fluoresces 1.8 times an equimolar quantity of zinc protoporphyrin correction of the peak areas gives: zinc protoporphyrin, 92% of total porphyrin and protoporphyrin, 8%. (**b**) H.p.l.c. of the same extract with fluorescence activation wavelength 417 nm showing the expected increase in the zinc protoporphyrin signal and decrease in the protoporphyrin signal.

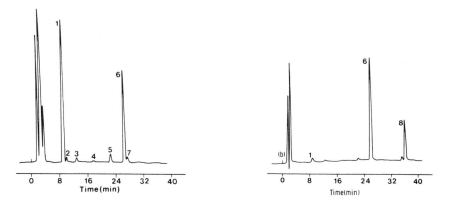

Figure 22. H.p.l.c. of (**a**) urinary and (**b**) faecal porphyrins from a congenital erythropoietic porphyria patient. H.p.l.c. conditions as in *Table 13*. Peaks: **1**, uroporphyrin I; **2**, uroporphyrin III; **3**, heptacarboxylic porphyrin I; **4**, hexacarboxylic porphyrin I; **5**, pentacarboxylic porphyrin I; **6**, coproporphyrin I; **7**, coproporphyrin III; **8**, protoporphyrin. From ref. 1 with permission.

isomers. In urine (*Figure 22a*) uroporphyrin and coproporphyrin I predominate, and in faeces (*Figure 22b*) the main porphyrin is coproporphyrin I. The resolution of type I and type III isomers is especially helpful in the unambiguous diagnosis of CEP.

5. ASSAYS OF HAEM BIOSYNTHETIC ENZYMES

5.1 Role of h.p.l.c.

The development of simple and effective h.p.l.c. systems for the separation of porphyrin precursors and porphyrins have allowed the development of reliable h.p.l.c. methods for assay of the haem biosynthetic enzymes. Methods for the assay of ALA synthase (31), ALA dehydrase (32) and the simultaneous determination of hydroxy-methylbilane synthase and uroporphyrinogen III synthase (33) have been developed by Lim and co-workers. The availability of effective h.p.l.c. systems for the separation of type I and type III isomers will assist in the development of assays for the remaining haem enzymes.

5.2 δ-Aminolaevulinic acid synthase (ALA-S)

ALA-S is a mitochondrial enzyme which catalyses the formation of ALA from glycine and succinic acid. Due to the low activity of ALA-S in the mitochondria of normal tissues, radiochemical methods have been developed in which ALA is purified prior to its quantitative determination. Lim *et al.* (31) have developed a h.p.l.c. method for the purification and isolation of ALA and applied it to the determination of the activity of ALA-S in mitochondria prepared by the sonication of normal human bone marrow cells. The isolated mitochondria are incubated with [^{14}C]α-ketoglutarate and the product [^{14}C]ALA formed is converted to a pyrrole. The pyrrole is separated and isolated by h.p.l.c. and its radioactivity determined by scintillation counting.

5.2.1 *Reagents*

[^{14}C]ALA hydrochloride and α-keto[5-^{14}C]glutaric acid as the sodium salt (Amersham International) are divided into aliquots containing 0.5 μCi (12.2 μM) and 2.5 μCi (0.8 μM), respectively, and the aliquots freeze-dried and stored under nitrogen at −20°C. Pyridoxal phosphate, α-ketoglutarate and co-enzyme A are obtained from Sigma Chemical Co. ALA-hydrochloride, EDTA, glycine, magnesium chloride, trichloroacetic acid (TCA) and Tris (hydroxymethylamine) are analytical grade reagents from BDH. Ethylacetoacetate is laboratory grade reagent from BDH. The ion-pair reagent 1-heptane-sulphonic acid (PIC-B7) is from Waters Associates.

The incubation medium contains EDTA (10 mmol/l), sucrose (0.25 mmol/l), magnesium chloride (5 mmol/l) and glycine (0.05 mol/l). The addition of pyridoxal phosphate (0.4 mmol/l) has no effect on the marrow enzyme activity in normal subjects. The medium is buffered with 0.04 mol/l Tris, adjusted to pH 7.55 at 20°C with 0.05 mol/l potassium dihydrogen orthophosphate. The final pH at 37°C is 7.4. Aliquots (20 ml) of the incubation mixture are stored at −20°C. When required, the mixture is thawed and co-enzyme A added to give a 0.25 mmol/l solution.

5.2.2 *Preparation of bone marrow*

(i)   Deliver 0.5−1.0 ml of marrow into 10 ml of PBS containing 250 U of preservative-free heparin.

(ii)   Pass the marrow suspension twice through a 21-gauge needle and centrifuge at 2500 *g* for 5 min.

(iii)   Remove the supernatant and wash the cells twice with cold isotonic saline.

(iv)   While washing, determine the cell volume and count the total nucleated cells (erythroblasts).

(v)   Suspend the washed cells in 2 ml of incubation medium and release the mitochondria with ultrasound from a 100 W ultrasonic disintegrator (MSE) using a 3/8 inch titanium probe for 15−18 sec.

(vi)   Adjust the volume of the marrow lysate by further addition of incubation medium so that each assay contains between 1 and 5×10^6 erythroblasts per ml.

5.2.3 *Incubation procedure*

(i)   Pre-incubate 0.9 ml of marrow lysate for 5 min at 37°C.

(ii)   Start the reaction by adding 0.1 ml (0.5 μCi) of 1.7 mmol/l [^{14}C]α-ketoglutarate in incubation medium.

(iii)   Stop the reaction at 1 h by adding 0.5 ml of 10% TCA and 0.1 ml (0.5 μM) of 5 mmol/l unlabelled ALA to act as carrier.

(iv)   Set up a blank where the reaction is stopped at zero time by adding 0.1 ml of ALA carrier followed by 0.1 ml (0.5 μCi) of [^{14}C]α-ketoglutarate and 0.5 ml of 10% TCA.

(v)   Set up separate tests and blanks to determine the loss of ALA during the incubation procedure by adding 0.0025 μCi (60 pM) ALA to the tests which are incubated for 1 h in the absence of α-ketoglutarate and to the blanks in which the reaction is stopped at zero time.

(vi)   Following the 1 h incubation and addition of TCA allow all tubes to stand for 10 min in an ice bath, add 1 ml of 1 mmol/l sodium acetate and allow to stand for a further 5 min.

5.2.4 *Isolation of ALA*

(i)   Centrifuge the tubes at 2000 *g* for 10 min.

(ii)   Transfer the clear supernatant to 10 ml test tubes and add 0.1 ml of ethylacetoacetic acid.

(iii)   Form the ALA-ethylacetoacetate pyrrole by heating at 100°C for 20 min.

(iv)   Extract the pyrrole twice with 3 ml aliquots of ether and transfer to another tube.

(v)   Evaporate the ether to dryness with a stream of nitrogen. The residue contains the pyrrole and unreacted ethylacetoacetate.

(vi)   Dissolve the pyrrole by mixing with 0.5 ml of water and then gently centrifuge to isolate the aqueous layer.

(vii)   Remove the aqueous layer and freeze-dry in preparation for h.p.l.c. isolation.

(viii)   Re-dissolve the residue in 50 μl of 50:50 (v/v) aqueous methanol and inject 20 μl onto the h.p.l.c. column.

5.2.5 *H.p.l.c. conditions*

A 10 cm $\times$ 5 mm Hypersil-SAS (Cl) column is used. The elution solvent is methanol$-$PIC-B7 (22:78, v/v) at a flow-rate of 1.5 ml/min. The PIC-B7 (ion-pair reagent) is prepared by diluting the 20 ml aliquots supplied to 1 litre with water. The ALA-pyrrole is monitored by u.v. detection at 252 nm as it elutes off the column with a retention time of about 5 min.

Collect the h.p.l.c. peak containing the pyrrole (2 ml) into 18 ml of Bray's scintillation fluid and count on an LKB Wallace 8100 liquid scintillation counter with adjustement for quenching by the channel ratio method.

5.2.6 *Recovery and calculation*

(i)   Perform a recovery experiment with each batch of analyses by converting 0.1 ml (0.5 μM) of unlabelled ALA (as used for the carrier) into the pyrrole derivative.

(ii) Separate the pyrrole formed from the unreacted ALA by the h.p.l.c procedure described above.

(iii) Calculate the percentage recovery from the d.p.m. of the pyrrole peak (the reference peak) and the d.p.m. of 0.025 μCi of unconverted [^{14}C]ALA.

(iv) Correct the area of the reference peak to give the area which would correspond to 100% recovery of 0.5 μM ALA.

(v)   Calculate the recovery of individual test samples by comparing the measured peak area of the test samples with the calculated peak area for 100% recovery, allowing correction of counts on each test sample as follows:

$$\% \text{ recovery test sample} = \frac{A_{TP}}{A_{RP}} \times \frac{C_{RP}}{C_{ALA}} \times 100$$

and

$$\text{corrected d.p.m. test sample} = \frac{C_{TP}}{\% \text{ recovery of test}}$$

where A_{TP} is the area of test pyrrole peak, A_{RP} is the area of reference pyrrole peak, C_{RP} is the d.p.m. of reference pyrrole peak, C_{ALA} is the d.p.m. of 0.025 μCi [^{14}C]ALA and C_{TP} is the d.p.m. of test pyrrole peak.

(vi) Calculate the blanks in the same way and subtract from the corrected test values. Calculate the amount of ALA formed as follows:

$$\text{pM ALA produced} = \frac{\text{d.p.m. ALA formed in assay} \times \text{initial pM } \alpha\text{-ketoglutarate}}{\text{initial d.p.m. } \alpha\text{-ketoglutarate}}$$

The activity of the enzyme is expressed as pM ALA/10^6 erythroblasts/h. Lim (31) reported a mean ALA-S activity in 10 normal subjects of 318.8 pM ALA/10^6 erythroblasts/h (SD $\pm$ 125.8).

5.3 δ-Aminolaevulinic acid dehydrase (ALA-D)

ALA-D catalyses the condensation of two molecules of ALA to form PBG. Lim (32) has used h.p.l.c. in the determination of this enzyme to separate the substrate (ALA) and the product (PBG). PBG is separated from ALA and an internal standard pyrrole by RP ion-pair chromatography on a SAS-Hypersil column.

5.3.1 *Reagents*

ALA hydrochloride and PBG are from the Sigma Chemical Co., Glacial acetic acid, methanol, sodium acetate trihydrate, sodium dihydrogen phosphate dihydrate, disodium hydrogen orthophosphate dodecahydrate and TCA are analytical grade reagents from BDH. Methylacetoacetate is laboratory reagent grade from BDH. The ion-pair reagent, 1-heptane sulphonic acid (PIC-B7) is from Waters Associates.

Make the pH 4.6 acetate buffer by diluting 57 ml of glacial acetic acid with 700 ml of water. Add 136 g of sodium acetate trihydrate and make up to 1 litre with water. Prepare the pH 6.8, 0.2 M phosphate buffer by mixing 0.2 M solutions of sodium dihydrogen phosphate dihydrate and disodium hydrogen orthophosphate dodecahydrate. Prepare the ALA substrate (20 mmol/l) by dissolving 335.2 mg of ALA-hydrochloride in 100 ml of water.

The internal standard pyrrole is 2-methyl-3-carbmethoxy-4-(3-propionic acid)-pyrrole. This is prepared by condensing ALA with methylacetoacetate as follows.

(i) Dissolve 2 mg of ALA-hydrochloride in 10 ml of pH 4.6 acetate buffer and 10 ml of water.

(ii) Add 1 ml of methylacetoacetate and heat in a water bath at 100°C for 20 min.

(iii) Freeze dry 1.0 ml aliquots of the mixture and store at 4°C.

(iv) Re-dissolve in 10 ml of water prior to use.

5.3.2 *H.p.l.c. conditions*

The h.p.l.c. conditions are similar to those described for the isolation of an ALA-derived pyrrole in Section 5.2.5. The same column is used. The elution solvent is methanol − PIC-B7 (22:78, v/v) at a flow-rate of 1.2 ml/min. A variable wavelength u.v. detector set to 240 nm is used for detection. This system will separate ALA, PBG and the internal standard effectively.

5.3.3. *Preparation of standards*

(i) Make a PBG solution of aoopproximately 100 μmol/l by weighing and then standardize by measuring the exact concentration with the Mauzerall and Granick method (19).

(ii) Dilute this standard stock solution to give a range of working PBG standards from 5 to 50 μmol/l.

(iii) Mix a 0.5 ml aliquot of each working standard with 0.1 ml of the internal standard and inject 20 μl into the h.p.l.c.

(iv) Construct a calibration curve by plotting PBG concentration against the ratio of peak heights of the PBG and internal standard.

5.3.4 *Incubation procedure*

Heparinized blood is used as the enzyme source and the packed cell volume measured. The blood samples are either used immediately or stored in an ice bath for up to 2 h.

(i) Haemolyse 0.5 ml of whole blood in 3.25 ml of water and use 1.5 ml of the haemolysate as the enzyme source. This corresponds to 0.2 ml of whole blood.

(ii) Add 0.5 ml of ALA substrate and 0.5 ml of phosphate buffer to each of three 10 ml test tubes (one blank and duplicate tests).

(iii) For the blank, add 1.0 ml of 10% TCA to one of the tubes.

(iv) Pre-incubate all the tubes in a water bath at 37°C for 5 min.

(v) Start the timed reaction by adding 1.5 ml of the haemolysate and mixing.

(vi) Following incubation for 1 h, stop the reaction by adding 1 ml of 10% TCA and mixing.

(vii) Recover the supernatant by centrifuging at 1500 g for 5 min and add 0.5 ml of supernatant to 0.1 ml of the internal standard.

(viii) Inject 20 μl of this solution into the h.p.l.c.

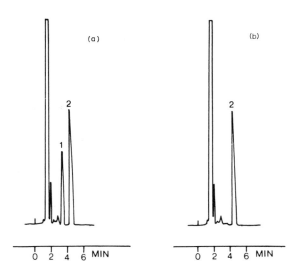

Figure 23. Separation of PBG and the internal standard pyrrole. (**a**) Test sample, (**b**) blank sample. Column, 10 cm × 5 mm Hypersil-SAS; eluent, methanol − PIC-B7 (22:78 v/v); flow-rate, 12 .ml/min; u.v. detection, 240 nm. Peaks: **1**, PBG; **2**, internal standard.

The separation of PBG and internal standard in test and blank samples of the incubation mixture is shown in *Figure 23*.

5.3.5 *Calculation*

The PBG concentration in the incubation mixture is read off the calibration curve in μM. The enzyme activity is expressed as μM of PBG formed per min per litre of RBC at 37°C. Calculate the ALA-D activity (μM PBG/l RBC/min) as follows:

$$PBG \times \frac{3.5}{0.2} \times \frac{100}{PCV} \times \frac{1}{60}$$

where PBG is the concentration of PGB (μM), 3.5/0.2 is the dilution factor, and PCV is the packed cell volume as a fraction of 100.

Lim (32) reported a mean ALA-D activity in 25 normal subjects of 17.50 μM PBG/l RBC/min (SD ± 3.84).

5.4 **Hydroxymethylbilane synthase (HMB-S) and uroporphyrinogen III synthase (UIII-S)**

The formation of uroporphyrinogen III from PBG is catalysed by two enzymes. HMB-S catalyses the first step which is the conversion of PBG into the unstable intermediate hydroxymethylbilane. UIII-S catalyses the conversion of hydroxymethylbilane into uroporporphyrin III.

Wright and Lim (33) have developed a method for the simultaneous determination of these two enzymes in which PBG is incubated with a buffered RBC haemolysate to give uroporphyrins I and III as reaction products. H.p.l.c. separation of uroporphyrin I and III isomers is used to accurately quantitate the individual isomers and total uroporphyrin concentration. Total uroporphyrin production is used to calculate red blood cell HMB-S activity, and the amount of uroporphyrin III formed represents the activity of UIII-S.

5.4.1 *Reagents*

PBG, uroporphyrin I and uroporphyrin III octamethyl esters and Triton X-100 are from Sigma Chemical Co. Ammonium acetate, acetic acid, TCA, magnesium chloride (anhydrous), sodium chloride, iodine, concentrated HCl and Tris (hydroxymethylamine) are analytical reagent grade from BDH Chemicals.

Prepare the incubation medium by mixing 1.5 g of magnesium chloride (anhydrous) and 1 ml of Triton X-100 in 1 litre of 0.05 M Tris-HCl buffer, pH 8.25. Prepare the PBG substrate by dissolving 3.32 mg of PBG in 2 ml of water.

5.4.2 *Preparation of RBC*

(i)   Centrifuge heparinized blood at 2000 *g* for 15 min at 4°C.
(ii)   Discard the plasma leucocytes (buffy coat) and wash the red cells twice with cold isotonic saline (0.9 g/100 ml), centrifuging at 2000 *g* for 10 min after each washing.

The red cells can be assayed immediately or stored at −20°C until required.

5.4.3 *H.p.l.c. conditions*

The h.p.l.c. conditions are described in *Table 11* for the isocratic separation of uroporphyrin isomers.

5.4.4 *Preparation of standards*

Standard solutions of uroporphyrin I and III are prepared using the procedure shown in Section 4.5.2. Construct calibration curves for the determination of uroporphyrin I and III by plotting peak area or peak height against concentration. Wright and Lim (33) confirmed linearity in the range 10−430 nmol/l.

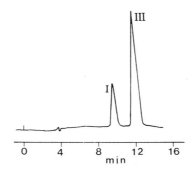

Figure 24. Separation of uroporphyrin I and III isomers in the incubation mixture used for the determination of hydroxymethylbilane synthase and uroporphyrinogen III synthase activities. H.p.l.c. conditions as in *Table 11*.

5.4.5 *Incubation procedure*

(i)   Accurately pipette 30 μl of washed red cells into a test tube and add 1.40 ml of incubation medium.

(ii) Mix to haemolyse the red cells and heat for 1 h in a 56°C water bath and allow to cool to room temperature.

(iii) Add a further 3 μl of washed red cells to the solution and mix well.

(iv) Pre-incubate the mixture at 37°C for 5 min and add 50 μl of PBG substrate to start the reaction.

(v)   Incubate for exactly 30 min at 37°C and stop the reaction by adding 1.5 ml of cold 10% TCA containing 0.5% (w/v) I_2.

(vi) Recover the clear supernatant following centrifugation at 2000 g for 15 min at 4°C.

(vii) Run two blanks with each set of analyses, one containing PBG and the haemolysate with the reaction stopped at zero time and one containing haemolysate without added PBG.

(viii) Inject duplicate aliquots of the clear supernatant into the h.p.l.c. system described in *Table 11*. The separation of uroporphyrin I and III isomers in the incubation mixtures is shown in *Figure 24*.

(ix) From the calibration curves, read off the concentration of uroporphyrin I and III (UI and UIII) in nM.

5.4.6 *Calculation*

HMB-S is heat stable, whereas UIII-S can be completely inactivated by heating. Wright and Lim (33) showed that if 33 μl of red cells were heated for 1 h at 56°C, the enzyme assay produced exclusively uroporphyrin I. If 30 μl of heated red cells plus 3 μl of unheated red cells are used, an identical amount of total porphyrin (uroporphyrin I plus uroporphyrin III) is formed. Thus the uroporphyrin III formed is a result of UIII-S activity in 3 μl of red cells, whereas the total porphyrin produced is due to the activity of HMB-S in 33 μl of red cells.

The enzyme activities are expressed as nM uroporphyrin/ml of red blood cells/h. The calculations are as follows:

$$\text{HMB-S} = (\text{UI} + \text{UIII}) \times \frac{2.983}{1000} \times \frac{1000}{33} \times \frac{60}{30}$$

$$\text{UIII-S} = \text{UIII} \times \frac{2.983}{1000} \times \frac{1000}{3} \times \frac{60}{30}$$

where UI and UIII are the concentrations in nM of uroporphyrin I and III formed and 2.983 is the final incubation volume in ml. Wright and Lim (33) reported preliminary reference range data on 25 normal subjects. The results for both enzymes showed a non-Gaussian distribution and the following results were obtained by logarithmic transformation of the data. The mean HMB-S activity was 29.1 nM uroporphyrin/ml of RBC (2 S.D. range 20.4−41.6). The mean UIII-S activity was 236 nM uroporphyrin III/ml of RBC (2 S.D. range 159−352).

6. ACKNOWLEDGEMENTS

We would like to thank W.H.Lockwood for assistance with the methods, May Lan Lee for typing the manuscript and Eleaner Leake for assistance with literature research.

7. REFERENCES

1. Lim,C.K. and Peters,T.J. (1984) *J. Chromatogr.*, **316**, 397.
2. With,T.K. (1976) In *Porphyrins in Human Diseases*, Vol. **II**, Suppl., Doss,M. and Nowrocki,P. (eds.), Freiburg, Falk, p. 272.
3. Petryka,Z.J. and Watson,C.J. (1978) *Anal. Biochem.*, **84**, 173.
4. Miller,V. and Malina,L. (1978) *J. Chromatogr.*, **145**, 290.
5. Seubert,A. and Seubert,S. (1982) *Anal. Biochem.*, **124**, 303.
6. Wilson,J.H.P., Van Den Berg,J.W.D., Edixhoven-Bosdijk,A. and Van Gastel-Quist,L.H.M. (1978) *Clin. Chim. Acta*, **89**, 165.
7. Day,R.S. and Eales,L. (1980) *Nephron*, **26**, 90.
8. With,T.K. (1975) *Dan. Med. Bull.*, **22**, 74.
9. Gray,C.H., Lim,C.K. and Nicholson,D.C. (1977) *Clin. Chim. Acta*, **77**, 167.
10. Christensen,N.G. and Romslo,I. (1979) *Scand. J. Clin. Lab. Invest.*, **39**, 223.
11. Lockwood,W.H., Poulos,V., Rossi,E. and Curnow,D.H. (1985) *Clin. Chem.*, in press.
12. Day,R.S., De Salamanca,R.E. and Eales,L. (1978) *Clin. Chim. Acta*, **89**, 25.
13. Lockwood,W.H. and Poulos,V. (1980) *Int. J. Biochem.*, **12**, 1049.
14. Scoble,H.A., McKeag,M., Brown,P.R. and Kavaranos,G.J. (1981) *Clin. Chim. Acta*, **113**, 253.
15. Hart,D. and Piomelli,S. (1981) *Clin. Chem.*, **27**, 220.
16. Garden,J.S., Mitchell,D.G., Jackson,K.W. and Aldous,K.M. (1977) *Clin. Chem.*, **23**, 1585.
17. Poh-Fitzpatrick,M.B., Sosin,A.E. and Bemis,J. (1982) *J. Am. Acad. Dermatol.*, **7**, 100.
18. Poulos,V. and Lockwood,W.H. (1980) *Int. J. Biochem.*, **12**, 1051.
19. Mauzerall,D. and Granick,S. (1956) *J. Biol. Chem.*, **219**, 435.
20. Straka,J.G., Kushner,J.P. and Burnham,B.F. (1981) *Anal. Biochem.*, **111**, 269.
21. Malina,L., Miller,V. and Magnus,I.A. (1978) *Clin. Chim. Acta*, **83**, 55.
22. Meyer,H.D., Jacob,K., Vogt,W. and Knedel,M. (1981) *J. Chromatogr.*, **217**, 473.
23. Chiba,M. and Sassa,S. (1982) *Anal. Biochem.*, **124**, 279.
24. Schreiber,W.E., Raisys,V.A. and Labbe,R.F. (1983) *Clin. Chem.*, **29**, 527.
25. Udagawa,M., Hayashi,Y. and Hirayama,C. (1982) *J. Chromatogr.*, **233**, 338.
26. Lim,C.K., Rideout,J.M. and Wright,D.J. (1983) *J. Chromatogr.*, **282**, 629.
27. Lim,C.K., Rideout,J.M. and Peters,T.J. (1984) *J. Chromatogr.*, **317**, 333.
28. Lim,C.K. and Peters,T.J. (1984) *Clin. Chim. Acta*, **139**, 55.
29. Fuhrhop,J.H. and Smith,K.M. (1975) In *Porphyrins and Metalloporphyrins*, Smith,K.M. (ed.), Elsevier, Amsterdam, Oxford and New York, p. 800.
30. Fuhrhop,J.H. and Smith,K.M. (1975) In *Porphyrins and Metalloporphyrins*, Smith,K.M. (ed.), Elsevier, Amsterdam, Oxford and New York, p. 798.
31. Tikerpae,J., Samson,D. and Lim,C.K. (1981) *Clin. Chim. Acta*, **113**, 65.
32. Crowne,H., Lim,C.K. and Samson,D. (1981) *J. Chromatogr.*, **223**, 421.
33. Wright,D.J. and Lim,C.K. (1983) *Biochem. J.*, **213**, 85.

CHAPTER 11

Bile pigments

SEAN McKAVANAGH and BARBARA H.BILLING

1. INTRODUCTION

Bile pigments originate mainly from the degradation of haem derived from the haemoglobin of effete red cells at the end of their life span. A small contribution comes from other haem proteins, immature erythroid cells and free haem which turn over at a faster rate. The conversion of haem to the bilirubin precursor, biliverdin IXα occurs in the reticulo-endothelial system by a complex series of reactions which are catalysed by the microsomal haem oxygenase system. In mammals the green bile pigment biliverdin IXα is reduced at its central methene bridge to bilirubin IXα by the cytosolic enzyme NADPH-dependent biliverdin reductase, which is present in most tissues. Other isomers of biliverdin and bilirubin can be formed *in vitro* and have been detected in the foetus.

Bilirubin IXα is virtually insoluble in aqueous solution at physiological pH due to a ridge-tile conformation which is maintained by six intra-molecular hydrogen bonds (*Figure 1*). It is, therefore, transported in blood tightly bound to albumin. In order to be excreted by the liver in the bile it has first to be converted to polar compounds so that the hydrogen bonding is reduced. This is normally achieved by esterification of one or both of the propionic acid side chains (C-8 and C-12) with uridine diphosphate glucuronic acid under the action of the microsomal enzyme bilirubin UDP-glucuronyl transferase (EC 2.4.1.17). Bilirubin mono-glucuronides and bilirubin diglucuronide,

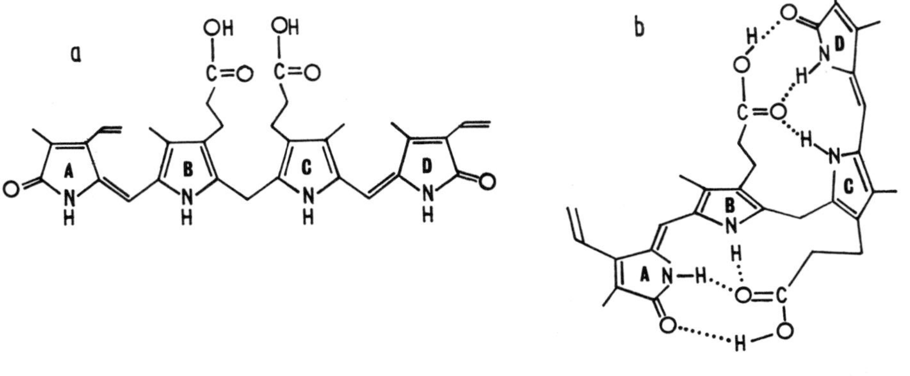

Figure 1. Structure of bilirubin IXα (**a**) linear representation; (**b**) three-dimensional structure with hydrogen bonding.

known collectively as bilirubin conjugates, are then deconjugated and reduced to urobilinoids in the intestine, as the result of bacterial action, and are excreted in the faeces.

In jaundice the nature of the bile pigment accumulating in the plasma is dependent on the abnormality in bilirubin metabolism that has occurrred. In haemolytic disease the increased production of bilirubin may be in excess of the capacity of the liver to excrete bilirubin and a mild unconjugated hyperbilirubinaemia will develop. Unconjugated bilirubin is also the dominant plasma pigment if there is a deficiency of the conjugating enzyme bilirubin UDP-glucuronyl transferase such as occurs in the newborn. Since bilirubin is toxic to the neonate other means of converting bilirubin to polar compounds have been sought. Treatment with blue light results in the conversion of bilirubin to a mixture of photobilirubins, including hydroxylated derivatives, and configurational and structural isomers in addition to di-pyrroles which can be excreted in bile or urine (1).

Raised plasma levels of bilirubin are a diagnostic feature in patients with a congenital deficiency of bilirubin UDP-glucuronyl transferase, who have no other detectable abnormality in liver function or evidence of overt haemolytic disease. In contrast, in patients with cirrhosis, hepatitis and obstructive jaundice, whose ability to excrete conjugated bilirubin is defective, both bilirubin mono-glucuronide and bilirubin diglucuronide are the dominant pigments in the plasma. In common with unconjugated bilirubin they are transported in the plasma bound to albumin but less tightly (2), so that they can be excreted in the urine. A conjugated bilirubin which is covalently bonded to albumin (δ-bilirubin, Bili-Alb)(3), has also been detected in the plasma of patients recovering from long-standing obstructive jaundice and is not excreted in the urine.

Until recently quantitative determinations of bile pigments have depended either on spectrometry (in the newborn) or on the Van den Bergh reaction. In this latter test bilirubin conjugates give a direct reaction with diazotized sulphanilic acid and form azo pigments while unconjugated bilirubin requires the presence of an accelerator (e.g. methanol or caffeine benzoate) to give an indirect reaction. Neither of the above procedures is suitable for differentiating between the various bile pigments, although the diazo reaction can be used to give an estimate of the relative amounts of unconjugated and conjugated bilirubin.

With the development of h.p.l.c. it is now possible to design accurate methods for the quantitative separation of all the different classes of bile pigments in biological material. The instability of the pigments and the need to separate the pigments in plasma from the circulating albumin have presented many problems which have not been entirely overcome. The value of h.p.l.c. determinations of bile pigments for the routine clinical laboratory has still to be determined.

2. STRUCTURE AND PHYSIO-CHEMICAL PROPERTIES OF BILE PIGMENTS

Bile pigments are referred to as linear tetrapyrroles and are schematically drawn as such, but in reality they have a convoluted structure which influences their solubility (*Figure 1*). They have a spectrum of colours depending on their degree of double bond conjugation which ranges from the colourless urobilinogens through the yellow rubins, orange-red urobilins, violet violins to the green-blue verdins (*Figure 2*). The most studied of these is the rubin, bilirubin IXα, which is responsible for the staining of tissues and body fluids in jaundice.

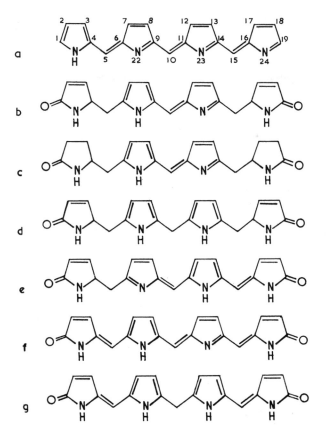

Figure 2. Structures of bile pigment classes: (**a**) numbering system for tetrapyrrole backbone; (**b**) urobilins; (**c**) stercobilins; (**d**) urobilinogens; (**e**) violins; (**f**) verdins; (**g**) rubins.

2.1 **Urobilins**

Urobilins are classified into the stercobilins, with two saturated pyrrolidone end-rings, the urobilins, with two unsaturated pyrrolenone end-rings and half stercobilins, with one saturated and one unsaturated end-ring (*Figure 2*). They can exist as (RS, SR) and (SS, RR) diastereoisomers, since the α-carbon atoms (4 and 16) are chiral, and the naturally occurring i-urobilin is a racemate of the RR and SS forms. They are orange due to the central dipyrromethene chromophore and the free bases or esters absorb maximally at 450 nm whereas the HCl salts absorb at 490 nm. They are polar compounds soluble in water and methanol, slightly soluble in diethyl ether and insoluble in petroleum ether. The HCl salts are particularly soluble in chloroform.

2.2 **Urobilinogens**

The urobilinogens are formed by the reduction of urobilins and have saturated methene bridges with conversion of the basic nitrogen atom in the pyrrolenone ring within the chromophore to an aromatic ring. The urobilinogens are colourless compounds, absorb in the u.v., and are lipophilic and soluble in petroleum ether, diethyl ether, chloroform and methanol. In aqueous solution at neutral or acidic pH they are insoluble but form soluble salts at high pH. Treatment with acids can cause rearrangement to form IIIα and XIIIα isomers. They also undergo dehydrogenation to the corresponding urobilins.

2.3 **Violins**

These pigments are violet in colour due to conjugation of three pyrrolenone rings via two unsaturated methene bridges. They are soluble in most organic solvents and have an absorption maximum in the range 564–587 nm.

2.4 **Verdins**

Verdins are green-blue in colour due to the presence of three methene bridges and therefore the chromophore incorporates the whole molecule. The absorption maximum of unesterified verdins is around 666 nm while that of their dimethyl esters is solvent dependent and is in the range 631–662 nm. Free or unesterified verdins are soluble in methanol but insoluble in chloroform, whereas the methyl esters are soluble in chloroform and hot methanol. In aqueous solution at high or low pH the free verdins are soluble as their sodium or HCl salts, respectively. Of all the bile pigments the verdins are chemically and physically the most stable.

2.5 **Rubins**

These are yellow in colour due to conjugation over two pyrrolenone rings connected by one methene bridge. The absorption maximum is around 450 nm for both the free and esterified pigments. Free rubins are insoluble in aqueous solution, at neutral pH and methanol due to six intramolecular hydrogen bonds, but are freely soluble in chloroform and dimethyl sulphoxide (DMSO) which can disrupt this bonding. They are also freely soluble in aqueous solution at high pH as their sodium salts. In contrast, esterified bilirubin (either as its sugar or alkyl esters) is soluble in polar solvents. Rubins are very labile and readily undergo oxidative degradation in the presence of atmospheric oxygen and traces of divalent metal ions: these reactions can be inhibited but not stopped by the addition of EDTA or anti-oxidants (4). In the presence of strong acids the IXα isomer undergoes dipyrrole exchange to give a mixture of the IIIα, IXα and XIIIα isomers (*Figure 3*).

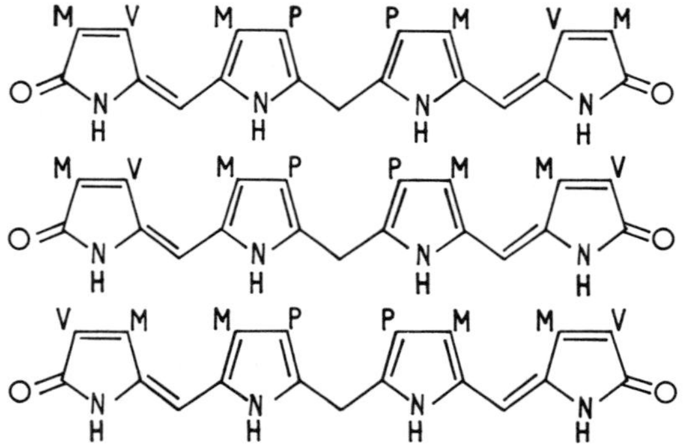

Figure 3. Bilirubin isomers: **1**, IIIα; **2**; IXα; **3**, XIIIα. M = CH$_3$-; V = -CH$_2$=CH$_2$; P =-CH$_2$CH$_2$CO$_2$H

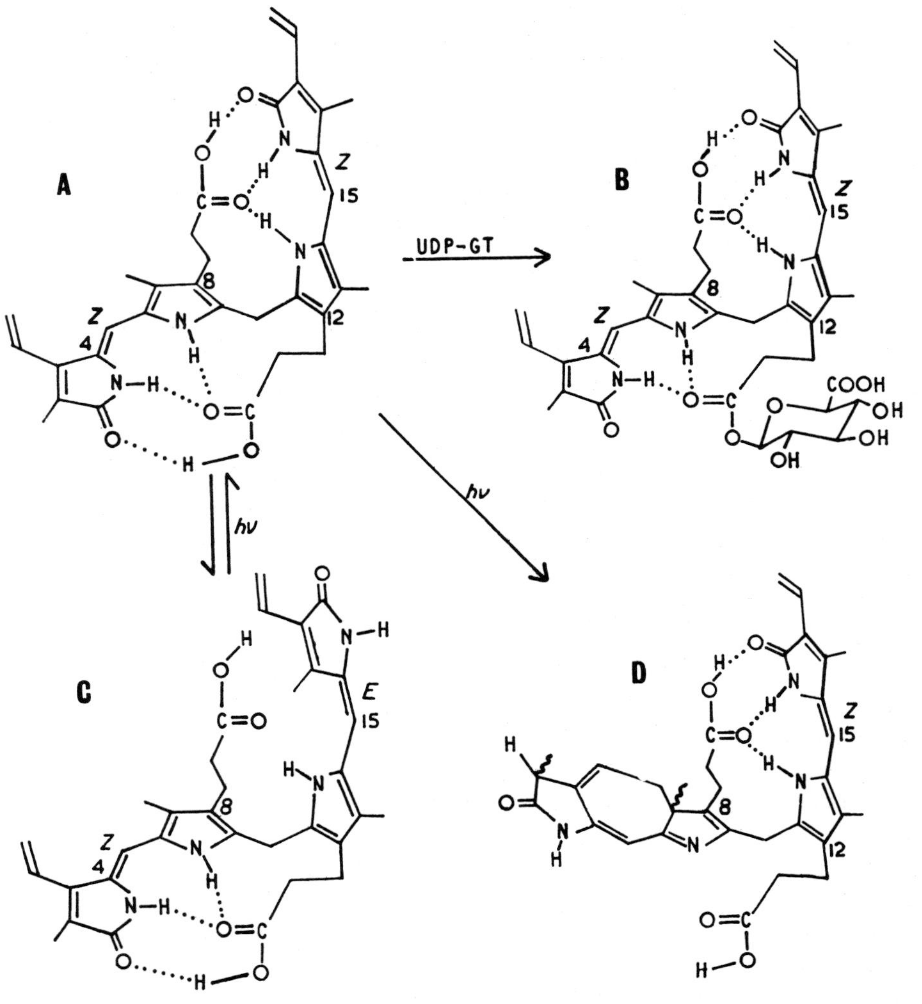

Figure 4. Reduction in hydrogen bonding in bilirubin IXα (Z,Z) (**A**) by UDP-glucuronyl transferase to give a monoglucuronide (**B**) and photochemically to give bilirubin IXα (E,Z) (**C**) and lumirubin (**D**). (Reproduced from ref.5.)

Bilirubin can photosensitize the formation of singlet oxygen with which it then reacts to form breakdown products (2). Bilirubin (Z,Z) also undergoes geometrical (Z→E), configurational and structural isomerization during photolysis to form bilirubin (E,Z) and lumirubin, respectively (*Figure 4*) (5).

In vivo rubins are esterified predominantly in the liver by the enzyme UDP-glucuronyl transferase to mono- and diglucuronides which are soluble in aqueous solution due to a reduction in the number of hydrogen bonds (*Figure 4*). The glucuronic acid moiety is bonded to the propionic groups via the l-hydroxy position as the β-anomer. At pH >6 there is migration of the site of esterification around the sugar ring to positions 2, 3 and 4 and also change from the β to α anomeric isomer (*Figure 5*) (6).

Indeed 80 chemically distinct glucuronic acid esters of the IXα type can arise from

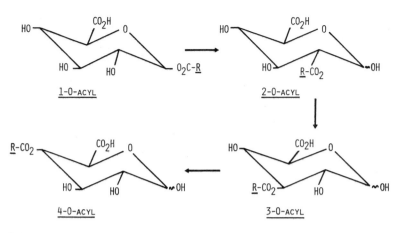

Figure 5. Sequential migration of bilirubin 1-O-acyl group to positions 2, 3 and 4 of glucuronic acid. R=bilirubin moiety.

acyl migration in a mixture of bilirubin IXα mono- and diglucuronides (7). Variable amounts of glucose and xylose esters are formed *in vivo* and may undergo the above reactions.

3. H.P.L.C. OF BILE PIGMENTS

Since 1975 a number of h.p.l.c. assays for bile pigments have appeared in the literature, the majority describing the separation of bilirubin and its esters. The development of satisfactory quantitative methods has been limited by the lack of commercially available reference compounds of high purity for the production of standard curves as well as by their instability.

3.1 Sample preparation

As outlined (Section 2) the bile pigments have to be handled with care. Nowhere is this more important than in the preparation of standards (8) and samples prior to analysis in order to prevent the formation of artefacts which will complicate the interpretation of chromatograms.

All manipulations of bile pigments should therefore be performed in dim, preferably, red light with deoxygenated solvents. Anti-oxidants such as ascorbic acid or butylated hydroxytoluene and a chelator such as EDTA should be added to all solutions. Extremes of pH should be avoided if at all possible and only weak acids and bases employed as buffers. Hydrolysis of conjugates can be avoided by buffering to pH values below 6 which also prevents acyl migration (6). Enzymatic hydrolysis of sugar esters by β-glycosidases can be prevented by addition of their aldonolactone inhibitors. When isolating pigments by solvent extraction the organic extracts should be dried as rapidly as possible under nitrogen or argon, stored at subzero temperatures under an inert gas and assayed as soon as possible.

Isolation of pigments is usually achieved by solvent extraction which is relatively straightforward for the unesterified bile pigments. In the case of bilirubin and its conjugates in physiological fluids there are complications due to their differing solubility characteristics.

Since both conjugated and unconjugated bilirubin bind tightly to albumin, with binding constants of $10^8/M$ and $10^6/M$, respectively (2), isolation of the pigments from protein-containing solutions demands vigorous solvent extraction and is not necessarily complete for conjugated bilirubin which is co-precipitated to a slight extent with

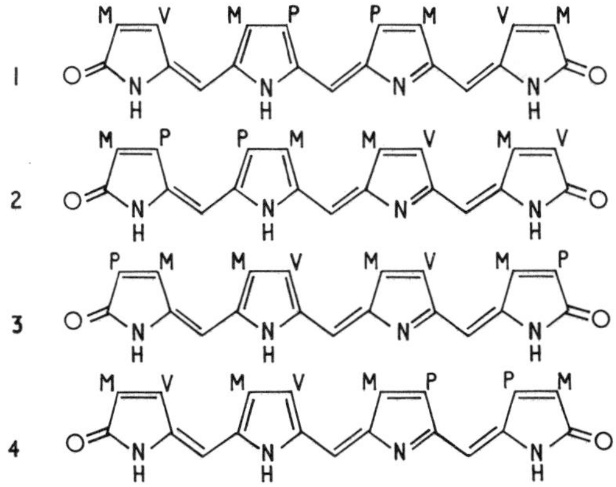

Figure 6. Biliverdin isomers: **1**, IXα; **2**, IXβ; **3**. IXγ; **4**, IXδ. M = CH$_3$-; V = -CH$_2$=CH$_2$; P = -CH$_2$CH$_2$CO$_2$H

Figure 7. Normal-phase separation of biliverdin dimethyl ester isomers. Column, Zorbax Sil-850 (250 × 4.6 mm): mobile phase, methylene chloride:methanol:water (99.0:0.9:0.1); flow,1.5 ml/min: detector, visible, 375 nm. **1**, IXβ; **2**, IXα; **3**, IXγ; **4**, IXδ. (Reproduced from ref. 12.)

311

the denatured protein, as is the covalent albumin complex 'Bili-Alb'.

Biliverdin also binds to albumin but not as strongly and is easily extracted by acidic methanol after esterification. The faecal pigments can be isolated from faeces by homogenization with glacial acetic acid followed by extraction with ether (9).

3.2 Separation of bile pigment methyl esters

3.2.1 *Biliverdin methyl esters*

Biliverdin IXα is the major product of the oxidative cleavage of haem accompanied by the formation of IXβ, IXγ and IXδ isomers as minor products (*Figure 6*). These isomers have been separated by adsorption and reversed-phase (RP) chromatography. An RP system (10) with acetonitrile:methanol:acetate buffer, pH 3.65 (1:1:1) as mobile phase on a C$_{18}$ column gave better resolution than a similar column eluted with methanol:water (78:22) (11). However the dimethyl esters are separated more efficiently using adsorption chromatography on silica with dichloromethane:methanol:water (99:0.9:0.1) as the eluent (12), (*Figure 7*). Biliverdin standard for chromatography can be prepared as described in *Table 1*. The method of extraction is shown in *Table 2*.

3.2.2 *Faecal pigment methyl esters*

A benzene:ethanol (29:1) solvent containing a trace amount of diethylamine separated the IIIα, IXα and XIIIα isomers of i-urobilin dimethyl ester on a silica (μ-Porasil) column and also resolved each isomer into pairs of diastereoisomers (13). Bull *et al* (14)

Table 1. Synthesis and purification of biliverdin.[a]

1.	Dissolve 100 mg of bilirubin in 10 ml of dimethyl sulphoxide (DMSO) and add rapidly to 82 mg of 2,3-dichloro-5,6-dicyano-1,4-benzoquinone (DDQ) in 10 ml of DMSO with continuous stirring.
2.	Stir for 5 min and then add 60 ml of 0.5% acetic acid to destroy excess DDQ and precipitate biliverdin. Wash the precipitate once with 60 ml of 0.5% acetic acid and then with water until no colour is extracted. Dry thoroughly by freeze drying.
3.	Pour a slurry of 15 g of silica gel G in 45 ml of methanol/acetone (1:1 v/v) into a glass Buchner funnel (400 mm i.d. × 50 mm high). Allow slurry to settle under gravity and drain the solvent to the top of the column using a water pump. Wash the column with 20 ml of methanol/acetone (1:1 v/v).
4.	Dissolve 100 mg of the crude biliverdin in the minimum amount of methanol/acetone (1:1 v/v), apply to the top of the column and apply a vacuum.
5.	Elute with 40 ml of methanol/acetone (1:1 v/v) followed by chloroform/methanol/acetic acid (7:3:0.03 by vol). Discard yellow-green or green eluates and collect the main blue-green band.
6.	Remove the solvent by distillaton under reduced pressure, re-dissolve the residue in 4 ml of 0.1 M NaOH, filter through a thin layer of celite, and wash with 0.1 M NaOH (3 × 1 ml).
7.	Add three drops of glacial acetic to the combined filtrates and collect the precipitate by centrifugation. Wash with water (3 × 7 ml) and again centrifuge.
8.	Mix the wet precipitate with 40 ml of acetone/water (8:2 v/v); add 40 ml of water and 5 ml of glacial acetic acid. Shake and leave for 10 min; collect the precipitate by centrifugation, wash with water (2 × 80 ml) and freeze dry.

[a]From ref. 2.

Table 2. Extraction and h.p.l.c. analysis of biliverdin methyl esters.

A. *Extraction*[a]

1. Dilute 1 volume of sample with 1 volume of water and adjust the pH to 3.8 with acetic acid. Add 10 g of talc and shake for 1 h at room temperature and filter.

2. Wash the talc with 2 × 25 ml of water and dry over silica gel in a vacuum.

B. *Preparation of esters*

1. Suspend the talc in 5% (v/v) sulphuric acid in methanol for 16 h at 4°C.

2. Filter and wash with methanol (2 × 5 ml plus 2 × 3 ml).

3. Dilute the combined filtrates with 70 ml of water and extract with chloroform (3 × 5 ml).

4. Wash the extract with water (4 × 10 ml), dry over anhydrous sodium sulphate and evaporate to dryness *in vacuo*.

5. Dissolve the residue in 3 ml of methanol, dilute with 7 ml of water and pass through a Sep-pak C18 cartridge (Waters Associates).

6. Elute methyl esters from the cartridge with 3 ml of methanol, evaporate the solvent and store at −20°C.

C. *H.l.p.c. conditions*[b]

Column: Zorbax Sil-850 (5 μm particle size silica; 250 × 4.6 mm).

Solvent: Dichloromethane:methanol:water (99.0:0.9:0.1 by vol).

Flow-rate: 1.5 ml/min

Detection: u.v. 375 mm

[a]From ref. 9; [b]From ref. 12.

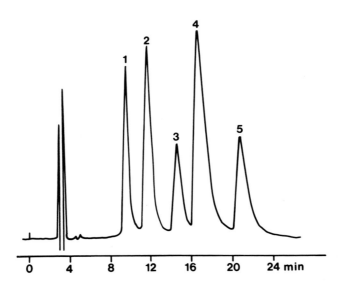

Figure 8. Separation of faecal pigment dimethyl esters. Column, Hypersil (250 × 5 mm): mobile phase, n-heptane:methyl acetate:methanol containing 1% diethylamine (75:25:2): flow, 1 ml/min, detector, visible, 490 nm. **1**, (SS)-stercobilin; **2**, (RR,SS)-half-stercobilin; **3**, (RR,SS)-urobilin; **4**, (RS,SR)-half-stercobilin; **5**, (RS,SR)-urobilin. (Reproduced from ref. 14.)

Table 3. Isolation and h.p.l.c. analysis of faecal pigments.

A.	*Extraction*[a]
1.	Grind faeces with glacial acetic acid until semi-liquid and add sufficient ether to obtain a clear supernatant. Decant and filter the ether extract. Repeat the extraction until the ether is colourless.
2.	Remove the ether by rotatory evaporation.
3.	Pour the remaining acetic acid solution into 6−8 volumes of 1% (v/v) HCl, let stand for 16 h at room temperature to precipitate fatty acids and then filter.
4.	Cover the filtrate with ether, add sodium acetate until the solution is negative to Congo Red and shake vigorously. Repeat the extraction five times. Then extract the remaining aqueous solution repeatedly with chloroform.
5.	Back-extract the chloroform with water. Filter the aqueous extract, make acid with 25% (v/v) HCl and extract into chloroform.
6.	Dry over anhydrous sodium sulphate, filter and concentrate on a water bath.
7.	Pour the concentrate into dry petroleum ether (15−20 volumes), collect the precipitate and dry.
B.	*Esterification*[b]
1.	Reflux a portion of material from step A.7 in 3 ml of methanol and 1 ml of boron trifluoride in methanol (14% w/v) for 10 min.
2.	Add 10 ml of water and extract into chloroform.
3.	Wash the chloroform extract successively with sodium hydrogen carbonate solution and water. Dry over sodium sulphate, filter and rotatory evaporate.
C.	*H.p.l.c. conditions*[b]
1.	Unesterified pigments (A.7) Column: SAS-Hypersil (C1, 5μm particle size, 100 × 5 mm) Solvent: acetonitrile−DMSO (50:50 v/v) Flow-rate: 1 ml/min Detection: u.v./vis 340 nm for mesobiliverdin and mesobiliviolin, 490 nm for urobilin
2.	Pigment dimethyl esters (B.3) Column: Hypersil (silica, 5 μm particle size, 250 × 5 mm) Solvent: n-heptane:methyl acetate:methanol containing 1% diethylamine (75:25:2 by vol) Flow-rate: 1 ml/min Detection: u.v./vis 490 nm

[a]From ref. 9; [b]From ref. 14.

described a system utilizing a silica column with n-heptane:methyl acetate:methanol (75:25:2) containing 1% diethylamine as eluent for separation of dimethyl ester stereoisomers. In both solvent systems the order of elution is the RR,SS forms before the RS,SR forms (*Figure 8*). *Table 3* summarizes the isolation and h.p.l.c. separation of faecal bile pigments.

3.2.3 *Bilirubin methyl esters*

Blanckaert *et al.* (15) first separated bilirubin methyl esters on a silica column with gradient elution using methanol (0−1%) in chloroform:acetic acid (199:1). The mono- and di-methyl esters were resolved into the IIIα, IXα and XIIIα isomers as were the positional (C-8 and C-12) isomers of monomethyl IXα (*Figure 9*). In 1983 Muraca and Blanckaert (16) introduced an RP method with gradient elution ion-pairing (IP);

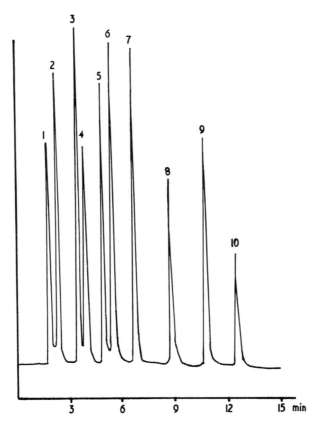

Figure 9. Normal-phase separation of bilirubin and its methyl esters. Column, Lichrosorb Si60 (250 × 4.6 mm): mobile phase, convex gradient from chloroform:acetic acid (199:1) to chloroform:methanol:acetic acid (197:2:1): flow, 1.5 ml/min: detector, visible 430 nm. **1**, β-carotene; **2**, bilirubin IIIα, IXα and XIIIα; **3−6**, monomethyl esters of bilirubin IIIα, IXαC-8, IXαC-12 and XIIIα, respectively; **7**, xanthobilirubinic acid methyl ester (internal standard); **8−10**, dimethyl esters of bilirubin IIIα, IXα and XIIIα, respectively. (Reproduced from ref. 15.)

starting condition methanol:water:tetrabutylammonium phosphate (65:35:1:1) and finishing condition methanol:ethanol:water:tetrabutylammonium phosphate (75:10:15:1.1). This system separated the dimethyl and monomethyl esters with no resolution of the IIIα and XIIIα isomers, nor was there any resolution of the positional isomers of monomethyl IXα (*Figure 10*). *Table 4* shows the method for the synthesis and purification of reference bilirubin methyl esters.

3.3 **Separation of unesterified bile pigments**

3.3.1 *Verdins, violins and bilins*

A mobile phase of acetonitrile:DMSO (50:50) or acetonitrile:DMSO:methanol (25:25:50) was used with a SAS-Hypersil (C1) column to separate mesobiliverdin, mesobiliviolin and urobilin to baseline resolution within 12 min. (14) (*Figure 11*).

315

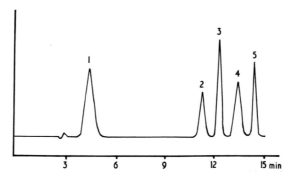

Figure 10. Reversed-phase separation of bilirubin and its methyl esters. Column, μ-Bondapak C_{18} (300 × 3.9 mm): mobile phase, convex gradient from methanol:water:PIC reagent A (65:35:1:1): flow, 1.5 ml/min: detector, visible 436 nm. **1**, bilirubin IXα; **2**, xanthobilirubinic acid methyl ester (internal standard); **3**, bilirubin monomethyl esters (C-8 and C-12 isomers); **4**, haemin; **5**, bilirubin dimethyl ester. (Reproduced from ref. 16.)

Table 4. Synthesis and purification of reference bilirubin methyl esters.

A.	*Synthesis*
1.	Dissolve 120 mg of bilirubin in 150 ml of chloroform with refluxing, cool, treat with excess ethereal diazomethane and rotatory evaporate to dryness at 35°C.
B.	*Purification*
1.	Wash four t.l.c. plates (20 × 20 cm) coated with silica gel G (0.75 nm) with methanol and reactivate at 120°C for 1 h.
2.	Dissolve the product from A.1 in chloroform and apply in streaks to the plates.
3.	Develop the plates in the dark using chloroform:methanol:acetic acid (97:2:1 by vol) for 18 cm.
4.	Scape the yellow bands with R_f values of 0.25 (dimethyl bilirubin IIIα, IXα and XIIIα) and 0.4−0.5 (monomethylbilirubin IIIα, XIIIα and XIα C-8 and C-12), extract the pigments with chloroform:methanol (40:1, v/v) and remove the solvent by rotatory evaporation.

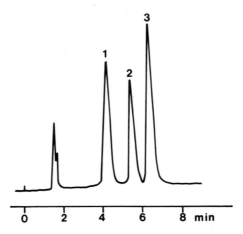

Figure 11. Separation of faecal pigments by RP-h.p.l.c. Column, SAS-Hypersil (100 × 5 mm): mobile phase, acetonitrile:DMSO (50:50): flow, 1 ml/min, detector, visible 340 nm for **1**, glaucobilin and **2**, mesobiliviolin and 490 nm for **3**, urobilin. (Reproduced from ref. 14.)

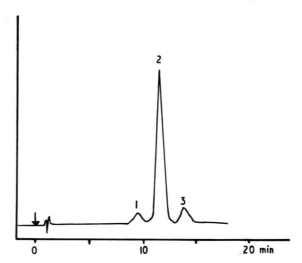

Figure 12. Separation of the IIIα, IXα and XIIIα isomers of bilirubin. Column, SAS-Hypersil (100 × 5 mm): mobile phase, acetonitrile:DMSO:water (30:30:40:) flow, 1 ml/min: detector, visible 450 nm. **1**. XIIIα; **2**. IXα; **3**, IIIα. (Reproduced from ref. 21.)

3.3.2 Bilirubin IIIα, IXα and XIIIα isomers

Commercial bilirubin preparations contain variable amounts of IIIα and XIIIα isomers (17) as impurities. A number of systems have been used for the separation of these isomers using RP and RP-IP chromatography (18−20). A gradient elution IP system utilizing acetonitrile (10−40%) in 0.01 M phosphate buffer containing 0.1% tetrabutyl-ammonium hydroxide, pH 8.0, on a Shimadzu PCH column (250 × 4.6 mm) was employed by Onishi *et al.* (18) but suffers from long retention times (120 min). Faster elution was obtained by a gradient of acetonitrile (25−80%) in 0.1 M acetate buffer containing 5 mM heptanesulphonic acid, pH 4.8, coupled to a stepped increase in flow-rate (19). Two C_{18} columns (200 × 4.6 mm) in series were used at 37°C and elution was completed in 35 min. Uesugi *et al.* (20) employed a C_{18} column (300 × 4 mm) and stepped gradient elution from methanol:acetonitrile:0.05 M citrate buffer, pH 5 (9:3:8) to (5:7:8) and buffer pH increased to 6.5.

An isocratic system using DMSO:acetonitrile:water (30:30:40) as the mobile phase on an SAS-Hypersil (C1) column, or (38:38:24) on a C_{18} support has been described by Lim *et al.* (21), (*Figure 12*). This system is rapid and gives good resolution.

3.4 Separation of conjugated and unconjugated bilirubins in body fluids

3.4.1 Bile

RP chromatography has been employed for the separation of bilirubin and its conjugates using either IP reagents or by manipulating hydrophobic interactions. Uesugi *et al.* (20) using citrate buffer containing methanol and acetonitrile were able to separate bilirubin diglucuronide IIIα, IXα and XIIIα isomers, monoglucuronide IIIα, XIIIα and IXα C-8 and C-12 isomers as well as mono- and di-glucoside and xyloside isomers. This separation took approximately 70 min which would mitigate against its use as a routine assay.

Onishi *et al.* (22) have described an IP system employing 0.1 M acetate at pH 4.0 containing 5 mM pentanesulphonic acid with an acetonitrile gradient (20−60%). Samples were prepared by precipitation of the proteins with acetonitrile and a portion of the supernatant was injected. Separation of bilirubin conjugates including the monoglucuronide isomers and unconjugated bilirubins were obtained. Chowdhury *et al.* (23) have also employed an RP-IP method using acetate buffer (pH 4.0) containing heptanesulphonic acid and a concave gradient of methanol (50−100%). The samples were treated with methanol to remove protein prior to their application to the chromatograph and after 70 min resolution of di- and mono-conjugates, but not the C-8 and C-12 isomers, was achieved together with unconjugated bilirubin.

Spivak and Carey (24) employed a C_{18} μ-Bondapak column with a linear gradient of methanol (60−100%) in ammonium acetate, pH 4.5 over 20 min and were able to resolve diconjugates (single and mixed sugar forms), monoconjugates (glucuronic acid, glucose and xylose) and unconjugated bilirubin. There was no separation of the positional isomers of the monoconjugates. Bile samples were injected directly into the chromatograph without prior protein precipitation and quantitation was achieved using response factors determined by chromatography of reference azo-pigments.

Gordon and Goresky (19) used a similar system to that of Onishi, with acetate (pH 4.8) and a stepped acetonitrile gradient and flow programming. Samples were extracted by the IP agent tetraheptylammonium chloride into chloroform prior to injectin. The procedure gave good resolution of monoglucuronide isomers, in addition to isomers of other glycosyl monoconjugates as well as mixed sugar diconjugates. Although the time for complete elution of the pigments was only 35 min, column re-equilibration required 20 min.

Two isocratic solvent systems have been described. Lim (25) described the separation of mono- and di- and unconjugated bilirubin within 20 min on a μ-Bondapack carbohydrate column with acetonitrile:water (90:10). Jansen's (26) method, on the other hand, requires 30 min and resolves the various sugar mono- and di-conjugates as well as mixed sugar diconjugates using acetonitrile:Tris containing 8 mM tetrabutyl-ammonium hydrogen sulphate (40:60) on a C_{18} column.

3.4.2 *Serum*

Blanckaert (15) and his associates described an assay for bilirubin and its sugar esters based on transesterification to their corresponding methyl esters using methanolic potassium hydroxide (27). The pigments are extracted into chloroform from acidic soluton (pH 2.7), dried and stored at −20°C. This method was a major breakthrough since the reference methyl esters can easily be prepared from commercial bilirubin in relatively large quantitites for pigment identification and quantification (*Table 5*). The RP system (*Figure 10*) (16) gives a simpler chromatogram than the normal-phase system but with increased sensitivity. It is not possible to ascertain whether the methyl esters were derived from glycosyl or glucuronyl conjugates of bilirubin. In both the normal and RP methods quantitation involves the use of xanthobilirubinic acid methyl ester (28) as an internal standard. A standard bilirubin solution in 5% serum albumin (8) may be prepared (*Table 6*) for constructing a calibration curve.

For serum, especially those containing large amounts of conjugates, there is loss of

Table 5. Extraction and h.p.l.c. separation of bilirubin methyl esters[a].

A. *Reagents*

1. Glycine/HCl buffer: add solid glycine to 0.4 M HCl to give pH 2.7.

2. Methanolic KOH: dissolve 2 g of KOH in 10 ml of methanol.

3. Internal standard solution: dissolve 5 mg of crystalline xanthobilirubinic acid methyl ester[b] in 1 l of methanol.

B. *Procedure*

1. Add 20 mg of ascorbic acid, a trace of EDTA, 0.2 ml of sample (serum, bile or amniotic fluid), 2.0 ml of internal standard and 2.0 ml of methanolic KOH to a 20 ml glass tube with a stopper.

2. Vortex mix for 1 min and leave for 1 min.

3. Add 2.0 ml of chloroform and 4.0 ml of glycine/HCl, shake vigorously and centrifuge at 2000 g for 5 min.

4. Remove the chloroform extract, evaporate to dryness (30°C) and store pigments under argon (−20°C).

C. *H.p.l.c. conditions*

Column: μ-Bondapak C_{18} (10 μm particle size, 300 × 3.9 mm) maintained at 40°C.
Solvent: Methanol:water:tetrabutylammonium phosphate (PIC ion-pair reagent A, Waters Associates) (65:35:1.1 by vol) containing 2 mM sodium ascorbate changing to methanol:ethanol:water:PIC reagent A (75:10:15:1.1 by vol) containing 2 mM ascorbate via a convex gradient during 9 min.
Flow-rate: 1.5 ml/min
Detection: u.v./vis 436 nm.

[a]From refs 15, 16 and 26; [b]From ref. 28.

Table 6. Preparation of bilirubin standard solutions[a].

1. Dissolve 20 mg of bilirubin in 4 ml of DMSO to give a stock concentration of approximately 5 mg/ml.

2. Add 2 ml of the DMSO stock solution to 40 ml of 5% (w/v) serum albumin solution (in water) in a 50 ml volumetric flask with continuous stirring and make up to the mark with 5% serum albumin solution.

3. Prepare standard solutions by quantitative volumetric dilutions of bilirubin−albumin solution with 5% serum albumin solution[b]

4. Dilute DMSO stock solution (1 in 1250) in chloroform, measure the absorbance at 453 nm using a 1 cm pathlength and calculate the concentration using 60 700 as the molar extinction coefficient (ϵ).

[a]From ref. 8; [b]From ref. 2.

pigments on the protein precipitated at the organic−aqueous interface which includes 'Bili-Alb'. To overcome this problem Lauff and co-workers (3) developed an assay that measures all four bilirubin species in serum by first precipitating high molecular weight proteins using saturated sodium sulphate (*Table 7*). The pigments were then separated on a C8 column using a gradient of propan-2-ol (0−19%) in 0.05 M phosphate pH 2.0 containing 5% 2-methoxyethanol (to prevent protein precipitation on the solid phase) at 41°C (*Figure 13*). In this method the individual pigments are reported as

Table 7. Assay of bilirubin, its mono- and di-conjugates and 'Bili-Alb'[a].

A.   *Reagents*

1.   Sodium sulphate solution: dissolve 27.7 g of anhydrous sodium sulphate in 80 ml of hot distilled water, adjust to pH 7.0 ± 0.2 with dilute sulphuric acid or NaOH and dilute to 100 ml. Keep at 37°C.

2.   Ascorbic acid solution: dissolve 5 g of ascorbic acid in 30 ml of distilled water, add 1 ml of 2 M phosphate buffer pH 6.7, adjust to pH 5.8 ± 0.2 with NaOH and dilute to 50 ml.

3.   Human serum albumin solution: dissolve 5 g of human serum albumin in distilled water and dilute to 100 ml.

B.   *Standard and sample treatment*

1.   Standards (from *Table 2*)
(i) Add 0.25 ml of solution, 7 ml of sodium sulphate solution and 0.5 ml of ascorbic acid solution to a 10 ml volumetric flask and make up to the mark with distilled water.

2.   Bile samples
(i) Dilute bile 1:10 with distilled water.
(ii) Add 0.25 ml of diluted bile, 14 ml of sodium sulphate solution, 0.5 ml of human serum albumin solution and 0.5 ml of ascorbic acid solution to a 25 ml volumetric flask and make up to the mark with distilled water.

3.   Serum samples
(i) Add 3.5 ml of sodium sulphate solution to 0.25 ml of serum
(ii) Seal the vial and heat for several minutes at 37°C in a water bath.
(iii) Remove the precipitated globulins by passing the contents through a 0.45 μm filter overlaid by a glass fibre pre-filter in an ultrafiltration cell (25 mm i.d.). Collect the filtrate into a 10 ml volumetric flask containing 0.5 ml of ascorbic acid solution
(iv) Stir the precipitate vigorously with 3.5 ml of sodium sulphate solution for 1 min, filter, combine with the contents of the flask and dilute to volume with distilled water.

C.   *H.p.l.c. conditions*
Column: Lichrosorb RP-8 (10 μm particle size, 250×4.6 mm) maintained at 41°C.
Solvent: 2-methoxyethanol:0.05 M phosphate, pH 2.0 (5:95 v/v) changing linearly over 16 min to 2-methoxyethanol:propan-2-ol:0.05 M phosphate, pH 2.0 (5:19:76 by vol).
Flow-rate: 1.4 ml/min
Detection: u.v./vis 450 nm for bilirubins; 280 nm for albumin

---

[a]From ref. 3.

percentages of the total pigment area detected at 450 nm and the actual values have to be calculated from the total pigment concentration determined by a standard 'diazo' technique. Although the chromatographic separation only takes 25 min the preparation of the sample is extremely time consuming and the method has not become generally available in spite of the fact that at present it is the only reliable method currently available for the estimation of Bili-Alb.

3.4.3 *Separation of photobilirubins*

The photobilirubins have been studied by Onishi *et al.* (18, 29−32) utilizing a gradient of acetonitrile (19−40%) in phosphate containing tetrabutylammonium hydroxide on a Shimadzu PCH column. McDonagh *et al.* (33) have separated photoproducts of bilirubin on a C18 column with 0.1 M octylamine in methanol as solvent.

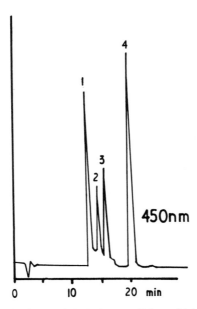

450nm

Figure 13. Separation of bilirubins from pathological serum. Column, Lichrosorb (250 × 4.6 mm): mobile phase, linear gradient from 2-methoxyethanol:0.05 M phosphate, pH 2.0 (5:95) to 2-methoxyethanol: propan-2-ol:0.05 M phosphate, pH 2.0 (5:19:76): flow, 1.4 ml/min: detector, visible 450 nm. **1**, 'Bili-Alb'; **2**, bilirubin diconjugate; **3**, bilirubin monoconjugates; **4**, unconjugated bilirubin. (Reproduced from ref. 3.)

4. CLINICAL SIGNIFICANCE OF THE SERUM BILE PIGMENTS DETECTED BY H.P.L.C.

In the normal subject, unconjugated bilirubin is the only serum pigment detected by the standard alkaline methanolysis technique (15,34,35) which gives a mean value of 8.1 + 2.9 μmol/l for total bilirubin. However, with the more sensitive Muraca and Blanckaert (16) technique, small amounts of bilirubin monoglucuronide (mean 0.10 + 0.04) and bilirubin diglucuronide (mean 0.12 + 0.06) have been demonstrated and they consist of approximately 3.0% of the total bilirubins. The values are slightly higher in men than women. Gilberts syndrome is the most common of the familial types of unconjugated hyperbilirubinaemia and occurs in 5% or more of the male population and to a lesser extent in females (36). The only non-invasive diagnostic test available is the demonstration that the jaundice is due solely to raised levels of unconjugated bilirubin (17−85 μmol/l) in serum. Since the diazo techniques tend to give false positive values the technique of choice is that of h.p.l.c. (15,34,35). It is also of value for the detection of the more severely jaundiced Crigler−Najjar syndromes and for determining whether jaundice in the neonate is due to prematurity.

Both bilirubin monoglucuronide and bilirubin diglucuronide have been found in the plasma of a proportion of patients with cirrhosis and metastatic liver disease even when the serum total bilirubin is normal or only slightly raised (34). The presence of these pigments may have diagnostic value. In hepatobiliary disease bilirubin diconjugates and the C-8 and C-12 isomers of bilirubin monoconjugates account for the majority of the bile pigments accumulating in the serum (37). Overall, the bilirubin conjugates

321

in serum consist of 30% C-8 monoconjugates, 37% C-12 conjugates and 33% diconjugates. Although the mono- and di-conjugates tend to be higher in patients with biliary obstruction than those with parenchymal liver disease, while the unconjugated bilirubin level is markedly less, there is a considerable overlap between the groups. This prevents the determination of the different conjugates from being diagnostically useful. It has, however, been shown that the specific measurement of bilirubin esters provides a more sensitive test for the detection of icteric and non-icteric hepatobiliary disease than any of the standard liver function tests such as serum bile acids, transaminases, alkaline phosphatase or glutamyl transpeptidase and is comparable in sensitivity to a combination of these tests (35).

In most hyperbilirubinaemic patients the total serum bilirubin levels, as determined by conventional diazo methods, exceed those obtained by h.p.l.c. This is due to loss of pigment on the protein precipitate during solvent extraction and the formation of 'Bili-Alb' (7, 38). Weiss *et al.* (39) showed that covalently bound bilirubin is an important fraction of total bilirubin (8−90%) in patients with hepatocellular and cholestatic jaundice as well as in patients with the Dubin−Johnson syndrome, and becomes a larger component (on a percentage basis) after it has disappeared from the urine. Albumin-bound bilirubin has not been detected in normal volunteers, neonates with physiological jaundice or patients with Gilberts syndrome or haemolysis and is only formed when the hepatic excretion of bilirubin is impaired.

5. REFERENCES

1. McDonagh,A.F. (1975) *Ann. N.Y. Acad. Sci.*, **244**, 553.
2. McDonagh,A.F. (1979) In *The Porphyrins.* Dolphin,D. (ed.), Academic Press Inc, London and New York, Vol. **6**, p. 293.
3. Lauff,J.J., Kaspar,M.E. and Ambrose,R.T. (1981) *J. Chromatogr.*, **226**, 391.
4. Compernolle,F. (1982) In *Bilirubin*, K.P.M. and Brown,S.B. (eds.), CRC Press Inc, Boca Raton, FL, Vol. **1**, p. 61.
5. McDonagh,A.F. and Lightner,D.A. (1985) *Pediatrics*, **75**, 443.
6. Blanckaert,N., Compernolle,F., Leroy,P., Van Houlte,R., Fevery,J. and Heirwegh,K.P.M. (1978) *Biochem. J.*, **171**, 203.
7. McDonagh,A.F., Palma,L.A., Lauff,J.J. and Wu,T.-W. (1984) *J. Clin. Invest.*, **74**, 763.
8. Billing,B.H., Halsam,R. and Wald,N. (1971) *Ann. Clin. Biochem.*, **8**, 21.
9. Watson,C.J. (1934) *J. Biol. Chem.*, **105**, 469.
10. Hirota,K., Yamahoto,S. and Itano,H.A. (1985) *Biochem. J.*, **229**, 477.
11. Noguchi,M., Yoshida,T. and Kikuchi,G. (1982) *J. Biochem. (Tokyo)*, **71**, 1479.
12. Rasmussen,R.D., Yokoyama,W.H., Blumenthal,S.G., Bergstrom,D.E. and Ruebner,B.H. (1980) *Anal. Biochem.*, **101**, 66.
13. Stoll,M.S., Lim,C.K. and Gray,C.H. (1976) In *High Pressure Liquid Chromatography.* Dixon,P.F., Gray,C.H., Lim,C.K. and Stoll,M.S. (eds), Academic Press, London and New York p. 97.
14. Bull,R.V.A., Lim,C.K. and Gray,C.H. (1981) *J. Chromatogr.*, **218**, 647.
15. Blanckaert,N., Kabra,P.M., Farina,F.A., Stafford,B.E., Merton,L.J. and Schmid,R. (1980) *J. Lab. Clin. Med.*, **96**, 198.
16. Muraca,M. and Blanckaert,N. (1983) *Clin. Chem.*, **29**, 1767.
17. McDonagh,A.F. and Assisi,F. (1971) *FEBS Lett.*, **18**, 315.
18. Onishi,S., Itoh,S., Kawade,N., Isobe,K. and Sugiyama,S. (1979) *Biochem. Biophys. Res. Commun.*, **90**, 890.
19. Gordon,E.R. and Goresky,C.A. (1982) *Can. J. Biochem.*, **60**, 1050.
20. Uesugi,T., Adachi,S. and Kamisaka,K. (1983) *J. Chromatogr.*, **277**, 308.
21. Lim,C.K., Bull,R.V.A. and Rideout,J.M. (1981) *J. Chromatogr.*, **204**, 219.
22. Onishi,S., Itoh,S., Kawade,N., Isobe,K. and Sugiyama,S. (1980) *Biochem. J.*, **185**, 281.
23. Chowdhury,J.R., Chowdhury,N.R., Gartner,U., Wolkoff,A.W. and Arias,I.M. (1982) *J. Clin. Invest.*, **69**, 595.

24. Spirak,W. and Carey,M.C. (1985) *Biochem. J.*, **225**, 787.
25. Lim,C.K. (1979) *J. Liquid Chromatogr.*, **2**, 37.
26. Jansen,P.L.M. (1981) *Clin. Chim. Acta.*, **110**, 309.
27. Blanckaert,N. (1980) *Biochem. J.*, **185**, 115.
28. Grunewald,J.O., Cullen,R., Bredfeldt,J. and Strope,E.R. (1975) *Org. Prep. Procedures Int.*, **7**, 103.
29. Onishi,S., Kawade,N., Itoh,S., Isobe,K. and Sugiyama,S. (1980) *Biochem. J.*, **190**, 527.
30. Onishi,S., Miura,I., Isobe,K., Itoh,S., Ogino,T., Yokoyama,T. and Yamakawa,T. (1984) *Biochem. J.*, **218**, 667.
31. Yokoyama,T., Ogino,T., Onishi,S., Isobe,K., Itoh,S. and Yamakawa,T. (1984) *Biochem, J.*, **220**, 377.
32. Itoh,S. and Onishi,S. (1985) *Biochem. J.*, **226**, 251.
33. McDonagh,A.F., Palma,L.A., Trull,F.R. and Lightner,D.A. (1982) *J. Am. Chem. Soc.*, **104**, 6865.
34. Jansen,P.L.M., Cuypers,H.T. and Peters,W.H.M. (1984) *Eur. J. Clin. Invest.*, **14**, 295.
35. Van Hootegem,P., Fevery,J. and Blanckaert,N. (1985) *Hepatology*, **5**, 112.
36. Owens,D. and Evans,J. (1975) *J. Med. Genet.*, **12**, 152.
37. Scharschmidt,B.F., Blanckaert,N., Farina,F.A., Kabra,P.M., Stafford,B.E. and Weisiger,R.A. (1981) *Gut*, **23**, 643.
38. Gautam,A., Seligson,H., Gordon,E.R., Seligson,D. and Boyer,J.L. *J. Clin. Invest.*,**73**, 873.
39. Weiss,J.S., Gautam,A., Lauff,J.J., Sundberg,M.W., Jatlow,P., Boyer,J.L. and Seligson,D. (1983) *N. Engl. J. Med.*, **309**, 147.

APPENDIX I

Suppliers of specialist equipments and reagents

The addresses listed here are those of the parent companies. The major companies all have subsidiaries or agents in other countries. Their addresses can be obtained by writing to the parent companies.

Amersham International plc, White Lion Road, Amersham, Buckinghamshire HP7 9LL, UK.
Anachem Ltd., Anachem House, 20 Charles Street, Luton, Bedfordshire LU2 0EB, UK
Analytichem International Inc., 24201 Frampton Avenue, Harbor City, CA 90710, USA
J.T.Baker Chemical Co., 222 Red School Lane, Phillipsburg, NJ 08865, USA
Beckman Instruments Inc., Altex Scientific Operation, 1716 Fourth Street, Berkeley, CA 94710, USA
BDH Chemicals Ltd., Broom Road, Parkstone, Poole, Dorset BH12 4NN, UK
Laboratorium Berthold, Calmbacher Str. 22, P.O. Box 160, D-7547 Wildbad 1, FRG
Bioanalytical Systems Inc., 2701 Kent Avenue, West Lafayette, IN 47906, USA
Bio-Rad Laboratories, 2200 Wrigh Avenue, Richmond, CA 94804, USA
Brownlee Labs Inc., 2045 Martin Avenue, Santa Clara, CA 95050, USA
Chrompack International B.V., P.O. Box 8033, Kuipersweg 6, 4330 EA Middelburg, The Netherlands
Chromatem (Touzart & Matignon), Rue Carle Vernet, B.P. 2, F-92310, Sevres, France
Du Pont Co., Concord Plaza-McKean Bldg., Wilmington, DE 19898, USA
Durrum Chemical Corporation (Dionex Corp.), 1228 Titan Way, Sunnyvale, CA 94088-3603, USA
EDT Research, 14 Trading Estate Road, London NW10 7LU, UK
ESA Inc., 45 Wiggins Avenue, Bedford, MA 01730, USA
Fisons plc, 41/45 Gatwick Road, Crawley, Sussex RH10 2UL, UK
Gilson Medical Electronics (France) S.A., B.P. 45 - 95400, Villiers-Le-Bel, France
Hewlett-Packard Analytical Group, P.O. Box 10301, Palo Alto, CA 94303, USA
HPLC Technology Ltd. (Applied Chromatography Systems Ltd.), 10 Waterloo Street West, Macclesfield, Cheshire SK11 6PJ, UK
IBM Instruments Inc., Orchard Park, P.O. Box 332, Danbury, CT 06810, USA
JASCO, Japan Spectro Co. Ltd., 2967-5, Ishikawa-cho, Hachioji City, Tokyo 192, Japan

Jones Chromatography Ltd., Colliery Road, Llanbradach, Mid-Glamorgan CF8 3QQ, UK

Kontron AG, Bernerstrasse Süd 169, CH-8010 Zurich, Switzerland

Kratos Analytical (Schoeffel), 170 Williams Drive, Ramsey, NJ 07446, USA

Locarte, 8 Wendell Road, London W12, UK

LDC/Milton Roy, P.O. Box 10235, Riviera Beach, FL 33404, USA

LKB-Prodokter AB, Box 305, S-16126 Bromma, Sweden

Macherey-Nagel, P.O. Box 307, Werkstrasse 6-8, D-5160 Dueren, FRG

E.Merck, Frankfurter Strasse 250, Postfach 4119, D-6100 Darmstadt, FRG

Millipore Corporation, 80 Ashby Road, Bedford, MA 01730, USA

Nuclear Enterprises Ltd., Bath Road, Beenham, Reading RG7 5PR, UK

Packard Instrument Company, 2200 Warrenville Road, Downers Grove, IL 60515, USA

Perkin-Elmer Corporation, Main Avenue (MS-12), Norwalk, CT 06856, USA

Pharmacia Fine Chemicals AB, P.O. Box 175, S-75104 Uppsala, Sweden

Phase Separations Inc., River View Plaza, 16 River Street, Norwalk, CT 06850, USA

Philips Analytical (Pye Unicam), York Street, Cambridge CB5 9BS, UK

Pierce Chemical Co., P.O. Box 117, Rockford, IL 61105, USA

Porphyrin Products Inc., P.O. Box 31, 195 South 700 West, Logan, UT 84321, USA

Radiometric Instruments & Chemical Company Inc., 5102 S. Westshore Boulevard, Tampa, FL 33611, USA

Regis Chemical Company, 8210 Austin Avenue, Morton Grove, IL 60053, USA

Rheodyne Inc., 6815 S. Santa Rosa Avenue, P.O. Box 996, Cotati, CA 94928, USA

Shandon Southern Products Ltd., Chadwick Road, Astmoor, Runcorn, Cheshire WA7 1PR, UK

Shimadzu Corporation, Shinjuku-Mitsui Building, 1-1 Nishishinjuku 2-chome, Shinjuku-ku, Tokyo 160, Japan

Sigma Chemical Company, P.O. Box 14508, St. Louis, MO 63178, USA

Spectra-Physics Autolab Division, 3333 North First Street, San Jose, CA 95134, USA

Supelco Inc., Supelco Park, Bellefonte, PA 16823, USA

Toyo Soda Manufacturing Company Ltd., TOSO Building, 1-7-7 Akasaka, Minato-ku, Tokyo 107, Japan

Valco Instruments Company Inc., P.O. Box 55603, Houston, TX 77255, USA

Varian Associates Inc., Instrument Group, 611 Hansen Way, Palo Alto, CA 94303, USA

Waters Chromatography Division, 34 Maple St., Milford, MA 01757, USA

Whatman Ltd., 9 Bridewell Place, Maidstone, Kent ME14 2LE, UK

INDEX

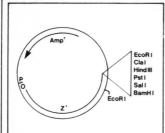

DNA cloning
(Volumes I and II)
a practical approach

Edited by D M Glover,
Imperial College of Science and
Technology, London

Published
in the
Practical
Approach
series

A STEP-BY-STEP GUIDE TO PROVEN NEW TECHNIQUES

Breakthroughs in the manipulation of DNA have already revolutionised biology; they are set to do the same for drug and food production. *DNA cloning* contains the background and detailed protocols for molecular biologists to perform these experiments with success. It supersedes previous manuals in describing recent developments with widespread applications that use *E coli* as the host organism.

Up-to-the-minute contributions cover the use of phage λ insertion vectors for cDNA cloning and the use of phage λ replacement vector systems to select recombinants for DNA cloning.

Two chapters evaluate *E coli* transformation and methods for *in vitro* mutagenesis of DNA cloning in other organisms including yeast, plant cells and Gram-negative and Gram-positive bacteria. Finally, the last three chapters of Volume II offer three different approaches to the introduction of cloned genes into animal cells.

Contents

Volume I

The use of phage lambda replacement vectors in the construction of representative genomic DNA libraries *K Kaiser and N E Murray* ● Constructing and screening cDNA libraries in λ gt10 and λ gt11 *T V Huynh, R A Young and R W Davis* ● An alternative procedure for synthesising double-stranded cDNA for cloning in page and plasmid vectors *C Watson and J F Jackson* ● Immunological detection of chimeric β-galactosidases expressed by plasmid vectors *M Koenen, H W Gresser and B Muller-Hill* ● The pEMBL family of single-stranded vectors *L Dente, M Sollazzo, C Baldari, G Cesareni and R Cortese* ● Techniques for transformation of *E coli* *D Hanahan* ● The use of genetic markers for the selection and the allelic exchange of *in vitro* induced mutations that do not have a phenotype in *E coli G Cesareni, C Traboni, G Ciliberto, L Dente and R Cortese* ● The oligonucleotide-directed construction of mutations in recombinant filamentous phage *H-J Fritz* ● Broad host range cloning vectors for Gram-negative bacteria *F C H Franklin* ● Index

Volume II

Bacillus cloning methods *K G Hardy* ● Gene cloning in *Streptomyces* / *S Hunter* ● Cloning in yeast *R Rothstein* ● Genetic engineering of plants *C P Lichtenstein and J Draper* ● P element-mediated germ line transformation of *Drosophila R Karess* ● High-efficiency gene transfer into mammalian cells *C Gorman* ● The construction and characterisation of vaccinia virus recombinants expressing foreign genes *M Mackett, G L Smith and B Moss* ● Bovine papillomavirus DNA: an eukaryotic cloning vector *M S Campo* ● Index

Volume I: *June 1985; 204pp;*
0 947946 18 7 (softbound)
Volume II: *June 1985; 260pp;*
0 947946 19 5 (softbound)
Volumes I and II; *0 947946 20 9*

For details of price
and ordering consult
our current catalogue
or contact:

IRL Press Ltd,
Box 1, Eynsham,
Oxford OX8 1JJ, UK

IRL Press Inc,
PO Box Q,
McLean VA 22101,
USA

◯**IRL PRESS**

Oxford · Washington DC